PYRAMID QUEST

ALSO BY ROBERT M. SCHOCH, PH.D.
WITH ROBERT AQUINAS MCNALLY

Voyages of the Pyramid Builders

Voices of the Rocks

PYRAMID QUEST

Secrets of the
Great Pyramid and
the Dawn of Civilization

ROBERT M. SCHOCH, PH.D.
AND ROBERT AQUINAS McNALLY

Jeremy P. Tarcher/Penguin
a member of Penguin Group (USA) Inc.
New York

JEREMY P. TARCHER/PENGUIN
Published by the Penguin Group
Penguin Group (USA) Inc., 375 Hudson Street, New York, New York 10014, USA • Penguin Group
(Canada), 10 Alcorn Avenue, Toronto, Ontario M4V 3B2, Canada (a division of Pearson Penguin Canada
Inc.) • Penguin Books Ltd, 80 Strand, London WC2R 0RL, England • Penguin Ireland,
25 St Stephen's Green, Dublin 2, Ireland (a division of Penguin Books Ltd) • Penguin Group
(Australia), 250 Camberwell Road, Camberwell, Victoria 3124, Australia (a division of Pearson
Australia Group Pty Ltd) • Penguin Books India Pvt Ltd, 11 Community Centre, Panchsheel
Park, New Delhi–110 017, India • Penguin Group (NZ), Cnr Airborne and Rosedale Roads,
Albany, Auckland 1310, New Zealand (a division of Pearson New Zealand Ltd) • Penguin
Books (South Africa) (Pty) Ltd, 24 Sturdee Avenue, Rosebank, Johannesburg 2196, South Africa

Penguin Books Ltd, Registered Offices:
80 Strand, London WC2R 0RL, England

Library of Congress Cataloging-in-Publication Data

Schoch, Robert M.
Pyramid quest : secrets of the Great Pyramid and the dawn of civilization /
Robert M. Schoch and Robert Aquinas McNally.
p.   cm.
Includes bibliographical references and index.
ISBN 1-58542-405-6
1. Great Pyramid (Egypt).   2. Egypt—Civilization—To 332 B.C.
I. McNally, Robert Aquinas.   II. Title.
DT63.S34   2005   2005041726
932—dc22

Printed in the United States of America
3   5   7   9   10   8   6   4   2

CONTENTS

PART FOUR: MYSTICS, ESOTERICS, AND INITIATES

PYRAMID
QUEST

Full West of the Citie [Cairo], close vpon those desarts, aloft a rocky leuell adioyning to the valley, stand those three Pyramides (the barbarous monuments of prodigality and vain-glory) so vniuersally celebrated.

George Sandys, 1621

As for the Pyramids, there is nothing to wonder at in them so much as the fact that so many men could be found degraded enough to spend their lives constructing a tomb for some ambitious booby, whom it would have been wiser and manlier to have drowned in the Nile, and then given his body to the dogs.

Henry David Thoreau, 1854

One

A DISTANT MIRROR

LIKE SO MANY PROJECTS, THIS BOOK ACTUALLY BEGAN with something else. When I first went to Egypt in 1990, the focus of my research was something other than the Great Pyramid. Rather, I studied a well-known structure that rests in the Great Pyramid's shadow: the Great Sphinx of Giza. Inexorably, however, the trail of research that began with the Sphinx led me to the Great Pyramid—and to this book.

I had come to Egypt as the guest of John Anthony West, a writer, travel guide, and scholar who has long acted as burr, goad, and gadfly to the respectable academics who study ancient Egypt. West wanted to solve a riddle no other living Egyptologist had even noticed. This riddle was one that only a geologist could unravel, yet it was also one that cut to the heart of the accepted history of ancient Egypt. Did the peculiar weathering patterns visible on the Great Sphinx, West wondered, indicate that the structure was much older than conventionally thought?

Before I had my own up-close look at the Sphinx, I was sure that the answer was no. For over a half-century, scholars had agreed that this immense statue dates to the Fourth Dynasty of the Old Kingdom, specifically to the reign of the pharaoh Khafre (known in Greek as Chephren) who ruled Egypt's Two Lands from 2520 to 2494 B.C.* Since the Sphinx can't be dated to a precise year, its construction is conventionally placed at circa 2500 B.C.

Only circumstantial evidence connects the Great Sphinx to Khafre and supports the 2500 B.C. date, but the clues do seem to point the same way. For one thing, the Sphinx sits closest to the second largest of the principal Giza pyramids, the one attributed to Khafre. For another, statuary likenesses of Khafre found in a nearby building add to the association of this particular pharaoh with the Sphinx. Third, there is a later, New Kingdom (c. 1400 B.C.) inscription on a pillar, or stela, that sits between the Sphinx's paws. When originally found, the stela—since damaged by time—may have contained a portion of Khafre's name, again linking the pharaoh to that magnificent, human-headed, lion-bodied monument. Unfortunately, the putatively Khafre-naming portion of the stela has flaked away. Fourth and finally, some authorities claim to see a similarity between the Sphinx's face and Khafre's features.

Still, there was a key fact all this evidence ignored: the Sphinx is made of stone. Like any stone, it offers evidence of the weather it has endured. Weather, in turn, can tell us a great deal about history.

Of all the recent scholars who have studied ancient Egypt, the only one who has paid attention to the stone reality of the Great Sphinx has been René Aor Schwaller de Lubicz (1887–1961). An Alsatian by nationality and a mathematician and philosopher by profession, Schwaller de Lubicz believed that ancient Egypt embodied an intellectual and artistic sophistication far exceeding anything we imagine. In the course of building his case for an advanced Egyptian civilization, Schwaller de Lubicz made a key observation at Giza. He noticed that the Great Sphinx was weathered differently from the other monuments at the same site, exhibiting a pattern that indicated erosion by water rather than sand ("the entire lion-like body of the Sphinx, with the exception of the head, provides indisputable evidence of erosion by water").[1] Schwaller de Lubicz asked: Did this difference in

---

*Scholars continue to argue about exact dates in ancient Egyptian history. Throughout this book, we are following the chronology used in the authoritative *Atlas of Ancient Egypt* (New York: Facts on File, 1980) by John Baines and Jaromir Málek.

weathering also indicate a difference in history? Lacking the right scientific training to find the answer, the Alsatian could only hypothesize.

John Anthony West shared Schwaller de Lubicz's wonder. West, who had long believed that the civilization of ancient Egypt had originated much earlier than commonly thought, knew that the climate in the eastern Mediterranean was far wetter in the millennia before 3000 B.C. than after. If the Sphinx showed evidence of erosion by water, then possibly it dated to this earlier, wetter period, proving that Egypt was home to a much older civilization.

But, like Schwaller de Lubicz, West couldn't investigate this hypothesis himself. Evaluating the Sphinx's erosion patterns required a geologist, and that was how West had come to me—through a mutual friend who knew I was a student of ancient history as well as a member of the science faculty at Boston University, and the holder of a doctorate from the Department of Geology and Geophysics at Yale.

When West and I met, I told him frankly that I was skeptical of his ideas. After all, a great many able scholars had studied the Sphinx, and surely they would have noticed something as obvious as water erosion. He insisted that I come to Egypt anyway and offered to pay my way. Certain that I was wasting his money only to undercut his ideas, I left for Cairo once my university duties for the spring semester of 1990 were over.

I had been in Egypt just a few days when I realized something. As capable as all those scholars who have studied ancient Egypt are, they don't know how to look at rock, stone, and soil the way a geologist does. I had a geologist's training, and my scientific eye told me there was something to West and Schwaller de Lubicz's ideas. Even as a tourist who could look at the Sphinx only from a distance, I saw that the monument exhibited obvious signs of heavy rainfall and water runoff, possibly the legacy of the wetter, pre–Old Kingdom climate. I also noticed that buildings dated unquestionably to Khafre and the Fourth Dynasty showed weathering and erosion primarily from windblown sand—the pattern to be expected from the dry, desert conditions that settled on Egypt after 3000 B.C. Superficially, the evidence suggested that the Sphinx dated to an earlier, wetter period than did the Fourth Dynasty structures. Still, I needed a much closer, much more scientific look to be sure.

It took two more trips to Egypt, a detailed research proposal approved by the Egyptian authorities, a seismic study to measure the depth of weathered rock surrounding the Sphinx, and months of data analysis to put the picture together. The results indicated that Schwaller de Lubicz and West's suspicions were correct. The oldest portions of the Sphinx were originally carved not in the reign of Khafre, circa 2500 B.C., but much earlier, somewhere between approximately 5000 and 7000 B.C., according to my best estimates. Since then, the original Sphinx has been heavily repaired and restored, both in ancient and modern times, and the pharaonic head is a recarving of an earlier one.

A WIDER CONTEXT

Although my geological research focused on the Great Sphinx alone, it suggested far wider implications. For the Great Sphinx exists not as a solitary monument but as only one component in an architectural and cultural complex representing the highest expression of one of the earliest and most enduringly fascinating civilizations.

The Giza Plateau, which sits on the west bank of the Nile River at the very edge of the Sahara outside modern-day Cairo, consists of a small city of sacred buildings and ancillary structures. In addition to the Great Sphinx, Giza boasts three major pyramids and six minor pyramids, plus dozens upon dozens of tombs, shrines, temples, walls, pits, causeways, and other remains from thousands of years of human occupation. In pushing back the date of the Great Sphinx, my thesis had called into question the accepted history not only of that one immense and stunning statue but also of every other structure and artifact at Giza. This realization led me to study the scholarship and science surrounding Giza and see how the redating of the Sphinx changed the conventional storyline of ancient Egypt.

In simplest outline, the orthodox point of view goes like this: what we conceive of as civilization—complex cities, elaborate social and political organization, and written language—began in approximately 3500 B.C. in Sumeria, which lay along the Euphrates River in what is now Iraq. Sumeria eventually collapsed under the weight of outside attack, but the ideas and

The pyramids of the Giza Plateau in the late nineteenth century, with the Great Pyramid in the front (east and north faces showing; viewer is looking toward the southwest), the Second (Khafre) Pyramid in the middle, and the Third (Menkaure) Pyramid in the back to the left. In the front the remains of the three small satellite or Queen's Pyramids that sit to the east of the Great Pyramid can also be seen. In the foreground is the plain below the Giza Plateau. Late-nineteenth-century photograph by Antonio Beato, 1825–1903. (*See D'Hooghe, and Bruwier, 2000, p. 32, for information on Beato; from Barber, 1900, facing p. 28.*)

techniques that informed its civilization followed the trade routes west, where the Egyptians proved eager learners.

In the fourth millennium B.C., as Sumerian ideas were making their way into northeastern Africa, Egypt was organized into small districts called nomes, which were strung out along the Nile like beads on a rosary. Each nome had its own chief and gods and, in the manner of much of human history, made war on the other nomes. A succession of alliances united the nomes into two kingdoms: Upper Egypt, which occupied the southern end of the Nile's long course, and Lower Egypt, which included the northern reach of the river and its delta, opening onto the Mediterranean Sea. Then, in about 3000 B.C., the legendary king Menes—whose name means "unifier" and is sometimes thought to be the same as the early ruler Narmer (although Narmer may have preceded Menes) and/or the ruler known as Scorpion—conquered both kingdoms, joined them as the Two Lands under his rule, named himself pharaoh, and established the First Dynasty. This

Aerial photograph looking straight down on the pyramids of the Giza Plateau, early to mid-twentieth century. North is toward the lower right-hand corner. From top to bottom, the three largest pyramids are the Third (Menkaure) Pyramid, the Second (Khafre) Pyramid, and the Great Pyramid. Photograph by the British Royal Air Force. (*From Grinsell, 1947, frontispiece.*)

triumph of central authority in the iron fist of a single male ruler was key to the progression of events that led, over the next five centuries, to Giza.

Before Menes, prominent Egyptians were buried first in pits marked by simple mounds of sand and gravel, later in neat boxes of mud brick sunk into the earth and divided into rooms and chambers. With the arrival of the pharaohs, the funeral pattern became more complex. Large pillars (stelae), mounds, and an imitation royal palace were built to house the spirit of the departed king and mark the place of his burial. During the Third Dynasty (2649–2575 B.C.), the last line of pharaohs during the Early Dynastic Period, these home-sized tombs made the leap into the monumental realm, as the first stepped pyramids were constructed. The Fourth Dynasty (2575–2465 B.C.), which ushered in the Old Kingdom (some authorities include the Third Dynasty as part of the Old Kingdom), made the building of pyramids the central activity of political, social, and religious life along the Nile.

Khufu (Cheops in Greek; reigned c. 2551–2528 B.C.), the second pharaoh of the Fourth Dynasty, abandoned the previous pyramid-building sites of Saqqara, Meidum, and Dahshur to focus on Giza. There he had his Great Pyramid and its associated temples erected, laying the groundwork for what would become ancient Egypt's most impressive ritual site. Although Khufu's successor Djedefre (also known as Rededef, 2528–2520 B.C.) built only a much smaller pyramid at Abu Roash, the next pharaoh, Khafre (2520–2494 B.C.) returned to Giza to construct the second largest pyramid there. Repeating the pattern in which activity at Giza skipped generations, Khafre's probable successor, Nebka (also known as Nabka or Bikka), started a large pyramid at Zawiyet el-Aryan, south of Giza, but never finished it, probably because his rule lasted a mere four years (2494–2490 B.C.). After Nebka came Menkaure (Mycerinus in Greek; 2490–2472 B.C.), who built the last and smallest principal pyramid at Giza.

STONE AND EGO

Just as there is no dance without the dancer, many believe that there is no pyramid without a pharaoh. In the orthodox view, every pyramid was erected to aid a pharaoh in his metamorphosis from mortal to god. The pyramid gave the pharaoh the wherewithal to achieve the divinity that was the ultimate prerogative of his office. The pyramids express the intersection of political philosophy and religion, where the man who rules the land in life becomes in death the god he was born to be. In this way, pyramids are monuments to royal ego, and the bigger the pyramid, the more expansive the ego behind it.

If this straightforward connection of size and ego holds, then Khufu must have been the greatest, or at least the most self-aggrandizing, of all the pharaohs who ever strode across the Two Lands. At approximately 756 feet on each of its four sides, an original height of 481 feet, and a volume of somewhere around 3 million cubic yards, the Great Pyramid is the largest stone building ever erected. It is also the largest religious structure yet built. Although the Great Pyramid is about the same height as the dome of Saint Peter's in the Vatican, it covers 13 acres, compared to Saint Peter's mere 4. Were the Great Pyramid hollow, it could easily enclose Saint Peter's, with enough space left over that a rearranged Westminster Abbey would fit inside as well.

Once the Great Pyramid was even more striking than it is today. When it was finished, the pyramid was reputedly sheathed in white limestone that gave the structure a smooth, gleaming surface. The limestone was also said to have been inscribed with hieroglyphics and symbols. Perhaps this was religious ornamentation, in the same way that biblical inscriptions decorate some Christian churches, but the "inscriptions" may simply have been graffiti from a period following the pyramid's construction. Unfortunately, the limestone sheathing didn't survive into modern times, as locals more interested in mosques, fortifications, and present comfort than past wonder carried the shining white blocks away to build the city of Cairo.

Despite this vandalism, the Great Pyramid still offers a unique beauty that transcends its phenomenal size and mass. Some scholars are convinced that the artistry of the structure incorporates the mathematical constants of pi (π) and the Golden Section (phi, ϕ), qualities that give it the same kind of inexplicable, lasting allure evinced by the Mona Lisa's smile or the Taj Mahal's perfect acoustics (see further discussion in chapter 9 and the appendices). And there is the matter of the Great Pyramid's peculiar internal structure.

Like the tombstones they are purported to be, the early pyramids were constructed over a room or rooms situated at, near, or under ground level and apparently intended to serve as a burial chamber. Often, a tunnel extended down through the body of the pyramid, presumably—so the traditional story goes—as a pathway for ritually conveying the pharaoh's remains to their final earthly resting place. In the Great Pyramid, this basic architecture becomes highly and unexpectedly elaborate. The structure incorporates a variety of passages, chambers, and shafts, as well as the Grand Gallery, constructed at different heights in the body of the pyramid, many also displaying exceptional and unusual attention to both grandeur and detail. No other pyramid, neither earlier nor later, contains so complicated or sophisticated an internal architecture.

There is another important question: Why is the Great Pyramid so big? Why, if the pharaohs were simply egotists par excellence who lived their kingly lives to outdo one another, did Khufu's successors settle for smaller mausoleums and surrender the ritual high ground to him? Why does the structure incorporate that variety of internal structures, when a basic tunnel and a stone room would serve more than adequately to preserve the pharaoh's mummy? Why, indeed, if the Great Pyramid was intended as a tomb, was no mummy ever found inside?*

These largely unanswered questions have led various writers, thinkers, and visionaries—and their many thousands of readers and fellow enthusiasts—to reject the Egyptological convention of the Great-Pyramid-as-great-tombstone and see something else in its size, complication, artistic accomplishment, and architecture. The list of something-elses, developed by writers often grouped as pyramidologists (as opposed to academic Egyptologists), is stunning in its length and variety. At one time or another, the Great Pyramid has been depicted as an ancient power plant, water pump, gargantuan resonance chamber, Bible in stone, architectural prophecy, eternal standard of weights and measures, landing beacon for colonizing extraterrestrials, hall of records for the sunken civilization of Atlantis, astronomical observatory, key component of a map of the constellation Orion, and monument to the prehistoric discovery of the speed of light.

If nothing else, pyramidology testifies to just how far imagination can carry us away from the mundane, grounding facts of empirical reality. Yet it also says much more. In the modern era, the so-called pyramidologists have studied the Great Pyramid in extraordinary detail, making exact measurements of virtually every chamber, passage, nook, and cranny of this magnificent structure. Arguably, no other single building has been studied in such detail by so many researchers, or had as many books devoted to it. It is beyond doubt—as the founder of modern Egyptology,

---

*There is indeed an Arab legend that a mummy was found in the Great Pyramid, but this is generally dismissed as not being accurate; see the appendices, section on "Where was Khufu actually buried?"

Sir William Flinders Petrie, demonstrated in the 1880s—that the Great Pyramid demonstrates extraordinary precision and exactness in its alignment (for instance, relative to true north) as well as the measurements of its internal chambers and passages. It would appear to be a finely tuned machine or measuring device on a gargantuan scale. Studying the Great Pyramid firsthand, I have heard the call that many pyramid researchers ultimately come to hear. The exacting details of the Great Pyramid, far from being random or simply the extravagances of a people following a primitive religion, must have a purpose, a meaning, a significance. Hence, the Egyptological convention, which holds that Khufu built the Great Pyramid solely to mark his grave and assure his divinity, fails to convince.

Then there is the problem of context. The evidence attributing the Great Pyramid to the pharaoh Khufu is far from definitive—much less so than most of the standard textbooks would lead one to believe. My research has demonstrated that the Great Sphinx was carved, recarved, and reworked many times and that its origins extend back thousands of years before Khufu and dynastic Egyptians. Could something similar be the case with the Great Pyramid? As we will see, compelling theories that align the pyramid with ancient cosmic events, and other evidence, suggest as much. Then there is the enduring question of how the Great Pyramid could have been constructed with the primitive technology generally attributed to the Old Kingdom Egyptians. Clearly, something we don't yet understand was going on at Giza. The task of this book is to explore what it was.

TERMS OF THE QUEST

In studying to become a scientist, I learned how to look at data, sift it for reliability, and develop the best theoretical explanation for what we know. When I used this approach to look objectively at the Great Sphinx of Giza, I found something much different from what I had been led to expect. In this book, my coauthor, Robert Aquinas McNally, and I will do the same for the Great Pyramid—sift through the facts and ideas attached to this singular monument to distinguish sense from nonsense and assemble the result into a picture as accurate as present knowledge can make it.

It is a daunting task. For one thing, we are investigating a complex, incompletely preserved monument that is no less than 4,500 years old. For another, our own preconceptions and unstated beliefs cloud our vision. As we shall see again and again, ancient Egypt has this way of bending under the weight of Western civilization's latest big idea.

For example, during medieval Christian times, the Giza pyramids were said to be the granaries in which the Hebrew patriarch Joseph stashed the bumper harvests of grain that carried Egypt through the terrible time of drought and hunger described in chapters 40 and 41 of the biblical book of Genesis. Given the worldview of medieval Christianity, in which biblical accounts served as literal history, explaining the pyramids as Joseph's granaries made sense. After all, if Joseph told the Egyptians to store their surplus, what else in the landscape of Egyptian civilization could have qualified as large enough to accept all that abundance?

The trouble is, the explanation hardly fits the facts. Had those medieval Christian scholars bothered to examine the pyramids, they would have discovered that they are ill suited to be granaries. Apart from the Grand Gallery of the Great Pyramid, the Giza pyramids lack the large internal hollows that make granaries suited for massive storage.

The modern study of ancient Egypt—which does involve actually looking at the pyramids—substituted a different point of view, but one that has also had its faith-based elements. What we think of as Egyptology began with Napoleon's invasion of Egypt in the early nineteenth century. Certain that he was making history with his ambition and his army, Napoleon took along not only soldiers but also a group of scholars, or savants, whose task it was to record what they saw. Much like the medieval Christian scholastics, Napoleon's savants had their own preconceived worldview, which they incorporated into their depiction of the pyramids. Appalled by what they saw as the squalid backwardness of the Islamic East and certain that they themselves were the founders of a great world civilization led by France, the savants created the image of a long-ago, long-lost, timeless Orient that had little or nothing to do with the Muslims they came to conquer and rule. Ancient Egypt proved not the historical magnificence of the modern East but its fall into decadence.

Although the terms of the description have changed, much the same process of seeing in the pyramids what we want to see continues. Consider

"The Ægyptian Pyramides and Colossus." Early seventeenth-century rendition of the Giza Plateau, showing the Great Pyramid (right), the other major pyramids, the Great Sphinx, and visitors traveling in the desert. (*From Sandys, 1621, page 128.*)

contemporary Egyptology, which makes the pyramids monuments to pharaonic ego built by a massively powerful theocratic state. It is intriguing that this perspective arose during the nineteenth and twentieth centuries, which witnessed the expansion of powerful imperialistic nations, major world wars, and the rise of two of the world's most vicious totalitarian states—the Soviet Union and Nazi Germany—both led by egos of cosmic proportions, Josef Stalin and Adolf Hitler, and guided by ideologies and symbols, Marxism-Leninism and Nazism, claiming the status, reverence, and universal reach of a state religion.

Much the same process goes on with pyramidology. If you believe in lost ancient wisdom and technology, submerged civilizations and Atlantis, the literal truth of the Old Testament, extraterrestrials in flying saucers, or the imminent occurrence of the Second Coming, what better place to find evidence of that belief than in the mute stones of the Great Pyramid?

In this book I attempt to cut through the noise and the nonsense, sift through what we know about the Great Pyramid, and discover as much of its truth as I can. This is a valuable enterprise. It tells us about the nature of a people who lived long ago and far away, of course. Equally important, it teaches us about the heritage of the civilization we live in and the nature of the humanity we share across the long reach of time.

Part One

WHO, WHAT, WHEN, WHERE, AND HOW

Two

THE STANDARD STORY

I T IS ONE OF THOSE UNSTATED ASSUMPTIONS OF HISTORIOG-
raphy that civilization as a whole grows more complicated and sophisticated over time, moving in a straight, upward line of progress
and complexity. Individual empires may rise and fall, of course, a process
famously memorialized in Edward Gibbon's *Decline and Fall of the Roman
Empire* and dramatized in popular culture by Hollywood epics depicting
Roman decadence. Still, in the wider, global view, we believe firmly that we
are more civilized today than our kind was a millennium ago or certainly a
millennium before that. This image of inevitable progression underlies the
accepted history leading up to the Great Pyramid. And, in fact, there is
something of truth to it—but only something.

LIFE AND DEATH

Say "ancient Egypt" to many people, and the first thing they think of is
embalming, mummies, and an endless preoccupation with death. In truth,
Egypt of the early days focused no more on death than have many other
cultures. Egypt's cities, villages, and farms were strung out along the Nile,

with its rich, ever-deepening soil and annual floods. Most of the artifacts of daily life, fashioned from wood, leather, cotton, and papyrus, quickly decayed and left little or no trace in that hot, fertile environment. But the ancient Egyptians took their dead to the desert, where heat and dryness helped to preserve both human remains and many of the objects used for funerals and burial. As a result, we know more about Egyptians in death than in life.

Still, this has proved a boon for scholars who study ancient Egypt, since the customs and rituals surrounding death provide important evidence of a culture's deepest religious beliefs and practices. As we follow the history of Egyptian funeral practices from the earliest days through the Giza pyramids and beyond, we witness not only the technological progress of a civilization but also its religious evolution.

BEFORE THE PYRAMIDS

In the Predynastic Period (c. 4500–3100 B.C.) before Menes united the Two Lands of Egypt under a single political power, Egyptians of south and north shared some funeral customs and differed on others. Throughout Egypt, both Upper (south) and Lower (north), graves were excavated in the sand, away from cultivated fields, in the form of oval or rectangular pits. The dead were laid to rest on their left sides, curled in the fetal position. Ritually, the grave represented a womb in the Earth Mother, and the buried corpse became the newborn awaiting rebirth. In Lower Egypt only the dead were placed in the tomb. But even before 4500 B.C. the people of Upper Egypt were burying various useful objects alongside corpses, probably in the belief that the dead would need them in the afterlife. This Upper Egyptian idea eventually spread throughout the Two Lands and became common practice across the whole country.

By the late Predynastic Period, bodies were placed, often on a reed mat or goat skin, so that they faced west, which was considered the direction of afterlife and rebirth. The goods buried along with the body represented the deceased's social standing—the more and classier the goods, the higher the dead one's position in the community hierarchy. Grave goods were useful objects: flint knives, scrapers, adzes, ornaments, grinding stones. These were things the deceased would need later.

Toward the end of this era, Egyptians were paying more and more attention to the grave itself. In some cases, they lined the walls of the pit with sun-baked mud bricks and plastered them with mud. As for the bodies themselves, they were not mummified, but burial in hot sand often effectively preserved them. Between desiccation by happenstance and purposely elaborate tomb-building, the Egyptians were working culturally toward establishing permanence in the face of death.

This trend became ever more elaborate during the Early Dynastic Period (2920–2575 B.C.). Egypt was united, but two power centers remained, one in the north, the other in the south. As a result, there were two burial areas: Saqqara in the north (near modern Cairo) and Abydos in the south (about 90 miles north of Luxor along the Nile). In the same way that Predynastic bodies faced west in their graves, both Abydos and Saqqara sit on the west side of the Nile. Scholars have long debated which of these ancient graveyards hold Egypt's earliest pharaohs. Today most of them are convinced that Abydos was the royal burial ground.

Abydos's earliest First Dynasty (2920–2770 B.C.) royal tombs are simply slightly more elaborate versions of the burial pits of the Predynastic Period. Gravediggers excavated a single pit and lined it with mud brick to receive both body and grave goods. Planks resting on wooden beams and posts roofed the pit, and a superstructure was erected atop the planks. No superstructures have survived, but they probably consisted of rubble and sand heaped into a mound, or tumulus, covered with mud brick to mark the grave.

The First Dynasty made a significant addition to the stock of grave goods: servants. In the case of Pharaoh Djer (also known as Dyer, c. 2900 B.C.), hundreds of servants were sacrificed, then buried, around his tomb. Since the point of grave goods was to provide the dead with everything they needed in the afterlife, a man who was used to being waited on hand and foot during mortal days would surely need a crowd of servants on the other side. Slaughtering a palace's worth of servants to make the journey with him made religious sense.

This custom of retainer burial, as it is often known, may have been imported from Mesopotamia, where it was a longstanding part of royal burial customs. In the case of Egypt, retainer burials faded out by the end of the First Dynasty. There is no evidence of retainer burials during the Old Kingdom, but the custom returned in Nubia, upstream from Abydos, between 2000 and 1700 B.C. when the area was a province of Middle Kingdom Egypt.

Some of the First Dynasty pharaohs built themselves two funeral monuments at Abydos. One was a tumulus burial pit, excavated in the ancestral cemetery known as Umm el-Saab ("mother of pots," in Arabic). The other was a palace constructed behind the town. At Saqqara, which is the better preserved of the two First Dynasty graveyards, the tumulus grave and the palace were united into one complex that shows a strong connection to the pyramids to follow. These massive mud brick structures are known as mastabas, from the modern Arabic word meaning "mud brick bench," which they resemble.

There are three main components to a mastaba. First is the substructure, a pit dug into the earth. Then comes the superstructure, the mud brick edifice that perches atop the excavated substructure. Finally, there are the ancillary, or auxiliary, buildings, which correspond to the separate palace buildings at Abydos.

The First Dynasty substructures of Saqqara are strikingly more permanent and more complex than the sand burial pits of the Predynastic Period. Cut from rock rather than simply dug out of the moving sands, the pit was large enough to be divided into separate rooms by walls of mud brick. Typically the large central burial chamber was surrounded by four storage rooms. Ornamentation, like inlaid gold work or colored mats, decorated some burial chambers, which held not only the body in a wooden coffin but also folded clothes in chests, furniture, and a funerary meal. This repast could be quite elaborate. The remains of one such final dinner uncovered at Saqqara included beef ribs, kidneys, pigeon stew, roast quail, loaves of bread, barley porridge, stewed figs, and berries. The storage rooms held jewelry, games, additional furniture, more food, tools, and weapons. The dead were taking all the gear of daily life into their new existence.

Wooden beams with planks at right angles roofed the substructures of the early Saqqara mastabas. As a result, the body and the grave goods had to be put inside the substructure before the roofing was complete and, possibly, even before the superstructure built. During the First Dynasty an innovation that solved this inconvenience took hold: a stairway starting outside the superstructure and leading into the burial chamber. The stairway meant that builders didn't have to wait until after the mastaba's owner died before building the superstructure. But it did have a disadvantage: robbers could make their way down the same entry to steal those sumptuous grave goods and turn a rich man of this world into a pauper in the next. To keep criminals out, mastaba builders lowered a series of stone slabs, or portcullises, down grooves cut into the stairway's walls after the body was interred to keep interlopers out of the burial chamber. The stairway proved to be such a good idea that it became the fashion at Abydos as well.

The typical mastaba superstructure sat at ground level and took the form of a mud brick rectangle that could range between 130 and 200 feet long and 50 to 80 feet wide. Partitions divided the interior into as many as 20 to 45 storerooms that held grave goods of less value than those that accompanied the dead underground. The sheer mass of stuff piled into these tombs can be stunning. For example, the Saqqara tomb known as 3035 was plundered in antiquity, yet its excavation by archaeologists still yielded 901 pottery vessels, 362 stone vessels, 493 arrows, 305 flint tools, 60 wooden tools, and 45 spindle whorls, as well as various pieces of ivory and textile fragments. Timber roofing protected the storerooms; then the builders added rubble infill and packing to bring the interior up to the height of the exterior walls, which stood about 25 feet tall.

The superstructure increased the mastaba's security by putting more material between any would-be robbers and the buried grave goods. But also, and perhaps more important, it carried religious significance. The Egyptians believed that creation emerged from chaos in the form of a mound. The mastaba's superstructure symbolized this primal mound, creating a center of regenerative power that transported the dead to rebirth in a new and better world.

According to Günter Dreyer, director of the German Archaeological Institute in Cairo, the architectural tension between the solid tumulus cresting the mastaba's superstructure and the wall surrounding it led eventually to the pyramid. If the outside wall was so high that it obscured the tumulus, the resurrection theme was likewise obscured. In a symbolic way of speaking, death triumphed. To resolve this tension between wall and mound in the direction of eternal life, tomb builders chose to raise the height of the mound and lay a new emphasis on the resurrection of the dead. When this idea triumphed fully—in the Third Dynasty, as we shall soon see—the pyramid came to be.

Two key elements of First Dynasty mastabas indicate the disparate sources that contributed to ancient Egyptian culture. The mastabas' exterior took the form of stepped niches known as the paneled façade design, a technique that probably originated in the religious architecture of Mesopotamia from the protoliterate period. All four sides of some Saqqara tombs boast low brick benches decorated with clay bull's heads festooned with real horns. This decoration is strongly reminiscent of the many bull's heads found in the ancient city of Çatal Hüyük, which flourished in the seventh millennium B.C. in what is now Turkey. The appearance of bull's heads in Egyptian mastabas is a strong reminder of the strong mixing of cultures and civilizations that characterized the ancient Middle East.

Curiously, much less is known about the Second Dynasty (2770–2649 B.C.) than the First. Only two royal tombs, those of Peribsen (Per Ibsen, c. 2700 B.C.) and Khasekhemwy (c. 2650 B.C.), have been identified at Abydos. Apparently, the unification of the First Dynasty had unraveled, and confusion, if not war, again descended upon Egypt. Two other kings may have been buried at Saqqara, but the remaining Second Dynasty tombs in that grave ground are apparently private, probably the tombs of highly placed officials. Tunnels reaching into rock replaced the excavated pits of the First Dynasty, mounds built of solid mud brick or mud brick over a rubble core served as superstructures, and the storerooms of earlier times disappeared.

STEPS TO THE TRUE PYRAMIDS

What we think of as the Egyptian pyramid began with the second pharaoh of the Third Dynasty (2649–2575 B.C.), Djoser (c. 2630–2611 B.C., also commonly known as Zoser or Zozer). Egypt had again become united and peaceful. The Two Lands extended their power outward and became increasingly wealthy in gold, copper, and fine stone quarried in the Eastern Desert. Given peace and prosperity, the pharaoh could turn his attention from subjecting the rebellious under his rule to achieving immortality through great works.

Originally Djoser followed his ancestors' ways by constructing a mastaba of sun-baked mud brick at Beit Khallaf, a little north of Abydos. Then Djoser moved his attention to Saqqara, where he began a new mastaba with an unusual design. It was basically a square, rather than rectangular like its predecessors. And Djoser built entirely with stone, in the end erecting a monumental building constructed entirely of this material.

In achieving this milestone of history, Djoser had help. It came from Imhotep (Imouthes in Greek), who was not only an architect but also a wise man and healer on such a scale that he became a figure of Egyptian mythology. After his death, Imhotep was made into a god, often identified with the Greek deity Asclepios, who is the patron of medicine and the bearer of the caduceus used as the emblem of the medical profession.

As Djoser and Imhotep explored the new possibilities stone offered as a principal building material, the structure—today known as the Step Pyramid—was something of a work in constant progress. The first draft of the structure was built with local rock faced with Tura limestone, a fine-grained, pure-white material quarried on the east side of the Nile. Unsure just how to work with stone, the builders kept the size of the blocks small. As they were apparently pleased with the results, a second casing of limestone some 13 feet thick was added, and then, through various extensions and additions, the mound was raised to four steps, each smaller than the one before and perched atop its predecessor like stacked blocks of decreasing size. More work later added two more steps and raised Djoser's Step Pyramid to 204 feet in height.

As in Second Dynasty mastabas, the burial chamber of the Step Pyramid lay at the end of a shaft cut almost 90 feet down into the bedrock. The top of the shaft was reached by a sloping ramp that also connected by stairs to a series of underground galleries ornamented with bas relief sculptures and tiles glazed in blue. The burial chamber itself was walled in pink

Aswan granite, and a hole was cut into one of the roof slabs to allow the body to be lowered into the tomb. A 3-ton granite block sat in a room above the burial chamber, apparently ready to plug the hole after the royal burial.

A mummy that is definitively Djoser's has yet to be discovered. In the early nineteenth century, skull fragments were found in the burial chamber, and in the 1920s splinters of foot and arm bones, but it is far from certain whether these skeletal fragments are the mortal remains of the pharaoh. Interestingly, however, in deep 30-meter shafts on the eastern façade, some 40,000 stone vessels of all types have been discovered, some bearing the names of rulers of the First and Second dynasties. Why they were buried within the Step Pyramid is unclear. Was Djoser reverently reinterring materials that his predecessors had ransacked from earlier royal tombs? Or were these vessels simply materials that had accumulated over the decades and centuries in royal storerooms and temple warehouses, and were now put into service for the deceased pharaoh?

The Step Pyramid is more than just a pyramid. It is a single component of an immense complex measuring approximately 1,640 feet by 820 feet and originally enclosed by walls over 30 feet high. The complex contained open courts, tombs, terraces, altars, underground storerooms for grain and fruit, and various ritual buildings. Apparently, the complex replicated the original pharaonic palace and recreated in death the place where the great king ruled in life. One of the structures was the *serdab*, a room that contained a seated statue of Djoser and was completely sealed except for two peepholes. In the event that the mummy were destroyed, the statue served as a secure repository for the pharaoh's spirit.

At least two similar stepped pyramid complexes were begun during Third Dynasty. The first, ascribed to Sekhemkhet (2611–2603 B.C.), Djoser's successor, was to consist of seven steps, but it was never completed, probably owing to the pharaoh's short reign. Yet another incomplete step pyramid was begun well up the Nile at Zawyet el Amwat, probably by Khaba (2603–2599 B.C.), another short-lived pharaoh. His successor, Huni (2599–2575 B.C.), the last pharaoh of the Third Dynasty, may have begun the pyramid at Meidum and, like his predecessors, left the project uncompleted. That task fell to his successor.

FIRST FLOWERS OF THE FOURTH

The transition from Huni to Sneferu (2575–2551 B.C.) was more than the usual passage of royal power from one king to another. Huni was the last pharaoh of not only the Third Dynasty but also of the Early Dynastic Period. Sneferu founded the Fourth Dynasty, which led off the Old Kingdom (2575–2134 B.C.)* and embodied the classic era of Egyptian pyramid building. His role in the progress of Egyptian history was so important that he went on to become not only a typical divine pharaoh but also a minor member of the wider Egyptian assemblage of gods and goddesses.

From a purely monumental perspective, Meidum may offer evidence of the transition from Huni and the Third Dynasty to Sneferu and the Fourth Dynasty. Some Egyptologists suggest that Huni built what was originally intended to be a seven-stepped pyramid and encased the structure in limestone, then decided to add another step and yet another limestone casing to the now eight-stepped structure. Workers laid the masonry of the stepped layers in courses that sloped in toward the center of the pyramid, a characteristic Third Dynasty style. Then, according to this hypothesis, Sneferu took Huni's pyramid over as his own and filled in the steps, creating the first smooth-sided, geometrically true pyramid of ancient Egypt. The shaped stones that effected this transformation were laid in horizontal courses, a Fourth Dynasty method of stone laying. Other Egyptologists, however, believe that the Meidum pyramid was actually begun by Sneferu himself and represents his first attempt at a pyramid.

The Meidum pyramid no longer stands as it originally did; much of the external structure has collapsed. Physicist and Egyptology enthusiast Kurt Mendelssohn argues that the collapse happened during construction, as the smooth-sided pyramid neared completion, and that it produced a terrible avalanche crushing all unlucky enough to be beneath it. There is important evidence, though, that the disaster occurred later, well after the pyramid was completed. The mortuary complex typical of a pyramid was completed

---

*Of course, the very concept of Egyptian dynasties and kingdoms is a later invention. The Old Kingdom Egyptians did not view themselves as of the "Old Kingdom."

at Meidum, an unlikely event if the pyramid had tumbled down during construction. It looks more probable that the pyramid was completed and used as a ritual center, with the collapse coming at some later date, perhaps because of an earthquake. Or possibly there was no wholesale collapse at all, and the pyramid weathered and eroded and was vandalized by later generations.

In undertaking a vigorous pyramid-building program, Sneferu was signaling his accession to power. He moved pyramid building onto the Fourth Dynasty's center stage, making it the primary and definitive activity of that period of ancient Egyptian civilization. With Sneferu, pyramid building wasn't simply a pious sideline for the monarchy to dabble in. It became the principal activity of each pharaoh's reign and the central economic engine of Egyptian society.

Sneferu demonstrated this shift by the sheer volume of his pyramid building. He did much more than simply build or rehabilitate an older structure at Meidum. He also built two massive pyramids at Dahshur, a little less than 30 miles north of Meidum and closer to the Old Kingdom capital of Memphis.

The more northerly of the two is sometimes known as the North Pyramid; it is also called the Red Pyramid, for the color of the stonework that was revealed when the original limestone casing was stripped away. The Red Pyramid stands about 340 feet tall, and when it was built, it ranked as the tallest pyramid in Egypt. However, its sides have an angle of 43° 22', which is much less vertical than the approximately 52° characteristic of the Great Pyramid at Giza. As a result, the Red Pyramid looks more squat than soaring.

Evidence suggests that the Red Pyramid was completed before Sneferu's rebuilding of the pyramid at Meidum and may well have been intended as the pharaoh's burial place. A north-side entryway leads down into the pyramid, then levels out at the structure's bottommost level and opens into three corbelled chambers. The first two are nearly identical in size, while the third is larger and may have been intended to serve as the burial vault.

Sneferu's original, and more interesting, effort at Dahshur is the Bent Pyramid, a name that conveys the building's unusual shape. The lower portion rises at an angle of about 54° 28'. Then, a little beyond the halfway point, the angle changes to a 43° 22' angle like that of the Red Pyramid. The overall shape looks something like a trapezoid with a triangle on top.

Various scholars have trotted out various explanations for the Bent Pyramid's shape. One theory is that the builders were running out of time, money, or stone, and decided to economize. The lower-angled upper portion consumes less rock and construction time than if the steeper angle had been extended all the way to the pyramid's uppermost course, and thus it shortened building time. However, this argument is unconvincing, in that Sneferu certainly had enough time and resources to build or rebuild both the Meidum pyramid and the North or Red Pyramid at Dahshur.

Then there is the safety argument. Mendelssohn, who holds that Meidum collapsed during construction, is of the opinion that the Bent Pyramid was already under construction and a little over half finished at the time of the disaster. Fearful, the builders altered the angle to prevent another such catastrophe.

Both the speed-and-economy and safety arguments overlook a key and unique fact about the Bent Pyramid: it contains two unconnected substructures, each reached by a separate entrance, and each clearly designed into the pyramid from the beginning of construction. The first entrance opens on the north side, the usual orientation for pyramid entries, then slopes down into the bedrock and ends in a corbelled chamber. The second entrance sits higher than the first and begins on the pyramid's west side. It leads down into another corbelled chamber built entirely in the body of the pyramid and positioned higher than, but not directly over, the bedrock chamber. Neither of these chambers has revealed any evidence of a burial or a sarcophagus.

I suspect strongly that the Bent Pyramid was meant to be bent from the beginning. Unlike any other ancient Egyptian pyramid, it expresses duality—two angles, two geometries, two tunnel and chamber complexes. There is something ritualistic and symbolic in this shape, a meaning we now find elusive. The Egyptians clearly found this meaning to be important. The craftsmanship of the Bent Pyramid achieves a high level, and the entire structure is beautifully wrought. Clearly, Sneferu and the Egyptians of his time were using architecture to express something of great importance, and they were giving this work their all.

We might also note that Sneferu's three pyramids do little if anything to help the theory of pyramids as tombs. Why does anyone need to be buried in three different structures? Furthermore, as the Egyptologist Miroslav Verner has written, "neither his [Sneferu's] bodily remains nor any convincing proof of his interment were found in any of them [the Meidum, Bent, or Red/North Pyramids]."[1]

APOGEE AT GIZA

Khufu, Sneferu's son and successor and the second pharaoh of the Fourth Dynasty (c. 2551–2528 B.C.), outdid his predecessor not in number of pyramids but in the size and elaboration of his single effort. Realizing that Dahshur was too small to hold the kind of grand pyramid complex he envisioned, Khufu chose the Giza plateau, which lay farther up the Nile, close to the point where the great river branches and braids into the delta that spills its great watery load into the Mediterranean. This area on the border between the dry Sahara and the verdant Nile Valley offered plenty of room and an abundant supply of high-quality limestone.

As we shall see later, there may have been additional reasons for Khufu's choice of Giza. For example, the presence of the Sphinx, the origins of which predate the Old Kingdom by at least 2,000 years, indicates that the area possessed ritual significance well before Khufu turned his attention to it. He may have been less going somewhere new than returning somewhere old.

Whatever brought him to Giza, it was there that Khufu launched the largest single building project of ancient Egypt (although, in sum, Sneferu's two or three pyramids were more ambitious) and one of the most monumental structures yet erected on this planet. The Great Pyramid—which the ancient Egyptians called Khufu's Horizon—is the only survivor among the Seven Wonders of the ancient world (see the appendices). It certainly qualifies, if only on quantitative measure. Even without its original white-limestone casing, the Great Pyramid contains approximately 2.3 million blocks of limestone. At an average per-block weight of 2.5 tons, the whole structure tips the scales at some 5.75 million tons. Originally reaching 481 feet in height, the Great Pyramid is the tallest pyramid, not only in

Photograph of the Great Pyramid taken by Francis Bedford on March 5, 1862; to the left
is the Second (Khafre) Pyramid. (*From Smyth, 1864, frontispiece.*)

Egypt but also in the entire ancient world. Until the construction of the
Eiffel Tower in 1889, it was the tallest building in the modern world, as
well. With its sides measuring almost 756 feet apiece in length, it also has
the largest ancient footprint of all, over 13 acres.

Two other aspects of the Great Pyramid make it stand out from all the
other pyramids, both of which we will examine in more detail later. One is
the extraordinary precision of the building. For example, the sides are oriented almost perfectly to the north–south and east–west axes, and they
vary in length by only a matter of inches. The second feature is the network
of passages and chambers that lie within and under the great stone structure. No other pyramid boasts an interior architecture anywhere nearly as
complex.

After Khufu, pyramid building declined in scale and, apparently, social
and religious importance. Only two more of the pharaohs of the Fourth
Dynasty built pyramids at Giza: Khafre, the fourth king in the line, and
Menkaure, the sixth. In addition to being smaller than Khufu's, these two
pyramids are less precise in their construction, less craftsmanlike, and sim-
pler, with less complicated tunnels and internal chambers.

Pyramid building continued in the Fifth (2465–2323 B.C.), Sixth (2323–2150 B.C.), and Seventh–Eighth dynasties (2150–2134 B.C.), but only one of the structures exceeded Menkaure's in size—and Menkaure's pyramid was but a fraction of the size of Khufu's. Likewise, the workmanship comes nowhere near what was exhibited at Giza. The high point had passed, and as in the Roman Empire depicted by Edward Gibbon and embellished by Hollywood, it was all downhill from there.

THE KINGS WHO WOULD BE GODS

There is more to the pyramids than the pyramids themselves. Surrounding the pyramids were complexes of temples, subsidiary tombs, causeways, walls, courtyards, and other structures. The pyramids and their ancillary structures were the centers of cult activities supported and administered by pious foundations. Each cult focused on statues of the dead pharaoh that were the basis of what amounted to an elaborate form of ancestor worship and that represented a shift in the nature of kingship from the First Dynasty to the Fourth.

In the early days, kingship among the Egyptians centered on military and physical prowess. To be pharaoh, the ruler had to be smart, strong, and sly; weakness meant the end of rule. The *sed* festival of early Egypt tested the king's mettle by requiring him to run the perimeter of a large courtyard, possibly several times. Since *sed* is rooted in the Egyptian word *sdi*, which means "slay" or "butcher," it is very likely that a king who proved less than vigorous was dead by the end of the *sed* festival, and a stronger rival had taken over the palace.

The philosophy of the pharaoh as the biggest, baddest guy on the Nile changed with Djoser and Imhotep. With a unified, peaceful Egypt, the king became less a military dictator who enforced order in the Two Lands than the man who was responsible for maintaining the fundamental order of the cosmos.

Since we see history as linear, we might assume that the emergence of the *benben* (the first land) from the original chaos set the universe on its course once and for all. The Egyptians, though, saw history as circular: what happened before will happen again. Chaos, or *isfet*, was always waiting to overwhelm creation and return the cosmos to formlessness. Existence depended on maintaining the balance between creation and chaos, a delicate, subtle, equilibrium the Egyptians called *ma'at*. Sometimes translated as "truth," *ma'at* has a meaning akin to Hebrew *shalom*, Arabic *salaam*, Sanskrit *om*, and Hawaiian *aloha*, implying balance on a scale that reaches from the individual to the cosmos. To preserve *ma'at*, everything in the universe required the balance of its opposite. Male had female, up down, night day, black white, mortal immortal.

To the pharaoh fell the cosmic task of bridging the gap between the two worlds of mortality and immortality, of this world and the afterlife. The pharaoh walked in the company of the gods, spoke their language, shared their wisdom, and enacted ceremonies daily that replicated the first instance of creation, thereby saving the cosmos from descent into chaos. Because the pharaoh attended to daily rituals that summoned the powers of creation against those of chaos, the natural world continued in its proper rhythms. When the pharaoh preserved *ma'at*, the Nile rose and fell as it should, the sun completed its daily passage from east to west, the moon always came back after three days of darkness, and prosperity and justice reigned in the Two Lands. The pharaoh's was an awesome task, and it was his to fulfill in death as well as life.

As befits the Egyptian sense of balanced duality, two worlds existed side by side. One was earthly existence—mortality, with its pain, illness, brevity, and impermanence. The other world was the afterlife—much like mortal life in its beauty and pleasure, yet eternal, populated by spirits the Egyptians called gods and lacking sickness, death, suffering, or worry. It was a blessed place to be, especially forever.

At the moment of conception, the two worlds combined to create a child. The mortal, physical world contributed the body, which could operate only because it was animated by the spiritual *ka*. The *ka* could leave the body during sleep or unconsciousness, but it always returned—at least until death, when the *ka* departed the body yet remained close to the grave or tomb. Since the *ka* had directed needs like hunger and thirst during life, it continued to need food and drink after death.

Each human also contained a *ba*, which lacked the personal identity of the *ka* and was a formless, cosmic energy that animated all beings. At death the *ba* returned to the universe, carrying no memory of its recent sojourn into mortality.

At death, the *ka* and *ba* fled the body and left it an empty shell. Mummification transformed this emptiness so that it could pass over into the afterlife. Mummification constituted a form of resurrection by reconnecting *ka* and *ba* to body and allowing the whole being to cross over.

Exactly where the realm of the afterlife was thought to exist changed over the course of the Old Kingdom, most notably during the reign of Khufu. Early on, the other world was located in heaven, among the stars. After death and burial, the mummified, resurrected pharaoh made his way to the stars and there joined the ranks of the gods. Later, however, the afterlife came to be literally an underworld. The sun moved from east to west during the day, then at night dropped below the horizon to appear again in the eastern sky at dawn. There, beneath our world, in that unknown place where the sun shone at night, the gods and the resurrected spirits passed their paradisiacal days for all eternity. The afterlife had moved from stars to sun.

Khufu was never known as a "son of Re," the sun god worshiped at the Egyptian holy city of Iunu (later known by its Greek name Heliopolis, "city of the sun"). But his Fourth Dynasty successors—Djedefre, Khafre, and Menkaure—bore that title. According to one interpretation, sometime between the death of Khufu and the accession of Djedefre, a major religious change occurred. A minor son of Khufu who came to the throne only after the untimely death of the most likely successor to the throne, Djedefre turned away from his father's complex at Giza to go his own way. The new pharaoh began a pyramid at Abu Roash (also spelled Abu Rawash), some 5 miles north of Giza and directly opposite the temple of Re at Iunu.

When Khafre, another minor son of Khufu, took the throne—possibly as a result of Djedefre's unexpected death, perhaps through a coup d'état— the pyramid of Abu Roash was left unfinished, and images of Djedefre were smashed. Something ferocious was going on in ancient Egypt, even as Khafre refocused the energy of the Fourth Dynasty on Giza and there built the pyramids associated with his reigns. He had come back to Khufu's ritual center, yet he and his Fourth Dynasty successors carried the title "son of Re," which the builder of the Great Pyramid had never borne.

Against this background, one interpretation is to view Khufu as the last defender of the old way, a fact that becomes all the more interesting when we look at the conflicting ancient stories surrounding him. Khufu is variously seen as a sacrilegious tyrant who opposed the religious ways of many of his people, or as a religious scholar who possessed a deep knowledge and yearning for the sacred. These competing interpretations of Khufu might be expected if he was a man of strong religious convictions—but not necessarily convictions shared by all of his people.

One ancient account of Khufu comes from the classical Greek historian Herodotus, who lived from about 484 B.C. until sometime between 430 and 420 B.C. According to Herodotus, Sneferu created a perfect state of justice— the social version of *ma'at*—and spread prosperity across Egypt. Khufu, though, "plunged into every kind of wickedness,"[2] shutting down all the temples, forbidding sacrifice, sending his daughter into prostitution when he needed money, and ordering all Egyptians to work for him, first in building a road, then on a burial vault on an island created by a canal from the Nile, and finally on the pyramid that now bears his name. Manetho, an Egyptian priest and writer of the third century B.C., who authored a history of the pharaohs from before the First Dynasty to Alexander's invasion, described Khufu as a scholar who wrote a holy book. Manetho claimed to have a copy, but unfortunately this work has not survived. Diodorus Siculus (c. 80–20 B.C.), a Graeco-Roman historian from the time of Julius Caesar and Augustus, maintained that neither Khufu nor Khafre was buried in the pyramid each built. Both pharaohs feared that because they were such tyrants, the people would rise up in revolt and desecrate their mummies. When they did come to die, they ordered their friends to bury them secretly in order to guarantee their passage into divinity.

It is important to recognize that these conflicting opinions of Khufu, though themselves ancient by our reckoning, were recorded long after the fact. When Herodotus wrote his account, approximately 2,100 years had passed since Khufu's rule. Herodotus was as far removed in time from Khufu as we ourselves are from Jesus of Nazareth. The accounts of Diodorus Siculus and Manetho are even farther from their point of origin.

Still, it is unlikely that the three writers were making up the story entirely. No doubt they were drawing on oral histories or folk tales, a source

Herodotus in particular relished. At a minimum, those stories, coupled with the Fourth Dynasty's religious upheaval, lead us to suspect that something curious and unusual was going on during Khufu's time, something the standard story—which posits the Great Pyramid as nothing more than a giant mausoleum—falls short of explaining. Once again, we must ask whether the Great Pyramid has more significance than simply being "a tomb for some ambitious booby," as Henry David Thoreau once expressed it.

FACTS THAT FIT, FACTS THAT DON'T

In part, the standard story works. The Two Lands did come together and form a dynamic political alliance that grew into an expanding kingdom, one that extended its rule into the neighboring regions of Africa and Asia. A powerful elite personified by the pharaoh ruled this growing kingdom, and the religious ideology of royal Egypt transformed the pharaoh into a god awaiting divine transformation at death.

It is in the next leap—that the pyramids served only to house the preserved bodies of dead pharaohs and help in their metamorphosis into a god—where the orthodox explanation falls short. Put simply, the standard story doesn't account for a number of realities, most strikingly in the case of the Great Pyramid.

To date, no unquestioned royal mummy has been found in the Great Pyramid, nor in any of the three large Giza pyramids for that matter. The best direct evidence for pharaonic interment in the larger Giza pyramids comes from the Menkaure Pyramid, where a basalt sarcophagus was discovered by the British colonel Howard Vyse in 1837 in one chamber, and human bones and the remains of a wooden coffin bearing the name Menkaure in another. Vyse had the sarcophagus shipped back to England for study, but the vessel foundered off the coast of Spain and took the sarcophagus to the bottom. The wooden coffin was probably a restitution from the Twenty-sixth Dynasty (664–525 B.C.), and, based on radiocarbon dating, the humans remains are from the Christian era. The Khafre Pyramid did contain a sarcophagus, but it housed the remains of not a human but a bull.

Perhaps robbers penetrated the royal tombs before archaeologists did and made off with the treasures they supposedly contained. The mummies themselves would also have been prizes. Even before history museums began adding mummies to their collections, mummy flesh was considered such a powerful medicinal ingredient in Europe that it fetched a stunning price. Thieves cleaned out more than a few ancient tombs, and the mummies of the pharaohs could have made up part of the supply that fed this ghoulish market.

But there is another explanation, one that has to be considered: the pyramids contain no mummies because they never were intended as burial sites. Diodorus writes that Khufu and Khafre were buried elsewhere. Perhaps they were hardly unusual in their choice of a final resting place somewhere other than the pyramids they are said to have built.

If so, then Khufu had another idea in mind with the Great Pyramid. Were he interested simply in building the biggest burial mound in human history, he certainly went to a great deal of unnecessary trouble, on both the inside and the outside of the structure.

The internal passages and chambers of the other pyramids of the Third and Fourth dynasties fit their putative purpose as burial sites. Basically, an entryway leads into one or more chambers located under the pyramid or close to its base. The Great Pyramid has a vastly more complex structure.

The original entrance begins on the Great Pyramid's north side, as is typical of pyramids in this era, then angles along the Descending Passage to an intersection just above the original bedrock foundation of the pyramid. There the First Ascending Passage angles up, while the Descending Passage continues well down into the bedrock. It ends in a rough-hewn, apparently unfinished room known variously as the Pit, the Subterranean Chamber, and the Cul-de-Sac.

Meanwhile, the first Ascending Passage rises to an intersection of three passages. The first, called the Well Shaft, heads steeply down through the pyramid, changes course more than once, and connects finally to the Descending Passage before it reaches the Subterranean Chamber. The second Passage follows the horizontal into what was dubbed the Queen's Chamber by the earliest Arab investigators of the pyramid. They gave it this name

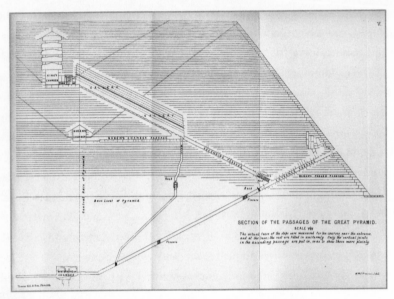

The passages of the Great Pyramid. (*From Petrie, 1885, plate v.*)

because it contained the kind of gabled roof used in women's tombs among the Arabs, rather than the flat roof found in men's.

The Great Pyramid currently contains 203 courses of blocks forming horizontal layers believed to run completely through the pyramid. The Great Pyramid does not come to a sharp point or apex, so it is often estimated that there may have been originally seven or eight additional courses, for a total of 210 or 211. The Queen's Chamber lies at the twenty-fifth course of masonry, and it is large, measuring 19 feet long, 17 feet wide, and 15 to 20 feet high (the ceiling comes to a peak). Its most prominent feature is a large niche cut into the eastern wall. The chamber is built of limestone blocks so precisely joined that it almost appears to have been carved from a single solid block of stone. One curious, and as yet unexplained, feature of the Queen's Chamber is the pair of vents, or airshafts, that begin 5 inches deep in the rock wall and lead over 240 feet, one north and one south, to within an estimated 20 feet of the exterior. The shafts, which are only about 8 inches square, are lined with limestone conduits. They weren't simply cut after all the courses of stone were in place. Rather, they were designed in and cut as the stones were put down layer by layer. Why the builders of the pyramid would have gone to so much trouble to route two shafts such a distance, only to leave them sealed at both ends, remains one of the Great Pyramid's many unanswered questions.

The third passage branching off the intersection horizontal to the Queen's chamber enters the Grand Gallery. This remarkable structure stretches for 157 feet at a 26-degree angle under seven-layered corbel walls that angle in on themselves dramatically through their 28-foot height. The Grand Gallery creates the effect of a long, exalted tunnel.

The Grand Gallery ends in a single immense stone block called the Great Step. Directly behind the Great Step lies a small opening, only 41 to 42 inches high and wide, that gives onto a small room known as the antechamber. Yet another small opening leads to the King's Chamber. Larger than the Queen's Chamber, the King's Chamber measures over 34 feet long, 17 feet wide, and 19 feet high, and it is built entirely of red granite from

The Grand Gallery looking south. Photograph courtesy of Robert M. Schoch.

Aswan, in Upper Egypt. The King's Chamber lies at the fiftieth course of masonry and is empty except for a lidless, rose-granite sarcophagus (also referred to as a coffer) widely considered to have received the mummy of Khufu. When Westerners first explored the King's Chamber, however, the sarcophagus was empty. As in the Queen's Chamber, two shafts lead from the interior space toward the pyramid's exterior. The King's Chamber's vents, though, do reach all the way to the surface and open into the chamber, creating a pathway for airflow between interior and exterior. No other pyramid has this feature.

Nor does any other pyramid have the five so-called Relieving Chambers constructed atop the King's Chamber. The uppermost of the five chambers has a pointed limestone roof that channels weight pressing down from above onto the sides and distributes it to the four chambers beneath. The engineering is ingenious. Various scholars have said that the King's Chamber would have collapsed under the weight of the rock above it without the Relieving Chambers. In fact, though, the Great Pyramid itself contains evidence against this argument. The Queen's Chamber lies 25 courses deeper in the pyramid and carries far more weight per square foot of roof area, yet it has survived for millennia. Perhaps the Relieving Chambers were an unneeded safeguard designed by an overly cautious architect. Or perhaps they served some other and still-unknown purpose.

Zahi Hawass, Secretary General of the Supreme Council of Antiquities in Egypt and Director of the Giza Pyramids Excavation, argues that the complexity of the Great Pyramid's interior resulted from indecision on the part of its builders. Hawass maintains that the Subterranean Chamber was the original burial chamber. Before this underground vault was finished, however, the builders decided to construct a new passage up into the body of the pyramid, then went horizontally to the Queen's Chamber, which was likewise left unfinished. Changing plans yet again, the builders constructed the Grand Gallery as an entryway to the larger, and even more magnificent, burial vault that became the King's Chamber.

This explanation, though, obscures a number of facts. For one thing, the entire internal structure shows forethought. As examples, the Ascending and Descending passages follow almost exactly the same angles, and the lidless sarcophagus in the King's Chamber is too big to have been moved up

The granite coffer in the King's Chamber. Photograph courtesy of Robert M. Schoch.

the passages. It had to be put into place before the chamber was finished. For another, the internal structure demonstrates a very high level of design and effort. In the other pyramids, passages serve only as paths for moving the royal remains and the funeral party into the burial chamber. If that were true for the Great Pyramid as well, why did anyone go to the trouble of building the exquisite Grand Gallery when an ordinary tunnel would have done just as well? And other details get in the way of accepting the King's Chamber as Khufu's burial vault. The sarcophagus, though too big to drag up the passages, is too small to accept a royal mummy and its customary multiple wooden coffins. And why, if this site were intended to bear the pharaoh's remains into eternity, is it supplied with shafts that apparently supply air? Among the dead an air supply merely hastens decay, a royal mummy's archenemy.

The exterior of the Great Pyramid shows a similar attention to details, many of which the standard story does not explain. One is the structure's extraordinary precision. The most accurate survey of the Great Pyramid, conducted in 1925 by J. H. Cole for the British colonial government in Egypt, found the north side to be 230.253 meters long, the south 230.454, the east 230.391, and the west 230.357. The variation from longest to shortest is but 0.201 meter, or just under 8 inches, over a distance well in excess of two football fields. The Great Pyramid comes about as close to a perfect square as human engineering, modern or ancient, can make it.

The same precision applies to the Great Pyramid's orientation. The four sides each point to one of the cardinal directions. The orientation to the north-south axis is just over 3 arcminutes to the west of true north—just over one-twentieth of a degree. Again, the Great Pyramid's orientation is about as perfect as human engineering can achieve.

Near perfection implies both intention and attention; such things do not happen by accident. The builders wanted the pyramid's squareness and cardinal orientation. They also wanted the slight concavity of its sides.

The Great Pyramid's sides do not run straight from one corner to the next above the base courses of masonry. Rather, they slope slightly inward, joining at the midline in a very shallow angle—the two planes of each "face" of the Great Pyramid meet at an angle of about 27' (about 0.45°) different from a perfectly flat plane. This slight concavity is virtually imperceptible to the human eye from ground level. It apparently transforms the pyramid into an indicator of the spring and fall equinoxes, those two singular days of the year when night and day are of equal length. At about 6 a.m. on the equinox, the rising sun striking the Great Pyramid briefly lights the west half of the south face, while the east half is still dark; then the entire face is in the light. At about 6 p.m. the lighting pattern is reversed, as the east half remains lit yet the west falls dark; then both sides fall dark. This phenomenon is sometimes referred to as the "flash" or the "flash effect." In ancient days, when the Great Pyramid's outer layer of white limestone was intact, the flash effect must have filled the exact day of the equinox with an extraordinary brilliance.

A final oddity of the exterior: alone of the three major pyramids on the Giza Plateau, the Great Pyramid lacks an apex. Instead of coming to a peak, it ends in a small rough platform. Some scholars argue that the pyramidion, the pyramid-shaped stone that should have capped the pyramid, and the uppermost core and casing stones were removed along with the rest of the outer white limestone centuries ago. This did not occur to the other two major pyramids on the plateau, however, despite their short stature and

The Giza Plateau photographed at sunset from 4,000 feet; early twentieth century. Note the concavity on the south side of the Great Pyramid. This unusual photograph caught the light of the setting sun on the Great Pyramid at just the correct angle to show that there are actually two "faces" on each side of the Great Pyramid. Photograph by Brigadier General P.R.C. Groves, British Royal Air Force. (*From Groves and McCrindle, 1926, p. 314.*)

therefore presumably easier accessibility. It makes me wonder whether the builders of the Great Pyramid ever intended a sharp apex capped by a pyramidion. If they did not, then it is but another bit of evidence pointing to the uniqueness of the Great Pyramid and the failure of the standard story to account for its fascinating singularity.

Three

THINKING OUTSIDE
THE SARCOPHAGUS

HERE IS NO DOUBT THAT THE GREAT PYRAMID IS NOT A
tomb alone, and may not be a tomb at all. This insight has come
to any number of contemporary writers who have pondered the
mysteries and peculiarities of this much-studied monument and realized
that the standard story simply fails to bear the weight of all the questions.

But if the Great Pyramid isn't just a tomb, then what is it? The many
answers to this question add up to an intriguing range of speculation about
the true purpose of the pyramid Khufu is said to have built. As we will see
in later chapters, some writers have sought the answer not strictly in terms
of burial rites but in the context of a broader mythological and religious
significance. Perhaps the Great Pyramid was not a tomb but a temple or, as
some posit, a site of initiatory rites, reflecting the liturgy found in the
Egyptian Book of the Dead, as suggested by Marsham Adams in 1895 (and
discussed further in chapter 11). Or, as researcher Alan Alford has suggested in his 2004 book *The Midnight Sun,* the Great Pyramid was part of
an ancient "cult of creation," the primary aim of which was a celebration
and reenactment of the myth of the creation of the cosmos. Other researchers have sought an explanation for the Great Pyramid outside the
realm of ancient Egyptian religious belief. This way of thinking often

shares a common starting point: minimizing or totally dismissing the structure's religious and mythological import. What if the Great Pyramid is something altogether different from a tomb and religious monument? What if it served a practical, even utilitarian function? In our own days of the early twenty-first century, immense building structures tend to serve useful secular functions, whether to generate energy (such as a hydroelectric dam or a nuclear power plant), or serve as a factory, or simply house people, as in an office building or apartment complex. Looking at ancient structures with modern eyes, many writers have asked: might not this have been the case thousands of years ago for mighty structures like the Great Pyramid?

PYRAMIDS, DEAD CATS, AND GOOD SHAVES

A common notion, and one that has made it into mainstream popular culture, is the idea of "pyramid power." In essence, the concept of pyramid power is that the very shape of a pyramid, especially one with the exact scale of the Great Pyramid, somehow can capture energy and perform practical functions, such as preserving food. As discussed in the section entitled "Pryamid Physics" in the appendices, a small but committed group of scientists takes this idea very seriously, and there may exist some empirical evidence, to a limited degree, supporting the concept of "pyramid power." Realistically, though, the jury is still out.

The modern concept of "pyramid power" begins with a Frenchman by the name of Antoine Bovis, who in the 1920s or 1930s stumbled onto something curious inside the Great Pyramid that no one else had ever noticed before. Bovis observed this phenomenon in the garbage cans set up inside the monument to handle the trash and castoffs of the tourist trade. Dead, discarded animals—sometimes a cat, sometimes a mouse, sometimes both a cat and a mouse, according to which version of the story you read—had dried into perfect mummies without putrefying and giving off the nauseating stench of death. Certain that this alteration of the usual physical reality of death came from the shape of the pyramid, Bovis returned to France, built a scale model of Khufu's monument, and deposited a dead cat inside. Sure enough, the phenomenon he had seen in Giza repeated itself, and the animal mummified without rotting. Bovis supposedly got similar results with slices of cheese and chunks of raw meat.

As far as I have been able to determine, Bovis never published his experiments. Yet word of them somehow made their way to Czechoslovakia, where, in the late 1940s, they caught the eye of Karl Drbal, a radio engineer interested in the regeneration of energy. Drbal attempted his own mummification experiments with meat, eggs, flowers, and small reptiles and amphibians, and reportedly found that the pyramid worked as Bovis advertised. Intrigued, Drbal located Bovis at his ironmonger's shop in Nice, on the French Riviera, and exchanged letters with him. Although Drbal found Bovis "'too magic'" for his taste,[1] he continued his own experiments. In the course of that work, Drbal made one of the longest logical leaps recorded in intellectual history: he decided that Bovis's work on dead cats had major implications for the sharpness of razor blades.

It all went back to Drbal's army service years earlier. Prankster soldiers got the best of one another by leaving straight razors out in the moonlight. According to military folklore, such treatment would dull the razor and turn the morning shave into a nick-filled misery. Drbal reasoned that a pyramid that dried a dead cat into a mummy without rotting would surely keep a razor blade from dulling after a few shaves, as the razor blades of those pre–stainless steel days did. How Drbal made this particular jump, from cats to razors, he himself has yet to explain.

Drbal built a model of the Great Pyramid and placed a used razor blade in it. Sure enough, he claimed, its sharpness returned. Once restored to its original keenness, the blade could be kept sharp for up to 200 shaves, just by storing it in the pyramid-shaped regeneration device between shaves. Drbal became so fascinated by this effect, and so convinced of its commercial possibilities, that he filed for a patent. Although initially unimpressed, the patent office in Prague eventually granted Drbal patent no. 91304 in 1959, 10 years after the original application, for a "device for maintaining the sharpness of razor blades and razors."[2] In the course of presenting evidence for his pyramid device, Drbal explained how it worked. "There is no magic involved in the functioning of the razor-blade pyramid," he wrote later, "nor of the mummification model pyramid. Rather, there are two main factors at work here."[3] One was fast dehydration; rapid drying saved the steel of the blade from rust and drew moisture out of the cat's tissues. In addition, the pyramid affected the microscopic structure of materials both living and dead, reorienting the steel to its original state and preventing the growth of microorganisms in the feline carcass. Both processes occurred, Drbal maintained, because the cavity of the pyramid resonated with cosmic microwaves concentrated by the earth's magnetic field. This is not an entirely implausible idea.

When word of Drbal's work penetrated the Iron Curtain and worked its way west, pyramid power extended beyond razor blades. Soon all kinds of people interested in the unusual and the paranormal were experimenting with pyramids for every purpose from preventing mold to preserving food without refrigeration. Pyramid-shaped tents became popular for meditation, and one New Age entrepreneur experimented with pyramid-shaped hats to boost brainpower. Erik von Däniken, the writer whose ideas about the extraterrestrial connections of pyramids appear in chapter 5, claimed he could use a pyramid to turn ordinary Bordeaux wine into a *grand cru*. Yet another writer reported that putting a pyramid under her boyfriend's chair transformed his fatigue into a pleasing sexual athleticism.

There are a number of problems with the pyramid power concept in terms of understanding ancient Egypt. If it worked, the mummification effect would clearly have been of value to the pharaohs and their people. But it's hard to imagine inhabitants of the Old Kingdom using pyramids to boost the longevity of copper razor blades, make bad wine good, or set the stage for an evening of romance—particularly when there are no depictions of such uses from ancient Egypt. There's good reason for that absence: a relative lack of solid and replicable evidence that all, or even most, of the positive effects attributed to pyramid power are real.

Most of the stories told about the power of pyramids to preserve dead critters or regenerate dull blades are anecdotes, tales told by one person to another, without any scientific control. They are as ephemeral and unreliable as the folklore of moonlight dulling army-issue straight razors. Moonlight has no known special property that dulls steel. More probably, leaving old-fashioned carbon steel out all night rusted the edge and stole its sharpness. When researchers from the Stanford Research Institute conducted experiments inside the Great Pyramid in 1977, biological samples deteriorated at predictable rates. There was no mummification effect. Still, this does not mean that there is absolutely nothing to the notion of pyramid power in a general sense. As I mention in the appendices under "Pyramid Physics," there exist some reportedly legitimate scientific studies supporting the concept of "pyramid power" to sharpen razors, affect biological materials, and so forth. Honestly, however, I have my doubts and believe more replication of such studies is needed before we can consider such affects verified. Furthermore, these modern studies of pyramid physics no more explain the true function and purpose of the Great Pyramid than the modern study of electricity explains the ancient respect for the power of lightning.

Whatever the deep power and allure of the Great Pyramid for many people, it has little to do with dead cats, bad wine, or dull razors.

THE GIZA WATER WORKS

According to the late hydraulic engineer Edward J. Kunkel of Warren, Ohio, who wrote a 1962 book called *Pharaoh's Pump*, the Great Pyramid served primarily to harness the power of water in moving great weights. The unique passages and chambers of the Great Pyramid's interior had nothing to do with transmitting the soul of the departed pharaoh into the next world. Instead, they created a huge pump that could spew water at tremendous pressure.

Kunkel's speculation began where many pyramid writers start out: Just how did the ancient Egyptians, who had no draft animals besides oxen and little metal other than copper and meteoritic iron, move stones weighing many tons? Pondering the 80-ton stone door to the Temple of Karnak, Kunkel decided that the answer had to be water. His idea was that the builders constructed a lock around the area where the door was to go, floated the monolith into place—presumably on some kind of barge—then let the water out to allow the stone door to sink into place. It was a simple solution, Kunkel declared, and because it was simple, it had to be correct.

Kunkel reasoned further that terraces at the Temple of Karnak were walled in to hold water and form a series of locks. Building blocks were moved up the terraces in much the same way that locks on canals like the Suez and the Panama fill or drain to raise or lower ships passing between bodies of water at different elevations.

Even though Kunkel offered no evidence to support this hypothesis other than its alleged simplicity, he stretched his line of reasoning farther. Monolith moving would take a great deal of water. Of course, water is a scarce commodity in a desert country like Egypt. Therefore, all building had to occur when the Nile was in flood stage and the river flowed close to the riverside building sites. Still, much more than a massive bucket brigade would be required to move water in the needed volume out of the river and into the system of canals, lakes, channels, and locks needed to bring stones up the sides of the pyramids and float them into place. Then he took another look at the internal architecture of the Great Pyramid.

"I contend," Kunkel wrote in an article published in the *Rosicrucian Digest,* "that the interior passages and chambers of the Great Pyramid of Gizeh were designed to be a water pump to provide water for the pools and locks whereby the immense blocks of stone could be floated into position and fixed."[4]

In Kunkel's view, two fountains spewed from the pyramid, one from its north side and one from its south, once the structure had been completed above the level of the King's Chamber. The fountains' spray formed a pool whose water spilled into a set of zigzag locks that extended down to the banks of the Nile—which was, of course, in flood stage and therefore close to the building site. Stone blocks brought down the Nile on barges could rise up the series of locks to the level under construction and be floated into place.

The key to Kunkel's water pump is the two diagonal tubes in the body of the Great Pyramid. The first, the Descending Passage, extends down through the body of the pyramid into the limestone bedrock below, where it ends in an apparently unfinished room. The Ascending Passage forms the second diagonal. It angles up from the Descending Passage, intersects with a horizontal passage to the Queen's Chamber, then continues on through the Grand Gallery in the direction of the King's Chamber. In terms of the hydraulic function of the diagonals, the Queen's Chamber serves as a compression chamber for the upper diagonal, and the bedrock chamber plays the same role for the lower.

By Kunkel's calculation, the lower diagonal tube of the Descending Passage could hold about 80 tons of water, the upper in the neighborhood of 300. A fire at the top of the tube would create a vacuum that caused the water to rise, and this rise continued because of the upward force of compressed air in the compression chambers. Eventually the water would reach the King's Chamber and travel up and out to the fountains through the misnamed airshafts—which were really water conduits.

In a laboratory, it is easy to demonstrate the basic physics of Kunkel's model. Fashion a diagonal tube with an air compression chamber at the bottom, then start a fire in an enclosure at the top. As a vacuum forms because of the fire, the compressed air at the bottom will push the water up. The movement will continue until the forces of vacuum, gravity, and air compression balance.

That's in the lab, however. Would the same hydraulics have worked inside the Great Pyramid of Giza?

Well maybe, if it were supplied with the necessary (and apparently now missing) valves, seals, and other apparatus. Still, many questions remain, and I am far from convinced that the pump theory is the best explanation for the Great Pyramid. Where was the fire built to create the vacuum? I have spent many hours exploring the chambers and passages of the Great Pyramid, and I would expect to find telltale damage to the stone in the passage or chamber where the fire was kept, yet I have failed to observe any such evidence in my investigations of the Great Pyramid (although I have observed fire damage to the stone walls of various ancient Egyptian temples elsewhere in Egypt, where, because they were inhabited as shelters, cooking fires were lit against the walls). And how was air supplied to the Queen's Chamber and the subterranean rooms to maintain air pressure? The shafts close to the Queen's Chamber never reach the chamber itself and could not have provided an air supply.

There is also the matter of the Great Pyramid's uniqueness. Kunkel argues that the interior of the pyramid is all about practical engineering, not religious significance. If that were true, and if the water pump worked as well as he said it did, why was it never repeated in another pyramid?

All of this points to the core problem with Kunkel's idea: a lack of compelling evidence. Theoretically, the Great Pyramid could probably be retrofitted to turn it into a monstrous water pump, but that does not mean it was either designed or used as a pump. There is simply no indication that the Great Pyramid ever contained the kinds of seals, valves, floats, and other devices a water pump requires. Kunkel's water pump theory is just a guess, and a highly speculative one at that.

THE POWER PLANT OF THE SANDS

Christopher Dunn, a master craftsman and engineer, follows another speculative path, developing an idea no less intriguingly outlandish than Kunkel's. Dunn's proposal, advanced in his popular 1998 book *The Giza Power Plant*, is that the Great Pyramid sat at the center of ancient Egypt's electrical grid. That's right: electrical. And this was not simply your usual smoke-spewing, coal- or gas-fired generator or water-damming hydroelectric turbine. Rather, it was a visionary, Jules Verne–worthy high technology that used hydrogen to convert the earth's own vibrations into microwaves, which were then beamed—by orbiting satellites, no less—across the Two Lands and beyond, perhaps even to the waiting machines and appliances of Atlantis.

The fantastical workings of Dunn's electrical power plant began in the Queen's Chamber, which produced hydrogen, the very same fuel many analysts are now proposing as the best replacement for gasoline, oil, and other fossil fuels. The hydrogen arose from a chemical reaction. Diluted hydrochloric acid was placed in one of the two Queen's Chamber shafts, and hydrated zinc chloride solution in the other. When the two compounds mixed in the Queen's Chamber and reacted, hydrogen gas filled the pyramid's passages. Waste materials from the spent chemicals flowed along the Horizontal Passage, then down the Well Shaft into the bedrock below the pyramid.

Meanwhile, unknown and now-missing equipment in the Subterranean Chamber primed the power plant by setting off vibrations tuned to the resonant frequency of the Great Pyramid. Once primed, the pyramid vibrated more and more in response, until its oscillations hit the same level as the earth's. Once synchronized, the pyramid drew vibrational energy from the planet itself and sent it up through the Great Gallery, which was also filled with now-missing equipment—vast arrays of Helmholtz resonators—to convert the vibrational energy into sound. An acoustic filter in the Antechamber ensured that only sound frequencies in harmony with the resonant frequency of the King's Chamber entered that room.

It was the King's Chamber where the heart of the Giza power plant beat. Quartz crystals in the chamber's red granite vibrated in sympathy with the incoming sound, stressing the crystals and setting up a flow of electrons through what is known as the piezoelectric effect. At this point, both acoustical and electromagnetic energy filled the King's Chamber, which had been previously pumped full of hydrogen gas from the ongoing chemical reaction in the Queen's Chamber. The gas absorbed this abundant energy, which vibrated at frequencies harmonic with the resonance of hydrogen. In response, the single electron in each atom of hydrogen rose to a higher energy state.

Even more energy was added to this potent mix from outside the pyramid. Originally lined with metal, in Dunn's scenario, the northern shaft in the King's Chamber channeled a microwave signal—possibly from the constant bombardment of the earth by atomic hydrogen—through a crystal amplifier and into the King's Chamber. There it interacted with the energized hydrogen atoms and forced them back into their natural, or unenergized, state. Happening over and over again billions and trillions of times, the energy released by the hydrogen atoms' reversion to their natural state was collected in a microwave receiver in the chamber's south wall, then beamed out of the pyramid through the southern shaft—which, like its northern counterpart, was also originally lined with metal.

As to how this power was distributed across Egypt to power machines and appliances, even Dunn admits uncertainty. He hypothesizes that electrical transmission was not a matter of the towers and insulated wires we know. Rather, Egypt got its power through a wireless system of the sort once envisioned, but never built, by Nikola Tesla, a contemporary of Thomas Edison. Electricity traveled across Egypt in much the same way satellites relay signals to television sets across the globe. And the Egyptians, Dunn is willing to argue, had satellites (where is the evidence? the critics ask), which bounced the energy beamed up from the Great Pyramid to the homes, factories, and commercial structures of the Old Kingdom's Two Lands.

Dunn even maintains that evidence in the cult temple of the cow-headed goddess Hathor in the Nile River town of Dendera in Upper Egypt actually depicts the ancient Egyptians' electrical technology. Wall carvings in the temple's lower crypt show three men holding transparent vessels supported on what are known as a *djed* pillars and decorated either with snake images or enclosing live serpents. A tether or rope connects the vessels to small statues of the god Atum-Ra, identified by the sun disk on his head. A baboon holds an upraised knife with the sharp side of the blade facing one of the vessels.

Dunn maintains that this carving represents not the symbolism of ancient Egypt's religion but a graphic record of a Crookes tube, also known as a cathode ray tube, a device developed in the 1870s by the Englishman Sir William Crookes. A Crookes tube consists of a partially evacuated glass tube or bulb with an anode and a cathode set into it. When an electrical source is properly connected to the tube, a stream of electrons will pass from the cathode to the anode. When the electrons hit a phosphorescent surface or screen in the tube, they form a visible image. The principle of the cathode ray tube formed the basis for a great deal of twentieth-century electronics, including old-fashioned radar tubes, oscilloscopes, and the tubes in certain televisions and computer monitors. As Dunn sees it, the Dendera wall carving is not a collection of religious symbols but the depiction of an electrical experiment.

He points to more evidence as well, phenomena that Dunn contends can be explained only if the Egyptians had access to electrically powered devices—some of which may represent a technology so advanced we can't even imagine it. Examples include the precise machining and polishing of very hard rock, such as the granite sarcophagus in the Great Pyramid's King's Chamber, and the ability of the ancient Egyptians to raise huge monoliths to great heights and maneuver them into place.

As great as these accomplishments are, they prove only that the Egyptians were clever and adept. They by no means make it certain, or even likely, that the Egyptians had and used electricity. And the evidence that they did fails to hold up to even casual scrutiny. One of the founders of modern Egyptology, Sir William Flinders Petrie, long ago called attention to the amazing stoneworking abilities of the ancient Egyptians,[5] yet seemed satisfied that it was within their capacity to have made such objects with their known technological level.

Consider the Dendera wall carving, for example. None of the symbols depicted in the relief, such as the snakes and the baboon, are unusual in Egyptian religious art. As a goddess of the sky, which was feminine in Egyptian mythology, Hathor became the deity of women, fertility, and sexual love. The Egyptians, like many cultures ancient and modern, connected snakes with fertility—because they renew themselves whenever they shed their skins—and with sexuality, because the body of a snake rising to strike is reminiscent of the penis hardening and erecting. As a result, carved images of snakes are hardly anything unusual or unexpected in the temple of Hathor.

Dating is also a major problem. Although the oldest foundation stones at Dendera date to 2600 B.C. and the Old Kingdom, the manifest temple was built and the carving made during the Ptolemaic period, which began with Alexander the Great's invasion in 332 B.C., more than two millennia later. It is a grand assumption to decide, without evidence, that the Ptolemaic builders followed the details of the original building at Dendera and replicated an earlier image accurately depicting a technological wonder over 20 centuries old. In our time, the equivalent would be a detailed engineer's drawing for a Roman catapult carved into a remake of the Coliseum.

The problems surrounding Dunn's power plant theory do not stop in Dendera. Consider just how much machinery has to be added to the pyramid to make the theory work. It begins with vibration equipment in the Subterranean Chamber and extends through banks of Helmholtz resonators in the Grand Gallery, an acoustic filter in the Antechamber, metal linings for both King's Chamber shafts and a crystal filter in the northern one, a microwave receiver in the King's Chamber, and a wireless transmission system that included relay satellites in earth orbit. As it is, none of this equipment now resides within the Great Pyramid. Even if it had been purposefully removed, some evidence should point to its prior presence.

Dunn's model faces yet another tall hurdle: in my assessment, his mechanics is questionable, and I am not at all certain that it would work. A central process in his theory is the production of hydrogen gas in the Queen's Chamber, a reaction fueled by chemicals placed in the so-called airshafts. These shafts, however, apparently connect neither to the exterior surface of the Great Pyramid nor, as far as we can ascertain, did they originally connect to the interior of the Queen's Chamber (see the appendices). Rather, the shafts stopped 5 inches short of connecting to the interior of the Queen's Chamber until Waynman Dixon discovered them in 1872; he removed the last 5 inches of stone. Dunn, however, speculates that originally there was a small hole connecting each of the shafts to the interior of the Queen's chamber, and these holes served to meter or measure specific amounts of fluids entering the Queen's Chamber. Even if the seemingly impossible were accomplished and chemicals were pumped into the airshafts (through the small holes that Dunn postulates were originally there, or perhaps if different, as yet undiscovered, shafts were used), I do not believe that they would mix and react exactly as Dunn requires.

NUKES IN THE OLD KINGDOM?

In an article published in the 2001 *Meta Research Bulletin*, chemical engineer Erica Miller, mechanical engineer Sean Sloan, and chemical engineer Gregg Wilson agree with Christopher Dunn that the Great Pyramid was a power plant. They have their own very different idea of the type of plant it was. As they see it, the pyramid produced fuel by nuclear fission in a breeder reactor, most likely for interplanetary export to Mars.

A breeder reactor is an extension of the kind of nuclear plant used to produce plutonium-239 for weapons. The process begins with uranium ore, which contains two primary isotopes, or forms, of uranium: slightly more than 99 percent uranium-238, and the tiny remainder uranium-235. Uranium-235 can be used to make a nuclear bomb, but extracting it from uranium ore requires so many steps that the military uses plutonium instead. In the presence of a moderating material like graphite or water, the natural fission of uranium-235 in uranium ore converts some of the uranium-238 into plutonium-239. Further fission reactions from the plutonium-239 convert even more uranium-238 into plutonium-239, "breeding" this desired material from the uranium. Unchecked, the reaction can lead to a runaway nuclear meltdown, such as the accident that destroyed the Chernobyl nuclear plant in Ukraine in 1986. But if engineers slow the reaction with water or graphite, they can produce either bomb-grade plutonium for weapons or plutonium fuel, which lacks the explosive potential of its bomb-grade cousin but can be used as an energy source.

Miller, Sloan, and Wilson maintain that the Great Pyramid was used in the ancient past to produce plutonium fuel. The evidence, they argue, is the monument's peculiar and unique internal geometry. The sarcophagus in the King's Chamber was packed with uranium ore, and the King's Chamber itself was flooded with water pumped in from outside the pyramid through the southern airshaft. The water reflected neutrons released by fission back into the nuclear pile, and it also slowed and controlled the reaction, preventing an ancient preview of Chernobyl along the Nile. The Relieving Chambers, which sit atop the King's Chamber, protected the structure against the explosive force of steam produced by fission in water. Water, steam, and gasses would have flowed out of the King's Chamber and down the Grand Gallery. Radioactive waste materials, such as strontium-90 and cesium-137, were carried away from the core, while steam and gasses escaped through the northern airshaft. The Grand Gallery also served as the pathway for raising new uranium cores into the King's Chamber and removing spent cores, probably by means of a hoist mounted in the ceiling.

The Great Pyramid even produced its own electrical power for lighting throughout the structure and electrical machinery in the Queen's Chamber. Radioactive water spilling down the Well Shaft turned a turbine in the Subterranean Chamber, which, the engineers argue, bears a striking resemblance to the support structure for a water-driven turbine electric generator.

Wear and tear on various parts of the Great Pyramid indicate that it produced power for a few hundred years, then it was purposely decommissioned and the internal machinery removed. Since there is no archaeological evidence of power stations or electrical grids in the ancient world, and since no one has yet stumbled across a stash of ancient Egyptian nuclear fuel, all the plutonium produced by the Great Pyramid in its centuries of operation must have been transported elsewhere, most likely to Mars, in the authors' view. And what better site for an interplanetary nuclear power plant than Giza? It lies near the equator, which simplified orbital landings and takeoffs. The Nile Delta's beneficent climate, predictable water supply, and fertile soil made it an ideal location for interplanetary travelers to assemble the human workers the nuclear project required. Miller, Sloan, and Wilson never specifically address the details of how the plutonium was transported to Mars. Presumably, the Martians who actually organized the construction and operation of the Great Pyramid had their own interplanetary means of travel.

Quite apart from the science fiction flavor of this idea, it suffers from a major problem: lack of evidence. Like Dunn's theory, the Giza nuke plant hypothesis rests on the supposition that the Great Pyramid once contained a vast array of equipment later removed without the least trace. That is hard to believe. What makes it even harder to believe is the absence of the evidence one would most expect in the vicinity of a nuclear power plant: radioactivity. The authors repeatedly cite Hanford, Washington, the primary production site for American nuclear weapons material during the Cold War, as an example of the kind of nuclear operation they have in mind. Nuclear production operations were shut down in Hanford in part because plutonium production had made it one of the most fiercely polluted places on earth. It will remain a dangerous hot spot for millennia. The half-life for plutonium-239—that is, the period it takes for the element to lose 50 percent of its radioactivity—is 24,000 years, and for uranium-238 about 4.5 billion years. Such long half-lives mean that even now, thousands of years after the Giza nuke plant shut down, the structure would be so radioactive that various phenomena should hold true. For one thing, the monument would glow at night inside. I have spent numerous hours in the Great Pyramid at night, and I can attest that it doesn't glow with radioactivity. For another, the expected high level of radioactivity might damage film and electronic equipment, but I have encountered no signs of such damage either in my own equipment or that of my colleagues who have spent much time in the Great Pyramid. Finally, the guards who spend years of their lives inside the pyramid should reveal an unusual cluster of cancers and radiation sickness. To my knowledge, no such incidents among the guards have ever been reported.

Miller, Sloan, and Wilson's fanciful idea is just that: a fancy, with no substantial evidence to support it.

THE DEATH STAR

Dunn's model of the Great Pyramid as an electrical power plant and Miller, Sloan, and Wilson's notion of the structure as a producer of nuclear fuel for interplanetary trade assume that the intention underlying Khufu's monument is benevolent. In his two books, *The Giza Death Star* (2001) and *The Giza Death Star Deployed* (2003), physicist Joseph P. Farrell offers an altogether different take on the beneficence of the Great Pyramid. Like the other writers, he sees the monument as evidence of a very high yet misunderstood technology. The people (or beings, for in his scenario it is not clear that they were humans) who used this sophisticated, ancient physics, however, were up to no good. The Great Pyramid, in Farrell's eyes, was a very bad weapon in the hands of very bad guys.

The civilization that built this weapon was, Farrell writes, "far too much like our own: capable of technological wonders, capable of mass destruction, and like our own, in almost complete moral decay. In that most profound sense, the Great Pyramid is a prophecy, and a warning."[6]

The theory that Farrell spins out begins with what he considers evidence of a global war fought with weapons of mass destruction in ancient times. He points to stories of reputed unnamed ancient cities of India turned to glass by extreme heat. And he cites vast fields of fused green glass—produced from sand by tremendously hot explosions—as proof positive that thermonuclear bombs were detonated in Egypt, other parts of the Middle East, and the Indian subcontinent. Three civilizations, based in India, North Africa and the Mediterranean, and either Antarctica or the Atlantic Ocean, were locked in a long world war and blasting away at each other.

Farrell maintains that this ancient war was fought with a weapon of frightening potential, one so powerful it could bust a planet in one blow. Something like Dunn's electrical power plant, Farrell's death star used the energy of hydrogen plasma to gather, oscillate, and harmonically resonate nuclear, electromagnetic, acoustic, and gravitational energy from the earth, the solar system, and even the galaxy itself, then direct it like an artillery piece at a distant target. When it fired, the pyramid was probably sheathed in a blue light that moved from the base of the structure to its apex, then disappeared into the atmosphere (possibly reflecting off of the atmosphere, or perhaps satellites) to strike down like a bolt of lightning at the target. There, literal hell would break loose. If the death star's commanders so wished, they could induce a violent reaction in the atomic nuclei composing the target's mass that would result in a nuclear explosion. Or they could cook the target with extreme heat, destroying the enemy without nuclear fallout. The commanders could even choose the size of blast they wanted: from small tactical detonations to full-scale big bangs that might threaten an entire planet's very existence.

Farrell's thermonuclear weaponry was only one of the many technological attributes of the ancient civilization whose various outposts were locked in this global war of long, long ago. They had at their fingertips a physics vastly more sophisticated than our own, possessed some kind of advanced computational technology and algorithms, and used their science to travel between the planets. In time, their dedication to evil purposes led to a destruction and downfall as great and awesome as Wagner's twilight of the gods or Plato's drowning of Atlantis. But before this civilization breathed its last, the death star's commanders removed the military apparatus and left the empty structure as a memorial to the evils of war, much as the preserved hulks of Auschwitz, Buchenwald, and Dachau remind us still of the horror of Nazism and the Holocaust.

Importantly, these now-vanished people or beings were not the ancient Egyptians of the Old Kingdom. Rather, they came earlier, although Farrell does not say precisely when. In *The Giza Death Star Deployed*, Farrell maintains that the Great Pyramid was built sometime before 10,000 B.C., perhaps even tens of thousands of years earlier. The Great Pyramid was already standing, in stripped, mute testimony, when the Fourth Dynasty moved its base of religious operations to Giza and invented the mythology of Isis, Horus, and Osiris to explain the presence of so great and mystifying a structure. The ancient Egyptians didn't realize it was a weapon; neither do traditional Egyptologists.

Yet the Great Pyramid's primeval purpose, Farrell says, is evident. The granite core of the pyramid functioned like an immense capacitor to build up a tremendous charge augmented by the windings of the stone courses forming the monument's exterior bulk. The asymmetric arrangement of the internal chambers and passages would amplify the shock wave, an effect explored experimentally by maverick inventor Nikola Tesla (1856–1943). Add acoustic resonators in the Grand Gallery, made of crystals engineered to resonate with the harmonics of gravity, much as Dunn imagined, and you have your death star, ready and able to immolate enemy nations at any distance.

Farrell draws heavily from Dunn's model, in fact, and he faces the same key problem as Dunn: absence of evidence. Even if the dubious physics behind his model worked, there are no indications that the Great Pyramid ever served as a high-energy howitzer. The death star theory rests on hypothesized machinery removed long ago from the Great Pyramid. No evidence points to such machines within the structure or anywhere else in ancient Egypt. Were the builders of the death star indeed trying to leave the emptied structure as a memorial, it is hard to understand why they were so secretive and cryptic about their eleventh-hour conversion from the path of evil.

There would certainly be good reason to search harder and wider for such machines if evidence suggested that ancient civilizations predating the Old Kingdom had fought a global thermonuclear conflict. Nothing points that way. Farrell asserts that the presumed fields of fused green glass (I question their existence) must have come from nuclear detonations, not exploding meteorites. Meteorites, he says, always leave a crater, because they explode on hitting the ground, not in the air like a nuclear weapon. But he's wrong. When comet P/Shoemaker-Levy 9 collided with the planet

Jupiter in July 1994, many of the fragments from the disintegrating object exploded in the Jovian atmosphere. The same phenomenon has been observed on earth—in the Tunguska explosion of June 30, 1908. The Tunguska object exploded between 3 and 5 miles above the earth's surface, and the heat and force of the blast burned or flattened trees across 850 square miles of Siberian forest. Had the Tunguska object detonated over the Sahara sands rather than Siberian taiga, it would have produced a vast field of fused green glass. Farrell's "evidence" of ancient thermonuclear blasts actually marks the impact sites of objects streaking into earth from space. It tells us nothing about the purpose of the Great Pyramid or the intentions of its builders.

FINDING THE PRESENT IN THE PAST

Since the ancient high civilization that built the Giza death star was global in its reach, Farrell often cites evidence from beyond Egypt to support his argument. He turns, for example, to a mural on the Sun Gate in the ancient city of Tiwanaku, on the Bolivian shore of Lake Titicaca. Scholars consider this drawing a portrayal of the god Viracocha. Farrell, however, sees a simple schematic for a thermonuclear bomb, complete with the implosion detonator needed to set off the device and the casing of fissile material, like plutonium, surrounding it. When Farrell parses this image, he locates the fissile critical mass in the god's eyes, the detonator in his headdress, and the fins in his feet.

Of course, we could all be missing something that Farrell has wisely and bravely perceived. But it is altogether more likely that he is seeing what he wants to. Like the neutral ink blots psychologists use to help patients project their deepest preoccupations and fears, the ancient world—and particularly the Great Pyramid of Giza—becomes a canvas on which modern writers project the key issues of their own time. Their work turns history into little more than a mirror image of themselves and their times.

Theories of the Great Pyramid as a razor blade preserver, water pump, electrical generator, nuclear fuel product facility, and long-range weapon of mass destruction reflect our world, not the ancient Egyptians'. The search for electrical and nuclear power for an energy-hungry civilization defined the technological growth of the twentieth century. Those same hundred years saw the bloodiest and most horrific wars of history, capped by the fiery destruction of Hiroshima and Nagasaki. The "discovery" of these same concerns and purposes in the ancient world points to a failure to see the civilization of long ago on its own terms.

Yet these same writers have done us a service, by helping to underscore the shortfalls of the orthodox theory of the Great Pyramid and to question when the monument was built, how, and by whom. The Great Pyramid is engineered to astounding precision, and at least the modern mechanistic, even if somewhat fantastical, theories attempt to account for this precision and exactness—something the standard theories fail to address. The pyramidological theories also question, either directly or indirectly, our understanding of the date and the builders of the Great Pyramid, subjects the traditional tomb theorists falsely assert have been resolved. Things are neither as clear nor definitive as modern academia would have it, and the pyramidologists are like gadflies—often fanciful, sometimes perceptive— who refuse to allow scholastic certainties to stand without challenge. If for no other reason, their ideas are worth considering.

Four

A CERTAIN AGE

CCORDING TO THE STANDARD STORY, KHUFU HAD AT
least two good reasons for choosing Giza as the site for his Great
Pyramid soon after he ascended the throne of the Two Lands in
2551 B.C. For one, the plateau provided a clean slate, an unused venue on
the west bank of the Nile, the direction of the setting sun, that opened into
the supernatural world of ancestors and gods. For another, Giza offered a
nearby supply of workable limestone to build the core of the pyramid, as
well as a firm foundation of bedrock to support the immense weight of this
massive monument. Having made his choice, Khufu put his people to work.
The project was massive, according to the much later account of Herodotus,
who wrote that construction cost the Egyptians the work of 100,000 men
over a 20-year period. The structure was completed before Khufu died in
2528 B.C., and, according to the conventional view, his mummy should have
been laid to rest in the King's Chamber of the Great Pyramid.

Although this story builds upon an ego of unusual grandeur, it is remarkable how little we actually know of Khufu. Few written records have
survived from his reign, and the only surviving image of this pharaoh of all
pharaohs is a 2½-inch tall ivory statuette uncovered by the famous Egyptologist Sir Flinders Petrie, not at Giza but at Abydos, in 1909. (Other images

of Khufu have been reported but are lost. Petrie himself told of a likeness of Khufu carved into a cliff in the Sinai, but it was smashed when ancient turquoise mines in the area were reopened for exploitation at the turn of the nineteenth and twentieth centuries.) In fact, apart from the account of Herodotus, written more than two millennia after the fact, the primary evidence at Giza linking the Great Pyramid to Khufu consists of nearby tombs and other structures dated to his reign, and a few graffiti within the body of the monument itself. These graffiti form the basis of a fascinating story, one that leads to as many questions as answers.

THE MARKS OF THE QUARRYMEN

To get the full measure of this story, we have to return to the time when the gentlemen of the British Empire considered the colonial world their nut to crack with cheap native labor and abundant gunpowder. Richard William Howard Vyse (1784–1853) was one of these imperial gentlemen.

Howard Vyse had unimpeachable blue-blood credentials. The son of General Richard Vyse and a grandson of Field Marshal Sir George Howard, Vyse rose through the ranks of the officer corps, ultimately becoming a general. Vyse served for a time under Wellington, and, like Wellington, he was described as artless and thorough. Those qualities proved useful when he came to work on the Great Pyramid.

Vyse arrived in Egypt in the 1830s as a tourist, but he soon became serious about understanding the mysteries of the pyramids' meaning and construction. At the time, a former sea captain from Genoa named Giovanni Battista Caviglia (1770–1845) was exploring Giza, seeking secret rooms inside the Great Pyramid and spinning theories about the hermetic purposes of the structure. Caviglia was said to be so devoted to his work that he took up residence inside the Great Pyramid in the first Relieving Chamber above the King's Chamber after he swept out several centuries' accumulation of bat guano. At the time, the first Relieving Chamber was the only one that had been discovered. Then and now it is called Davison's Chamber, after Nathaniel Davison, a British diplomat, who discovered it in 1765.

Intrigued by Caviglia's ideas about the Great Pyramid, Vyse set up his own camp in a tomb close to the Great Pyramid and hired Caviglia to oversee hundreds of workmen clearing and exploring the monument. In time the Englishman and the Italian parted ways, and Vyse took complete control of pyramid explorations. He approached the task as would any good general. In the words of a contemporary, he "'sat down before the Great Pyramid as a fortress to be besieged.'"[1]

After extensive and expensive excavation elsewhere in and around the Great Pyramid, Vyse turned some of his workmen to exploring an anomaly in Davison's Chamber: a reed 3 feet long could be run up through a crack in the stone ceiling. Thinking that this curiosity might indicate an unknown chamber above, Vyse ordered his men to chisel through the granite. The stone proved too hard, however, and the chamber was too low to give them enough room to maneuver. Then the Englishman resorted to gunpowder. He blasted up through the softer, surrounding limestone until he discovered an unknown room atop Davison's Chamber. Continuing his explosive upward journey, Vyse and his crew discovered three more layers of chambers and revealed the structure of the Relieving Chambers to the modern world. Vyse himself first posited the theory that the chambers had been built to alleviate the immense weight of rock bearing down on the King's Chamber below.

What proved as interesting as the chambers themselves was a series of hieroglyphics, including cartouches crudely painted in red on the walls of the upper chambers. Vyse decided they were quarry marks that told workmen where to place the stones after they had been cut and shaped. Since one of the cartouches named Khufu explicitly, Vyse and others viewed them as proof that the Great Pyramid was indeed the work of the pharaoh Khufu, second monarch of the Old Kingdom's Fourth Dynasty.

Not everyone is convinced of this fact, however. A number of writers have followed the lead of pyramidological gadfly Zecharia Sitchin in accusing Vyse of forgery. As they see it, the Englishman planted the marks to solidify his place in the annals of Egyptology.

I have never been persuaded by Sitchin's scholarship—or, more accurately, his lack thereof—but I jumped at the chance to see the inscriptions for myself in late November 2003 and again in May 2004. Those examinations convinced me that the cartouches, including the one that spells out the name Khufu, are indeed ancient and not a forgery by a nineteenth-century English explorer, no matter how narcissistic or ambitious. Portions of the cartouches are obscured by incrustations, unlike the abundant nineteenth- and twentieth-century graffiti found in the Relieving Chambers. In addition, it is clear that some of the stones were marked before they were put into place, a sequence of events that rules out modern forgery. Most of the inscriptions are upside down, a peculiar orientation for forgeries. One runs upward before it is cut off by the chamber's roofing blocks, while another runs downward before it is cut off by the chamber's flooring blocks (which are actually the blocks making up the roof of the chamber below). In addition, the marks are crude, painted swiftly, most likely at the quarry where the stones were prepared.

Yet, given that the marks Vyse discovered are authentic, the critical question is What do they tell us? Only that the Great Pyramid from the Relieving Chambers up was the work of someone associated with Khufu.

Still, this may or may not have been the second pharaoh of the Old Kingdom's Fourth Dynasty. Several of the cartouches, for example, read not "Khufu" but "Khnum-Khuf." Khnum refers to the primal Egyptian god of creation, the deity later identified with Amon (also spelled Amun); *Khuf* is a variant spelling of *Khufu*. Why was Khufu associating himself with Amon? Is this a reference to a given individual king, or does it have something to do with the original religious mystery that underlies the pyramid itself?

In fact, the hieroglyphic cartouche for the name Khufu was a powerful charm found on any number of tombs and monuments throughout Egypt, many of them accurately dated to long after the Fourth Dynasty, some as late as a few centuries before Christ. The Khufu cartouche was used as a holy symbol in the same way that the cross was inscribed here, there, and everywhere by Christians in later centuries. The Relieving Chambers inscriptions don't necessarily prove that Khufu built the Great Pyramid. They could mean that Khufu was himself named after the Great Pyramid, which existed before he did.

Support for this reverse order of events comes from the Inventory Stela, which was uncovered at Giza and dates from the sixth or seventh century B.C. According to the inscription on the stela, Khufu discovered and rebuilt an existing temple sacred to Isis, the great goddess of Egypt: "He [Khufu] found the House of Isis, mistress of the Pyramid, by the side of [the] cavity [house?] of the Sphinx, on the north-west of the House of Osiris [the great god of Egypt and Isis's consort]."[2] The inscription also suggests that a pyramid already stood on the site where Khufu built a pyramid for himself and another for Princess Henutsen, his wife. But which pyramid does the stela refer to—the Great Pyramid itself or one of the smaller pyramids close by, one of which was indeed intended for Princess Henutsen? If the inscription is correct, then, like the Great Sphinx, which certainly is, the Great Pyramid may also be older than Khufu.

Most Egyptologists dismiss the Inventory Stela as a Late Period forgery and refuse to take its redating of the standard story seriously. They are refusing to look seriously at several lines of evidence indicating that nothing at Giza is as simple as they want to believe.

BUILDING OR REBUILDING?

Curious physical evidence relevant to the dating of the Great Pyramid comes from a carbon-14 study performed in the mid-1980s by the American Research Center in Egypt under the direction of prehistorian Robert J. Wenke of the University of Washington. Carbon-14 dating works only with organic materials and therefore cannot be used on stone. The cores of the pyramids, which are out of sight and less precisely fitted than the outer courses of stone, are held together with large amounts of mortar, which often contains charcoal, wood, and reed. The mortar, like stone, cannot be dated, but the organic material embedded in it can. Wenke's team took mortar samples from the exteriors of all three Giza pyramids and the Sphinx Temple for testing at Southern Methodist University in Dallas, Texas, and the Eidgenössische Technische Hochschule (Federal Technical University) in Zurich, Switzerland.

The results were puzzling. Despite careful refinement and calibration, the samples averaged 374 years earlier than the accepted dates of the pharaohs with whom they were associated. Even more anomalous were the individual findings within single monuments. Two charcoal samples from an upper course in the Khufu pyramid dated to 3809 B.C., with a margin of error either way of 160 years. This means that the samples could date to as early as 3969 B.C. A wood sample from the same site, however, tested to 3101 B.C. (± 414 years). Another 13 samples, all but two of them charcoal, from lower in the Khufu pyramid spanned a range from 3090 to 2853 B.C., with a margin of error of between one and four centuries. Seven samples from the Khafre pyramid were dated to 3196–2723 B.C.; six from the Menkaure pyramid to 3076–2067 B.C.; and two from the Sphinx temple to 2746–2085 B.C.

Some of these curious findings may be due to the technical difficulty of carbon-14 dating. The concentration of carbon-14 in the atmosphere is not constant, and samples can be contaminated with carbon from the environment that is younger or older than they are. It can also be the case that the organic materials do not in fact date from the same time period as the inorganic object being studied. For example, wooden beams used in the tracks over which stones were hauled to build the pyramids at Lisht were much older than the Twelfth Dynasty, during which those pyramids were built. Apparently the pyramid builders were using wood from trees felled long before, possibly taking advantage of the same timbers over and over again, a recycling strategy that makes eminent sense in a country as little forested as Egypt. It is possible that the same pattern was followed at Giza, with charcoal being made from wood that was already a few hundred years old when the mortar surrounding it was mixed. However, the researchers involved in the project noted that at least some of the samples used to arrive at dates included reeds and other short-lived materials, which would be unlikely to yield the same results as presumably old wood.

The David H. Koch Pyramids Radiocarbon Project,[3] the detailed results of which have still not been released, undertook a second radiocarbon survey of the Giza Plateau in 1995. Preliminary reports, however, suggest that while the discrepancies are not as great as in the 1980s study, radiocarbon dates from the Old Kingdom pyramids are generally a century or two older than the traditionally accepted dates. The researchers involved in this latest study concluded that the Old Kingdom Egyptians must have utilized massive quantities of wood, so they took whatever they could find, including wood that was already hundreds of years old. This, they suggested, gave the anomalously old dates.

But other explanations for the curious carbon-14 findings are possible. Many of the Giza samples from the 1980s study are much older than the pharaohs who supposedly commissioned the monuments. If we take the results of the radiocarbon dating at face value, the charcoal-tainted mortar at the top end of the margin of error in the upper course of the Great Pyramid was put into place over 1,400 years before Khufu became pharaoh. In the case of Khafre, the difference is almost seven centuries. There is also the matter of the long span of dates within individual monuments, which reaches almost a millennium for the Menkaure and Khufu pyramids. And there is the curious finding that the samples from the area toward the top of the Great Pyramid are older than those at the bottom. If we assume that the Great Pyramid was built all at once, then this finding implies that the structure was constructed in an unlikely top-down order.

The older samples at the top do make sense, however, if we assume that the Great Pyramid was built, rebuilt, and rebuilt yet again in stages. While there is yet no definitive proof that this is the case, various pieces of evidence suggest that the major pyramids were purposely constructed over something older.

The pattern begins with the Red Pyramid at Dahshur. Although the body of this pyramid is dated confidently to the reign of the Third Dynasty pharaoh Sneferu, the pyramid appears to be built around a room or chamber composed of very ancient (older than the Third Dynasty), weathered megalithic stonework. Completely enclosed within the pyramid, this chamber should not have weathered appreciably since the pyramid was built. Indeed, other Red Pyramid chambers, and even the more recent roof of this chamber, do not show the same weathering. I believe the Red Pyramid of Dahshur was constructed to enclose, house, and protect a much older, highly sacred structure.

The same pattern extends to Giza. My research suggests that the lowest layers of the Khafre Pyramid may well predate the Old Kingdom. Close examination shows that the courses close to the pyramid's base differ distinctly in style from the upper tiers. Furthermore, the Second Pyramid's base or foundation is faced with red granite, which appears to date to no later than the Fourth Dynasty. The rest of the pyramid, however, was faced with fine white limestone, so that in Khafre's time a horizontal red stripe ran around the base of the otherwise-white pyramid. Why this difference in color and material? The answer may come from the ancient Egyptians' preference for granite to renew or refurbish older structures. Possibly the Fourth Dynasty Egyptians were rebuilding and adding to a much older, preexisting structure, with the red granite demarcating the older, refurbished from the newer, white-limestone pyramid above.

Likewise, the Menkaure Pyramid has a surviving outer casing of granite on its lower courses. Was it, too, refurbished, either by generations after the Fourth Dynasty (during the Twenty-sixth Dynasty, c. 600 B.C., according to one suggestion) or possibly by Fourth Dynasty Egyptians working on a site and structure that predated their own time? Furthermore, after studying the Tomb of Queen Khentkaus at Giza (late Fourth Dynasty), I believe that this tomb is built on and incorporates an older structure dating from very early dynastic or predynastic times.

Robert Bauval, the author of *The Orion Mystery* and a serious scholar of Giza, is of the opinion that the same pattern holds true of the Great Pyramid, an idea he shared with me when I spoke with him in Cairo in May 2004.

It has long been known that the Great Pyramid was erected around and atop a mound of bedrock. Egyptologists argue that the strategy of incorporating the mound into the pyramid's structure served purely practical reasons—saving the Fourth Dynasty builders the work and expense of filling in that portion of the monument with courses of stone. An engineer by training, Bauval scoffs at the idea. From an engineering point of view, a flat, level site is far easier to build on, because it distributes weight evenly and allows clear lines of sight for surveying—no small issue with the Great Pyramid because of its precise orientation to the cardinal directions. Bauval told me that it would have made much better engineering sense to excavate the mound, level the site, and then build the pyramid.

According to Bauval, the builders of the Great Pyramid built around and atop the mound—and the Descending Passage and Subterranean Chamber that lie within and beneath it—because the complex was an already existing holy site. The Fourth Dynasty builders wanted to incorporate it into their structure; for the same reason, they located the Great Pyramid dangerously close to the cliff that marks the northern edge of the Giza plateau. Moving the site 100 meters south would have made the pyramid a less risky building project, but then incorporating the mound and placing the Subterranean Chamber directly under the pyramid's apex would have been impossible. Putting the pyramid where it is makes better sense, though, if for religious purposes it needed to be located over an already existing sacred spot.

Bauval's ideas make sense, particularly when we consider the strongest evidence that Giza served as a holy site well in advance of Pharaoh Khufu and the Great Pyramid: the Great Sphinx.

PULLING BACK TIME'S VEIL

The immense Great Sphinx of Giza—66 feet high, 240 feet long, and with a headdressed human face 13 feet wide, all carved from solid limestone bedrock—has been dated since the 1950s to Khafre, the second pharaoh after Khufu. A number of lines of evidence support this attribution.

For one, the Great Sphinx fits into a ground plan that also includes the Sphinx Temple, the Valley Temple, Khafre's Causeway, and the Khafre Pyramid. Given the artistic unity of this portion of the Giza site, the assumption is that one builder assembled the entire complex. In addition, an exquisite sculpture of Khafre was discovered in the Valley Temple in 1860. The sculpture, it is argued, adds to the likelihood that Khafre was the pharaoh responsible for the temple and, by association, for the Great Sphinx as well.

Further evidence is provided by the Dream Stela, an inscribed pillar of granite that was carved and set between the Sphinx's paws by the New Kingdom pharaoh Tuthmosis IV (Thutmose IV) in approximately 1400 B.C. A significant legend surrounds the stela.

The body of the Great Sphinx lies below the level of the Giza Plateau

Late-nineteenth-century photograph of the Great Pyramid,
Great Sphinx, and partially excavated Valley Temple. Photograph by Frank M. Good. (*From Good, no date [1880?].*)

in a pit—the so-called Sphinx enclosure—from which limestone was quarried to build other structures. Sand carried into the enclosure by the constant desert winds gradually fills the enclosure if it is not removed
regularly. This is exactly what happened in the social and political break-
down that followed the collapse of the Old Kingdom in about 2150 B.C.
After a few decades, only the head of the Sphinx, as enigmatic as ever, pro-
truded above the sand.

The story goes that a young prince of Egypt riding in the desert paused
for a nap in the shade of the buried Sphinx. While he slept, Khepera, a
form of the sun god Ra and the divinity that occupied the Sphinx, came in
a dream and told the prince that if he cleared away the sand, he would ascend to the throne of Egypt. The prince did as the Sphinx bade him, and
he, although not the natural heir to the throne, did become pharaoh. To
honor the vision that brought him to power, Thutmosis IV had the Dream
Stela carved and placed in front of the Sphinx.

Unearthed in the nineteenth century, the Dream Stela was reported to contain the first syllable of Khafre's name. Unfortunately, this particular part of the inscription has flaked away and can no longer be studied except from reports made at the time of the discovery. Even if Khafre's name did appear on the stela, however, its presence does not prove that he was the Sphinx's creator. He may simply have been associated with a preexisting Sphinx, just as Thutmosis IV was over a thousand years later.

The next line of evidence comes from Mark Lehner, of the University of Chicago, and other Egyptologists who maintain that the face of the Sphinx is a sculpted portrait of Khafre. Using a computer program to reconstruct the damaged face of the Sphinx, Lehner claimed the image "came alive" when he gave it Khafre's features.[4]

This likeness-to-Khafre argument is the weakest proof of the three. For one thing, it amounts to circular reasoning. When Lehner made the face look the way he thought it should look, then it looked the way he thought it should look. Lehner's notion has been further refuted by Frank Domingo, then a forensic officer with the New York City Police Department, who went to Egypt in October 1991 to do what forensic officers do—develop an image of the Sphinx's damaged face as if he were reconstructing a criminal's likeness from the victim's fractured memory. Domingo concluded that Khafre and the Sphinx are not only different people but different races. Khafre had a distinctly European face, yet the Sphinx looks African, with a heavier jaw positioned at a different angle and a wider nose.

While the other lines of evidence ascribing the Sphinx to Khafre are marginally better, it remains the case that there is no direct, unassailable, physical evidence linking the monument to that particular pharaoh. Indeed, my own research into the best physical evidence available, and corroboration from other scientists, indicates that the Great Sphinx of Giza is much older than the Fourth Dynasty and even the Old Kingdom. It all comes down to how weather affects rock and when that weather happened.

As the Alsatian mathematician and philosopher René Aor Schwaller de Lubicz (1887–1961) first noted, the monuments of the Giza Plateau are subject to two kinds of weathering. In Egypt the wind blows steadily during certain parts of the year and propels sand that scours and wears. Wind-driven sand often weathers stone unevenly, abrading away the softer layers and leaving the harder ones, sometimes yielding a pronounced steplike pro-

file. Water from rain and runoff weathers stone differently, typically creating a rolling, undulating surface that gives the rock a coved appearance,
often with pronounced vertical fissures that are wider at the top than the
bottom.

Different monuments at Giza display different patterns of weathering.
For example, structures dated unambiguously to 2600–2300 B.C.—the early
and middle Old Kingdom—and built from the same limestone as the
Sphinx show prominent weathering by wind and relatively little by water.
That pattern fits with the current Egyptian climate, in which arid, windy
conditions are broken only by rare, scant rainfall.

The Sphinx too shows wind weathering, particularly on the head, which
lies above the level of the plateau and receives the full force of every breeze
and gale that blows in off the Sahara. Below that level, on the body of the
Sphinx, there is little wind weathering. However, weathering by rainfall,
with its striking coved appearance and deep vertical fissures, is marked
and obvious on the walls of the surrounding Sphinx enclosure, particularly
the one to the west. This was the anomaly that caught Schwaller de
Lubicz's eye.

Assume for the moment that the Sphinx and its enclosure were excavated at the same time as the indubitably Old Kingdom structures, and
you'll realize that something very strange must have been happening at
Giza. Some structures weathered one way, and others weathered another,
both at the very same time. That just doesn't make sense—unless, of
course, different structures were built at different times under different
climatic conditions.

Further evidence that this could be the case comes from the Valley and
Sphinx temples, which are situated in front of the Sphinx. It is absolutely
certain that the limestone blocks used to build the Sphinx Temple were
quarried from the enclosure when the body of the Sphinx was first carved,
and highly probable that the limestone blocks of the Valley Temple were as
well. The temple limestone blocks were subsequently faced over with an
outer layer of granite ashlars marked with Old Kingdom inscriptions dated
to the approximate time of Khafre's reign. Interestingly, the ashlars are
weathered very differently from the underlying limestone blocks. The
granite shows only minimal wind weathering, yet the limestone beneath

reveals the uneven surface to be expected from long-term exposure to rainfall. Egyptian stonemasons actually fitted some of the ashlars to the wavy surface of the limestone to make a smooth and esthetically pleasing outer layer. Clearly, the limestone had been subject to rainfall weathering much like the Sphinx, and then was repaired with the granite outer layer at a later date—possibly during the reign of Khafre.

The words *Egypt* and *rain* do not usually appear in the same sentence, yet Egypt has not always been the desert it is today. When the most recent Ice Age ended, circa 13,000 B.C., heavy rain typified the climate of the Mediterranean, until 9500 B.C. What is now desert in Egypt was then green, well-watered grassland dotted with clumps of trees. A drier period followed, between 9500 and 7000 B.C., as the temperate zone's rain belt moved north. Then came another rainy period, from 7000 B.C. until between 3000 and 2350 B.C., when arid conditions more or less the same as the current climate set in, and water weathering yielded to wind.

This climatological history, combined with the weathering and erosional features seen on the stone, indicates that both the Great Sphinx and the Sphinx and Valley temples were originally built at a time when Egypt was wet and rainy. And they must have been built far enough back in that rainy period to allow the obvious, substantial water weathering to develop.

Data indicating just how far back came from seismological testing conducted in the Sphinx enclosure by seismology expert Thomas Dobecki in 1991. The data gave Dobecki and me a look at a cross-section of the structures under the Sphinx, and revealed an interesting pattern of uneven weathering. The Sphinx itself faces east. The northern, southern, and eastern floors of the Sphinx enclosure are weathered to a depth that varies between 6 and 8 feet below the surface. The western floor, however, is weathered less deeply, to a maximum of just 4 feet. The difference isn't due to variations in the rock; the exposed floor of the enclosure on all sides belongs to the same stratum of limestone. Rather, the western floor has been weathering for a shorter period of time. Obviously, it must have been excavated at a considerably later date.

The western end of the Sphinx enclosure shows further evidence of two-stage construction. There are two excavation walls at this end of the enclosure. The higher wall, which lies farther west, is deeply coved and fissured by rain and runoff. It must have been dug out when Egypt's climate was wet and rainy, well before the Old Kingdom. The second, lower wall, which is closer to the Sphinx's rump, shows much less precipitation weathering. It was along the base of this lower wall that the western seismic line, showing a depth of only 4 feet of weathering, was taken. The lower wall may have been excavated later than the higher wall—and certainly the western floor of the enclosure, where we took our seismic readings, was excavated later than the remainder of the enclosure—at a time when Egypt had already turned dry, perhaps during the Old Kingdom.

The evident two-stage construction of the Sphinx enclosure and the Valley and Sphinx temples gives rise to a likely scenario. All three structures were built well before the reign of Khafre—and Khufu, for that matter— when heavy rain regularly washed across Egypt. Then Khafre claimed this corner of Giza for himself by refurbishing the temples and altering the Sphinx. Originally, I suspect, the sculpture's body emerged from the bedrock as if it were an integral part of the plateau. By carving the rump and digging out the western enclosure to a second, lower level, Khafre divided the monument from the rock and gave it its own separate esthetic existence.

The two-stage construction hypothesis also helps explain another anomaly of the Sphinx: the curious size of its head. When the sculpture is viewed from the side, the head appears disproportionately small. This is by no means a convention of Egyptian art; all the monuments I know of have a correct body–head balance except, notably, the Great Sphinx. When I inspected the head up close, I saw relatively recent (Old Kingdom versus earlier) chisel and tool marks. This evidence, along with the appearance of the stone itself, have led me to believe that the current head, complete with the dynastic headdress of a dynastic pharaoh, was recarved from an earlier, larger head—perhaps, given the leonine form of the rest of the sculpture, that of a lion. This recarving possibly took place at the same time as the excavation of the rump, or it may have happened during earlier dynastic times.

The Sphinx and the temples had to have been built long enough before Khafre that the rains could weather them sufficiently to require repair in c. 2500 B.C. Just how long would that take? In other words, how old is the Sphinx?

The seismology data provide a scale. It has taken 4,500 years for the subsurface weathering at the younger, western floor of the Sphinx enclosure to reach a depth of 4 feet (comparable to the weathering depth found around Old Kingdom structures of c. 2500 B.C.). Since the weathering on the other three sides is between 50 and 100 percent deeper, it is reasonable to assume that this excavation is 50 to 100 percent—or approximately 2,200 to 4,500 years—older than the western end. If we accept Khafre's reign as the date for the western enclosure, then this calculation pushes the date for the Great Sphinx's original construction back to the 4700 to 7000 B.C. range, or 6,700 to 9,000 years ago.

REACTION AND REBUTTAL

A number of scholars have argued that my research is wrong. According to them, I have misinterpreted the evidence.

One of those scholars is Mark Lehner, who is director of the Giza Plateau Mapping Project, is affiliated with the University of Chicago, is a research associate at the Harvard Semitic Museum, and is sometimes cited as the world's most prominent authority on the Egyptian pyramids. Lehner has said that present climatic conditions in Egypt account for the weathering of the Sphinx. The country has been industrializing rapidly, and Cairo is growing by leaps and bounds because of a high birthrate and steady immigration from rural areas. Extreme air pollution makes the small amount of rain that falls during the Egyptian winter very acidic. As we know from pollution studies in other areas, limestone holds up poorly against acid rain. Thus, Lehner argues, I am mistaking the destructive weathering of the present for past damage, and confusing the new with the old.

Two fundamental problems plague Lehner's argument. For one, acid rain wouldn't produce the runoff patterns obvious on the walls of the Sphinx enclosure. For another, how is it that the acid rain has done so much damage to the Sphinx alone, when indisputably Old Kingdom structures constructed from the same limestones are holding up much better under the same chemical assault?

K. Lal Gauri, a University of Louisville geologist, maintains that the weathering of the Great Sphinx came not from rainfall but from the various effects of chemical weathering, particularly something known as "exfoliation," or the flaking away of the limestone surface. According to Gauri, dew forming at night on the rock dissolves soluble salts on its surface, making a liquid solution drawn into tiny pores in the stone by capillary action. During the heat of the day, the solution evaporates, and salt crystals precipitate in the pores. The forming crystals exert pressure that causes the surface of the limestone to flake away.

This process is, in fact, an important current weathering factor on the Giza Plateau. However, it alone cannot account for all of the weathering features seen in the Sphinx enclosure or, more important, for the specific weathering features in the Sphinx enclosure, such as the more intense weathering, erosion, and degradation in the western end of the Sphinx enclosure. In addition, the weathering processes Gauri proposes have their maximum effect under extremely arid conditions when the Sphinx is exposed to the elements. If the Sphinx and Sphinx enclosure are buried under a layer of sand—as they have been for much of their existence—they are largely protected from these effects. Interestingly, the exfoliation Gauri proposes should be operating on all the limestone of the Giza Plateau, yet somehow no other surface shows the same type of weathering and erosional profile as the Sphinx enclosure. While salt crystal growth is indeed damaging the Sphinx and other structures at present, this mechanism does not explain the ancient degradation patterns seen on the Sphinx's body and in the Sphinx enclosure.

James Harrell, a geologist at the University of Toledo, gives a different spin to the same line of logic as Gauri's argument. According to Harrell, the culprit is sand piled for centuries against the Sphinx and wetted by rainfall, Nile floods, and capillary action. Flooding, though, would have undercut the base of the Sphinx and the enclosure, yet there are no such features. Nor does wet sand around the base of the Sphinx explain the obvious and pronounced weathering on the upper portions of the enclosure walls and the body of the monument. Indeed, there is no documented mechanism known by which wet sand piled against a limestone surface will produce the weathering and erosional profile seen on the body of the Sphinx and on the walls of the enclosure. Sand, even wet sand, may actually have done more to preserve the Sphinx. Capillary action, far from being a mechanism capable of keeping numerous feet of piled sand wet over many centuries, is negligible in loose sands in arid areas. Furthermore, according to Harrell's theory, the Twenty-sixth Dynasty (c. 600 B.C.) tombs cut into the back wall of the Sphinx enclosure should show a similar weathering profile to that seen on the Sphinx and Sphinx enclosure walls. They do not, however. Harrell's wet-sand theory is all wet.

There is another major problem with the work of Harrell and, for that matter, Gauri. Neither exfoliation nor wet sand can make the coved rock and vertical fissures, or runnels, that are wider at the top than at the bottom and are a prominent feature of the western end of the Sphinx enclosure. Runnels come only from water that is running.

Farouk El-Baz, a geologist who directs Boston University's Center for Remote Sensing, argues that the Sphinx was carved from already-weathered rock. The Great Sphinx is, he maintains, what we geologists call a yardang, a hill of stone harder than the surrounding rock and carved out by weathering over the eons, like the mesas of the American Southwest. This idea, though, flies in the face of the obvious fact that all but the head of the Great Sphinx lies below the level of the Giza plateau and had to be excavated from the limestone bedrock. The head, it is true, may have been a yardang carved in place by ancient Egyptian stonemasons. The rest of the sculpture had to be excavated first, then carved.

Finally, there is the counterargument of Zahi Hawass, the Egyptian archaeologist who is the director of the Giza Plateau. Hawass claims that the Sphinx was built from limestone of such poor quality that it needed repair almost immediately. The Sphinx has indeed been repaired repeatedly. The question concerns when those repairs occurred, and what they signify. According to Hawass, the poor quality of limestone explains the apparent erosion, but not everyone agrees.

The earliest repairs to the Great Sphinx utilized limestone blocks that conform to the style followed by Old Kingdom masons. Hawass maintains that the repairs were done during the Old Kingdom, most likely soon after Khafre had the Sphinx carved from the limestone bedrock. Lehner disagrees. He holds that New Kingdom masons scavenged Old Kingdom blocks from other Giza sites and used them for the repairs.

Lehner's hypothesis raises logical problems, however. Since each repair block had to be shaped to fit, using existing material would have saved no labor over new. This makes it reasonable to assume that Hawass is right, and that the first repairs to the Sphinx were made during the Old Kingdom.

This solution, however, presents Hawass with a new and serious problem. How could the Sphinx have weathered so fast that it needed repair almost immediately after construction? The Sphinx is carved from what geologists call a competent limestone, one that stands up well enough to weathering to perform effectively as a building material. In addition, tombs adjacent to the Sphinx and cut from the same limestone during the Old Kingdom did not require the same kind of immediate repair the Sphinx did. How can it be that the same material weathered so differently at the same site?

The limestone is not the issue. Rather, the Sphinx had already been in place for so long that it was severely weathered by the time of the Old Kingdom and needed refurbishing. When Khafre set to work, the Sphinx was already old.

As John Anthony West has pointed out, another problem plagues the counterarguments: they are inconsistent with one another. The Sphinx cannot have been weathered because of capillary action, modern acid rain, wet sand, ancient yardang processes, *and* particularly poor-quality limestone. Each of the arguments, weak on its own merits, contradicts some of the others. They are all attempts to salvage the circumstantial case that Khafre built the Sphinx. To allow that the Sphinx is older than Khafre is to admit the inadmissible: something big was happening in Egypt well before Egyptologists think it was.

Two more recent geological studies of Giza add to the evidence for a Great Sphinx much older than Khafre. Writing in 1998 in the journal *InScription*, geologist David Coxill confirms my observations of the weathering patterns at Giza and supports my hypothesis that the Sphinx must date to a time of heavy rainfall well before the Old Kingdom. Coxill hesitates to push that date back to the 5000–7000 B.C. range on the basis of seismological data, but he agrees that the Sphinx "is clearly older than the traditional date."[5] How much older he does not say.

Colin Reader, a geological engineer educated at London University, comes to a similar conclusion in a 2001 issue of the journal *Archaeometry*, following a meticulous study of Giza's weathering patterns and the hydrology of the plateau. He also adds a significant piece of physical evidence. Agreeing with my analysis of the weathering patterns, Reader notes correctly that the enclosure is most heavily weathered and precipitation-eroded at its far western end, in the area behind (that is, west of) the lower wall, which was presumably carved when Khafre fully excavated the rump of the Sphinx and repaired the statue. The explanation for this particularly severe weathering and erosion is surface runoff from rain storms. Since the Giza plateau tilts down from the north and west, runoff headed directly toward and through the Sphinx enclosure on its way to the Nile Valley—or at least it did so until the reign of Khufu. This pharaoh removed large quantities of stone from quarry pits immediately upslope from the Sphinx enclosure. After the pits were abandoned, wind-blown sand filled them and soaked up any runoff heading down toward the Sphinx enclosure. Therefore, the heavy weathering and degradation of the western end of the Sphinx enclosure had to occur before the quarries were excavated during Khufu's reign.

Reader also argues that the Sphinx is hardly the only Giza monument that predates Khufu. According to his analysis, Khafre's Causeway (which runs from the Sphinx area up to the Mortuary Temple on the eastern side of Khafre's pyramid), a portion of the Mortuary Temple itself, and the Sphinx Temple all predate Khafre, who is thought by conventional Egyptology to have been responsible for them. Interestingly, John Anthony West and I too had earlier come to the conclusion that part of the Mortuary Temple is older than Khafre, on the basis of what appear to be two stages of construction in the temple: to an early, now heavily weathered, core of gigantic megalithic blocks, stylistically Old Kingdom masonry has been added. Reader has arrived at the same conclusion on his own, using similar evidence. For his part, Reader is unwilling to push the date of the Sphinx back beyond the latter half of the Early Dynastic Period, or circa 2800–2600 B.C., and there he goes wrong. If the Sphinx was carved in the 2800–2600 B.C. period, then there had to be sufficient heavy rainfall during that time to heavily weather the monument and its enclosure. The height of the rainy period had ended by 3000 B.C., however, and Egypt was well on its way to becoming desert by

2800 B.C. Mud-brick mastabas built on the Saqqara Plateau, only 10 miles up the Nile from Giza, and dated indisputably to circa 2800 B.C., show little rain weathering, even though they are built from a much softer and more vulnerable material. It is impossible that the Sphinx could have been carved as late as 2800 to 2600 B.C. and weathered so badly, under scant rainfall, that it required extensive repair by the time Khufu was building his pyramid circa 2550 B.C.

Still, despite the disagreement over the era of construction, Reader, like Coxill, corroborates the fundamental truth about the Sphinx: the monument belongs to a time much older than Khafre or Khufu.

A FINAL ANALYSIS

One of the most intriguing predynastic sites in Egypt—and one that indirectly corroborates my dating for the Great Sphinx—lies far from Giza, in a now-desolate place called Nabta Playa, about 65 miles west of Abu Simbel, in southernmost Egypt's Western Desert. The playa is a basin that filled with water when rainfall was sufficient. Beginning in about 9000 B.C., cattle herders brought their animals to the playa during the wet season and grazed them until water and grass dried up. By 7000 B.C. the nomads had settled in the area, dug deep wells to allow year-round habitation, and built villages of small huts arranged in straight lines. Following a major drought, the villagers abandoned the playa; they were replaced circa 5500 B.C. by people with a social system more complex than any yet seen in Egypt. Their religion centered on sacrificing young cows and interring them in roofed chambers marked by burial mounds. Nabta grew into a ceremonial center that drew people from all over the Western Desert to participate in rituals that probably confirmed social and religious unity. At some point, the people of Nabta turned to erecting large stones in alignments, building a calendar circle of megalithic stones to mark the summer solstice—the earliest astronomical measuring device known in Egypt—and constructing over 30 complex structures.

According to an analysis by Thomas G. Brophy in his book *The Origin Map,* three of the stones inside the Nabta calendar circle represent the belt of Orion. They show how these three stars would have appeared on summer solstice nights between 6400 B.C. and 4900 B.C. as they crossed the meridian—the imaginary line in the sky that runs from north to south through the zenith. Someone standing at the north end of the calendar circle on the meridian line of sight would see the stars of Orion's Belt represented by the stones just as they would look when he or she looked upward to gaze at the real meridian halving the nighttime sky.

I find Brophy's analysis convincing. And it is intriguing that his range of dates corresponds to the same period when my research indicates that the Sphinx was under construction. That same individual who saw the map of Orion's Belt in the stones of Nabta could have made the journey down the Nile to see the Sphinx emerging from the limestone bedrock of the Giza Plateau. And, as we shall see in chapter 6, the link between Giza, Nabta, and Orion is both fascinating and very much to the point of understanding the mystery and purpose of the Great Pyramid.

It is clear that three pharaohs of the Fourth Dynasty—Khufu, Khafre, and Menkaure—had an important hand in shaping the Giza Plateau that we see today. And it is equally clear that when Khufu turned to Giza to memorialize his rule, he wasn't initiating a new religious site. He was instead returning to a sacred place that was already very, very old.

Five

NAMING THE BUILDER

CONSIDERING THE GREAT PYRAMID SIMPLY AS AN EXERCISE in engineering, it is easy to see how it qualified as one of the Seven Wonders of the ancient world. For one thing, there is the sheer mass of the structure—about 2.6 million cubic meters (approximately 90 million cubic feet), enough to enclose Saint Peter's in the Vatican and Saint Paul's Cathedral in London with plenty of room left over. Although it is impossible to pluck the Great Pyramid up and set it on a scale, the weight of the monument has been estimated at around 6 million tons. Its footprint extends over more than 13 acres, and it contains upward of 2 million blocks of stone, a few of them weighing in the neighborhood of 50 or more tons.

Yet the wonder of the Great Pyramid extends to more than size. The structure's precision is striking and practically unparalleled. Despite its immense size, the Great Pyramid is as close to perfectly square as any building that has ever been made. Its orientation is also extraordinarily close to perfect. Each side faces one of the cardinal directions: north, south, east, and west. Modern builders would have trouble hitting the directions so well.

How, one wonders, did the Egyptians accomplish all this, those many millennia ago? The answer, some writers say, is simple: the Egyptians had nothing to do with it.

ARCHITECTS FROM AFAR

In his book *The Great Pyramid: Man's Monument to Man*, ancient mysteries researcher Tom Valentine summarizes well this dissenting point of view: "If one takes the time and effort to really study the Great Pyramid at Giza, the first conclusion must be that no people whose culture was only one step removed from the Stone Age could have possibly designed and built such a monument."[1]

Ancient people as we know them were not up to the task, Valentine argues. Given the Great Pyramid's extraordinary size and perfect complexity, someone other than the Egyptians of the Old Kingdom or the Predynastic Period must have been responsible.

Historically, the first candidate for true builder was God. The earliest modern writer to advance this idea was John Taylor (1781–1864), whose day job was editing the *London Observer.* Taylor was also a publisher; the great English poet John Keats numbered among the writers he brought to the reading public. Taylor was already in his late fifties when Vyse returned to England and created something of a stir. Taylor devoted much of his remaining life to studying the Great Pyramid—without ever actually going to Egypt and looking at the monument firsthand. His ideas appeared *The Great Pyramid. Why Was It Built? & Who Built It?* first published in 1860 (although dated 1859 on the title page).

As we shall explore in more depth in chapter 8, Taylor was one of those who saw in the Great Pyramid's measurements—height, perimeter, area, angle of slope, and so forth—an elaborate code carrying a universal, even infinite message. He wrote that the pyramid was built to *"make a record of the measure of the Earth"* and that the monument's builders knew our planet's circumference, expressed in units derived from the accurate spherical dimensions of the earth.[2]

This assertion left Taylor in something of a theological quandary, however. He was a profoundly religious Protestant, a fundamentalist who believed in the literal factuality and truth of the Bible. As Taylor saw it, God created Adam and Eve circa 4000 B.C. and loosed Noah's flood upon the earth circa 2300 B.C. Since the historians of Taylor's day dated the Great

Pyramid to about 2000 B.C., that left only 300 years for humankind to have arisen from the watery erasure of the deluge to a complete, accurate knowledge of the planet's spherical dimensions. To make matters worse, the ancient Egyptians were pagan unbelievers. It was too much to believe that so unholy a people could have made such a major scientific advance so quickly.

Taylor was convinced they hadn't. Rather, he wrote, "it is probable that to some human beings in the earliest ages of society, a degree of intellectual power was given by the Creator, which raised them far above the level of those succeeding inhabitants of the earth."[3] He indicated, too, that these God-guided builders were not the pagan Egyptians who later enslaved the Hebrews. Instead, the Great Pyramid was built by men from "the *chosen race* in the line of, though preceding, Abraham; so early indeed as to be closer to Noah than to Abraham."[4]

Although Taylor's ideas proved unpopular in England, they inspired Charles Piazzi Smyth, another true Christian believer, who was the astronomer royal of Scotland, at the Edinburgh observatory. Smyth took Taylor's fascination with the Great Pyramid's numbers to a high art and devoted four months and most of his life savings to measuring and photographing the monument. As we will explore in more detail in chapter 8, Smyth discovered his own personal validation of the Bible's timelines in the lengths, angles, and marks of the Great Pyramid and furthered the message of John Taylor. In its way, as Smyth saw it, the Great Pyramid exceeded scripture in the importance of its revelation.

"In the Great Pyramid," Smyth wrote in the 1880 edition of *Our Inheritance in the Great Pyramid,* "the world now possesses a *Monument* of Inspiration, as it has long possessed a *Book* of Inspiration, one dating altogether, and the other partly, from primeval times."[5] The Great Pyramid was not a pagan monument. No Egyptian designed the Great Pyramid or lifted uninspired its limestones and granites into place: "the Great Pyramid was yet prophetically intended—by inspiration afforded to the architect from the one and only living God."[6]

Despite his excellent scientific credentials, Smyth fared no better with his ideas than John Taylor had. Today, only a few religious zealots, prophets, and extreme visionaries would hold to a theory of divine inspiration underlying the Great Pyramid. Yet Taylor's and Smyth's notions have survived, dressed up in the clothing of contemporary culture.

In his 1975 book *The Great Pyramid*, Tom Valentine, who, like Taylor and Smyth, rejects the idea that the Old Kingdom Egyptians could have built the Great Pyramid on their own, argues that the monument is actually the work of an unknown, very high civilization called the Hyksos, a Greek word sometimes mistranslated as "shepherd kings." The Hyksos are known historically, although not in the form Valentine gives them. They were a group of Canaanites or Syrians, most likely displaced by wars in their homeland, who settled in Egypt and later took control of Memphis, the capital, in the middle seventeenth century B.C. and founded the Fifteenth Dynasty during the Second Intermediate Period (c. 1640–1532 B.C.). Valentine sees them as much more than outside invaders who exploited chaos to establish political control over Lower Egypt for a significant time. To him, they were an enlightened people who had survived the deluge recounted in the biblical story of Noah. The Hyksos brought goodwill, harmony, and prosperity wherever they visited. Their wisdom was bestowed most abundantly on the Egyptians, who built the Great Pyramid under their guidance as a temple of human potential. Their work done, the Hyksos faded away, confident that a later civilization in search of enlightenment— one like our own, for example—would solve the mystery of the Great Pyramid and embrace its encoded message.

Of all lost civilizations—real or imagined—none is more famous than Atlantis, which has become an oft-cited, if little proved, source of the Great Pyramid. The copious contemporary literature on Atlantis is often based on Plato, who recounts the tale of a sunken continent in two dialogues written sometime around 360 B.C.: the *Critias*, which is more detailed but was never finished, and the *Timaeus*, which mentions Atlantis only in passing and goes on to discuss the greater issues of the ideal political state and the nature of the universe. Even Plato noted a connection between Atlantis and ancient Egypt. Plato writes that the story he tells was brought to Greece by the great Athenian lawgiver, poet, and traveler Solon (638–559 B.C.), who learned it during his time as a student of the priests of Egypt. The Great Pyramid, however, never figures into Plato's account.

In a time closer to our own, the American psychic Edgar Cayce (1877–1945) drew a direct connection between Atlantis and the Great Pyramid. A believer in reincarnation, Cayce worked by entering a trance state and recounting stories purportedly rooted in the past lives of people who came to him for counseling. Of his over 14,000 recorded readings, more than 700 mentioned Atlantis and over 1,100 described ancient Egypt around the time of the building of the Great Pyramid, some of them with great detail and specificity.

According to Cayce, an alliance of peripatetic Atlanteans, native Egyptians, and migrants from the Caucasus built the Great Pyramid somewhere between 10,490 and 10,390 B.C. Raising the stone blocks posed no problem for these superior beings. They used levitation to neutralize gravity and lift the blocks into place. The Great Pyramid was no tomb but a temple with many functions, one of which was the preservation of knowledge at risk of being lost. Knowing that Atlantis was itself soon to be swallowed by the sea, the builders of the Great Pyramid encoded that doomed nation's wisdom within it.

Other mechanisms besides levitation have been put forward as the advanced, ancient technologies used to build the Great Pyramid: hydrogen balloons, magnets, and aircraft, including planes and helicopters. The helicopter and plane idea comes from images carved into a support beam in the Temple of Seti at Abydos, which indeed do look something like modern-day aircraft. In fact, though, these images result from the recarving of hieroglyphs and do not represent flying machines.

In the second half of the twentieth century, a new twist on the idea of construction by divine power or lost civilization appeared. Even as we first began to probe space, extraterrestrials became the geniuses who built the Great Pyramid and left it behind for the ancient Egyptians to puzzle over and expropriate to their own decadent, latter-day mythology. Three writers have done the most to preach this idea.

Zecharia Sitchin, primarily on the basis of his analyses and translations of ancient texts, argues that the Middle East's two high ancient civilizations, Sumeria and Egypt, were the product of cultural, even genetic, influence from beyond planet Earth. A race of beings from an undiscovered planet in our own solar system came to earth on an emergency mission, which was later threatened by a mutiny among part of the crew. To save the mission, the leader of the extraterrestrials fashioned the first humans from the available genetic material as a race of workers. This solution worked for a time. Then, in yet another political upheaval, one faction of the extra-terrestrials wanted to rid the earth of the new beings—by means of a great flood, no less—while another group wished to preserve the new species by teaching a few of them how to build a boat. The preservationist group be-friended the flood's survivors by passing on to them their own culture and equipping them to inherit the earth the extraterrestrials were now aban-doning. Yes, this is another version of the story of Noah, with a sci-fi twist.

Best-selling author Erich von Däniken connects his own notions of vis-itors from outer space to ancient Egypt and the pyramids. According to von Däniken, the mythology of ancient Egypt recounted the alternating confu-sion and enlightenment of humans struggling to come to terms with an extraterrestrial reality. For example, the pharaohs had seen beings from outer space fly across the heavens in their spaceships, so they built them-selves sun ships to figuratively sail the skies. Going into the realm of the gods at death meant becoming like the extraterrestrials, who had brought the Egyptians the technological marvels of their world. The Egyptians recorded these gifts in images, like the solar barque and the sun disk, that we now call symbols and interpret in religious terms. That, Von Däniken says, is missing the point.

Maverick researcher Richard Hoagland draws a direct connection be-tween the pyramids of ancient Egypt and the putative "pyramids on Mars," members of a series of peculiar forms photographed on the red planet by the *Viking* probe in 1976. One is the so-called Face on Mars, identified by astronomer Tobias Owen on a photo of an area some 34 by 31 miles, taken at around 40° north latitude on the Martian surface, a region known as Cydonia. Nearby lies the so-called Fort, which has two distinctive straight edges; the City, an arrangement of massive structures interspersed with smaller pyramids; the NK Pyramid, about 25 miles from the Face and on the same latitude as the D & M Pyramid; and the Bowl, which is approached by a long ramp reminiscent of the stairways on Mayan and Aztec pyramids. Most intriguing in terms of studying the Great Pyramid is the D & M Pyra-mid (called this by Hoagland and others in honor of astronomers Vincent

DiPietro and Gregory Molenaar, who have studied the structure in detail on photographs), which is located about 10 miles from the Face and aligned almost perfectly north–south along Mars's axis, much like the Great Pyramid. The location of all these features in one relatively confined area adds to the enigma. Can it be by chance that so many seemingly artificial shapes are found so close together? Doesn't this fact alone speak to the presence of a guiding, intelligent hand? Hoagland argues that it does, and that there is a clear and obvious link between the pyramid monuments of Mars and those of ancient Egypt.

The biggest problem with Hoagland's idea is less the science-fiction nature of the hypothesis than the facts themselves. Apparently yielding to pressure to provide additional data on Cydonia and rising to accusations that the agency had been suppressing information about Martian cities and altering its photographs to cover up the evidence, the National Aeronautics and Space Administration dispatched the *Mars Global Surveyor* to fly over the controversial area and take a new series of photos. These images, snapped in 1998 at 10 times the resolution of the original *Viking* photographs and under different conditions of light and shadow, stripped away much of the Cydonia mystery. Now the Face looked less like a face than a weathered landform.

The more I have looked at the images, the more I am convinced that they are quite interesting but entirely natural features. Arguing that they are artificial is a very long stretch, one simply not supported by the evidence to date. On the basis of what we now know, the Cydonia "pyramids" are natural features formed by geological processes under Martian conditions, which differ from those on earth and produce shapes of an appearance other than what we are used to.

All these writers, from Taylor to Hoagland, underscore yet again how the Great Pyramid becomes a Rorschach test from antiquity. Taylor and Smyth, for example, faced an assault on traditional Christianity prompted by the scientific revolution of the nineteenth century. In response to Darwin's book *On the Origin of Species* intimating—but never saying—that humans were but another animal species lacking any special blessing from on high, they sought rock-solid assurance that God would triumph over the naturalist who collected finches on the Galápagos. Sitchin, von Däniken, and

Hoagland come from a time when traditional religion has given way to fundamentalism and only science offers intellectual credibility. They cloak their work in supposedly scientific jargon yet seek from extraterrestrial life the same sort of cosmic transcendence Taylor and Smyth wanted from their very Protestant and completely Anglo-Saxon divinity.

One key unstated assumption informs the work of all these authors: the people of Old Kingdom Egypt were incapable of building the Great Pyramid on their own. So we now turn to the question: Could they have done it all by themselves?

OLD-TIME HEARSAY

The sole ancient description of possible building techniques used to erect the Great Pyramid comes from the Greek historian Herodotus. The father of history asked around about the construction of the immense monument, when he traveled to Egypt a century before Alexander the Great arrived with his Macedonian military machine and a conqueror's glint in his eyes.

Here is what Herodotus had to say, according to one translation:

Cheops [the Greek name for Khufu], coming to reign over them, plunged into every kind of wickedness. . . . He ordered all the Egyptians to work for himself. Some he, accordingly, appointed to draw stones from the quarries in the Arabian mountains down to the Nile, others he ordered to receive the stones when transported in vessels down the river and to drag them to the mountain called the Libyan. And they worked to the number of a hundred thousand men, each party during three months. . . . Twenty years were spent erecting the pyramid itself. . . . This pyramid was built thus: in the form of steps, which some call crossae [tiers], some bomides [terraces]. When they had first built it in this manner, they raised the remaining stones by machines made of short pieces of wood. Having lifted them from the ground to the first range of steps, when the stone arrived there, it was put on another machine that stood ready on the first range; and from this it was drawn to the second range on another machine; for the machines were equal in number to the range of steps; or they removed the machine, which was only one and portable, to each range in succession, whenever they wished to raise the stone higher; for I should relate it in both ways as it is related. The highest parts of it, therefore, were first finished, and afterward they completed the parts next following, but last of all they finished the parts on the ground, and that were lowest.[7]

Herodotus made no secret that he worked from hearsay. He went looking for stories, collected them as they were told to him, and often leaned to the one that seemed the most likely or the most interesting to him. This heritage is obvious in his account of the pyramid's building. For example, he is unsure whether the wooden machines were left on each level of the pyramid or moved from one to another. He was told two stories, and he repeats them both, not being engineer enough to choose between them.

All historians, no matter how conscientious, implicitly reflect the concerns of their times. As the father of history, Herodotus began the trend. He created the image of the pyramids built by a 100,000-man army of seasonal workers, often said to be pressed into labor and thus effectively slaves, who spent three months of each year—presumably the time when the Nile was in flood and the fields unworkable. Josephus, the Jewish historian of the first century A.D., reinforced this image by suggesting that his ancestors in Egypt had been forced to build various structures, including pyramids. It is an image that has persisted to our day. A fabulous Hollywood example is Cecil B. Demille's *Ten Commandments,* which shows a scene of pyramid building in which sweating, rag-clad, sunburned slaves toil in dark crowds as numerous as ants scuttling across an immense, sand-colored colony. This image doesn't fit, however, with what we know of the Old Kingdom.

As far as we know, there were no hordes of ill-fed slaves in the Egypt of the Fourth Dynasty. Poor people did exist, but they weren't slaves. The poor were Egyptian citizens, and they enjoyed the same rights as all citizens, including the right to turn to the king to redress grievances.[8] People who can ask the pharaoh for help are not slaves. In telling stories of slavery, Herodotus and later writers were reflecting the concerns of their own time, not the reality of ancient Egypt. The Greeks had fought mightily for centuries to protect themselves against enslavement by Persia. Josephus was writing at a time when the Jewish nation was struggling, and even actively waging rebellion, against the Roman Empire. Josephus himself was a complex character, at various times governor of Galilee, leader of a band of resistance fighters during the Jewish uprising of 66 A.D., and later a recipient of the patronage of the Roman emperor Vespasian (ruled 69–79 A.D.). Such writers were more than prepared to find yet another example of despotism in Khufu.

In addition, slavery was hardly a sensible strategy for building the Great Pyramid. The precision of the building and the efficiency needed to erect it swiftly are not the attributes of underfed, ill-treated slaves. Raising this immense monument took the skills of highly accomplished craftsmen, who, the evidence indicates, worked in gangs or crews and moved from site to site as their abilities were needed. Part of the pyramid labor force was organized in the same manner as boat crews. The team, or crew, consisted of about 200 men organized into five groups that were further subdivided into gangs. Each of the groups had a name, which sometimes referred to the men's place of origin and sometimes to such required virtues as stamina, strength, and endurance. Another system was also used in construction; it divided an unknown number of men into gangs named after three of the four cardinal directions. There is no evidence of any eastern teams, perhaps because "east," like "left" and "13" in our culture, carried connotations of bad luck, or because "east" was too sacred to be used for such mundane purposes. These organized groups spent their lives at the work of building and became masters at what they did.

Excavation of the workers' cemetery at Giza by Zahi Hawass has uncovered skeletons with joints worn by years of hard work. One of the skeletons came from a man who had suffered several fractures, all of which had healed well and straight. Evidently, the pyramid workers received medical care that was as good as it could be for that time in history.

Sneferu, Khufu's father and the purported builder of three pyramids, first organized the labor pool for this pyramid-building industry. He had conquered the armies of Nubia, or modern Sudan, and driven some 7,000 defeated men, along with their families and animals, into Egypt. Rather than let these new subjects spend their days idling about and causing trouble, Sneferu turned them into Egyptian citizens and encouraged them to become skilled workers who benefited from a system of privilege. A stela

Sneferu erected at Dahshur explains how he did it: "The settled Nubians working on the two pyramids of Sneferu are given tax exemption."[9] But how did they actually erect pyramids? How did they raise all that stone into the sky and line it up so precisely?

AN INCLINED PLANE
TO THE SQUARE

On the issue of how the pyramids were actually constructed, Herodotus, who never laid claim to being an engineer, is more than a bit vague. His phrase "machines made of short pieces of wood" tells us so little that Egyptologists for decades have dismissed the description as too flawed to be useful. They have come up with their own ideas, which are all variants of that mainstay of high-school physics: the inclined plane. They call it a ramp.

The ramp theory has any number of variants, but they all fall into one of three basic concepts. The first is a long, straight ramp that slopes up against one face of the pyramid. The workers placed stones on sledges and dragged them uphill in gangs. The advantage to this ramp strategy would be that three sides and all four corners would remain unobstructed and make it easier for the builders to keep the structure square and true. The problem is that as the pyramid grew, the ramp would have to extend an incredibly long distance. To preserve a slope of 1 in 10 all the way to the top of the Great Pyramid, the ramp would have to reach approximately 1,600 yards, or almost a mile.

To solve the length issue, some Egyptologists have argued for a spiral ramp. Four ramps, each beginning at a corner of the pyramid, spiraled upward and rested for support on the outer casing blocks.

A third idea combines the straight and spiral ramps. A straight ramp ran from the mouth of the Giza limestone quarry to a point about 100 feet up the Great Pyramid, then a spiral ramp climbed the rest of the structure's height.

All three ramp ideas suffer from fatal flaws. There is the length problem with the long ramp, of course. There is also a major issue with volume and mass. Even if the slope were a relatively steep 1 in 7, a ramp that reached from ground level to the apex of the Great Pyramid would require over 5.5 million cubic meters of material. That's more than twice the volume of the Great Pyramid itself!

And what could such a ramp be built with? Mud brick or tamped earth would collapse under its own weight and years of heavy traffic before the ramp reached its maximum height. Rock chips or trimmings from the pyramid would also prove as unstable as scree deposited at the base of a cliff. The only workable alternative is dressed stone, which means that the Egyptians would have had to build a ramp more than twice as big as the Great Pyramid in order to erect the Great Pyramid itself. As close to the Stone Age as they were, the Old Kingdom Egyptians would have quickly figured out that this approach amounted to an engineering black hole.

The spiral ramp, even when combined with a long ramp, is no better a solution. As the ramp rose with the growing pyramid, the distance between turns would decrease at each level, and the ramp would become steeper and steeper. In addition, the corners would be so sharp that the workers, no matter how large or muscular their gangs, could not drag the stones around them. With nothing but the outer casing stones for support, ramps would soon crumble away or fracture into uselessness. A spiral ramp would have also obscured the sides and corners of the pyramid and made it impossible to check squareness and alignment. Had they used a spiral ramp, the builders might have pulled it down at the end—itself a major feat of demolition and waste disposal—only to find they had erected something that was far from the near perfection seen in the existing pyramids. The Egyptians clearly knew better.

One alternative theory, promoted in, among other sources, a 1988 book entitled *The Pyramids: An Enigma Solved*, by Joseph Davidovits and Margie Morris, and in Moustafa Gadalla's *Pyramid Handbook*, is that the Egyptians didn't cut and lift stones. Rather, what we think of as stones are in fact molded blocks made of high-quality, manufactured limestone concrete. The pyramid builders made this material by combining silico-aluminate cement mortar with fossil-shell limestone in much the same way that modern-day cultured marble is made by mixing ground limestone into a polymer base. The Egyptians hauled materials up the pyramid, the way hod carriers do on contemporary construction sites, and cast their "stones" where and when they were needed. Herodotus's "machines" should actually be translated as "molds," Gadalla writes.

Of course, casting the masonry wouldn't actually solve entirely the pyramid construction problem. Even if the Egyptians were pouring stones rather than hauling them as blocks, they would still have to haul the same mass of material up the pyramid in the form of mortar and fossil-shell limestone. Admittedly, it might be easier to haul as small bundles of rubble rather than large blocks, but a lot of work and time would still be involved.

Yet, even though this strategy offers little advantage, Gadalla cites a variety of evidence to support it. He maintains, for example, that the Great Pyramid's building blocks do not match the Giza limestones and that the copper tools the Egyptians used couldn't cut enough limestone to build the structure within a single pharaoh's lifetime.

Gadalla is wrong on both counts. Other geologists and I have studied the pyramids and ancient quarries (which retain evidence of the ancient rock-cutting activities), and we know the natural sources of the stone used in the Great Pyramid and the methods used to remove it from the quarry and transport it to the building site. Both fell well within the technological competencies of the Old Kingdom.

The inner core of the Great Pyramid was assembled from blocks of yellowish limestone quarried at Giza. This stone is relatively easy to remove because of the weak zones and planes natural to this particular limestone. Limestone is a sedimentary rock; it often forms from the layered accumulation of shells and other calcareous materials. The Egyptians learned to exploit the relatively weak zones between certain layers of limestone and peel the rock off stratum by stratum. They dug a grid of trenches cross-hatching the limestone deposit, each trench just wide enough to allow a stonecutter to mark the blocks and cut them to the same approximate depth. Then, starting with the row of blocks on the end, a wedge—probably made of hard wood, like acacia, sheathed in copper—was driven into the weak zone marking the layer, and the block was split from the underlying rock. The quarrymen then dragged the freed blocks one after another over a layer of quartz sand spread over the quarry surface. This abrasion smoothed the tops of the next layer of blocks, which were then trenched and removed just as the layer above had been. The whole procedure exploited limestone's natural characteristics, and it produced blocks that, layer by layer, were of roughly the same dimensions. Various courses of the Great Pyramid are of different thicknesses, reflecting the origin of the blocks in strata whose depth varied naturally.

The fine white limestone that made up the outer polished and finely fitted outer layer didn't come from Giza. Its source was the Mokattam (Mokhattam, Muqattam) Hills (Jebel Mokhattam), on the other side of the Nile, near the modern cities of Tura and Maasara.[10] This stone was harder to remove than the Giza material, because it lay under the surface and could be mined only by digging tunnels, some of which went more than 50 yards below ground level. The quarrymen removed the limestone in a steplike fashion, wedging the blocks off and tumbling them down. The stone could be further trimmed and shaped with copper chisels and short, single-handed saws bearing a blade about $\frac{2}{10}$ inch thick.

The rock that caused Egyptian masons the greatest difficulty was the granite used in a few parts of the Great Pyramid, such as the King's Chamber. An igneous rather than a sedimentary rock, granite is much harder than limestone. Yet even it has weak points, natural cleavage lines that carve the stone into pieces with usable shapes. At Aswan, one of the principal sources for the granite used in the Great Pyramid, the rock bed breaks apart in layers that are nearly parallel and take a variety of shapes, including blocks, beams, and balls. Egyptian stonemasons could work these stones into the forms they needed.

Not that this didn't take a lot of elbow grease and sweat. Granite is so hard and difficult to work that it was reserved for those areas of the Great Pyramid, such as the great beams roofing the Relieving Chambers, where its ability to span an unusual distance or support great weight was required. Still, when they needed granite, the Egyptians knew how to prepare it for use. The process began with handheld balls of dolerite, a stone harder even than granite, which the stonemason pounded against the rock. A block could be further shaped by sawing, as is evidenced by the granite coffer or sarcophagus in the King's Chamber, which shows signs of having been cut with a blade at least 8 feet long. Copper by itself is too soft to cut granite. Hard sharp materials, such as bits of diamond, may have been inserted into the blade, or a slurry of sand, emery, or diamond dust could have been worked into the cut.[11] Experimental trials of such devices have shown that they work, and the Egyptians could have used them to create the masonry we see today throughout the Great Pyramid.

Once the blocks of limestone or granite were quarried and at least roughly shaped, they next had to be transported to the building site. For the limestone, it was but a short distance from the quarry to the pyramid. The granite, however, was floated down the Nile from Aswan in Upper Egypt. Very few depictions of working wheels are known from the Old Kingdom. The archaeological evidence to date indicates that the Egyptians of the pyramid-building era most likely transported stone blocks on sledges rather than wheeled vehicles. Depictions from the Eighteenth Dynasty show oxen dragging a stone block on a sledge and groups of men pulling sledge-mounted, heavy funerary statues of the dead. The single bas relief showing the transport of the 58-ton stone colossus of Djehutihotep has 178 men roped to a massive sledge with four hawsers and supplying the power. In most of these images, including that of Djehutihotep, an individual pours liquid in front of the sledge. Perhaps this libation served a symbolic purpose; it may have also been practical. Covering the route with silt that was wetted just before the sledge slid onto it would have reduced friction and made pulling that much easier. And, although few rollers have been found in ancient Egypt, the stone transporters of the Old Kingdom did use wood tracks.

Sledges moved the Giza limestones to the building site, and the Tura and Aswan blocks to the Nile, where they could be barged to the plateau, then sledged up from a riverside dock to the growing pyramid. But once they were there, they still had to be lifted up and put into the right place. A ramp wouldn't solve that key problem for the pyramid builders of ancient Egypt. What method or tool did they use?

THE POWER TO MOVE THE WORLD

There is the thing itself; then there is the story about the thing. In the case of the lever, the story dates to the third century B.C., when the Greek mathematician and engineer Archimedes (287?–212 B.C.) first described it. The lever did not, however, begin with Archimedes. His genius lay in figuring out its physics. The lever had been around for a long, long time, and it was an understanding of its usefulness and power that led to the quotation ascribed to Archimedes centuries after his death: "Give me a place to stand, and I can move the earth."

The earth is vastly larger than even the biggest block of stone in the Great Pyramid, and the lever is the key to how each of the more than 2 million stones in the monument were moved into place. This is the hypothesis advanced by Peter Hodges in his 1989 book *How the Pyramids Were Built.* I find his approach convincing.

Hodges came to the pyramid-building problem not as an antiquarian scholar but as a man who spent his life in construction. He trained professionally at the School of Building in Brixton, England, then served with the British Army's Royal Engineers as a sapper officer dealing with field fortifications during World War II. When peace came, he worked with a number of building firms and eventually took over and ran a long-established construction business. He understood building from the inside and knew firsthand how it feels to work stone with hand tools. Still, when Hodges came to Egypt, he accepted the ramp theory of construction. Given how many eminent academics accepted it, why wouldn't he?

Then, as always happens in construction, anything that can go wrong will. Staying in a hotel within sight of the Great Pyramid, Hodges was felled by a dose of dysentery that gave him three full days flat on his back to think about how the builders of the Old Kingdom would go about putting up a pyramid. In that time, he figured out the basis of his approach, which he elaborated over the following years and developed into a book that was published after his death.

Hodges realized that the Egyptians had figured out something that Archimedes later immortalized and every sapper officer knew from experience: a few levers with a few men can lift crushingly huge weights. During his wartime service, Hodges had often watched as four sappers pumping two simple lever jacks readily and quickly raised the end of a 30-ton Bailey bridge to place rollers or permanent bearing plates under the lifted end. The handle on jacks the sappers employed raised the bridge about ⅓ inch with each stroke, then caught on a ratchet to hold the slightly higher weight in place. Another stroke, another ⅓ inch, and in a matter of minutes, four men could boost the bridge upward inch by inch and foot by foot.

The Egyptians, as far as we know, lacked the ratchet, but they could gain the same advantage by packing materials in under the block. Say, for example, two levers were inserted under the end of a typical 2½-ton pyramid building block. One or two men on each lever pushed down, raised the end of the block a short distance, and inserted a piece of wood into the space between the block and the surface it was sitting on. The same procedure of jacking and packing was followed on the other end of the block. Again and again, the block was jacked and packed. Do this enough times, and the block rises to the next course of stone, where it can be moved horizontally—again with the levers—onto the higher surface. The crew removes the now-freed packing, puts the levers under the block yet again, raises it the first increment, and puts some of the packing underneath. Again and again the process is repeated. This would work, as the sides of the unfinished pyramid courses formed a series of steps. Working in a finely tuned rhythm, Hodges figured that a crew of four could boost a typical building block halfway up the pyramid in a day's work.

Hodges experimented with various kinds of levers, and he favored a design that looked something like a club-footed hockey stick, with the weight-bearing lower end sheathed in copper to add strength. Julian Keable, Hodges's editor, preferred a straight lever; it lacked the obvious weak point in the bend of the curved lever. Whichever design the Egyptians may have used, the basic physical principles remain the same.

The exceptionally large, very heavy pieces of stone used in the Great Pyramid pose no stumbling block to the lever theory. A heavier stone is also a larger stone; that many more men can find foothold around the load and work their levers. Forty levers manned by one or two workers apiece could lift even the 50-ton, or more, red granite blocks that roofed the Relieving Chambers.

One of the fascinating aspects of the lever strategy is that it eliminates ramps or scaffolding. The pyramid itself becomes the platform on which the men work as they raise the stone blocks from one level to the next. When they put the last stone in place, they simply pick up their tools and go home. There was no ancillary structure left to remove. As soon as the pyramid is done, the project is finished.

Curiously, Hodges's idea fits with Herodotus's description that "they [the pyramid builders] raised the remaining stones by machines made of short pieces of wood" and "they removed the machine, which was only one and portable, to each range in succession, whenever they wished to raise the stone higher."

SCRIBING THE SQUARE

Of course, lifting the stones is only part of the challenge of building a pyramid. The builders had to be sure that they were raising the right shape into the sky. They wanted to know that when they were finished, they could step back and see the shape they intended, not that of a collapsed angel-food cake.

Fashioning the right shape began with leveling the ground to create a flat, firm base in the bedrock. The first step was marking the approximate directions and length of each of the four sides. The builders then probably selected one side as a baseline and set their men to work cutting a broad, level track about 6 feet wide and at least 50 feet longer than the approximately 756-foot eventual length of the Great Pyramid's side. As the baseline was cut, the builders could measure the level with the same principle masons and carpenters use today: checking the horizontal against a liquid. As you probably know, a level uses a bubble in a heavy liquid to indicate the horizontal. If the level is off, the bubble moves to one side or the other, depending on the direction of slope from the horizontal. The ancient Egyptians could have exploited a similar principle by building a narrow channel about one foot wide and 50 feet long and filling it with water—whose surface is, of course, level. Stones were placed at each end of the channel just flush with the surface of the water. Two men carrying flat-topped rods of exactly equal length placed the butts of the rods on the stones in the water, while other men with the rods of the same type and length set them at approximately equal intervals along the baseline. A worker sighting along the rods could use the level established by the two rods in the water to determine the amount of rock that needed to be removed farther down the line to make the base level. Although the work of removing the bedrock with the tools the Egyptians had to work with was difficult indeed, repeated rechecking allowed them to establish the level precisely.

With the baseline cut and level, the time came to determine the orientation and length of each of the four sides. One way to do this would be to determine the center point of the baseline, establish the true north–south axis of the pyramid, and orient the site plan so that the axis crossed at the center point. This orientation determined the rest of the square, which had to be marked before the real work could begin.

The square began by setting two right angles at the center point of the baseline. Three cords of at least 50 feet in length were set out, each from the center point marked into the rock. One followed the north–south axis exactly, the other two what would be the halves of the side. The builders marked the cords at exactly the same distance from the center point and placed the side cords as close to a right angle as eyeballing could make them. Next they measured the angle of the hypotenuse of the triangles formed between the marks on the side cords and the mark on the axis cord and adjusted the side cords until the hypotenuses were equal and both angles truly 90°. The same procedure was used to determine the right angles at the corners of the baseline, then around the remaining three sides of what would be the pyramid. Most likely, the pyramid builders placed sighting stones away from the corners but in line with the sides. This allowed them to check the right angles even when the original corners were covered with masonry and no longer visible.

The next task was determining the length of the baseline side, a solution that probably proved to be relatively simple. It could have been a matter of taking two rods of exactly the same length and laying them end to end over and over again until the predetermined length was reached. Most likely the rods were capped with metal to lessen wear and tear; they could also be filed to achieve exactness in length. Wooden measuring rods are known from the New Kingdom, although there is no evidence of their use in the Old Kingdom. Still, the solution is so simple and obvious that the ancient Egyptians were likely to have had such devices.

With the square marked and the baseline now level, the procedure of rough cutting followed by water leveling and sighting along the rods could be repeated around the three remaining sides of the pyramid site. This work began at the level established by the baseline, so that the whole square was brought to that one level. When this work was finished, the four sides had been leveled and measured, yet within lay them nearly 13 acres of rough, ragged bedrock. Leveling this part of the site became the next task, one that must have taken a great many men months to complete. And in a sense, they did not finish the task. One rocky prominence, which extends two dozen feet upward from the base, remains under the pyramid. Containing the lower portion of the Descending Passage, as well as the Subterranean Chamber and the Grotto, it was left in place, probably for important religious reasons (we will explore these further in chapter 6).

SHINE IN THE SKY

Even with the base squared and much of the underlying site leveled, the Egyptians faced the challenge of putting all those many block of stones in the right place. Stepped pyramids like Djoser's at Saqqara were erected essentially by starting at the center and raising a core that was wider at the bottom and narrower at the top for stability. The outer layers leaned in against the core and acted as buttresses to hold it in place. The core rose faster than the outer layers, so that the center of pyramid was reaching into the sky sooner than the exterior faces. Some Egyptologists have argued that the Old Kingdom builders erected the core of the Great Pyramid in the same way, then evened up the outer walls to give a smoothly sloping outward appearance. Engineer Peter Hodges doesn't think so, and I agree. Squaring off a stepped pyramid after the fact would have made it very difficult to ensure that the corners rose as they must to place the apex directly over the center of the pyramid. Building instead course by course and completing each tier in turn would make it easier to verify the building.

Once again, this approach fits with Herodotus's account: "This pyramid was built thus: in the form of steps, which some call crossae [tiers], some bomides [terraces]." In other words, the builders laid one course completely, then set the next course atop it. They worked not from the center out but from the bottom up.

Each course in the Great Pyramid is a square that sits atop the slightly larger square of the course beneath it, center aligned to center. Put another way, each course angles precisely in from the course below it. The angle is the key. If it's right, the pyramid is on track; if it's off, there's trouble that gets worse, course by course. One solution to the problem of setting each course at the correct angle is to raise the corners first, then fill in the straight reaches between the corners. The pyramid builders must have laid the four corner blocks of each course and checked the angles before laying the rest of that course and moving to the next course above, beginning again at the corners. Probably the pyramid builders used a plumb frame to check the corner angle, a triangular frame constructed to the correct 52° angle and equipped with a plumbing device to ensure vertical accuracy.

It was also possible to double-check the positioning of each corner by sighting from outside the pyramid. Because of the pyramid's geometry, the corner hip line (where two adjoining sides meet) looks vertical to an observer standing opposite the hip and looking toward the pyramid. Old Kingdom engineers could sight the corner hip lines from the pyramid's base against a vertical marker. If the corners were all rising vertically at the same angle to the horizontal, then the four would meet at the apex. If one of the hips was off, that corner could be adjusted before the structure reached any higher. As long as each step was parallel, equal, on the correct gradient, and straight along its hip line, the shape was guaranteed to grow into a correct pyramid.

An advantage to this approach is economy of effort. Setting the corner stones for each course was a demanding task; the stone had to be set in by a precise distance in two directions to maintain the hip line. But, since the Great Pyramid has 200 courses and four corners to each course, precision alignment of a total of 800 stones determined the shape of the entire structure. The 100,000 facing blocks lined up behind the corners, while the remainder of the pyramid—over 2 million pieces of stone—consisted principally of fill that required vastly less precision and care. The Egyptians put their effort where it showed, and economized on the hidden rest.

Besides pointing to the use of levers and the course-by-course construction of the Great Pyramid, Herodotus reported that it took 20 years to build the structure. A great many writers have argued that this is far too fast a pace, particularly when the project included the vast ramps thought to be necessary. Peter Hodges again disagrees. He calculated that 125 teams of men working 350 days a year could raise the Great Pyramid in 17 years.

After all stones were lifted and placed, a final step remained—the white limestone facing that once graced the surface of the Great Pyramid and turned it into a shining mountain under the midday sun. Many writers have assumed that the facing stones were cut to a sloping angle on the ground, then raised into place from the bottom to the top to encase the completed pyramid core. There is a better alternative, however, one that Hodges favored. As he saw it, rectangular blocks of white limestone were laid as the outward-facing stones in each course in the rising pyramid. When the topmost course was finished, masons working with hammers and chisels trimmed the white limestone blocks by cutting off the pro-truding step each block formed and smoothing the surface to the pyramid's 52° slope. This work began from the top of the pyramid. The masons could stand on the step of the course below as they trimmed one course, then move down yet another course to work on the one that had just served as the platform for their work. Trimming, Hodges calculates, would have taken three years, which adds up to the 20 Herodotus reported.

Circumstantial evidence supports this idea. By Hodges's calculations, trimming the Great Pyramid would have produced 56,000 tons of stone dust and chips. Archaeologists Michael and Angela Jones found large quantities of chips—including chips of Tura

Some of the original facing blocks at the base of the north side of the Great Pyramid. Photograph courtesy of Robert M. Schoch.

limestone, the very stone used for the casing—at the base of the Great Pyramid during their excavation of the nearby Temple of Isis. And the trimming method fits with Herodotus. "The highest parts of it, therefore, were first finished," he writes, "and afterward they completed the parts next following, but last of all they finished the parts on the ground, and that were lowest."

THE INTERCONNECTION OF WHO AND WHEN

It is apparent that building the Great Pyramid didn't require helicopters, levitation, extraterrestrial help, or divine intervention. An organized, highly motivated civilization using tools as basic as water levels, copper chisels, dolorite balls, and levers was capable of building the Great Pyramid. But answering the question of whether the ancient Egyptians could have accomplished this feat does not necessarily mean it was done during the time of Khufu or even during the Old Kingdom.

Construction of the Great Pyramid falls within the technical competence of a long-ago people. But exactly when this ancient civilization did its work is an issue we still need to resolve.

The path toward resolution lies partly in understanding how the ancient Egyptians oriented the Great Pyramid so perfectly to the cardinal directions. To grasp that, we need to look up—to the heavens that fascinated Taylor and Smyth and the distant planets and stars that drew Hoagland, Sitchin, and von Däniken.

Part Two

AS
ABOVE,
SO BELOW

Six

TRACKING
THE HEAVENS

W HEN THE BUILDERS OF THE GREAT PYRAMID FACED
the challenge of orienting the structure to the cardinal directions, they couldn't simply take a compass bearing. As
far as we know, there were no such instruments in those days. But even if
the pyramid builders had laid their ancient hands on a compass, it wouldn't
have given them the information they needed. A compass points to magnetic north, which deviates from true north by a significant amount, depending on the bearing-taker's position on Earth. To use a compass to
obtain geographic north (as opposed to magnetic north) in a certain region,
you must know how much magnetic north deviates from true north, which
means you must know the direction of true north in the first place.

Three fundamental methods of determining true north as accurately as
it is incorporated into the Great Pyramid were most likely available to
these long-ago builders. One approach, which has a number of possible
variations and has long been used in India, focuses on shadows cast by the
sun at midday, most accurately near the winter solstice. The other two
methods make use of the movement of the stars across the heavens. The
first involves sighting a single star against an artificial horizon, such as a
perfectly level wall, as it rises and sets, then dividing the arc between them.

The second is based on bisecting the extreme uppermost (highest) and lowermost positions of a circumpolar star, one that turns in a small circle about the north celestial pole. Exactly between these two extremes will lie the north celestial pole—or, to find the direction of geographical north on Earth, one can sight on the highest or lowest culmination of the star itself.

Not long before the turn of the nineteenth century, a British astronomer made a good argument for the circumpolar star method. His analysis underscores the fact that the Descending Passage points to a star near the celestial north pole, and in asking when—that is, at what period or periods—this occurred, he takes us back to the question of just how old the Great Pyramid really is.

STRETCHING THE CORD

English astronomer and science popularizer Richard A. Proctor (1837–1888), like many scientists of the Victorian era, began his career as a well-read amateur. One of the writers Proctor delved into was Proclus (A.D. 411?–485), a Neoplatonic philosopher, mathematician, and astronomer. Proclus reported in his commentary on Plato's *Timaeus*—one of the two Platonic dialogues that mention Atlantis, by the way—that the Great Pyramid had been used as an astronomical observatory before it was completed. Proctor realized the idea made inherently good sense. If the pyramid had been built course by course the way Peter Hodges proposes, the raised square structure would have made an excellent platform for observing movements in the heavens. To make those observations precise and replicable, ancient astronomers needed a baseline. That's where true north came in.

From the point of view of an earthbound observer who knows nothing of the Big Bang, an expanding universe, or the awesome immensity of interstellar distances, the night sky looks like a great vault, a rotating sphere in which we find ourselves at the very center. Stars, like the sun, rise in the east and set in the west. The eastern and western horizons provide the outer boundaries of their observable movements. The meridian line, which stretches between the north and south celestial poles, marks the exact center between the two horizons and divides the dome of the sky into two halves. Since a time in antiquity that probably lies far beyond the building of the Great Pyramid, astronomers have made the north pole of the earth and the north pole of the sky one and the same in direction. Determining true north allowed an ancient astronomer—or a modern one, for that matter— to trace the meridian across the heavens and record when the stars and planets crossed it in their transit across the sky.

Locating the north celestial pole is easy enough in theory. It is the point around which the stars seem to turn in their transit from east to west. The closer to the pole one looks, the smaller the circle the stars travel around it. In our time, the single star Polaris nearly occupies this point, and appears to be stationary. But, for reasons of celestial mechanics we will discuss later in this chapter, stars move on and off the celestial north pole. At the time of the Old Kingdom's Fourth Dynasty, no single star occupied the sky's north pole. Rather, a small number of circumpolar stars circled round the pole, neither rising from the horizon nor setting below it. The Egyptians knew these stars as the Imperishables. Select the Imperishable with the smallest circumpolar circle, determine the easternmost and westernmost (or northern- most and southernmost) points of its turning, then divide the angle between them in half. The result is true north.

It appears likely that this act of measuring and dividing is the substance of a little-understood ancient Egyptian ceremony known as the stretching of the cord. Depictions of the ceremony show the god Thoth holding a shoulder-high pole in one hand and a club in the other and facing the god- dess Seshat, who is holding the same kind of pole and club. Between the poles a circle of cord is stretched. Presumably, the poles are sighting rods driven into the ground with the clubs to mark the east–west extremes of a star's circumpolar circle. An inscription from Edfu, a Nile River town about 70 miles north of Aswan, that accompanies an image depicting the stretch- ing of the cord reads: "I hold the peg. I grasp the handle of the club and grip the measuring cord with Seshat. I turn my eyes to the movement of the stars. . . . I make firm the corners of thy temple."[1] Although this depic- tion and its inscription date from long after the pyramid age, the ceremony's roots have been traced to the Second Dynasty.

The stretching of the cord allowed the pyramid builders to transfer the meridian of the sky to the earth. A chalk line would blow away, however, and a simple string like the ceremonial cord could be moved. The builders needed something more permanent. This, Proctor realized, was what they were after with the Descending Passage.

The Descending Passage extends from the north-facing entrance of the Great Pyramid through the lower courses of the monument until it enters bedrock, penetrates deeply into the earth itself, and ends in the Subterranean Chamber. As Proctor saw it, the builders began the Descending Passage at ground level, long before the first course of pyramid masonry was laid. The diggers set the line and angle of descent according to the circumpolar star that they had used to determine true north.

"From the middle of the northern side of the intended base [of the pyramid]," Proctor wrote, "they would bore a slant passage tending always from the position of the pole star at its lowest meridional passage, that star at each successive return to that position serving to direct their progress."[2]

Proctor assumed that this star was Alpha Draconis, which, though faint, circled only 3° 43' from the celestial north pole around 2140 B.C. and earlier around 3440 B.C. At the Great Pyramid's latitude, the light from Alpha Draconis at the southern extreme of its nightly circle would have struck the earth at an angle of about 26° 16'–26° 17'. Within the accuracy that the less-than-perfectly-smooth Descending Passage can be measured, this is the angle of the tunnel. The deeper the builders dug and the longer their excavation, the more limited the field of vision and the more accurate their orientation on Alpha Draconis. Indeed, this explains the Descending Passage's consistent angle and straightness. It has been claimed that originally the straightness varied less than ¼ inch, and the roof slope by under ³⁄₁₀ inch, throughout the tunnel's 350-foot length.[3] Even if these claims are somewhat exaggerated, the passage is carved with remarkable precision. With the Descending Passage dug, the builders could have used simple trigonometry to place the center of the pyramid over the Subterranean Chamber, set the corners of the pyramid's square, leveled the site, and begun laying the masonry.

Extending the Descending Passage up through the rising masonry ensured that the structure remained oriented correctly as it rose. This technique ended, though, once the Descending Passage exited the pyramid core at the nineteenth course.

The Ascending Passage, Proctor argued, extended the usefulness of the Descending Passage's orientation to the celestial north pole. The Ascending Passage rises at nearly the same angle at the Descending: just over 26°. The pyramid builders maintained this angle by following the light of Alpha Draconis in a reflecting pool formed at the junction of the Ascending and Descending passages, according to Proctor. They plugged the Descending Passage, then filled the area above the plug with water. By following the reflection of Alpha Draconis in the pooled water, the builders were able to head south with the same accuracy with which they had earlier gone north.

The Ascending Passage ends in the Grand Gallery, which Proctor saw as the core and genius of the Great Pyramid's astronomical usefulness. From the point of view of a watcher of the heavens, before its southern end was enclosed, the Grand Gallery was a huge, graduated, vertical slot exactly bisected by the celestial meridian. Looking up along and through the Grand Gallery at the open end, observers could watch the constellations of the zodiac pass through the sky in their nightly east-to-west journeys. The most important measure in such observations is the exact moment when the object being observed crosses the celestial meridian. A Grand Gallery observer could note the time when the star first appeared—which could have been measured with a device as basic as an hourglass or swinging pendulum,

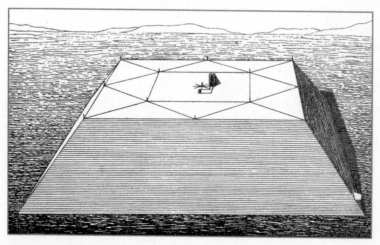

Reconstruction of the lower portion of the Great Pyramid as an astronomical observatory. (*From Proctor, 1883, frontispiece.*)

with an attendant perhaps chanting out times by the second—then note when it disappeared, divide the time of passage in half, and know precisely when the star crossed the celestial meridian. Do this often enough, for enough stars, and the result is an accurate map of the zodiac and surrounding stars made well before the days of telescopes and fancy mechanical chronographs.

The pyramid's utility for star mapping would have been augmented by placing observers on the flat platform of the structure, where wooden posts or other markers designated the cardinal directions. There they could have recorded the risings and settings of the stars, data that were then combined with the meridian observations of the other observers stationed inside the Grand Gallery to complete the star map. Knowing the positions of the fixed stars, ancient astronomers could have also traced the paths of the planets, which moved according to very different dynamics from those driving the zodiac and the other constellations.

The Grand Gallery's contributions didn't end with the stars and the planets. It also furthered knowledge of the sun's movements. The falling rays of midday sunlight on midsummer's and midwinter's days and on the vernal and autumnal equinox would have set up distinct and useful patterns

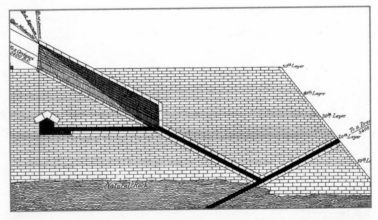

Vertical north-south section of the Great Pyramid through the Grand Gallery, Ascending and Descending passages, and Queen's Chamber, illustrating how a partially completed Great Pyramid could be used as an astronomical observatory. (*From Proctor, 1883, facing page 155.*)

of light and shadow and told the users of the Great Pyramid's astronomical observatory where they stood in the turn of the year.

THE SUN AND THE STARS

A contemporary of Proctor, Sir Norman Lockyer (1836–1920), devoted most of his astronomical career to studying the sun. He was director of the solar physics observatory at England's Royal College of Science, leader of eight British government expeditions to observe total solar eclipses, and winner of a medal from the French government for codiscovery of the spectroscopic method of observing solar prominences in daylight. But there was another aspect to his career. Lockyer focused on the astronomical connections of ancient monuments, looking at Stonehenge in his native land and also directing his attention to Greek and Egyptian temples. His books and papers, including *Dawn of Astronomy*, published in 1894, conferred upon Lockyer scholarly status as one of the founders of archaeoastronomy, the discipline that investigates the relationships between ancient monuments and the skies of their times. Much of our contemporary understanding of Stonehenge began with Lockyer's pioneering work.

Lockyer made two fundamental findings in his work on Egypt. The first reinforced Proctor's argument. Many Egyptian monuments, Lockyer realized, were oriented to the heavens, whether sun or stars. His second discovery was that the Egyptians knew that the skies were anything but constant. They changed, slowly to be sure, but changed nonetheless.

Heading for Egypt on his academic summer holidays, Lockyer began his research at the temple of Amen-Ra at Karnak. The temple was built in such a way that on the summer solstice—the longest day of the year, or the day with the greatest length and extent of sunlight—the sun's rays entered the temple at sunset, traversed its length along the building's axis, and penetrated the sanctuary. Working backward from his knowledge of the slowly changing tilt of the earth's axis, Lockyer estimated that the Karnak temple, or at least the original foundation upon which it is built, had been erected circa 3700 B.C., as opposed to the currently widely accepted dating of much of this temple, which was continually being built and rebuilt, to the Middle Kingdom through Greek period, circa 2000 to 300 B.C.

Other temples, Lockyer argued, were oriented to the points where certain stars rise just before sunrise—a phenomenon called heliacal rising—on the vernal equinox. Among these stars was the one we know as Sirius, the Dog Star, the brightest star in the sky, forming part of the constellation Canis Major, which is located near the constellation we call Orion. The ancient Egyptians knew Orion as Osiris, their great god, and Sirius was the star of Isis, Osiris's wife and goddess mother of all Egypt.

There is an issue with orienting a temple to a star's heliacal rising on the vernal equinox, however: the star's orientation changes over the centuries. The reason is a complex intersection of natural phenomena.

Our planet isn't really round. It flattens at the poles and bulges at the equator, so that a radius drawn from the earth's center to the equator is about 14 miles longer than one drawn to either pole. This extra roll around the middle makes the earth not a true sphere but, technically, an oblate spheroid. In addition, the earth's axis of rotation tips relative to the plane (or ecliptic) of its orbit around the sun. The sun, the moon and, to a much smaller degree, the other planets tug gravitationally on the greater mass of the earth's bulging equatorial middle and slowly move the axis of rotation. Because of these forces, the earth spins not like a wheel on an axle, around and around in the same plane, but like a top wobbling across a table or floor.

This slow wobbling movement is called precession, and it affects how we on Earth see events in the heavens. The stars slowly shift relative to the celestial north and south poles and trace paths that come full circle about every 26,000 years. For example, in 12,000 B.C., the North Star was Vega. In 3000 B.C., the closest candidate was Alpha Draconis. At the height of Greek civilization in the fifth and sixth centuries B.C., the North Star was Beta Ursae Minoris. Currently the North Star is Polaris (also known as Alpha Ursae Minoris), at the tip of the constellation of Ursa Minor (also known as the Little Bear or the Little Dipper). By about A.D. 14,000, Vega will again occupy the position of North Star, as the precessional circle closes.

Precession affects not only the position of the North Star but also the relative positions of the constellations. Over time, constellations rise in new points on the eastern horizon, then follow new paths across the meridian to changed setting points in the west. And precession affects the position of the stars relative to the sun, a phenomenon that is often most carefully observed on the spring equinox. In our era, the sun rises in the constellation of Pisces on the spring equinox; This is why, by the conventions of astrology, we live in the precessional age of Pisces, which began in about 60 B.C. The next precessional age, Aquarius, will commence when the sun first comes up against that constellation, sometime between A.D. 2060 and 2100, depending on the method of calculation.

Historical convention confers the honor for detecting precession to Hipparchus, a brilliant Hellenistic mathematician and astronomer of the second century B.C. Watching the sky one night, Hipparchus saw a star where he was certain no star had been charted before. He carefully catalogued the nearly 1,100 fixed stars he knew, positioned them by celestial longitude and latitude, then compared his star chart with one made by a Greek astronomer some 150 years earlier. Calculating that all the stars had shifted position by approximately 2° in the intervening time, Hipparchus named the change precession.

It is hard to believe, though, that the Egyptians, with their careful observations of the heliacal risings of key stars, didn't know about precession long before the idea first came to Hipparchus. In fact, the Egyptians routinely reoriented star temples every 200 to 300 years, when precession had disconnected a temple from the star it was built to mark. The great temple of Luxor, Lockyer discovered, had undergone four distinct changes of orientation as it was built and rebuilt over the centuries. "This change of direction," Lockyer wrote, "is one of the most striking things which have been observed for years past in Egyptian temples."[4]

Because he understood precession's effect on the positions of sun and stars, Lockyer could date temples and other structures by determining when the skies fit their specific orientations, and the dates he came to were often considerably older than the standard Egyptological beliefs. The ancient Egyptians were very probably doing the same thing—that is, aligning with astronomical objects, in order to memorialize the changing heavens—in monuments other than their temples, including, perhaps, the Great Pyramid.

THE OLD SKIES OF THE ANCIENT GOD

Lockyer's work met considerable academic resistance from classical Egyptologists of the time, especially since they were generally not trained as scientists; and for some decades afterward, archaeoastronomy was little honored and less pursued. The field wasn't resurrected until the late twentieth century, and then was popularized in large part by the work of a nonacademic aficionado of the Great Pyramid who paid careful attention to an oddity of Giza: the three pyramids don't line up.

The effect is most pronounced in an image of the pyramids taken from above. Take a ruler or straight edge, and connect the apexes of the Khufu and Khafre pyramids, and you'll notice that the Menkaure pyramid sits well off the line. As attentive as the pyramid builders were to cardinal directions, perfect squares, and precise corners, this divergence must have been intentional. But why did the pyramid builders purposely misalign the three pyramids of Giza?

The answer came to Robert Bauval, a construction engineer of Belgian background who was born in Egypt. As he looked up at the stars one night in the startlingly clear skies of the Arabian Desert, a friend pointed out that the three stars forming Orion's Belt are offset. The dimmest of the three lies at a slight distance from the axis formed by the two brighter stars. Suddenly Bauval realized he had the model for the site plan that placed the three Giza pyramids in their curious, intended positions: the three pyramids replicated Orion's Belt in both alignment and relative size.

There was nothing arbitrary or trivial about this choice. The people of the Old Kingdom recognized some of the same constellations we do, but they knew them by different names. Our Orion was their Osiris, an identification that takes us to the core of religious belief in the third and fourth millennia B.C. In the religious mythology that underpinned ancient Egypt, the story of Osiris was the key myth, as central as the story of Jesus to Christianity or Moses and the Exodus to Judaism.

Osiris was the eldest son of Nut, goddess of the sky, a man as well as a god. He became ruler of Egypt and, following the royal custom, married his sister Isis. Osiris was the essence of the good king. He spread *ma'at* (truth and justice) throughout the kingdom and through his vizier, the equally divine Thoth, taught humans the arts of civilization, prosperity, and happiness. However, Osiris's goodness angered his brother Seth (also known as Set). Seth murdered Osiris treacherously and cut his body into small pieces, which he scattered across Egypt.

Isis gathered all the many pieces of Osiris's corpse from the far corners of the country and reassembled them. Then, in the brief span of life this return to wholeness afforded her husband, Isis coupled with Osiris and became pregnant with their child. His task on earth done, Osiris transformed himself into a star being—the constellation we know as Orion— while Isis, her body swelling with a son who would be called Horus, took refuge in the Nile marshes to escape Seth. Horus grew into a powerful young prince who challenged Seth to personal combat to determine who should rule Egypt. The fight was fearsome: Horus lost an eye, and Seth's testicles were torn off. Horus was the victor and became the pharaoh of Egypt.

This story, with its themes of the battle of good and evil, of dismemberment and rejoining, and of revenge and the return of justice across the generations, created the religious ethic of the pharaoh's rule. Each subsequent pharaoh, including Khufu, saw himself as the reincarnation of Horus, the fighter who struggles to reestablish balance and good order. At his death, the Horus-king was transformed into Osiris and, like the first god of the Egyptian pantheon, took his place among the stars.

In the years following that clear Arabian night, Bauval joined forces with author Adrian Gilbert, set about writing *The Orion Mystery*, and furthered his research into the Great Pyramid's Osiris-Orion connection. Bauval realized that the star map of Orion extended beyond Giza to encompass all the major pyramids coming up the Nile from Dashur to Abu Roash, with the Nile itself standing in for the Milky Way. That was the big picture. On a smaller scale, he made note of the fact that the shafts extending through the Great Pyramid from the King's and Queen's chambers lined up with stars that furthered the Orion connection. The northern shaft from the King's Chamber pointed to Alpha Draconis, the southern shaft pointed to Orion's Belt. In the case of the two Queen's Chamber shafts, the northern pointed on the correct bearing for Beta Ursae Minoris, and the southern for Sirius, which was sacred to Isis. By Bauval's calculations, these alignments fit the sky in approximately 2450 B.C., close to the conventional date assigned for the construction of the Great Pyramid and an apparent corroboration of the Egyptological orthodoxy.

But that wasn't all, as became clear when Bauval explored the position of the stars, taking precession into account and going back thousands of years. Returning to the epoch of circa 10,400 B.C., Bauval found that "the pattern of Orion's Belt seen on the 'west' of the Milky Way matches, with uncanny precision, the pattern and alignments of the three Giza pyramids!"[5] Bauval continues: "In *c.* 2450 B.C., when the Great Pyramid was built, the correlation was experienced when Orion's Belt was seen in the east at the moment of heliacal rising of Sirius, the perfect 'meridian to meridian' patterns, i.e., when the two images [terrestrial and celestial] superimpose in perfect match; this is when we see the First Time of Orion's Belt in *c.* 10450 B.C.," a date that marks the "start of the great precessional cycle at 10450 B.C."[6] Knowing precession and following a master plan handed down through the millennia, were the Fourth Dynasty Egyptians recording, memorializing, and reconfirming the period of the so-called First Time of Osiris (c. 10,400–10,500 B.C.) in the positions of their great architectural achievements on the Giza Plateau? This appears to be the case.

One thing that feeds skepticism about Bauval's theories, as he himself acknowledges, is that his date lines up a little too precisely with some interpretations of Plato's chronology for the destruction of Atlantis, and with the time that psychic Edgar Cayce assigned to the building of the Great Pyramid by locals helped by wanderers from Atlantis. Such an association only gives critics ammunition. Still, Bauval's ideas have met skepticism in conventional Egyptological circles less because of their psychic connections than because they indicate that the Egyptians of the pyramid age—and earlier—understood precession long before our version of history says they should have. But precession may be only the very beginning of what they understood.

CLOCKING THE ZODIAC

Bauval's ideas underscore two fundamental concepts about the Great Pyramid and Giza. The first idea is that the Giza monuments, and perhaps all of the Old Kingdom pyramids, form a complex whose meaning can be understood better in the whole than in the parts. The second is that later monuments were erected to memorialize or record much earlier arrangements of the constellations in the round of precession.

I didn't fully realize how far across Egypt the astronomical complex might extend, or how far back into prehistory that memorialization might reach, until November 11, 2001. On that day physicist Thomas G. Brophy sent me a copy of an article he had written about the stone circles of Nabta Playa in southern Egypt. In his cover e-mail, Brophy wrote, rather academically, "I think you may find interest in the results of the attached pre-submission manuscript." That proved to be an understatement. I found his work—which later grew into the book *The Origin Map*— fascinating.

Nabta Playa, about 65 miles west of Abu Simbel in southernmost Egypt's Western Desert, is a desolate, hot, difficult place that is now practically lifeless for much of the year. The archaeological significance of the site was discovered quite by accident in 1973–1974. A group of scientists headed by Southern Methodist University anthropologist Fred Wendorf had stopped for a break while driving from the Libyan border to the Nile. As Wendorf later wrote, "we were standing there minding our own business, when we noticed potsherds and other artifacts."[7] Throughout the 1970s and 1980s Wendorf returned to excavate Nabta Playa, uncovering one of the most fascinating and fruitful archaeological finds of Stone Age Egypt.

The playa, which forms a basin that fills with water when there's enough rain, has been inhabited by humans, at least seasonally, since about 9000 B.C. In circa 5500 B.C., a time when rainfall was regular and ample, the area was permanently settled by pastoralists with a social system more complex than any previously seen in Egypt. These people erected large stones in alignments to build a calendar circle that marked the summer solstice of about 4500 B.C. Charcoal in hearths around the circle has been dated to circa 4800 B.C., another indication that the area was used extensively in the fifth millennium B.C. as a ritual center. That is at least 1,000 years before Stonehenge, a much better known monument with a calendar circle marking the solstice.

Brophy proposes that the stone circle at Nabta Playa is more than a calendar marking the first day of summer, however. As he sees it, three of the stones inside the Nabta Playa circle represent the belt of Orion—in the same way that the three major Giza pyramids symbolize the very same stars. The Nabta Playa stones demonstrate how these three stars would have appeared as they crossed the meridian on summer solstice nights between 6400 B.C. and 4900 B.C. Significantly, in 4940 B.C., the inclination of Orion's Belt on the meridian was at its smallest angle. Even more significantly, that same year also marked the only time in the entire precessional cycle when Orion Belt's lies on the meridian close to sunrise on the summer solstice.

The residents of Nabta erected three other stones inside the circle. These monoliths, Brophy argues, diagram the configuration of Orion's head and shoulders as they appeared in circa 16,500 B.C. That, too, is a significant date. In the skies close to that time in distant prehistory, the inclination of Orion's Belt on the meridian was at its greatest angle. Overlay the shapes of Orion at the summer solstice in both 4940 B.C. and 16,500 B.C., and you'll see how the stones making up the circle and standing within it outline the constellation at both points. Whoever built this circle understood the precession of Orion in its entire 25,900-year cycle—thousands of years before Hipparchus is reputed to have discovered it.

Although Nabta Playa lies 400 miles from Giza, the cultural links between the two sites are very strong, indicating that the culture that erected the Nabta Playa monoliths contributed directly to Predynastic and Old Kingdom Egypt. For example, cattle played important religious roles in both cultures, and both cultures laid great importance on the constellation Orion, which the ancient Egyptians called Sahu and associated with Osiris. It is likely that when the Egyptian climate turned extremely arid in the late fourth millennium B.C., the people of Nabta Playa migrated toward the Nile and became one of the groups that contributed to the cultural mélange from which ancient Egypt arose.

In his way, Brophy supports Bauval's hypothesis that Giza memorializes the sky of a distant era, but he adds an intriguing complication to this basic idea. When Brophy matched the layout of the pyramids to the changing image of Orion's Belt as it crosses the celestial meridian, he found that the ground map matched the sky in 11,772 B.C., not 10,500 B.C. As for the shape of Orion's Belt when it rose from the horizon on the spring equinox, that configuration matched the pyramids' in 9420 B.C.

Other important astronomical alignments mark both dates as well. If an observer in 9420 B.C. were standing at the center of the site where the Great Pyramid now sits, he or she would see Orion's Belt rise over the rump of the Sphinx. Then, at the time of the sun's rising, the shape of Orion's Belt sighted over the Menkaure Temple would match the ground orientation of the three main Giza pyramids. Finally, Orion's Belt would set alongside the three smaller, or satellite, pyramids alongside the Menkaure Pyramid.

Now move the date back to 11,772 B.C., and what does an observer in the same position as the Great Pyramid see? Again Orion's Belt comes up over the horizon atop the Sphinx's rump. If he or she looks due south—along the same line as the celestial meridian—as the Belt passes the meridian, the arrangement of the stars exactly matches the ground orientation of the three main Giza Pyramids. Finally, once again the Belt drops below the horizon over the Menkaure Pyramid's three satellite pyramids.

Where Bauval says Giza points to one date in the ancient sky, Brophy argues that Giza sets bookmarks or brackets around the 2,352 years between 11,772 and 9420 B.C. This period has two important points of significance. For one, it marks a single precessional age. That is, since the horizon is a circle of 360°, and since the zodiac contains 12 constellations, each constellation accounts for an average of 30° of precession, which is a little less than the amount marked by the turning of the heavens during between 11,772 and 9420 B.C. The second point makes this particular time even more significant. It marks the highest position, or northern culmination, of the Galactic Center in 10,909 B.C., the date of the shift in precessional age from Virgo to Leo.

The Galactic Center is just what its name implies: the center of our galaxy, the point around which the millions and millions of stars that make up the Milky Way spin in their long orbits. It is a mysterious place, full of dust and gas clouds, and possibly the home of a black hole. And, equally important from the perspective of the study of ancient civilization, the Galactic Center cannot be seen with the naked eye, at least not in our time. Still, despite its apparent invisibility, the Galactic Center has other connections to Giza.

First, dial the precession clock back to 13,101 B.C., assume that the Galactic Center can be seen, and place one observer on the site of the

Menkaure Pyramid and another on the Great Pyramid. The Great Pyramid observer would see the Galactic Center rise over the Khufu Valley Temple, while the Menkaure observer watched the same phenomenon over the Sphinx. And the shape of Orion's Belt as it rose over the horizon would match the ground plan of the three satellite pyramids next to the Great Pyramid.

The builders of the Great Pyramid were still keeping track of the Galactic Center millennia later, by means of the shafts emanating from the King's and Queen's chambers. In circa 2370 B.C., the southern King's Chamber shaft aligned with the Galactic Center, while the northern King's Chamber shaft pointed to Thuban (Alpha Draconis, the visible star closest to the north celestial pole at that time) and the southern Queen's Chamber's shaft aimed directly at Sirius. The northern shaft in the Queen's Chamber, which has been measured less precisely than the others, appears to have been sighted at the ritually significant star Kochab (Beta Ursae Minoris) at the same time. If Brophy is correct about the alignments—and, as far as I can tell, he is—it can hardly be a random event that four shafts are aimed at important stars or celestial points on the same date. Somebody— somebody very sophisticated—knew what he or she was doing.

What does all this analysis of Giza add up to? It tells us that not only did the builders of the Giza monuments mark the northern culmination of the Galactic Center and the southern culmination of Orion's Belt; they also understood the length of a precessional age and calibrated precession's cycle from the northern culmination of the Galactic Center. In the same way that both hands of the clock turning to 12 mark the beginning of a new day, the Galactic Center's northern culmination started the cycle of the zodiac all over again. When Virgo gave way to Leo as the Galactic Center reached its northernmost point in 10,909 B.C., precession had started again on its long cycle through the cosmic millennia.

MEMORY'S LONG STRETCH

Constellations have remarkable staying power. Although the names we give to the constellations come down to us from the classical Greeks, arranging the stars in patterns that carry significance is a very old piece of human culture. This point was first brought home to me in the mid-1990s by Frank Edge, a high school and community college teacher of mathematics and cosmology. Edge studied the magnificent frieze in the Hall of Bulls inside the Lascaux cave, a fascinating archaeological site in France's Dordogne Valley dating to circa 15,000 B.C. Where other scholars saw a hunting scene of bulls, stags, buffalo, and ponies, Edge recognized the star cluster we know as the Pleiades and the constellation we call Taurus. Taurus means "bull" in Latin, and the constellation is appropriately depicted as an immense bull.

"So striking is the resemblance of this ice age bull to the traditional picture of Taurus," Edge writes, "that if the Lascaux bull had been discovered in a medieval manuscript rather than on a cave ceiling, the image would have been immediately recognized as Taurus."[8]

Other portions of the Hall of Bulls captured other constellations. The figure known as the Unicorn, for example, came from combining stars we now place in Scorpio, Libra, and Sagittarius. Put all the paintings within Lascaux together, and you have an accurate picture of the summer night sky in approximately 15,000 B.C. The cave dwellers, Edge suggests, used this star chart to follow the path of the moon and determine the summer solstice.

Recent research indicates that modern constellations reach even farther back into prehistory. Michael Rappenglueck, a former University of Munich researcher known for his work on star charts in ancient caves, argues that a tiny tablet of inscribed mammoth ivory dating to between 30,000 and 36,000 B.C. charts the constellation Orion. The ivory, discovered in German's Ach Valley in 1979 and attributed to the little-known Aurignacian people, who supplanted the Neanderthals, shows a man with what could be a sword hanging between his legs. The man's shape is curious: The right leg is longer than the left, and the waist is unnaturally slim. Connect the stars of Orion as if they were dots, and you'll see that the left leg is shorter than the right, the sword hangs between the legs, and the waist is surprisingly slim. In the same way that Lascaux depicts Taurus as a bull, the Ach Valley ivory shows Orion as a hunter, the very image we still have, over 30,000 years ago.

Like Edge's and Rappenglueck's research, Brophy's work deepens our understanding of the antiquity of astronomical knowledge, from the names and shapes of the constellations to the precise movements of heavenly bodies. And he implies that people of the old times knew a great deal more than we give them credit for.

It is clear from Brophy's research, as well as that of Bauval and the groundbreaking work of Jane Sellers, author of *The Death of Gods in Ancient Egypt: A Study of the Threshold of Myth and the Frame of Time* (first published in 1992 and later revised), that the ancient Egyptians understood precession, recognized what it meant, and measured the shift from one precessional age to the other. They knew the paths the stars followed in their transits and the way those paths shifted year by year—so precisely that they could plot lines of sight through layer upon layer of masonry to stars with ritual significance. They understood how to determine true north from observations of circumpolar stars, and how to transfer the north–south meridian from sky to earth. And they could locate the Galactic Center, which is no easy undertaking.

Does this mean that the ancient Egyptians possessed telescopes or extraterrestrial assistance? It does not. Robert Temple and Thothnu Tastmona (pseudonym of Paul T. Platt) have both suggested that the ancients may have used telescopes, but few scholars have been persuaded by their arguments. Brophy indicates that people who watched the heavens carefully over long periods of time might be able to locate the Galactic Center—and its opposite, the Galactic Anticenter, the point in the plane of the galaxy that lies directly opposite the Galactic Center and is found close to the bright star Alnath in Taurus. In modern times, the Galactic Center was first found by William Herschel (1738–1822), who counted stars in the Milky Way (our galaxy) and grouped them by magnitude (degree of brightness) to find where they were most dense, thereby locating the direction to the center of the galaxy. The ancient Egyptians may have done something of the same, perhaps as a result of their extensive star mapping.

Or they may have been able to see the Galactic Center, at least after a fashion. Physicist Paul LaViolette argues in his 1997 book *Earth under Fire* that the Galactic Center emits periodic outbursts of particles and electromagnetic radiation. One of these events, which spanned several thousand years, climaxed in about 12,200 B.C. Where we now see nothing in the Galactic Center, the ancients may have seen a significant glow that did not escape their astute and constant observations.

Does the work of Bauval and Brophy mean that the Great Pyramid was actually built not in the third millennium B.C. under Khufu but much earlier? Should the time of construction be pushed back, as Edgar Cayce prophesied, to the middle of the eleventh millennium B.C., within the very time when many of the astronomical events memorialized at Giza actually occurred?

No, in and of itself, it doesn't necessarily change the date of construction. But it does mean we have to alter how we view the "rise" of ancient Egypt.

The Giza site as we see it shows that a tremendous amount of construction, including the bulk of the Great Pyramid, went on during the Old Kingdom, most likely during the Fourth Dynasty. This date is reinforced by both the Khufu cartouches in the upper Relieving Chambers and the Great Pyramid's shaft alignments to the stars of the middle third millennium B.C.—which gives us at least a functional date for the pyramid, if not the time of its actual construction. That said, however, these monuments were erected not on a virgin site but on one that had been used, perhaps like Nabta Playa, for a long, long while. This hypothesis would explain the older date for the Sphinx, the differing construction of the lower layers of the Khafre Pyramid, and the rain-weathered stone blocks in the Valley and Sphinx temples. When Khufu came to Giza, he was building atop a site whose ritual use probably dated back millennia. Each of the monuments most likely incorporated structures and markers already there, such as the Descending Passage cut into the bedrock, with its perfect star-based orientation to true north.

This scenario also addresses one of the key anomalies of the Great Pyramid's construction: why the builders left the bedrock prominence that occupies the center section of the lowest courses. From an engineering point of view, leveling the bedrock would have made more sense. But if that prominence had been a religious site, probably one dedicated to ritual observations of stars and sun, leveling it would have been a blasphemy. Incorporating it into the structure, however, added old energy to new and made the structure even more powerful and awe-inspiring.

Typically, the cultural ascendance of the Old Kingdom is portrayed as a sudden event, an unexpected and unpredictable rise from ignorance and anarchy to glory. The astronomy that underlies the Great Pyramid and the other Giza monuments tells a different story. The astronomical, astrological, and religious knowledge the Old Kingdom represented had been gathered over thousands of years and passed down, no doubt in an oral tradition that was, even by the standards of antiquity, very old. It began far back with stargazers in places like Nabta Playa studying the night skies, memorizing what they saw, and handing that knowledge on to their successors. With each new generation of sky sages, this ancient science grew, deepened, and became more sophisticated, and from it rose a mythology that lent the heavens religious significance. Finally, this knowledge made its way to the Nile Valley, where it became a key component of what we know as Predynastic through Old Kingdom Egypt.

Giza isn't the birth of something new. It is instead the full flower of something old. And we can gain an even greater appreciation of its wonder when we turn from what Old Kingdom Egyptians and their predecessors understood of the skies to what they knew of earth.

Seven

BOUNDARIES OF SEASONS AND THE EARTH

O RPHANED WHEN ONLY TWO YEARS OLD, MOSES COTS-
worth (1859–1943) received some of his first lessons in measuring time from the grandparents and great-grandparents who
raised him. Distrustful of newfangled mechanical methods for telling
time, Cotsworth's elders relied on shadow pins, noonmarks, and hourglasses
to gauge the passing day, and they intrigued their young ward with a family collection of old calendars. Cotsworth carried his ancestors' interest in
the march of time into his career with the British railroads. There his tal-
ent for numbers led to an assignment to revise railway rates in the early
1890s and later to a project to improve the system of railroad statistics.

In the course of his work, Cotsworth encountered constant complaints
from managers and directors about monthly fluctuations in income and ex-
penses. It wasn't Cotsworth's fault; it was the calendar's. Months can be 28,
29, 30, or 31 days in length, and there is no correspondence between date
and day of the week—the first can be a Saturday in one month, and a Tues-
day in the next, for example. Certain that there had to be a better way of
arranging time to suit the statistical and accounting needs of business,
Cotsworth followed Charles Piazzi Smyth's lead and set out to explore the

possibility that the Great Pyramid served as a perfect almanac for register-ing the seasons and the year.

Working from his childhood experience with sundials and noonmarks, Cotsworth began his research by fashioning model cones and pyramids to see what kinds of shadows they threw in light of various angles. He real-ized that at the Great Pyramid's latitude of almost exactly 30°, an ordinary obelisk acting as a giant sundial could tell the time of day tolerably well. It would, however, have to be of an unwieldy height, some 450 feet tall, to throw a shadow that would change by a sufficient amount (about a foot a day) during the course of the year to accurately measure the length of a year. A pyramid worked better for the purpose of designating seasons. Its northern face would remain in shadow through the six winter months. That shadow would extend farther and farther as the sun approached the winter solstice, then shrink after the solstice until it reached a minimum on the equinox sometime in March. To gauge this shadow, Cotsworth figured, the pyramid builders needed a flat surface laid on the structure's north side and marked in a geometrical pattern that allowed them to record the shadow's daily progress. So Cotsworth took off for Egypt in November 1900 to look for the shadow floor his theory predicted.

And he found it—a pavement of flat stones laid out in half-squares from the base of the pyramid platform to the remains of the old wall that once surrounded the entire complex. The width of every paving stone was close to 4.45 feet, the distance the noontime shadow moved each day as it progressed toward the March vanishing point. This pattern allowed the priests who managed the pyramid complex to count the days of winter and, with a little mathematical manipulation, determine the length of the year fairly exactly.

Cotsworth left Egypt to champion his 13-month calendar, which fea-tured months of 28 days' length that always began on a Sunday and ended on a Saturday. Cotsworth won the support of George Eastman, founder of the Eastman Kodak camera company, who was convinced that the irra-tional calendar cost business tremendous sums of money. Eastman's interest in the calendar, like Cotsworth's, was practical, not religious or mythologi-cal. The British railway statistician understood that an accurate calendar was a great aid to people who depended upon the turn of the seasons to know when the Nile was likely to rise and when to prepare for planting. It took another practical man to demonstrate that the Great Pyramid could be used not only to determine the changing seasons but also to accurately resurvey the land after each annual Nile flood.

THE OLD KINGDOM'S SURVEY CREW

In the late nineteenth century, Robert T. Ballard, an Australian by nationality, was sitting on a train steaming past Giza when he noticed something fascinating about the three principal pyramids. Because the monuments cut clear lines against the sky, and because their angles constantly changed with the viewer's position, the pyramids could easily have served the ancients as instruments—theodolites, in a surveyor's vocabulary—for surveying and triangulating the land.

A railroad engineer by profession, Ballard knew a great deal about surveying routes and determining property lines. He realized, too, that property lines would have been no small issue along the Nile, particularly in Lower Egypt, where the river's annual flood poured over the land and wiped out the markers dividing one farmer's plot from another. Resetting the boundaries each year would have been a major task, one that the pyramids made easier. The only instrument surveyors would need, Ballard wrote in his grandly titled *The Solution of the Pyramid Problem*, published in 1882, was a moveable scale model of the Great Pyramid in the center of a circular board marked with the cardinal directions. Point the north end of the board toward the north, orient the model so that it shows the same pattern of light and shade as the real pyramid, and read the bearing. It was that easy. Ballard also realized that the pyramids could be used for something surveyors do all the time: measure land by means of right-angle triangles with whole-number sides, such as 3-4-5.

Ballard's insights underscore the accuracy of a comment by Herodotus in his writing about ancient Egypt. The country was heavily populated along the fertile areas of the Nile Valley—by some estimates, with nearly 700 people per square mile. To create balance and justice, Herodotus writes, this king divided the land . . . so as to give each one a quadrangle of equal size and . . . on each imposing a tax. But everyone from whose part the river tore anything away . . . he sent overseers to measure out how much the land had become smaller, in order that the owner might pay on what was left. . . . In this way, it appears to me, geometry originated, which passed thence to Greece.[1]

Herodotus and Ballard recognized that geometry—a word that comes from Greek roots meaning "measuring the earth"—had its origins not in academic mathematics but in such practical, day-to-day business as determining where one farmer's fields ended and another's began. What Ballard didn't realize, but Herodotus may have, was that this annual geometric exercise came to have religious import. Each year's flood signaled the return of the watery chaos from which the cosmos had emerged, rising up as the original mound of creation and seeking the justice and order of perfect *ma'at*. Geometry restored the order lost to the flood and returned an off-kilter universe to its proper balance. Geometry gave to the earth the same harmony the pharaoh bestowed upon his subjects.

One name the ancient Egyptians gave their homeland was To-Mera, meaning "the land of the *mr.*" The word *mr* originally referred to the median triangle of a pyramid and by extension to the pyramid itself. The core meaning of this ancient name is that Egypt was the measured land, a region of the planet known by a unique geometry. The people of the Old Kingdom knew the shape of the Two Lands in astounding detail, and they incorporated their knowledge into the design of the Great Pyramid.

THE TWO MEASURED LANDS

As we shall explore, it appears that the Great Pyramid reveals that the ancient Egyptians realized the earth is round. If you were raised on the historical tale of brave Columbus sailing west in his three tiny ships toward a possible plummet off a flat earth into the cosmic void, this statement comes as an almost unbelievable claim to intellectual sophistication in the ancient world. Actually, the story of Columbus and the flat earth tell us more about the backwardness of fifteenth-century Europe than about antiquity. The adepts of ancient Egypt knew full well the earth wasn't flat, at least 40 centuries before Columbus worked up the courage to bet his life on a theory.

One wonders why it took the Europeans so long, because, frankly, it's not that difficult to tell that the earth is round, and indeed educated people throughout history realized that the earth is a sphere. Look at the moon when it is full, and you may ask yourself "Why should the earth have a different shape?" Watch a ship steam toward the horizon, and you'll see its hull disappear long before the last radar dish on the superstructure slips out of view. The stars also reveal the earth's shape. As you head north from a starting point in the northern hemisphere, the north celestial pole rises in the sky, and all the stars in their nightly transits rise with it. Head south, and they descend. Such an observation requires an explanation.

It's one the ancient Egyptians were well equipped to work out. They had been dedicated stargazers, Nabta Playa tells us, for at least several millennia by the time the Old Kingdom began. And they inhabited a country that ran north and south. Stars that sit on the horizon in Upper Egypt (to the south) will shine higher in the sky in Lower Egypt (to the north). The Egyptians noticed this difference, and they understood the implications of their observation.

They also used it to site the Great Pyramid—or, perhaps, unknown and undiscovered structures, even more ancient, that underlie it. The Great Pyramid sits at almost exactly 30° north latitude. The operative word is "almost"; the site is slightly south of the actual line. Richard Proctor realized why during his investigations of the astronomical utility of the Great Pyramid. If you journey steadily northward from the equator, the north celestial pole rises in the sky until, at the North Pole, it stands directly overhead. It appears easy enough to measure latitude by determining the angle of the north celestial pole above the horizon. If the north celestial pole lies 30° above the horizon, then the latitude must be 30°. That's not quite right, however, because the atmosphere gets in the way. When you are gazing at the horizon, you look through more atmosphere than when you look straight up. Because of this slight refraction, sightings of the celestial pole angle have a built-in error that lessens as you move from equator to pole. At 30° north latitude, you would think you are very slightly farther north than you really are. On the other hand, Proctor demonstrated that if you use the sun and shadows to determine your latitude without compensating for atmospheric effects, you will think you are located very slightly south of your actual latitude. The Great Pyramid is about a mile and a third south of perfect alignment with 30° north latitude. Proctor considered this strong evidence that the ancient Egyptians used the circumpolar stars to place themselves along a north–south line on a spherical earth.

But once the Egyptians knew that the earth is a sphere and where they stood on it, they were likely to ask another question: How big is the earth?

In theory, the answer isn't that difficult to determine. First, you set up astronomical observatories at different latitudes. Ideally, the observatories are directly north and south of each other, but, with the proper mathematical analysis, the determination works even if they're not. Next, select a suitable star and measure its highest point in the sky from each observatory. Alternatively, measure the angle of the sun at its noontime high point at a definite mark in its annual cycle, such as solstice or equinox. Simple geometry reveals that the difference between measurements depends on the latitudinal difference between the two observatories in degrees. Repeat these measurements again and again for a variety of stars or a succession of solstices or equinoxes to ensure reliable data. The third step is measuring the geographical distance between the two observatories on the ground. From this, one can determine the geographical distance equivalent to a change in 1 degree of latitude. Finally, multiply the distance per degree by 360—the number of degrees in a circle. The result is the circumference of the earth through the poles.

Conventional scientific history credits the first measurement of the earth's circumference to the Greek-speaking astronomer Eratosthenes in about 250 B.C., well over two millennia after the Fourth Dynasty and the great age of pyramid building. Eratosthenes made his measurements in Egypt, using the angles of the sun at summer solstice in the cities of Alexandria, on the Mediterranean, and Syene, on the Nile in Upper Egypt. His result was 250,000 stadia, a somewhat problematical outcome, since no one is now certain just how far a stadion is. Most classicists assume that 1 stadion (a Greek term; in Latin it is *stadium*) equals ⅒ mile, which makes Eratosthenes' calculation of the earth's circumference equal to 25,000 miles.

That's within approximately 200 miles of our current measurement, or an error of less than 1 percent.

Given what we know of Egyptian astronomy and mathematics, there is no doubting that the elites of the Predynastic through Old Kingdom periods had the wherewithal to measure the earth's circumference. But saying that the Egyptians could have done it is hardly the same as proving that they did. Academic Egyptologists have long rejected the notion that the Egyptians were anything but flat-earthers who could handle little more than simple arithmetic, despite the evident architectural achievements they left us. But there is another, maverick tradition that says the Egyptians knew and they proved their knowledge in the Great Pyramid. This line of thinking began in modern times with an insightful and unconventional Frenchman named Edmé-François Jomard (1777–1862). Jomard was only in his early twenties when he accompanied Napoleon's army as one of the *savants* who turned the military invasion of Egypt into a major event of Western intellectual history—resulting in the immense, multivolume, multiauthored work *Description de l'Égypte.*

One of the tasks that fell to Jomard during Napoleon's occupation was measuring the exterior dimensions of the Great Pyramid. That was a difficult task; mounds of debris had built up along the monument's sides. Still, Jomard and his colleagues made their measurement and came up with a length of 230.902 meters, or 757.5 feet, to a side. Next Jomard climbed the pyramid, then measured down each step. His result was 144 meters, or 481 feet, for the pyramid's height. With basic trigonometry, Jomard calculated the Great Pyramid's slope at just over 51°—51° 19' 14", to be exact. A further calculation told Jomard that the apothem, the distance from the center of the pyramid's apex to the midpoint of any one of its sides, was 184.722 meters. Of necessity, Jomard was guessing a bit. Since the outer casing of the pyramid had been removed, he had to estimate the thickness of that last layer of limestone and work the number into his calculation.

Jomard's result of 184.722 meters (606 feet) rang a bell in the young Frenchman's classically trained mind. He knew that the historians Diodorus Siculus (c. 80–20 B.C.) and Strabo (c. 63? B.C.–A.D. 24?) said that the Great Pyramid's apothem equaled 1 stadion (stadium), or about 600 feet, which was a basic unit of land measure in the ancient world. The Greeks of

Alexandria—the community that had given rise to Hipparchus, the putative discoverer of precession, and to Eratosthenes—made the stadium equal to approximately 185.5 meters (608.6 feet), a number tantalizingly close to Jomard's own measurement for the pyramid's apothem. Was this coincidence, or was it the product of the pyramid builders' intention?

Some of Jomard's colleagues corroborated his understanding of the pyramid's geodetic utility. When the surveyors among Napoleon's *savants* realized that the monument was oriented correctly to the four cardinal directions, they used the north–south meridian running through the Great Pyramid's apex as the base line for their measurements of the country. This led to a fascinating discovery: the meridian through the apex divided Lower Egypt neatly in two, while diagonals drawn from the pyramid's corners completely enclosed the Nile Delta.

But other colleagues of Jomard torpedoed his ideas. When they remeasured the base of the pyramid, they found it to be 2 meters longer than Jomard had. They also made a new measurement of the height. Their result was higher than Jomard's, which made his angle of incline too low and his apothem too short. The exactness Jomard had claimed fuzzed into sloppy approximation.

Jomard, though, didn't give up easily. He argued that the Descending Passage was an observatory for watching circumpolar stars—an idea that we now know makes good sense—and that the coffer in the King's Chamber was not a sarcophagus but a monument of measure: something of an Old Kingdom Bureau of Standards.

Still, modern Egyptologists have largely dismissed Jomard's ideas on the Egyptians' knowledge of the earth as so much wishful thinking. It was only in the second half of the twentieth century that a line of curiously esoteric research revealed that Jomard was onto something after all.

THE IMPORTANCE OF THE CUBIT

The late Livio Catullo Stecchini had the kind of career even academics consider academic. The son of a law professor at the University of Catania in Italy, Stecchini studied Latin and Greek in secondary school, then pursued philosophy in Germany at the University of Freiburg, where the great existentialist philosopher Martin Heidegger (1889–1976) was teaching. Stecchini, though, was less intrigued by the philosophical nature of being than by the study of ancient measurement, a subject that had first drawn his interest back in high school. Forced to leave Germany by Hitler's attacks on the autonomy of the universities, Stecchini returned to Italy, earned a doctorate in Roman law, and held an academic position at the University of Rome. World War II brought Stecchini to the United States, where he became a candidate for a second doctorate at Harvard, this time in ancient history. While his professors were enamored of the Greeks for their literary and philosophical greatness, Stecchini was drawn more to the utilitarian and practical aspects of their lives. He wrote his dissertation on the origin of money in Greece. The thesis was accepted, and Stecchini got his degree, but the Harvard faculty felt he should lop all the numbers out of his manuscript before he published it, as the classicists of the time had no particular interest in what seemed nothing more than a bunch of extraneous arithmetic.

Stecchini, though, loved numbers, particularly old units of measure, and he continued his research into measurement in the ancient world. He progressed from the study of Greek monetary weights to the operation of Greek mints to the dimensions of Greek temples to ancient geography and geodesy. All the while, his fellow classicists told Stecchini that numbers didn't count as evidence in ancient studies. Stecchini went off on his own, ignoring their advice, working in what he called "splendid isolation."[2]

In fact, Stecchini's painstaking and solitary research demonstrates that numbers do matter. And in the case of the Great Pyramid, they matter a great deal.

The French surveyor *savants,* Stecchini showed, had detected only the beginning of the ancient Egyptians' proclivity toward precise measurement of the land they inhabited. They were right in discovering that the meridian running through the Great Pyramid's apex neatly divided the Nile Delta into two. In fact, this line served as the prime meridian for the entire country. The Egyptians extended it from Behdet, a Predynastic capital close to where the Nile empties into the Mediterranean at 31° 30' north latitude, to the Great Cataract of the Nile, which lies directly south on the same line of longitude. The southern boundary of the country was set at 24° 00' north, near the point where the Nile crossed the Tropic of Cancer, which then lay at 23° 51' north latitude (it has since moved slightly), close to the First Cataract of the Nile at Aswan. The eastern and western boundaries of the country extended north–south from the edges of the Nile Delta along lines parallel to the prime meridian. The result was a country shaped like a long, thin rectangle and defined by right angles.

Geodetic knowledge in Egypt was so advanced that the country's prime meridian became the baseline not only for cities and temples within the country but also for the rest of the eastern Mediterranean. It served the same earth-orienting purpose in the ancient world as the 0° longitude line running through Greenwich, England, in our own times. Mount Gerizim, an early Hebrew holy site that continues to be the ritual center of the Samaritan sect, lies exactly 4° east of the Egyptian prime meridian. Delphi, one of the two oracular centers of classical Greece and the geodetic cen-

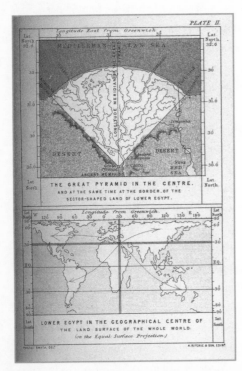

ter of the ancient Hellenes, is 7° north of Behdet along the same line of longitude as the Egyptian prime meridian, while Mecca, the sacred center of Islam (but dating back well before the time of Muslim culture), is both 10° east of Egypt's western boundary and 10° south of Behdet. In a very real way, Egypt anchored the ancient world.

The geodetic system of ancient Egypt evidenced the unification of the two lands. In the Predynastic Period, the Egyptians measured the distance between their northern boundary (set at Behdet, 31° 30' north latitude) and their southern (set at 24° 00' north lati-

The location of Giza and the Great Pyramid relative to the Nile Delta and to the earth as a whole. (*From Smyth, 1880, plate II.*)

tude) as 1.8 million geographical cubits. Therefore, one geographical cubit equaled approximately 1.5 modern feet, or, more precisely, about 461.7 millimeters. The cubit, represented by a hieroglyphic picture of a forearm (transliterated as "mh"),[3] was not a basic unit of length only in ancient Egypt. The term *cubit* that we use is derived from the Latin *cubitum* (elbow). Each cubit was made up of 6 palms (also known as hands), which were further subdivided into 4 fingers (also known as digits). When the country was unified, a second geodetic system came into use, one that measured the distance from the base of the Nile Delta (31° 06' north latitude) to the southern boundary of Egypt (24° 00' north latitude) as 1.5 million cubits. In the new, longer measure, a single cubit, or "royal cubit," was 524.1483 millimeters (or about 20.6 modern inches, or about 1.72 modern feet). This longer royal cubit was commonly divided into 7 hands, still with 4 fingers to each hand.

The royal cubit is significant because it is the measure used to lay out the Great Pyramid. It is also a base-seven unit, important because the number 7 was sacred to the Egyptians as a cosmic number, one that joined earth and sky. For example, it was a matter of no small importance to the people of the Old Kingdom that Upper Egypt extended 6° of longitude up the Nile, and Lower Egypt another 1°, a total of 7° that mirrored the sacred dimension. The sacred order of the sky replicated itself on the Two Lands in a visible demonstration of *ma'at.*

The Egyptians also incorporated an aspect of the sky into the way they defined the boundary between Upper and Lower Egypt, an issue that helps explain the location of the Great Pyramid. In the Old Kingdom, the southern frontier of Egypt was seen as not one boundary but a composite of three lines. The southernmost was the Tropic of Cancer at 23° 51'. When the sun reached its noontime zenith on the summer solstice, it stood at 24° 6',* which is also the latitude of the lower edge of the First Cataract. That was the northernmost of the three lines. In between lay 24°, the latitude of the upper edge of the First Cataract.

For the sake of cosmic symmetry, the Egyptians duplicated this tripli-

---

* As Stecchini explains, in calculating the position of the noontime zenith on the solstice, the ancient Egyptians introduced a 15' correction, since the sun is not a point in the sky but has an apparent diameter of a little over 30'.

cate system at the boundary of Upper and Lower Egypt. They created three lines, each 6° north of the corresponding southern boundary limits: 30° 6', 30°, and 29° 51'. Significantly, the band between 30° 6' and 29° 51' fell within the jurisdiction of none of the local districts, or nomes, of either Upper or Lower Egypt. The boundary zone was something like the United States' District of Columbia or Mexico's Distrito Federal, a national capital over which no single town, city, or state had political sway.

Hieroglyphics represented the boundary district as a rectangle that either stood empty or enclosed water or fish. This is an image or icon found all over the world for the Square of Pegasus, a sky region of four stars that form a square. The stars are associated with water and fish because they are part of the constellation Pisces (which means "fish" in Latin). In ancient times, the Square of Pegasus represented the starting point for mapping the sky. The Egyptian "fishpond" district stood for the same point in mapping the earth, and it centered the Two Lands.

It is no accident that the Great Pyramid sat in this district's center at 30°—or as close to it as the ancient Egyptians could measure. The structure occupied a balance point between Upper and Lower Egypt, exactly on the meridian, its corners defining the limits of the Nile Delta and thus the eastern and western boundaries of Egypt—all at a point exactly one-third of the way between the equator and the pole. Any one of these correspondences could have happened by accident, but so many happening in one spot is no coincidence.

You could come away from all this thinking that the Old Kingdom Egyptians were a narcissistic bunch. After all, they saw their land as the starting point of earth mapping, in the same way that the Square of Pegasus performed that function in the sky, and established their own prime meridian as the center of the ancient world. Yet the Egyptians saw beyond their own country. According to Stecchini, they incorporated into the Great Pyramid a model of the Northern Hemisphere.

The model begins in the Great Pyramid's perimeter. Based on the lengths for the sides measured by J. H. Cole in his 1925 survey, the perimeter of the monument is 921.455 meters. That value is almost exactly our current measurement for ½ minute of latitude at the equator: 921.463 meters. And if the Old Kingdom Egyptians knew what ½ minute of latitude was at the equator—1,758 royal cubits, to use their unit of measure—they did indeed know the circumference of the earth.

They understood more as well, particularly that the earth isn't a sphere but an oblate spheroid. A radius drawn from the center of the planet to the equator is longer—6,378,758 meters, by one reckoning—than a radius drawn from the center to one of the poles: 6,355,858 meters, by the same reckoning, or a difference of 22,900 meters. The clue lies in the height of the Great Pyramid, which—it generally agreed—was intended to be 280 cubits. That was a cosmically pleasing number to the Egyptians, because 280 is divisible by 7. But, Stecchini argues, the Great Pyramid didn't actually reach this height, topping out a bit short at approximately 279.5 cubits. By taking that half-cubit off the predicted and pleasing height, the Egyptians were indicating the slight flattening of the earth at the poles. They knew, too, that a degree of latitude at the equator was longer than a degree of latitude at the pole due to the polar flattening of the earth (see the appendices, section entitled "Latitude and Polar Flattening Expressed in the Shape of the Great Pyramid").

Since elementary school, we have all seen what is called the Mercator projection, a map that takes the nearly spherical form of the earth and converts it to a flat rectangle. The Egyptians were doing something of the same with the Great Pyramid. They projected the dimensions of the Northern Hemisphere onto four triangles, where the apex represented the pole and the perimeter the equator. The scale was 1:43,200, a number chosen because it represented the length of one-half day (1 day = 24 hours = 1,440 minutes = 86,400 seconds; 86,400 seconds / 2 = 43,200).

In the middle of the third millennium B.C., the ancient Egyptians were demonstrating knowledge about the shape of the planet that wasn't predicted until the seventeenth century A.D. by Isaac Newton—and not demonstrated experimentally until the eighteenth century.

NUMBERS AND MESSAGES

By the time of the Old Kingdom, it is clear that the Egyptians had amassed a detailed knowledge of the earth and were sufficiently sophisticated to incorporate this knowledge into the Great Pyramid. From their point of view, this knowledge wasn't recent, either. The geodetic reform that accompanied the unification of the Two Lands, when the seven-based royal cubit supplanted the geographical cubit, points to a body of earth-based knowledge that originated well before Menes pulled the unruly nomes into one political entity. The astronomical sophistication of ancient Egypt reaches back at least to the stargazers of Nabta Playa. The geodetic knowledge is probably every bit as old.

The Great Pyramid stands as a reminder of the extent and the antiquity of this knowledge, both of earth and sky, and it passes on to us at least the outlines of their knowledge. It's enough to make one wonder: Was there anything else they were trying to tell us?

Part Three

A CODE FOR THE BREAKING

Eight

GOD'S NUMBERS

PRACTICALLY FROM THE TIME NAPOLEON'S INVASION RE-
stored ancient Egypt to the western intellectual landscape, various
writers and scholars have looked to the pyramids of Giza, and
particularly the Great Pyramid, as a source of wisdom. We have seen already
how the monument embodies a remarkable level of astronomical and geodetic science. Yet some writers have taken this line of thought even further
and proposed that the Great Pyramid provides answers to those ultimate questions about the universe usually assigned to theology and religion. To them,
the Great Pyramid is more than an ancient marvel. It is a modern revelation.

THE EGYPTIAN ETERNITY

John Greaves (1602–1652) would never have been one to say that religious
interests brought him to explore the Great Pyramid in 1638 and 1639. An
Anglican at a time when holy wars between Catholic and Protestant drenched
much of Europe in blood, Greaves had no compunction about visiting the
Vatican in the course of his research into ancient measures. Even though

the archbishop of Canterbury was one of Greaves's major sponsors, his stated purpose in going to Egypt was secular. He wanted to standardize the weights and measures of all nations, ancient and modern, once and for all.

Greaves was one of the few scholars in Europe who had the credentials to accomplish the task he set for himself. A 36-year-old professor of geometry at Gresham College in London, Greaves was a master of the ancient astronomical literature in Latin, Greek, Hebrew, Arabic, and Persian. As a mathematician, Greaves understood the implications of the uncertain standards of measure for the world he lived in. As an antiquarian, he thought of Egypt as a place that had escaped the ravages of time and preserved the original measures the modern world needed. Seeking to define those original measures and pass them down for all posterity, Greaves resolved to "have recourse to such monuments of Antiquity, as have escaped the injury, and calamity of time" and to establish the standard for metrology on "the most lasting monuments of the Ancients."[1] Listing the monuments that "have stood unimpaired for many hundred years, and are likely to continue many more," Greaves put the Great Pyramid at the top, less because of its alleged astronomical and astrological connections than its mountainous, timeless stolidity.[2] Greaves entered the Great Pyramid as if he were passing into metrology's inner sanctum.

What he sought there was elucidation of the English foot, which would then shed light on all units of measurement, ancient and modern. Along the way to Egypt, Greaves researched the Roman *pes*, or foot, and determined that it was just slightly shorter than the English foot. If the English foot were divided into 2,000 parts, the Roman foot was as long as 1,944 of them. It was also important that the Roman foot was $^{24}/_{25}$ of the Greek foot used in building the Parthenon, that most perfect example of Athenian architecture.

To measure the Great Pyramid, Greaves had taken with him a 10-foot measuring rod, further divided into 10,000 equal parts, that was based on the foot standard preserved in Guild Hall in England. He used it to measure the pyramid's base, which was so obscured by drifted sand and accumulated rubble that he came up well short, at only 693 feet, despite the accuracy of his instrument. Inside the pyramid, Greaves paid particular attention to the King's Chamber, whose workmanship awed him. "The structure of it hath been the labour of an exquisite hand," he wrote later.[5] Greaves meticulously and assiduously measured the King's Chamber and its peculiar coffer, climbed the pyramid to estimate its height, and counted the exterior courses of limestone.

On his return to England, Greaves recorded his measurements, observations, and musings in *Pyramidographia: Or, a Description of the Pyramids in Ægypt* (1646). *Pyramidographia* is a fascinating mix of learned treatise and travel story that stands out even today for its scholarly quality. It also established a key idea that has influenced thinking and writing about the Great Pyramid ever since: that ancient Egypt had somehow extricated itself from the ordinary passage of time. Even for a scholar as nonsectarian and heterodox as Greaves, the Great Pyramid represented a kind of eternity, a zone of timelessness where the usual laws of decay and corruption held little power.

Isaac Newton (1643–1727), that giant of science known for gravity, calculus, and the clockwork universe, seized upon Greaves's work for his own purposes. His study of Greaves's data led him to believe that two different cubits were used during antiquity: a "sacred" cubit, utilized by the Israelites, and a "profane" cubit, utilized by non-Israelite nations. Even though Newton came close to Stecchini's insight about different types of cubits, namely geographical and royal, Newton's interest was less in ancient measure per se than it was in establishing once and for all the circumference of the earth, a number he hoped was encoded in the Great Pyramid. Newton needed this value for his theory of gravitation. Since Newton connected the power of gravity in part to the mass of the object exerting it, he needed to know the circumference of the earth to determine its gravitational pull. He hoped that by establishing the size of the cubit he could calculate the exact length of the classical stadium, which, according to some classical authors, was related to a geographical degree. With that number, Newton planned to compute the earth's circumference to the degree of accuracy he needed.

Newton was stopped by the same obstacle that had prevented Greaves from getting an accurate measurement of the Great Pyramid's base and perimeter: accumulated sand and rubble. Until the monument was properly cleared, there was no telling exactly where the bottommost course of masonry lay, and measurement was little better than speculation. When

Newton didn't find what he wanted in the ancient data, namely the value of a geographical degree that would give the size of the earth, he had to rely on the work of a French surveyor who in 1671 produced a highly accurate measurement of 1° as 69.1 miles. Newton used that value to complete his computations of the earth's circumference and gravitational pull and to publish his work on gravity.

Despite his lack of success, Newton had furthered the idea that the Great Pyramid's dimensions offered a timeless key for unraveling the deepest mysteries of the universe. It fell to another astronomer to take this idea in a direction Greaves and Newton never had in mind.

"... SUBSERVE A HIGH PURPOSE FOR THESE LATTER DAYS"

Charles Piazzi Smyth (1819–1900) was born to a career in science and exploration. His father, William Henry Smyth (1788–1865), achieved renown as naval vice-admiral and surveyor of coastal Sicily, Sardinia, and North Africa. Born in Naples during his father's long professional sojourn in Italy, Charles took his middle name from his godfather, Giuseppe Piazzi (1746–1826), the Roman Catholic cleric and astronomer who discovered Ceres, the first and largest asteroid, in the belt between Mars and Jupiter. Charles Piazzi Smyth was also the uncle of Robert Baden-Powell, famed British military officer and founder of the Boy Scouts and the Girl Guides.

An accomplished scientist, Smyth became astronomer royal of Scotland and professor of astronomy at the University of Edinburgh when he was only 24 years old. Later in his scientific life he became a leading investigator in the then-new field of spectroscopy. Nowadays, though, Smyth is known in many circles less for his scientific research than for the rigor and meticulousness he brought to arguing for his fundamentalist religious beliefs.

The link Smyth drew between the science of the Great Pyramid and his theology originated in a relationship with John Taylor (1781–1864), the writer, editor, and publisher who spent the later years of his life studying the Great Pyramid from afar. As we saw in chapter 5, Taylor was convinced that the Great Pyramid encoded the spherical dimensions of the earth and that this knowledge had been imparted to the monument's builders by divine inspiration to be passed on to later generations. Over the last few weeks of Taylor's life, he and Smyth carried on an intense, idea-filled correspondence. After Taylor died, Smyth decided that the only way to validate Taylor's assertion of the Great Pyramid's scientific accuracy and divine origin was to do what Taylor had not done: go to Egypt himself and measure the monument with the care this important task required.

Smyth was no stranger to long-range scientific expeditions. As a teenager he had gone to South Africa to assist in observations of Halley's Comet, and he later investigated the advantages of mountaintop astronomical observatories on Tenerife in the Canary Islands. For the journey to Giza, he prepared an extraordinary armamentarium of measuring rods, clinometers, cords, theodolites, telescopes, and thermometers and added to it the most advanced tools of a then-new technology: photography. Unable to line up outside funding, Smyth paid for the trip out of his own pockets, which were none too deep. He and his wife set up housekeeping in an abandoned tomb on the Giza Plateau's eastern face as 1864 became 1865 and spent the next four months measuring, recording, and photographing.

The result was the most accurate survey of the Great Pyramid up to that time. Working from his expertise as an astronomer, Smyth explored the monument's connection to the circumpolar stars. He asserted that the monument must have been built when the Pleiades reached their zenith at midnight on the autumnal equinox of 2170 B.C. He came up, too, with a precise measurement of the Great Pyramid's latitude, showing it to be just south of the thirtieth parallel. And he was convinced that Taylor was right in finding the value of pi incorporated into the Great Pyramid, an idea we will explore in the following chapter.

In his work *Our Inheritance in the Great Pyramid,* Smyth wrote that understanding the Great Pyramid required three keys. The first two were pure mathematics, like pi, and applied mathematics, such as astronomy and physics. The third was "positive human history . . . as supplied . . . by Divine Revelation to certain chosen and inspired men of the Hebrew race, through ancient and medieval times; but now to be found, by all the world, in THE

OLD AND NEW TESTAMENTS."[4] Should mathematics say something different from what scripture did, then scripture won.

Take, for example, Smyth's conundrum over the perimeter of the Great Pyramid. To begin with, he was convinced that the pyramid's builders had used the same cubit as Noah in constructing his ark, a measure equal to 25.025 British inches (see the appendices for a discussion of the various values for the cubit assumed by different authors). Since $\frac{1}{25}$ of this cubit was almost exactly the same as the British inch, Smyth was convinced that the British were still using a divinely ordained unit of measurement that had come down to them from the time of the Hebrew patriarchs. He was further convinced, as John Taylor had been, that the perimeter of the Great Pyramid in inches encoded the correct length of the solar year, or 365.242 days, multiplied by 100. To get this number and to adjust for the slight difference between the pyramid inch based on the cubit and the British inch, each side of the pyramid needed to be 9,140.18 British inches long. That was a problem. The French *savants* and Vyse had come up with numbers within 6 inches of each other, indicating a fairly high degree of accuracy, but they were about 2 feet too long to prove Smyth's point. In hopes of getting the number he needed even though he was about to leave Egypt, Smyth commissioned two Scottish engineers to survey the Great Pyramid's base. He didn't get their results until he was back in Edinburgh, but one can imagine his reaction. At only 9,110 inches, the side was 2.5 feet short. So Smyth decided that the real value had to be the mean of his surveyors' number and Vyse's 9,168. That came out to 9,139, a little more than 1 inch short of the value he was looking for but close enough to add cogency to Smyth's hypothesis.

Actually, there was nothing scientific about the mean. It wasn't a factual measurement, only a mathematical midpoint between conflicting data. In an argument that demanded extreme exactness, Smyth was willing to split the difference, as long as this exercise in applied mathematics fit his take on divine revelation.

Still, for all his willingness to wink at unfriendly data, Smyth was right in concluding that the builders of the Great Pyramid were scientifically adept in ways history failed to recognize. The Great Pyramid "revealed a most surprisingly accurate knowledge of high astronomical and geograph-

ical physics . . . nearly 1,500 years earlier than the extremely infantine beginning of such things among the ancient Greeks," he wrote.[5] Since there
was no adequate human-based theory for such a premature manifestation
of advanced scientific understanding, the only explanation was the workings of God. "The Bible tells us that in very early historic days, wisdom,
and metrical instructions for buildings, were occasionally imparted perfect
and clear, for some special and unknown purpose, to chosen men, by the
Author of all wisdom."[6] The Old Testament recorded God's precise instructions to Noah on building the ark; something of the same had happened with
the Great Pyramid. Smyth pronounced it "that inspired scientific Appendix
to the Sacred Scriptures."[7]

This left Smyth with a theological problem, however. How was it that
the Great Pyramid was built by the Egyptians, a people condemned in the
scriptures as the worst of pagan idolaters and enslavers of the chosen Hebrew people? Smyth worked out an answer. The Egyptians had nothing to
do with it: "the Great Pyramid, though *in* Egypt, is not, and never was, *of*
Egypt—that is, of, belonging to, or instructing about Pharaonic, idolatrous,
and chiefly Theban, Egypt."[8] Rather, according to Smyth, the Great Pyramid was the work of Philitis, a divinely inspired royal priest or prince.
Philitis had been mentioned by Herodotus not as the ancient builder, nor as
a royal priest or prince, but simply as a shepherd who herded his flock near
the pyramids. But in Smyth's interpretation, Philitis became much more
than a simple shepherd. When Philitis (sometimes equated by Smyth with
Melchizedek, a king mentioned in Genesis 14) finished building the Great
Pyramid, he retired to what would become the kingdom of Israel. There he
selected the site of Jerusalem and built that holiest of Jewish cities.

The message of the Great Pyramid was encoded in such a manner that
it meant nothing to the people of that time. "The Great Pyramid was yet
prophetically intended . . . to remain quiescent during those earlier ages;
and, only in a manner, to come forth at this time to subserve a high purpose
for these latter days."[9] Humankind needed to achieve scientific sophistication before it could crack the Great Pyramid's divine code.

There was good reason why the Great Pyramid's inspired message was
encrypted in its "*ancient* length, breadth, and angles."[10] This was a "means

most efficacious for preventing the parable being read too soon in the history of an, at first, unlearned world; but for insuring its being correctly read, and by all nations, when the fullness of prophetic time, in a science age, has at last arrived."[11]

Smyth's work took Greaves and Newton's metric analyses in a direction they never could have imagined. He elevated the vague, implicit sense of timelessness they ascribed to the Great Pyramid to the realm of divine eternity. He also served the needs of the British Empire, although unwittingly. It was hard to believe that a colonial people like the Egyptians could have built anything as magnificent as the Giza pyramids. Smyth provided a religious explanation showing that they had had nothing to do with it. In terms of the history of divine inspiration, the Egyptians were interlopers in their own land.

Another undercurrent informs Smyth's writings. He was living in an age in which science contended with faith. In 1859—the year before John Taylor brought out his *The Great Pyramid. Why Was It Built? & Who Built It?* and less than six years before Smyth departed for Egypt—Charles Darwin published *On the Origin of Species.* Darwin undercut the theory of special creation and implied that humans were but another animal species evolved from yet other animal species. Even without Darwin's overarching theory, many geologists were convinced that the earth was much older than the 6,000 years biblical fundamentalists claimed was the planet's scripture-based age. Like Taylor, Smyth wanted to show that science served the cause of Christianity and that it gave the British a special place in religious history. As the inheritors of an inch passed down from the Hebrews and sanctified in both Noah's ark and the Great Pyramid, the British stood as a bulwark of faith against what Smyth called the "atheistical French metric system."[12] The Great Pyramid was one more reason for the British to look down their noses at their neighbors, and sometime enemies, across the English Channel.

Smyth's colleagues received his work with admiration for his meticulousness, and with skepticism and derision for his religious explanation of the Great Pyramid builders' scientific sophistication. Among scientists, his research went nowhere. But among true believers, it spawned a line of prophetic writing about the Great Pyramid that stretched Smyth's ideas even farther than he meant them to go.

THE DISCIPLES' ZEAL

Jumping on Smyth's ideas soon after the first edition of *Our Inheritance* was published in 1864, Robert Menzies (?–1877) argued that the interior passages and chambers of the Great Pyramid replicated the chronology of divine history. The key to understanding the correspondence lay in realizing that one inch equaled one year. The lengths of the passages and the dimensions of the chambers told the exact story of the Bible, year by year by year. For example, the Grand Gallery represents the Christian era, which began with Christ's birth. Proceed 33 inches up the gallery from its starting point, and you come to the Well, which stands for the tomb in which the crucified body of Christ was interred. Some observers claimed that the rock around the mouth of the Well looked as if it had been blown out in an explosion. In a scriptural manner of speaking, it had, according to Menzies, since the Well embodied the great burst with which the resurrected Christ had emerged from the sepulcher on Easter morning in his thirty-third year.

David Davidson, an English engineer who considered himself agnostic, took on Menzies to prove him wrong. In the end, though, Davidson became convinced that Menzies was right and that the Great Pyramid was "an expression of the Truth in structural form."[13]

At least a millennium before the Hebrews, the builders of the Great Pyramid predicted the coming of Christ. "In all essential features, the ancient Egyptian prophecy concerning the Messiah, the Hebrew Old and New Testament prophecies relating to Him, and the Pyramid's symbolism are in complete agreement," Davidson wrote in *The Great Pyramid, Its Divine Message: An Original Co-ordination of Historical Documents and Archaeological Evidences* (1st ed. 1924; reprinted many times since), a book he coauthored with H. Aldersmith.[14] Equally important, this ancient civilization had achieved an extraordinary degree of scientific accomplishment, not through the hit-or-miss of hypothesis and experiment scientists use but through a thorough, inspired understanding of natural law. Like Smyth, Davidson saw the Great Pyramid as a form of revelation purposely encrypted by God until our civilization had achieved sufficient knowledge to parse its hidden meaning and accept the revelation. Seen in this way, the Great Pyramid becomes God's time capsule.

The overlapping expositions of Smyth–Menzies–Davidson have created a tradition that portrays the Great Pyramid as the product of the same divine inspiration that led to the Bible. What the Bible says in words, the Great Pyramid says in stone, so that these two great gifts of inspiration reinforce one another. Although the various writers who have contributed to this tradition have their own emphases and hobbyhorses, certain common ideas unite them.

The first is the certainty that scripture itself connects the Bible to the Great Pyramid. For example, Charles Taze Russell (1852–1916), a founder of the Watchtower Society, which evolved into the modern Jehovah's Witnesses, wrote biblical commentaries about the Great Pyramid. He put great stock on two verses from the prophet Isaiah: "That day, there will be an altar to Yahweh in the center of the land of Egypt and, close to the frontier, a pillar to Yahweh, which will be both sign and witness to Yahweh Sabaoth in the land of Egypt" (Isaiah 19:19–20). Russell argued that, even though this passage never uses the word *pyramid,* it can refer only to Khufu's monument in Giza. The pyramid, Russell wrote,

> is by no means an addition to the written revelation: that revelation is complete and perfect, and needs no addition. But it is a strong *corroborative witness* to God's plan; and few students can carefully examine it, marking the harmony of its testimony with that of the written Word, without feeling impressed that its construction was planned and directed by the same divine wisdom, and that it is the pillar of witness referred to by the prophet in the above quotation.[15]

Located as it is in the boundary zone between Upper and Lower Egypt, the Great Pyramid is in the center as well as on the frontier, as Isaiah prophesied. And Egypt stands for both a historical land and the souls who need to be saved. "Egypt," Russell wrote, "represents the empire of Sin, the dominion of death . . . which for so long has held in chains of slavery many who will be glad to go forth to serve the Lord."[16]

H. Spencer Lewis, whose 1936 book *The Symbolic Prophecy of the Great Pyramid* was published by the Rosicrucians, cites another Old Testament text: "You [Yahweh] performed signs and wonders in the land of Egypt" (Jeremiah 32:20). And a writer closer to our own time, Paul Lemesurier, the author of *The Great Pyramid Decoded* (1977), finds references in the New Testament as well as the Old. For example, the great messianic Psalm 118 contains the verses "It was the stone rejected by the builders / that proved to be the keystone; / this is Yahweh's doing / and it is wonderful to see" (Psalms 118:22–23). The rejected stone mentioned in the psalm is the Great Pyramid's missing capstone, or pyramidion, according to Lemesurier. In Matthew 21:42, Jesus quotes these lines in reference to himself and, according to Lemesurier, to the Great Pyramid's centrality in the Old Testament prophecy predicting the arrival of the messiah. Lemesurier finds yet another reference to the Great Pyramid in Luke's gospel. As Jesus was entering Jerusalem in the days leading up to his crucifixion, some Pharisees told him to silence his disciples, whose sung praises of Jesus as God struck them as blasphemous. Jesus snapped back, "If these keep silence, the stones will cry out" (Luke 19:40). The stones, Lemesurier argues, could refer to the stones of the Great Pyramid. He also thinks that the three magi, or kings, who visited the newborn Jesus in Bethlehem are veiled references to the three pyramids of Giza and that the guiding genius of the Hebrews' escape from Egypt named as Yahweh in the book of Exodus is one and the same divine being as Khufu. Thus, saying that the Great Pyramid is the work of Khufu is the same as saying that it is the work of Yahweh, the God of the Old Testament.

Lemesurier discovers further validation of the correspondence between the Bible and the Great Pyramid in a bit of geographical geometry. Draw a true east–west meridian through the Great Pyramid, then take a northeast bearing off this line at 26° 18' 9", the angle of the Descending and Ascending passages. This line, Lemesurier asserts—as do many of his predecessors and contemporaries, including John and Morton Edgar, Charles S. Knight, A. J. Ferris, Adam Rutherford, Raymond Capt, and Thomas Foster— crosses the northern end of the Red Sea at the site where the waters parted to allow the fleeing Hebrews across and then rushed back in to drown Pharaoh's army hot on their heels. Extend the line even farther, and it runs first through Bethlehem, where David and Jesus were born, then across the ford on the Jordan River where Joshua, Moses' successor, first led his Hebrew army into the Promised Land of Canaan.

Lemesurier is demonstrating a second key belief among writers who share his point of view: the message of the Great Pyramid is to be found in its dimensions. "The Great Pyramid speaks to us," Charles Taze Russell wrote, "not by hieroglyphics, nor by sketches, but only by its location, its construction, and its measurements."[17]

The pyramid's exterior gives us God's divine understanding of the measures of our planet, as John Taylor argued, while the interior passages and chambers recount the story of salvation told in the Old and New Testaments with that precise chronology in which one inch equals one year. Following this logic, by one interpretation the Great Pyramid was calibrated with a datum point in 2144 B.C., as indicated by certain scored lines found in the upper part of the Descending Passage. The 630 inches down the Descending Passage between the scored lines and the junction with the Ascending Passage demonstrate that the flood that floated Noah's ark occurred 630 years before the Exodus, when the Hebrews made their way out of Egypt with help from the Almighty. Another 1,542 years, or inches, passed between the Exodus and the birth of Jesus, which occurs at the opening of the Grand Gallery, the symbol representing the Christian age. Add in the inches for the rest of the Grand Gallery, and you get the year 1914. That, Charles Taze Russell said, would be a critical time in the history of our planet and the story of salvation. "Thus," he wrote, "the Pyramid witnesses that the close of 1914 will be the beginning of the time of trouble such as there was not since there was a nation—no, nor ever shall be afterward."[18] Given that 1914 witnessed the beginning of World War I, which was until then the bloodiest and most apocalyptic struggle in history, Russell's prediction appears eerily prescient. Of course, worse things have happened since.

Some writers have gotten vastly more explicit in the level of historical detail they see both predicted and recorded in the Great Pyramid's inches. A prime example is H. Spencer Lewis. According to Lewis, the Great Pyramid recounts practically the whole of European history in the first half of the twentieth century nearly year by year. Without giving exact measurements, Spencer finds in the Great Pyramid the August 1909 agreements between Czar Nicholas of Russia and various European countries; outbreaks of violence in the Balkans in 1912 and 1913 that set the stage for World War I; the Treaty of Bucharest on August 10, 1913; England's declaration of war on Germany in August 1914; the entry of the United States into the war in 1917; General Allenby's capture of Jerusalem from the Turks on December 11, 1917; the founding of the Soviet Republic on January 18, 1918, in St. Petersburg; the kaiser's flight into Holland on November 10–11, 1918, with the signing of the armistice ending World War I soon thereafter; the Big Four postwar conference in December 1919; the Treaty of Sèvres on July 11, 1920; the Turkish Treaty on August 10, 1920; and the world-renowned stock market crash of October 1929.

Writing in 1936, Lewis predicted that that very year would be a very big one, according to measurement signs given by the Great Pyramid. The United States would adopt a modified dictatorship with a strong tendency toward state socialism—probably a sign that Lewis was less than enchanted with Franklin Delano Roosevelt and the New Deal. Later that year, though, a major event would occur, something that would especially benefit the people of the United States, Great Britain, and Israel. (At the time, Israel was not a nation, only a passionate idea in the minds of Zionists with ambitions on British-controlled Palestine.) Lewis never said what that something was, and it's hard to know which historical event would correspond to his prediction. He also put great stock in September 31, 1947, as the beginning of an era when church and state would be reconstructed in Great Britain and the United States. Lewis neglects any mention of World War II in the intervening years, the kind of oversight that leaves a reader wondering.

Indeed, that is but one of many things in this line of writing about the Great Pyramid as the product of divine inspiration that leaves the theory wanting.

TAKING A STEP BACK

Is the Great Pyramid really a monument conceived in the mind of the Judeo-Christian God? Is it mentioned in the Holy Scriptures? Let's start with the Old and New Testament texts that supposedly mention the Great Pyramid. In every case, the verses have been taken out of context and twisted to support a predetermined point of view.

The best example is the key text in this argument, the second half of chapter 19 of the book of Isaiah, which supposedly names the Great Pyramid as a pillar and altar raised in the center and at the boundary of Egypt. Every reading of this text from Smyth down fails to notice a central fact about the passage: it is written in the future tense. "That day, there *will be* an altar to Yahweh in the center of the land of Egypt and, close to the frontier, a pillar to Yahweh, which *will be* both sign and witness" (Isaiah 19:20, italics added). The passage tells not of what God has done but of what God will do. That description hardly fits the Great Pyramid, which was close to two millennia old when Isaiah wrote in the middle of the eighth century B.C.

In addition, the passage contains clear references to the current events of Isaiah's time. The kingdom of Israel was living under the threat of invasion by the Assyrians, who eventually occupied much of the Middle East, including Upper and Lower Egypt. Isaiah saw conflict between Assyria and Egypt looming, and he predicted its outcome: "Assyria will have access to Egypt and Egypt have access to Assyria. Egypt will serve Assyria" (Isaiah 19:23).

When the Old Kingdom pyramid builders set about their work, Assyria did not even exist. Isaiah is writing about a pillar and an altar in the Late Period Egypt of his time, not Khufu's. He is describing a battle between the two international superpowers of his day and age, not of the Old Kingdom. This passage has to be removed from its historical context and reshaped into an anachronism in order to apply it to the Great Pyramid. It doesn't fit.

As for Psalm 118, it doesn't fit either. There's nothing about a keystone—which is the central stone in an arch—that has anything to do with the Great Pyramid's pyramidion. As for the story from Luke that says that the stones will cry out if the disciples are silenced, Jesus is obviously referring to the stones in the place where he was standing on the Mount of Olives, a notably rocky place in a stony land, and not to an ancient masonry building far away.

Lemesurier's passage on the angle line rests on the same kind of speculation. No one knows where the fleeing Hebrews crossed the Red Sea. We don't even know if they actually crossed the waters. The same, of course, goes for Joshua's invasion into the Promised Land. Maybe it happened where Lemesurier says it did, and maybe not. The choice has more to do with faith than fact.

Then there's the question of the inch. The prophetic view that begins with Menzies rests on the assumption that one inch equals one year. If you were using the metric system, then—assuming that the prophetic writers are right—a year would equal approximately 2.54 centimeters. That's not a quantity that exactly rolls off the tongue; it lacks elegance. Smyth saw the metric system as atheistic, something he blamed on the anticlerical French. The inch was part of the Great Pyramid's revelation, because the original Hebrew inch had come down to the British, practically intact and certainly sacred. H. Spencer Lewis takes this idea to its logical conclusion:

> since the Anglo-Saxon race had adopted the ancient Hebrew inch it would indicate that this race descended from the Hebrew. And it would indicate also that the Egyptians in adopting such an inch realized that the Anglo-Saxon races would be the first to recognize the unit of measurement and therefore look upon the messages concealed in the Great Pyramid as intended for them principally.[19]

Where Smyth saw scientific sophistication as central to unraveling the Great Pyramid's cryptic message, Lewis sees the inch. And it is one more proof that the monument has little to do with Egypt. "Later generations of the Egyptians looked with as much astonishment upon the mystery of the Great Pyramid as we do today, indicating that they lacked the wisdom which was required to build the Great Pyramid or it would not have so mystified them," Lewis writes.[20] In short, the Great Pyramid was meant for the British and the Americans, because they have the inch and the Egyptians didn't have the brain power.

That probably explains why the inch prophecies in the Great Pyramid's passages hold so true for European history in the first third of the twentieth century and for various predictions about the late 1930s and 1940s in the United States. Certainly, you would get very different results if the one inch, one year equation were applied to, say, Latin American or East Asia. Those regions of the earth, though, don't rely on the inch. The God Lewis is writing about plays ethnic favorites.

This God also has a very specific focus. It is amazing that Lewis finds correspondences between lines and marks in the Great Pyramid's passages and events like the czar's 1909 agreements with the European powers, Allenby's entry into Jerusalem, and the Treaty of Sèvres. Ask people on the street these days what the Treaty of Sèvres was about, and you'll get one blank stare after another—unless you happen across a specialist in modern European history who knows that the agreement ended World War I between the Allies and Turkey and was later supplanted by the Treaty of Lausanne. At the time, these events appeared momentous, even defining. Now these are the stuff of footnotes in doctoral dissertations.

There is in all the prophetic writing about the Great Pyramid a presumption that divine energy focuses upon the writer's time. Like Lewis finding the Treaty of Sèvres in the Great Pyramid, Charles Taze Russell was sure that the resurrection of souls predicted in the Great Pyramid and signaling the end time had begun in 1874, during his own lifetime. Smyth likewise argued that the Great Pyramid served a prophetic purpose for "these latter days." He felt as if he were standing at the end of days and watching the prophecy come to pass while he lived. Lemesurier equates the Great Pyramid with the great "Messianic Plan." He is waiting for the sign, and "when that sign comes it will be the final signal, hoisted upon the mountains, that the long-awaited Messiah and Great Initiate is at hand, and that the last great act in the present cycle of the human drama is about to begin."[21]

We all share an urge to see our time as the most critical historical period ever. That urge reveals itself powerfully in the prophetic writing about the Great Pyramid. This came out almost ironically in a used copy of Lemesurier's book I was reading. A previous owner of the volume had underlined a passage where Lemesurier wrote: "both Bible and Pyramid agree that the second advent will be preceded by a time of unprecedented death and destruction"[22] and penned "AIDS?" in the margin. Think about this. The centuries since the building of the Great Pyramid and the writing of the Old and News Testaments have seen far too many examples of death and destruction on an unprecedented scale. Consider the Black Death, the religious wars of medieval and early modern Europe, the 1918 influenza epidemic, the European invasion of the New World, the 20 million Russian dead in World War II, the fire-bombing of Tokyo and Dresden, the Holocaust, Hiroshima and Nagasaki, the killing fields of Cambodia, the Rwanda genocide—the list goes on and on. But that unknown reader who came before me wrote AIDS, because this terrible disease is the prime contemporary example of widespread death. The issue is less the horror of the epidemic than the fact that it is *our* epidemic.

And that is the failure of the prophetic writing about the Great Pyramid. It tries to appropriate this amazing structure to a religious perspective the monument itself does not share. The challenge in understanding the Great Pyramid is taking it on its own terms, as an achievement of the third millennium B.C. in the Old Kingdom, and not on the basis of the modern prejudices and ideologies we bring to it.

But we have to give the prophetic writing credit for one important understanding. From Greaves to Lemesurier, this tradition shows that the numbers in the Great Pyramid matter—but only when we attempt to understand them as the great builders did. This brings us the question of pi and the Golden Section.

Nine

PI AND THE
GOLDEN SECTION

O CHRISTIAN FUNDAMENTALIST AND PYRAMID SCHOLAR John Taylor, one of the numbers that counted toward his proof of the Great Pyramid's divine origin was pi (π). Pi expresses the relationship between the circumference of a circle and its diameter. If C is the circumference and d is the diameter, then $C / d = \pi$. Since the radius (r) of a circle equals half the diameter, or $2r = d$, this equation can also be written as $C / (2r) = \pi$.

The beauty of pi is that it allows you to calculate the circumference of a circle from the measurement of the radius. Begin with the $C / (2r) = \pi$ equation, then go through the usual algebraic operations to solve for C. This makes the equation for calculating the circumference from the radius $2\pi r = C$.

Pi has another important and fascinating mathematical characteristic: it is an incommensurable number. Take it out to as many places as you want—modern computers have performed the calculation to hundreds of thousands of places—and it just keeps going on, and on, and on. Stop anywhere in that lengthy calculation, no matter how far out, and the number you end up with is in some manner an approximation. For practical reasons, modern mathematicians use 3.14159+ as the best six-digit value for pi ($= 3.14159265358979\ldots$).

According to the standard history of science, the Babylonians were the first to discover that pi exists. They also worked out the first approximation, 3.125, in about 2000 B.C. It was another 1,700 years before Archimedes of Syracuse (287?–212 B.C.), by many reckonings the most brilliant mathematician of antiquity, found a method for determining pi to any desired accuracy. In the fifth century A.D., the Chinese mathematician Tsu Chung-Chi determined that the exact value of pi was both greater than 3.1415926 and less than 3.1415927, a degree of accuracy that wasn't achieved in Europe until the sixteenth century.

Given this history, John Taylor was surprised when he played with numbers from the Great Pyramid and discovered what he thought just had to be pi, long before anyone was supposed to have known it existed.

THE PI THEORY

Even though Taylor took credit for the pi theory, it almost certainly didn't originate with him. He probably borrowed it from another much more obscure writer, H. Agnew, who in 1838 published a book with the delightful title *Letter from Alexandria on the Practical Application of the Quadrature of the Circle in the Configuration of the Great Pyramids of Egypt*. Little is known of Agnew except that he spent the year 1835 in Cairo, which was under quarantine because of an outbreak of the plague. Rather than idle about, Agnew used the time to analyze the Giza pyramids, which were conveniently close to the shut-down city. By the time he finished, Agnew decided that the mathematical ratio between the Menkaure Pyramid's height and its perimeter depended on the constant pi.

John Taylor never credited Agnew with this insight, but he appeared to make use of it in his study of the Great Pyramid (Agnew's ideas are discussed in Vyse, 1840, which Taylor had read). He discovered that dividing the perimeter of the Great Pyramid by twice its height gave 3.144 as the quotient. Since this value lies in the same neighborhood as 3.14159+ (if rounded to 3.142, pi is only 0.002 from Taylor's quotient), and since the pyramid's height had the same relationship to its perimeter that a circle's circumference has to its radius, Taylor argued that the intended value was pi—perhaps in the then-current Egyptian approximation. He argued further that the builders had incorporated pi into the pyramid by design. In fact, Taylor saw the emergence of pi, centuries before its putative discovery, as further evidence that God, and not a raggedy bunch of idol-worshipping Egyptians, provided the inspiration for the Great Pyramid. Taylor's most enthusiastic follower was Charles Piazzi Smyth, who, like Taylor, seized upon the pi theory as further proof that the Great Pyramid was God's handiwork.

Against the backdrop of Victorian England, such a claim sounded more plausible than it might now. Unlike the French or the Germans, the English saw mathematics as both central to a liberal education and woven from the same fabric as theology. English gentlemen typically received at least a basic education in mathematics, and they were of a mind to look for proofs of divinity within it. In their world, the existence and nature of God were seen as immutable as geometric truth. Science gave humans an insight into the nature of the divine; geometry, like all science, functioned not only as a standard of immutability but also as a direct path to God. John Henry Cardinal Newman (1801–1890), who was both a leading Victorian intellectual and a prominent Roman Catholic churchman, wrote that "religious doctrine is knowledge, in as full a sense as Newton's doctrine is knowledge." He even alluded to John 3:16, a gospel verse much beloved by fundamentalist Christians, when he wrote "God so loved the world that He made it good, and gave man a mind with which to investigate and display God's goodness in the form known as knowledge, scientific knowledge, even technical knowledge."[1]

As a result, Taylor's and Smyth's ideas received a careful hearing, and they circulated far outside Christian and fundamentalist circles in the English-speaking world. They gave rise to the pi theory of the Great Pyramid, which to this day attracts a great deal of attention. Despite their flimsy evidence for their prophetic theory of pyramid building, Taylor and Smyth may have made an important observation. Sometimes people with the wrong models come up with the right theories, and the pi theory deserves a close look.

It goes like this: the pyramid's shape was determined by, first, setting its height to equal the radius of a hypothetical circle, then setting its base perimeter to equal the circumference of the same circle. Assuming that all four of the pyramid's sides are of equal length, each side equals one-quarter of the circumference of the same hypothetical circle. This set of relationships determined the pyramid's slope.

The calculation is simple and direct. Let L be the length of one equal side and let h be the height of the pyramid. Therefore, $2h\pi = 4L$, or $\pi = 2L / h$. Now let a stand for the horizontal distance from the middle of one side of the Great Pyramid to a point directly below the apex; then $2a = L$. Next, substituting the value $2a$ for L into the first equation gives $\pi = 4a / h$. The tangent of the slope of the Great Pyramid can be determined by rearranging this equation to give $h / a = 4 / \pi$.

The equation that summarizes the pi theory, $h / a = 4 / \pi$, gives the run relative to the rise (or rise over run). That is, it tells how much the pyramid had to rise, a measure of vertical displacement, for every given unit of run, a measure of horizontal displacement. The equation tells us that for every rise of 4, the pyramid had to show a run of π. This relationship works well on the blackboard or in an electronic calculator, but 3.14159+ is a tough value to use in a quarry for cutting and measuring blocks, or on a hot, dusty building site teeming with work gangs. Whole numbers are a lot easier to handle. The units you use for those numbers, whether cubits or pyramid inches or meters, do not matter, since they cancel out mathematically. As a result, the Egyptians may have settled for 22/7 as a practical value for pi, even if it is not quite so accurate as 3.14159+. If they used 22/7 as a convenient approximation for π, then $h / a = 4 / \pi = 4 / (22 / 7) = 28 / 22 = 14 / 11$. All the Egyptians had to do was to set a rise of 14 units for every horizontal run of 11 units, and they were building a pi-theory pyramid.

Of course, the rise-to-run ratio set the slope of the pyramid. If the modern approximation of pi was incorporated into the Great Pyramid, the slope would be 51.854°. But if it was 22/7, the slope would be approximately 51.843°. The difference is small, but it is a difference. Theoretically, if we can just measure the slope of the Great Pyramid, we can determine how close it is to the modern or 22/7 approximation of pi, and then decide on the basis of the evidence whether the Old Kingdom Egyptians knew what pi was all about. The trouble is, the reality of the Great Pyramid is less than cooperative.

Since the original casing stones have been removed from the Great Pyramid and we are looking at the imprecise core, we don't know with real accuracy what the original slope was. Sir Flinders Petrie (1853–1942), whose methodical archaeological studies of the Great Pyramid were motivated by a desire to test the biblically based theories of Taylor and Smyth, calculated slopes based on the few remaining casing stones on the north face and one on the south. On the north side, Petrie came up with values that ranged from 51.736° to 51.889°, while the south face had a slope of 51.958°. From this fairly meager evidence, Petrie concluded that the mean slope of the Great Pyramid was 51.866°.

That value is only 0.012° off the 51.854° slope for the modern approximation of pi and 0.023 ° from the 51.843° slope for the 22/7 value. Unfortunately, these results doesn't prove very much, because there is another way the Egyptians could have gotten to the same value, even without having a handle on pi.

THE QUESTION OF THE *SEKED*

In 1858 Alexander Henry Rhind, a Scottish antiquary traveling in Egypt, purchased a papyrus that has proved to be one of the oldest mathematical documents known. Today, because of its historical importance, that papyrus resides in the British Museum. Dated to approximately 1550 B.C. in the Fifteenth Dynasty, or about one millennium after the construction of the Great Pyramid, the Rhind Papyrus is also known as the Ahmes (or Ahmose) Papyrus, after the name of the scribe who copied it from an original that was about 300 years older. The Rhind Papyrus gives insight into the nature of mathematics in the latter half of the Twelfth Dynasty, about 700 years after the completion of the Great Pyramid.

The Rhind Papyrus is what we would call a manual of mathematical techniques. It shows, through numerous examples, how to solve basic kinds of problems in arithmetic and geometry. A great deal of variation exists in the text, so it may show techniques developed at different historical times.

Certain sample problems in the papyrus dealing with pyramids incorporate a concept known as the *seked*. The *seked* measures the run of the pyramid relative to a rise of one cubit, the Egyptian measure we encountered in chapter 8. One cubit consists of 7 palms, each of which is divided into 4 fingers; 1 cubit, therefore, equals 28 fingers. According to the concept of the *seked* in the Rhind Papyrus, producing a pyramid with the approximate angle of the Great Pyramid at Giza requires a run of 5 palms and 2 fingers for every cubit of rise. In other words, for every 28 fingers the pyramid rose vertically, it had to extend 22 fingers horizontally. Mathematically, this is *seked*: 28 / 22 = 14 / 11. This is exactly the same run-to-rise ratio that comes from a 22/7 approximation of pi.

The *seked* is essentially a practical rule for architecture and construction, one that delivers a useful value even if you have no idea of the complex geometry that lies behind the concept. Modern construction is full of the same sort of rules. Ask anyone with a general contractor's license how high and strong the retaining wall has to be if you take 6 feet off the slope of a particular hill, and he or she can give you the right answer even without knowing very much about the theory of gravity or the angle of repose. All you have to know is that dirt has an urge to slide downhill, and it will take a wall of a certain height and strength to stop it. The *seked* had the same sort of value. It told pyramid builders how to angle their structures for greatest esthetic effect, even if they had no idea what pi to six places was or even why that incommensurable number is so central to plane geometry.

Unsurprisingly, Egytologists have seized upon the *seked* theory to explain the slope of the Giza pyramids. Small wonder; it lessens the stature of the Old Kingdom Egyptians as mathematicians but provides a workable explanation for why the Great Pyramid seems to incorporate pi. In effect, the modern *seked* theory says that pi is indeed part of the Great Pyramid, but the ancient Egyptians had no idea what they had stumbled across. The architects of the Old Kingdom had made a lucky find by tinkering, not by doing the math.

Kurt Mendelssohn, a physicist who studied at the University of Berlin under Max Planck and Albert Einstein and did important work in low-temperature physics and the transmutation of elements, also took an interest in the Great Pyramid, offering a variation of this pi-by-practicality theory. Mendelssohn assumes that the ancient Egyptians measured height and distance in different units. Height was stated, of course, in the cubit of

28 fingers. Distance was measured with the rolled cubit. The pyramid builders constructed a drum that was 1 cubit in diameter, then measured the rolled cubit as one revolution of this drum.

Let's try out the mathematics of Mendelssohn's theory. The 2-to-1 ratio of height to the length of a side suggests that the intended height of the Great Pyramid was 280 cubits and the length of a single side 140 rolled cubits. The side length would be equal to 140 x π, or 439.8 cubits. In this scenario $h = 280$ cubits and $a = 70$ rolled cubits, so $h / a = 280 / (70\pi) = 4 / \pi$. That is, of course, exactly the value suggested by the pi theory, but again it is found by the Egyptians stumbling upon it rather than understanding the mathematics.

The biggest drawback to Mendelssohn's theory is lack of evidence. Nothing indicates that the Old Kingdom Egyptians used different units of measure for height and vertical distance or that rolling a drum was their preferred way for determining ground distances. Lack of evidence is also the first of three problems that plague the modern *seked* theory.

Mathematician Roger Herz-Fischler, the one scholar who has investigated the *seked* question, reports that his extensive search of the archaeological literature failed to turn up clear proof that the Egyptians of the Fourth Dynasty used the *seked* as an architectural and construction technique. They could have, but there's no good evidence to support the contention that they did.

In the absence of evidence, contemporary Egyptologists who argue the *seked* theory are making the assumption that what was true of Twelfth Dynasty Egyptians must have been true for Fourth Dynasty Egyptians. They are dismissing as irrelevant the severe decline in cultural and intellectual skills that accompanied the collapse of the Old Kingdom and the eventual rise of the Middle Kingdom from political anarchy and social chaos. Compare the buildings of the Middle Kingdom with those of the Old, and you see a marked decline in esthetics and construction. The newer structures are like poorly done sketches of masterworks. The same kind of upheaval and decline probably occurred in Egyptian intellectual life.

Remember what happened in Europe in late antiquity and the medieval period. Although the artistic and intellectual accomplishments of Greece and Rome now seem like a fundamental part of European civilization,

Europe completely lost contact with the Greek and Roman classics through-out the Dark Ages, which followed the collapse of the Roman Empire in the fifth century A.D. If it hadn't been for contact during the Crusades with Arab scholars who continued to study Greek writers and the reintroduction of classic Latin texts from Irish monasteries that had faithfully preserved and copied them for centuries, modern Europeans still wouldn't know who Cicero or Aristotle was.

There is every chance that something of the same occurred in Egypt. The Middle Kingdom Egyptians may well have lost the pi the Old King-dom Egyptians had and settled for the *seked* as a reasonable facsimile.

Which leads us to the final problem with the *seked* theory: the intriguing suggestion that pi wasn't the only mathematical constant the Old Kingdom Egyptians understood.

THE GOLDEN SECTION

Since the Renaissance it has been called the Golden Section, or phi (ϕ). Phi isn't a number that can be worked out with arithmetic, but it can be deter-mined with nothing more than a compass and a ruler. First, draw a line, which we call AC. Now divide the line AC at a point B such that AC / AB = AB / BC. In other words, the ratio of whole to the longer part is the same as the ratio of the longer part to the shorter part. Both ratios equal phi, which is 1.618033988749895 ... This irrational and incommensurable number is the Golden Section, also known as the Golden Mean, Primordial Scission, and the Divine Proportion.

Phi can also be demonstrated with the geometry of the square. Take a square with a side of 1 unit, and cut it in half from one side to the other, forming two rectangles of 1 x ($\frac{1}{2}$). The diagonal of one of the rectangles plus 1 / 2 equals ϕ. Let's call this diagonal W, and apply the Pythagorean theo-rem to it. Now we know the relationship of W to the other two sides: $W^2 = 1^2 + (1 / 2)^2$. This can also be written as $W^2 = 1.25$, so $W = \sqrt{1.25}$ and $\phi = \sqrt{1.25} + (1 / 2)$. However, $\sqrt{1.25}$ can be multiplied by 1 in the form of $\sqrt{4} / 2$ to arrive at $\sqrt{4 \times 1.25} / 2 = \sqrt{5} / 2$. Now substitute $\sqrt{5} / 2$ for $\sqrt{1.25}$ in the equation $\phi = \sqrt{1.25} + \frac{1}{2}$, and we arrive at $\phi = (1 + \sqrt{5}) / 2$.

One of the most fascinating things about phi is that $1 + \phi = \phi^2$. Carry out some simple algebra on this equation, and you get $(1 / \phi) + 1 = \phi$, an equation that leads to an additive series of numbers known as the Fibonacci series. It is named for perhaps the greatest mathematical genius of the Middle Ages, Leonardo Fibonacci (c. 1270–1240 A.D.), an Italian also known as Leonardo of Pisa. Fibonacci introduced Europe to the Hindu-Arabic numbers we know and use, and he traveled widely, even to Egypt, and studied the mathematical techniques he encountered. It may have been in Egypt that Fibonacci first encountered the sequence that bears his name and discovered its relationship to both phi and pi.

The Fibonacci sequence looks simple enough: 0, 1, 1, 2, 3, 5, 8, 13, 21, 34, 55 . . . Each number after the first 1 represents the sum of the two preceding numbers. Intriguingly, the ratio of each term to the one that goes before yields an approximation of phi. As you go up the series, the approximation gets more and more accurate. The ratio of 1:1 is 1, 3:2 is 1.5, 5:3 is 1.666, and by the time you work up the series to 55:34, the ratio is 1.61747, much closer to the actual value of 1.6180339.

Through the Fibonacci series, phi shapes many natural phenomena, such as the growth curve of a nautilus shell, the seed whorls in a sunflower or aster, and the structure of a spiral galaxy. Plato in his dialogue *Timaeus*—which also discusses Atlantis—says that the Golden Section is the most binding of all mathematical relationships and that it is a key to the physics of the cosmos. The Golden Section is also an important compositional element in many Renaissance paintings, including works by Fra Lippo Lippi (1406–1469), Leonardo da Vinci (1452–1519), and Raphael (1483–1520). It formed the basis of the grid system used by Le Corbusier (1887–1965), the great Swiss architect who designed, among other buildings, the United Nations headquarters in New York City.

The classical Athenians used the Golden Section in constructing the Acropolis, and the elaboration of the mathematics behind it is associated with the Greek geometers Pythagoras (c. 569–475 B.C.) and Euclid (c. 325–265 B.C.). But the Great Pyramid and other monuments suggest that the Egyptians of the Old Kingdom understood phi, and its relationship to pi, more than 2,000 years earlier.

Perhaps the first writer to make this assertion was René Schwaller de Lubicz (1887–1961), the Alsatian mathematician and philosopher whose observation of water erosion on the Great Sphinx was the roundabout reason I first came to Giza. Consider, for example, a relief Schwaller studied on the east side of the temple of Luxor, which received more of his attention than any other ancient Egyptian structure. The relief shows a group of priests carrying the solar barque of the king through a gate in the temple of Karnak.[2] According to Schwaller's computations, if the width of the gate from one outside wall to another is taken as 1, the external height of the gate is 2, while if the width of the gate from one inside wall to the other is taken as 1, the height of the inside of the gate is $\phi^2 \times 1.2 = 3.1416$.

That's the value of pi, of course, and it means that the ancient Egyptians understood the relationship of pi to phi as $\pi = \phi^2 \times 6 / 5$. Take two approximations of ϕ in the Fibonacci series in sequence and substitute then into this equation, and you can produce a good approximation of pi (the pi approximations, like the phi approximations, get closer as you move further along in the Fibonacci series). This gives us at least one approximation of pi apparently used in the Great Pyramid, namely $(34 / 21) \times (55 / 34) \times (6 / 5) = (55 / 21) \times (6 / 5) = (11 / 21) \times 6 = 66 / 21 = 22 / 7$.

To Schwaller's credit, he based his revelation of phi in Old Kingdom Egypt on more than one observation. Many depictions of the pharaohs show the Egyptian king wearing a curious kind of triangular loincloth. Schwaller de Lubicz measured the angles of dozens upon dozens of these depictions and always came up with two values: ϕ and $\sqrt{\phi}$. It is no symbolic accident that the loincloth was the article of clothing chosen to represent phi. Because of phi's importance in shaping everything in the world from nautilus shells to spiral galaxies, the number is commonly seen as the seed power of the universe. Phi is phallic.

Schwaller also argued that phi appears in the cross-section of the Great Pyramid, which forms a triangle comprising the height of the structure, half its base, and the apothem. If the half-base is 1, then the apothem is ϕ, and the height is $\sqrt{\phi}$. The cross-section of the Great Pyramid, therefore, expresses the same angles as the pharaohs' loincloths and embodies the same masculine principle of the shape-forming seed.

Livio Catullo Stecchini, the measures-obsessed classicist we met in chapter 7, added an additional wrinkle to the presence of phi in the Great Pyramid and its relationship to pi. Most Great Pyramid researchers assume that the structure was intended to have a perfectly square base with sides that rose to the apex at equal angles. Stecchini questioned these fundamental assumptions. He believed that a starting point for the design of the Great Pyramid may have been a base length of 440 cubits and a height of 280 cubits, but that these dimensions were then modified in the final plan and construction. The basic length of each side was changed to 439.5 cubits, and the perimeter of the Great Pyramid was therefore meant to be 1,758 cubits (921.453 meters). You will remember from chapter 7 that Stecchini said that this value was meant to equal a half-minute of latitude at the equator. The ancient Egyptians calculated this value as 3,516 cubits, which translates to 1,842.905 meters, extremely close to our contemporary measurement of 1,842.925 meters.

But Stecchini goes further. The Cole Survey of 1925 shows that the Great Pyramid isn't quite perfectly square. Most Egyptologists ascribe this slight variation to accident or inaccuracy. After all, it's difficult to put that much stone into place and get it all right down to the last cubit or two. Stecchini, however, says that the Great Pyramid's base was designed to be slightly different from a perfect square, and that the purpose behind this variation has to do with pi and phi.

As Stecchini sees it, the axis for the alignment of the Great Pyramid's western side was laid out first, then the northern side was drawn to be perfectly perpendicular to it. The eastern side, however, was intentionally positioned at an angle 3 arcminutes greater than perpendicular to the northern side. In other words, the northeast corner was meant to be 90° 03' 00", not 90°. As for the southern side, it was intended to be a half-arcminute greater than perpendicular, so that the southwest corner measured 90° 00' 30", for according to Stecchini's analysis, not all of the sides were at the exact same angles.

Stecchini also analyzed a small line on the pavement at the base of the Great Pyramid near the middle on the north side. Some writers have assumed that this was the original north–south axis of the Great Pyramid.

The data from the Cole Survey show that the axis line is located 115.090 meters from the northwest corner and 115.161 meters from the northeast corner, so that it is a little off center, a variation typically dismissed as human error. Stecchini concludes that this was no mistake. Rather, the Great Pyramid's north–south axis was off center on purpose. Therefore, the apex was also off center—again, on purpose—by about 35.5 millimeters to the west. As a result, each of the four faces of the Great Pyramid has a slightly different slope from the others, an idea that also occurred to Petrie in the course of his measurements but one he never pursued.

It is this difference between the sides that allows the Great Pyramid to incorporate both pi and phi into its exterior design. The western face of the Great Pyramid was designed with the factor pi, the northern face with the factor phi.

Here's how the math works out for the western, or pi, side of the Great Pyramid. Let Z be the horizontal length from the middle of the western side at the base to a point directly under the apex of the Great Pyramid, which equals 115.090 meters, according to the Cole Survey. To say that the western face was designed with pi in mind means that 2 times value Z times 4 divided by 2 times pi equals the height of the Great Pyramid, or $(2 \times 115.090$ meters $\times 4) / (2 \times 3.14) = 146.6$ meters. If a more accurate value of pi is used in this equation, such as 3.14159, then the calculated height is 146.537 meters. Using the approximation of 3.1420 for pi, the calculated height is 146.518 meters.

Now let's look at the north side, which Stecchini says is based on phi. Let Y be the horizontal length from the middle of the northern side at the base to a point directly under the apex of the Great Pyramid. Y equals one-half of the standard base length of 439.5 cubits divided by 2. In metric terms, that is 230.363178 / 2, or 115.181589 meters. To say that the northern face was designed with phi in mind means that Y divided by the square root of 1 over phi, $\sqrt{1/\phi}$, equals the height of the Great Pyramid, or 115.181589 meters / $\sqrt{1/\phi} = 146.512$ meters.

That is only 0.006 meters from the pyramid's height calculated from pi on the western wide. Both calculations prove themselves empirically by coming out to values within such a small margin. Stecchini's final analysis suggests powerfully that both pi and phi are part and parcel of the design of the Great Pyramid.

The Egyptians of the Old Kingdom were doing more than relying on the handy-dandy *seked* to calculate the slopes of the Great Pyramid. They understood pi and phi as important mathematical constants. But why were they using them? Was there something they were trying to tell us?

Part Four

MYSTICS,
ESOTERICS,
AND
INITIATES

Ten

SECRET KNOWLEDGE

THE GREAT PYRAMID WAS HARDLY THE MOST BURNING ISsue on the mind of Edward Said when he wrote *Orientalism* in the 1970s. A Palestinian born in Jerusalem and a highly regarded American professor of comparative literature, Said wanted to explore the complex and painful relationship between the imperial powers of Europe and North America and the regions of Asia and Africa those western nations colonized. Said uncovered two important aspects of western academic and popular thinking about the East that bear strongly on our interest in the Great Pyramid. The first was that even serious students of the Orient were interested less in what existed now than what had gone before, in what they saw as a time of classical greatness. In other words, the present represented a decadent descent from a magnificent past. It fell to the scholar, thinker, and writer to resurrect that past and pass it on despite the depredations of the present. Hence, Napoleon's *savants* thought it their duty to rescue an accurate image of ancient Egypt from a miserably poor, degenerate Egypt that lacked both motivation and intellect to understand its own patrimony. This same Orientalism also explains the many attempts to interpret the pyramids as something other than Egyptian and to make them the handiwork of an Old Testament God, colonizing extraterrestrials, or wandering Atlanteans.

This assumption contributed to the second aspect of Orientalist thinking. The East existed less in itself than in books and accounts that described it, often in imaginative, even fictional terms. This writing upon writing upon writing created a self-fulfilling universe that bore only a passing relationship to the East in reality. What mattered wasn't what scholars, writers, or thinkers saw or experienced in that great stretch of colonized earth from Egypt to China. Rather, what mattered was what they read about it, and what they took away from their reading:

> the Orientalist attitude in general . . . shares with magic and mythology the self-containing, self-reinforcing character of a closed system, in which objects are what they are *because* they are what they are, for once, for all time, for ontological reasons that no empirical matter can alter or dislodge.[1]

In other words, facts from the Orient too often matter less than stories and beliefs about the Orient. In the case of the Great Pyramid, what we believe about Egypt and its monuments commonly trumps what we empirically determine.

To give an example, let us return to John Greaves (1602–1652), the English geometer and antiquarian. We encountered Greaves in chapter 8 as he conducted the first survey of the Great Pyramid and launched the numerological legacy that enthusiasts of a biblical interpretation have found so intriguing. On the one hand, Greaves was dedicated to the facts. He approached his work with an exquisitely calibrated and verified 10-foot measuring rod, and he recorded his measurements of the inside and outside of the pyramid with meticulous care. On the other hand, Greaves sometimes put as much stock in the manuscripts of antiquity as he did in his own observations. Regarding a causeway to the Great Pyramid that Diodorus Siculus said had disappeared in his day, the first century B.C.—even though observers from as late as the eighteenth century A.D. reported its existence—Greaves agreed with Diodorus, without taking a look for himself. In Greaves's work, fact and belief about the Great Pyramid tug at one another. It is a struggle that has been going on for a long while.

ANCIENT ROOTS

Egypt as the source of ultimate wisdom; the ancients as bearers of sacred, mystical, and practical knowledge that has been lost to time; a Golden Age pre-dating recorded history—each of these are themselves very ancient and longstanding concepts that have been drawn upon by thinkers through the ages. And who is to say with certainty that these traditions are wrong? Indeed, their robustness and continued reoccurrence would suggest that there is more than a grain of truth underlying such notions. Egypt has beckoned to thinkers of all stripes for thousands of years.

When Herodotus (484–425 B.C.) arrived in Egypt in the fifth century B.C. with his ear tuned for good stories from the past, Egypt's difference from the rest of the world he knew impressed him. Its lifestyle, culture, and animal worship looked strange even to a well-traveled Greek. "Concerning Egypt," he wrote, "I will now speak at length, because nowhere are there so many marvelous things, nor in the whole world beside are there to be seen so many things of unspeakable greatness."[2] Ever the historian, Herodotus stood in awe of a land where historical memory reached more than a hundred generations into the past.

In part because of this long history, Plato (427–347 B.C.), who wrote his dialogues well after Herodotus, saw Egypt as a primary cultural source. In the *Timaeus* and the *Critias*, the dialogues that lay out the story of Atlantis, Plato says that Solon (died 559 B.C.), the great Athenian lawgiver of the sixth century B.C., journeyed to Egypt to learn from priests who claimed a 9,000-year-old tradition. (Given what we know of the age of the Sphinx, that may have been no idle boast.) In the *Phaedrus* and the *Philebus*, Plato tells of an Egyptian god or divine man who gave the human race numbers, calculation, the alphabet, mathematics, and astronomy. Plato calls him Theuth, a corruption of the Egyptian Thoth.

Diodorus Siculus (c. 80–20 B.C.) extended the tradition of Egypt as a source of Greek learning by listing all the famous men of ancient letters and sciences who, like Solon, spent formative time along the Nile. Some of these figures were mythical. One was Orpheus, the son of Apollo and Calliope and the god of music who tried to rescue his lost love from the underworld;

another was Musaeus, a minor Greek deity who was either the son or the pupil of Orpheus. Others in the list were historical, beginning with Homer (c. 800 B.C.), the poet of the *Odyssey* and the *Iliad;* Lycurgus (c. 600 B.C), the father-king of the militaristic Spartan state; Thales (c. 624–547 B.C.), the philosopher and mathematician; Plato, of course; Pythagoras (c. 569–475 B.C.), reputed to be the world's first pure mathematician; and Eudoxus (c. 400–347 B.C.), the mathematician and astronomer known as the first Greek to map the stars.

Whether these great men of Greece actually went to Egypt is irrelevant. What matters is that Greek speakers of the Hellenistic and Roman periods saw Egypt as the source of learning central to what we call civilization. In addition, some of this knowledge came from a particularly ancient tradition—the 9,000 years Plato cites, for example—and it was often considered secret. Pythagoras, who sought to merge mathematics and philosophy, swore his students to a pervasive silence that cloaked his work in a continuing mystery.

The god the Hellenistic Greeks saw as the divine embodiment of wisdom and the fountain from which this secret Egyptian knowledge sprang was Thoth, the very name Plato had misheard as Theuth. In the most ancient Egyptian myths, Thoth sprang from the head of Seth after he inadvertently ingested the semen of Horus. Thoth carried within him the conflicting traits of these eternally battling opposites, Horus representing order and justice, Seth chaos and greed. In the Old Kingdom, Thoth's violent characteristics predominated. He was described as a lord of killing who overthrew the armies of Asia and trampled his enemies underfoot. The Pyramid Texts, which were inscribed on tombs at Saqqara during the Fifth, Sixth, and Eighth dynasties, describe him slicing off heads and cutting out hearts, a fierce butcher of Egypt's enemies. But Thoth, often depicted with the head of an ibis or baboon on the body of a man, also served as a judge and messenger of the gods and the guardian of the eye that Horus lost in his epic struggle with Seth, an eye that came to symbolize knowledge and wisdom. During the Twelfth Dynasty, the priests of Thoth's temple in Hermopolis created the *Book of the Two Ways* (part of the larger collections of writings commonly referred to collectively as the Coffin Texts), a volume of esoteric learning that described the afterlife and was a precursor to the better known *Egyptian Book of the Dead.* The Coffin Texts, which consist of spells written on the coffins of Middle Kingdom officials, add to the reputation of Thoth as the author of sacred texts. By the time of the New Kingdom, Thoth had grown from a devotee of violence into the god who created all culture, the role from which Plato recruited him into his dialogues.

The *Book of the Two Ways* is often described as the earliest hermetic writing—that is, it is associated with the teachings of a figure, sometimes human and sometimes divine, that began as Thoth and eventually evolved into the personage known as Hermes Trismegistus. When the Greeks encountered Thoth, they were reminded of their own god Hermes, but Thoth seemed greater still. Hence they referred to the Egyptian Thoth as the "thrice-great Hermes," or Hermes Trismegistus, thus creating the Greco-Egyptian Thoth-Hermes. The root *Hermes* appears in both *hermetic* and *Hermopolis*, the latter meaning "city of Hermes" in Greek. Like Thoth, Hermes is the messenger of Olympus, the one who carries word from the gods and goddesses on high to humans below. The Romans took Hermes into their pantheon as Mercury, giving him winged sandals to speed his flight between heaven and earth. They attached his name to the planet that circled closest to the sun as a way of symbolizing Hermes-Mercury's proximity to divinity and his quick movements (the planet Mercury has the shortest and fastest path relative to the sun).

CHRISTIANS AND ALCHEMISTS

By the time Hermes Trismesgistus received his full name, Egyptian spirituality was already making its way out into the wider world, first the Hellenized eastern Mediterranean, then the larger Roman Empire. Osiris, who had become not only the god of the underworld but also the lord of the sun, took on a new name: Serapis. Serapis assumed aspects first of Zeus, top god of the Greeks, then of Jupiter, top god of the Romans, turning into a divinity who blended Egyptian, Greek, and Roman elements.

Isis, Osiris's wife, likewise took on an expanded divinity. She went from being the mother of Egypt to the mother of the world, a universal goddess who was, according to a Roman inscription from the Italian city of Capua, "the one who is all." In *The Golden Ass,* written by Lucius Apuleius (c. 123/124?–after 170? A.D.) toward the middle or end of the second century A.D. and the only surviving Roman novel, Isis appears to the protagonist and describes herself:

> I am Nature, the universal mother, mistress of all the elements, the initial progeny of worlds, primordial child of time, sovereign of all things spiritual, queen of the dead, queen also of the immortals, the single manifestation of all gods and goddesses that are. My nod governs the shining heights of Heaven, the wholesome sea-breezes, the lamentable silences of the world below. Though I am worshipped in many aspects, known by countless names, and propitiated with all manners of different rites, yet the whole round world venerates me. The primeval Phrygians call me Pessinuntica, Mother of the gods; the Athenians, sprung from their own soil, call me Cecropian Artemis; for the islanders of Cyprus I am Paphian Aphrodite; for the archers of Crete I am Dictyanna; for the trilingual Sicilians, Stygian Proserpine; and for the Eleusians their ancient Mother of the Corn.
>
> Some know me as Juno, others Bellona of the Battles; others, as Hecate, others again as Rhamnubia, but both races of Aethiopians, whose lands the morning sun first shines upon, and the Egyptians who excel in ancient learning and worship me with ceremonies proper to my godhead, call me by my true name, Queen Isis.[5]

Christianity became the state religion of Rome after the conversion of the emperor Constantine (reigned A.D. 307–337), who recognized the value of uniting the empire under one religious symbol. Naturally, this threatened pagan religions and cults. The Serapis and Isis cults, however, fared better than most, slipping into the Christian world through the back door of mythological similarity. Many Christians saw common ground between the sufferings of Jesus on the cross, followed by resurrection, and the dismemberment of Osiris, again followed by resurrection. Horus, too, bore more than a passing similarity to Jesus in that both had been born miraculously—one from the Virgin Mary, the other from Isis coupling with her reassembled and resurrected husband. Isis was even depicted in the same manner as Mary, the one breastfeeding Horus, the other suckling the baby Jesus. The Madonna was Isis and Mary, the child Horus and Jesus. Mary, in effect, became the goddess Lucius Apuleius described; she was Isis dressed up as a Christian.

The Osiris-Isis-Horus complex was only the beginning of what Egyptian pagan belief contributed to early Christianity. Egypt's ornate conception of the afterlife, which stood in marked contrast to the shadowy underworld of the Greeks, helped shape the Christian image of heaven. Egyptians of the New Kingdom believed in a fiery hell, another idea they added to the growing Christian belief system. The story that Jesus descended into hell after his death, a postmortem journey that is not recorded in the gospels but became a part of the official creed in A.D. 359, was possibly based on legends that originated in Egypt. Mummification even continued in Egyptian Christian circles until Islam swept out of Arabia and across North Africa in the seventh century A.D.

Origen (A.D. 185?–254?), one of the most influential and important of the early theological writers known as the Church Fathers, maintained that Jesus had gone to Egypt as an adult and learned there the magical arts he later used to create his miracles. Augustine (A.D. 354–430) dedicated several chapters of his *City of God* to Hermes Trismegistus, who by this time had become a great human—and mortal—mind rather than a god. Of all the Church Fathers, Augustine had the most profound influence on the Christian tradition. Hence, his serious discussion of the opinions attributed to Hermes Trismegistus helped propel the discussion of hermetic ideas into the works of the scholastic theologians of the twelfth and thirteenth centuries, as well as later writers on matters of God and humankind. During the Renaissance, the teachings attributed to Hermes were resurrected, and extraordinary enthusiasm surrounded the translation of hermetic texts. Hermes Trismegistus served as a philosophical authority of great ancient learning, cited by Peter Abelard (A.D. 1079–1142), Albertus Magnus (or Albert the Great; A.D. 1200–1280), Thomas Aquinas (A.D. 1225/1227–1274), Nicholas of Cusa (A.D. 1401–1464), Marsilio Ficino (A.D. 1433–1499), Giordano Bruno (A.D. 1548–1600), and Bonaventura (c. A.D. 1598–1647).

This openness to Egyptian ideas and images, and a curious overlap with Christian thinking, allowed another hermetic tradition to flourish in medieval and modern Europe. That tradition was alchemy. The origins of alchemy are lost, but clearly it extends back thousands of years. An important figure associated with alchemy in late antiquity is Zosimus of Panopolis (c. A.D. 300), an Egyptian city now called Akhmim. Although Zosimus is a historical figure, nothing is known of his life. Some of his writings have survived, however, and they name a number of sources, including Hermes. Early alchemical texts, some dating as far back as the second century B.C., are written in Greek rather than Egyptian, but they often mention the Egyptian gods, particularly the holy family of Osiris, Isis, and Horus. Khufu is actually named as the author of one work on alchemy, even though it is written in Greek, and during the Roman occupation of Egypt, the Great Pyramid was associated with alchemy.

All in all, alchemy possessed a distinctly Egyptian flavor, with roots that probably reach into the New Kingdom and perhaps earlier. Even in the Old Kingdom, Egyptians saw minerals not as inert material but as living beings. The *Pyramid Texts*, for example, describe lapis lazuli as growing like a plant, and they depict the bodies of the gods as constructed from gold and lapis lazuli.

Alchemy turned, in part, on the transformation of base metals into precious ones—most famously, lead into gold. The Great Pyramid was reputed to work the same magic, but with different materials. It began with the corpse of the pharaoh, which under ordinary circumstances was destined to decay into dust. Mummification of the body arrested this natural process, and the magic of the pyramid transformed the dead pharaoh into a star being who lived in the heavens with Osiris. Christianity did something of the same. Every time a priest said Mass, ordinary bread and wine became the body and blood of Christ. In both instances, an imperfect, destructible world was made perfect and immortal.

The alchemical transformation of lead into gold is not the true end unto itself; it's not simply about turning a box of fishing weights into a glistening fortune. Rather, alchemy at its best involves the transformation of the individual human from a lower to a higher spiritual state. Carl Jung (1875–1961), the great Swiss psychiatrist who broke from Sigmund Freud to explore the spiritual aspect of human nature, considered alchemy an extended metaphor for psychological transformation into higher levels of awareness and self-knowledge.

ROSY CROSSES AND FREEMASONS

In many of the ancient cultures from which the modern traditions descend, the path to psychological transformation and spiritual awareness is through initiation. The individual begins in an unenlightened state and passes through a series of rituals until, in the last step, he or she ultimately gains enlightenment. This was true in the theology of ancient Egypt, and I believe has an important bearing on the meaning and purpose of the Great Pyramid.

Initiation is found in many spiritual traditions the world over. In both Buddhist and Christian monastic practice, for example, the prospective monk must pass through a sequence of steps in order to become a full member of the religious community. The system of differently colored belts in martial arts recognizes the same kind of progression through disciplined training from beginner to master. Initiation itself is hardly new. The modern attempt to rediscover ancient Egyptian initiation rites (along with the sacred mysteries and knowledge that underlie them, which may indeed be connected with, and incorporated into, the Great Pyramid) has involved over the last several centuries a line of thinking, writing, and analysis that often mixes a legendary Egypt with aspects of alchemy and the hermetic tradition. These hermetic traditions have been expressed in the Rosicrucian and Freemasonic movements.[4]

While no hermetic tradition arises from a vacuum with a single individual or myth, it is sometimes argued that Rosicrucianism began with a legendary individual named Christian Rosenkreuz (also spelled Rosencreutz), who was allegedly born in the late fourteenth century, studied in Egypt, Yemen, and Morocco, and left a secret book in his tomb for later generations to find. Rosenkreuz means "rosy cross" in German, and that surname, along with Christian, links Christ's death on the cross to the rose as a symbol of resurrected life, an association that was popularized by Martin Luther. Early Rosicrucians like Johann Valentin Andreae (1586–1654), Adam Haslmayr (1562?–1630), and Michael Maier (1566–1622) mixed ideas from a number of sources, including the teachings of the Swiss alchemist Paracelsus (1493–1541), the Kabbala, Arabian alchemical ideas, and hermeticism. They soon added an appeal to Egypt as the font of all wisdom.

The central early work of Rosicrucianism is *The Chymical Marriage of Christian Rosenkreuz in 1459*, which was written in the early seventeenth century by Andreae. This work purports to be an autobiographical account of Christian Rozenkreuz's initiation into wisdom, and it concludes with rebirth and a mystical marriage. A portion of the story—in which royal couples who have been beheaded by an axe-wielding black man journey across a lake to a square island—draws heavily on the myth of Osiris and Isis.

The early Rosicrucian movement embodied a desire for unity in a Europe torn apart by bloody religious wars between Catholics and Protestants. Although the movement claimed a Christian mantle, it was variously condemned and attacked by the various religious powers. The High Theological Faculty of Paris even went so far as to condemn both Paracelsus and Hermes Trismegistus. Forced underground, the Rosicrucians reemerged in the later half of the eighteenth century in a movement called the Gold and Rosy Cross of the Ancient System, which was particularly influential in Prussia. This group conceived of a way to eliminate the pagan cast in Egyptian learning, a stumbling block to Christians averse to any unbaptized belief. According to the history promoted by this order, an Egyptian priest from Alexandria named Ormus was converted to Christianity by the apostle Mark and later cleansed Egypt's teachings of their heathen elements. As a result, members of the order saw no conflict between their practice of alchemy and "Egyptian" beliefs and rituals, the Kabbala, and Christian belief.

In the late nineteenth and early twentieth centuries there were a number of offshoot societies that claimed a connection to Rosicrucian traditions. In 1915, Harvey Spencer Lewis (1883–1939) founded the Ancient and Mystical Order Rosae Crucis (AMORC). Since 1927, AMORC has been headquartered in San Jose, California, and now occupies a group of buildings constructed in an Egyptian style and housing an impressive collection of ancient Egyptian artifacts. More than any other group in the Rosicrucian tradition, AMORC explicitly connects Egypt, alchemy, and Christianity. The organization says that it draws on a tradition dating to about 1500 B.C., when the pharaoh Tuthmosis II founded the Rosicrucian order. The pyramids, in its view, were not tombs but temples of knowledge and mystical initiation. And Lewis, whose book *The Symbolic Prophecy of the Great Pyramid* was discussed in chapter 8, claimed common ground between the mystical tradition of the Great Pyramid and Christianity. Lewis saw Jesus as one of many initiated and enlightened beings who drew their wisdom from the traditions embodied in the ancient Egyptian monuments.

Although not officially a part of the Rosicrucian movement, the Freemasons were open to its ideals and even borrowed some of its ideas, including the system of high degrees and the notion of a brotherhood that transcended person or religion. Although there were likely forunners in the seventeenth century and earlier, the Masonic movement is sometimes seen as beginning on June 24, 1717, in a London tavern, where four lodges in the south of England chose one Anthony Sayer as the first grand master.[5] Although the earliest Masons attached themselves primarily to biblical traditions, particularly the temple of Solomon, the seal of a lodge in Naples, Italy, displayed a pyramid and a sphinx. A group of German Masons called the Afrikanische Bauherren, headed by Carl Friedrich Köppen (Koeppen; 1734–1797) and Johann Wilhelm Bernhard von Hymmen, went farther.[6] Köppen and von Hymmen created a complicated path of seven degrees of initiation based on information about the Egyptian priesthood gleaned from classical writings. The initiate began as a pastophoris, or apprentice, and ended up as a prophet, a stage to which he gained entry with the password "ibis," an animal form of Thoth and Hermes Trismegistus. Although Köppen, tired of squabbling among the German lodges, later left the Masons altogether, his initiation scheme continued to exert considerable influence and helped shape the rituals Freemasons practice today.[7]

The man who most closely connected Freemasonry to Egypt was a stunningly controversial figure known far as Count Cagliostro (1743–1795). Born Giuseppe Balsamo in Palermo, on the island of Sicily, Cagliostro founded one "Egyptian" Masonic lodge after another in France, Poland, the Baltic states, and Switzerland. Cagliostro claimed that he learned his secret knowledge—the same lore Moses had acquired—in vaults hidden beneath the Egyptian pyramids. He also said that he had been educated in Medina, the city on the Arabian peninsula that had sheltered Mohammed when the people of Mecca cast him out for teaching Islam. There he said he met priests from underground Egyptian temples and acquired ancient statues of prominent Egyptian masons originally displayed in a temple to Isis. Cagliostro's putative teacher was Althotas, a name he may have derived from Thoth and *Séthos*, a popular novel of the time. The novel, published by the French Hellenist Abbé Jean Terrasson in 1731, told the tale of a young man who was initiated into the mysteries of Isis inside the Great Pyramid. Cagliostro borrowed heavily from this fiction written by a priest.

In the end, though, he ran afoul of the Church. Because Freemasonry was anticlerical, the Roman Catholic Church condemned it as a heresy almost from the beginning. In 1791, the Inquisition condemned Cagliostro to death for propagating Egyptian Masonry, but a lenient Pope Pius VI reduced the sentence to life imprisonment. Cagliostro died in 1795 in a papal prison near Urbino.

Many of the most prominent writers and thinkers of the time recognized Cagliostro as a fraud and con man. Johann Wolfgang von Goethe (1749–1832) satirized Cagliostro in his play *The Great Cophta* (1791) after he had personally gone to Palermo and uncovered the count's less-than-noble origins. Still, despite Cagliostro's unsavory reputation, he helped reinforce an undeniably Egyptian element that already existed in Freemasonry. And since Freemasons were influential and active in the arts and politics, the Egyptian aspect of the movement revealed itself in both public and intellectual life.

In eighteenth-century North America, Freemasonry was important as a political and religious force, informing the anticlerical religiosity held by many of the founders of the United States. George Washington, Thomas Jefferson, and Benjamin Franklin all belonged to the order, as did many lesser figures among the United States' founders. The Egyptian element in Freemason practice can be seen clearly in the Washington Monument, which took its shape from the obelisks of ancient Egypt, and, of course, on the back of the $1 bill. The reverse of the Great Seal of the United States printed on the bill shows an unfinished pyramid topped by an all-seeing eye. The Latin phrases *Annuit coeptis* and *Novus ordo seclorum* surround the image. The phrases, which echo lines from the Roman poet Virgil (70–19 B.C.), mean, "He has approved our undertakings" and "A new order of the ages." The seal symbolizes the conception that the ideas on which the United States was founded draw from a tradition reaching back to ancient Egypt. Designed in the new nation's early days from 1776 to 1782, the seal gave the fledging country the legitimacy granted by antiquity and the significance lent by Egypt.

In monarchical Europe, Freemasonry's Egyptian connection manifested itself more in art. Wolfgang Amadeus Mozart (1756–1791) joined the Masons in Vienna and tapped into his Masonic learning when he composed the music for *Die Zauberflöte* (The Magic Flute). The opera, whose libretto was written by Mozart's fellow Mason Emanuel Schikaneder, features the mysteries of Isis and dramatizes initiation inside a pyramid.

In 1797 Friedrich Schiller (1759–1805), Goethe's close friend and collaborator, published an influential poem entitled "Das verschleierte Bild zu Saïs" (The Veiled Image at Sais) that is still studied in college classes on German classical literature. The poem tells of a young would-be initiate in the temple of Isis at Sais. By reputation, the temple's statute of Isis bore an inscription saying "I am what is, and what will be, and what has been. No one has lifted my veil. The fruit I bore was the sun." Schiller's initiate, a headstrong young man certain of his indestructibility, slips into the temple at night and raises the veil. Unprepared for what he sees, he falls mortally ill and warns everyone else against approaching ultimate truth while still in a state of guilt and uncleanness. Egypt's secret knowledge held both allure and danger.

THE UNVEILING OF ISIS

Although distinct from both the Freemasons and the Rosicrucians, the theosophists borrowed heavily from their ideas. Of all the inheritors of hermetic knowledge, they considered themselves sufficiently cleansed of wrongdoing to approach the ancient image and lift the veil without fear of an untimely death. Helena Petrovna Blavatsky (1831–1891), the central figure in the founding of the theosophist movement, titled her masterwork *Isis Unveiled: A Master-Key to the Mysteries of Ancient and Modern Science and Theology* (1877). She intended to dare what had killed Schiller's rash initiate: to see into the occult power of nature, and to open Christianity to the truths of eastern religious philosophies.

Blavatsky had a colorful and peripatetic background. The daughter of an imperial army colonel and a noblewoman, she was born in the czarist Ukraine in 1831 and as a young woman married well, to the vice governor of Yerevan in Armenia, then also a part of the Russian empire. The marriage, though, lasted only a few weeks. Blavatsky fled to Constantinople, beyond the reach of the Russian authorities, and later appeared in Cairo. She claimed to have spent seven years in Tibet studying as an initiate under a master, although this story may have been a fabrication. Blavatsky came to the United States in 1873, departed some years later for India and Europe, then settled in England, where she lived until her death in 1891. During her time in England she befriended a great many influential people, including William Butler Yeats, the Irish poet and Nobel laureate.

Blavatsky argued that ancient cultures contained a sacred, lost wisdom that needed to be brought to light again. In part, she was drawing from the textual history created by the Freemasons and the Rosicrucians. But she was also making use of the writings of serious students of Egyptology, which had begun with the work of the French *savants* and extended to such nineteenth-century scholars as Richard Proctor and William Flinders Petrie. This scholarly work was revealing—by pulling back the veil, in a manner of speaking—the complexity and sophistication of ancient Egypt. She drew, too, on religious traditions outside Egypt, particularly Christianity, Buddhism, and Hinduism. Blavatsky attempted to distill them all into a spiritual essence that could hold its own against the materialist scientific determinism of her day.

She even went so far as to reconstruct the early spiritual history of humankind. Blavatsky placed Adam, Eve, and the Garden of Eden on the lost continent of Lemuria, and described Atlantis in detail in *The Secret Doctrine* (1888), her second major book.

As fits a philosopohical (and arguably religious) movement that took its inspiration from the great mother goddess of all, Theosophy possessed a strongly feminist message. Rather than accept a husband she disliked, Blavatsky abandoned her marriage and her country for a life on her own terms. That willful energy attracted Annie Besant (1847–1933), a prominent English feminist who shared something of Blavatsky's history. As a young woman she had married a clergyman and borne two children, but she soon found that her independent spirit clashed with her husband's orthodoxy. When she refused to attend communion, he threw her out of the house. Completely rejecting Christianity, Besant became an ardent advocate for birth control, the rights of the oppressed, and the cause of socialism. She joined the Theosophical Society and became Blavatsky's closest collaborator. Besant moved with Blavatsky to India, where she learned Sanskrit, and after Blavatsky's death she wrote *The Ancient Wisdom: An Outline of Theosophical Teachings* (1897). Although she was drawn primarily to Indian teaching, Besant published works on Hermes Trismegistus, including the *Gospel of Hermes*, by Duncan Greenlees.

The educator and mystical scholar Rudolf Steiner (1861–1925) was an early theosophist who drew heavily from Blavatsky's and Besant's writings and saw Egypt as spiritual homeland for all human beings. In a long series of lectures, Steiner indicated his belief in reincarnation by saying that "we ourselves probably once lived in ancient Egypt."[8] Since ideas, like souls, recycle, he also said that "our modern truths are reborn Egyptian myths" and that "all modern culture seems to us to be a recollection of that of ancient Egypt."[9]

WHEAT FROM CHAFF

As Edward Said points out, much of the history of the East, and of the ideas swirling about the Great Pyramid, is a textual invention. Working less with a microscope than a mirror, various thinkers, writers, and philosophers have attached their ideas to ancient Egypt and the pyramids as a way of giving them the patina of antiquity and authority. Now those ideas have taken on a life of their own quite apart from what we know empirically of the Great Pyramid, and of ancient Egypt itself. This doesn't mean, however, that every idea that has come down through the hermetic and theosophical traditions is wrong. In fact, the hermetic traditions may have preserved elements of the initiatory and theological aspects of antiquity that would have otherwise been overlooked or disregarded by the materialistic approach that came to dominate academic Egyptology. Add to the hermetic interpretation a close look at the accounts of experiences inside the Great Pyramid, and the idea of this monument as a site of ritual and initiation takes on even deeper meaning.

Eleven

AN ENTRY INTO
THE MYSTERIES

For Napoleon, Egypt represented not only a strate-
gic possession but also a way of placing himself alongside the
great men of history. As the occupier of Egypt, he joined the
ranks of conquerors like Alexander the Great and Augustus, and he raised
France to the same level as the fabled Macedonian and Roman empires. No
doubt such impressive historical company was on his mind when, on August 12, 1799, Napoleon visited the Great Pyramid in the company of a
Muslim cleric and a group of French officers and soldiers. Entering the
King's Chamber, he asked to be left alone with his thoughts.

Some time later, he emerged, pale, faint, unwilling to speak. When one
of his aides asked whether he had seen anything mysterious, Napoleon refused to say anything in detail, intimating only that he had experienced a
preview of his fate. Throughout his rule he kept silence about what happened inside the King's Chamber. Just before his death from cancer on St.
Helena in 1821, Napoleon appeared on the verge of telling a close friend
what had happened 22 years earlier in the King's Chamber. Then he
stopped. "No," he said with a shake of the head. "What's the use? You'd
never believe me."[1]

Both before and after Napoleon's time, the Great Pyramid has been seen as a place of initiation, a mechanism to receive visions and knowledge, a conduit to the sacred and estoreric, an entry to the mysteries, a pathway to the gods.

THE VISION QUEST OF PAUL BRUNTON

Unlike Napoleon, Paul Brunton (pen name of Raphael Hurst, 1898–1981) trusted that we would believe him and so wrote of his experiences in the Great Pyramid. A Briton by nationality, Brunton began his career as a journalist, then turned to writing about Eastern religion and mythology. His 13 books were instrumental in introducing yoga and meditation to the West and explaining their philosophical backgrounds in lucid, nontechnical language. One of his books, *A Search in Secret Egypt* (1936), contains Brunton's detailed account of a night spent in the King's Chamber, as alone as Napoleon.

After convincing the local police that he would pose no danger to the pyramid and the pyramid no danger to him, Brunton was locked inside at nightfall—standard practice to protect the structure against thieves and vandals. After exploring the various passages, Brunton made his way into the King's Chamber, carrying a thermos of hot tea, a couple of water bottles, a notebook, and a pen. Taking off his shoes and hat, folding his jacket, and turning off his flashlight, Brunton settled in for the night.

First there was the darkness, absolute and palpable, and the feeling that the chamber had "a strong atmosphere of its own, an atmosphere which I can only call 'psychic.' "[2] Brunton became acutely aware of the silence, both outside and inside: "The stillness which descended on my brain rendered me acutely cognizant of the stillness which had descended on my life."[3]

As time passed, Brunton grew cold, both because temperatures plummet at night in the desert and because he had fasted for the three days prior to his night in the pyramid, leaving him with little fortification against the chill. As Brunton shivered, the still, dark space of the King's Chamber turned ominous and dangerous. It filled with unseen beings, the spirits, Brunton thought, that guarded the pyramid. Then it got worse. The guardian spirits gave way to hostile, evil beings that filled Brunton with dread and apprehension. One of these images advanced on Brunton and gave him a long, sinister look.

"At last the climax came," he wrote. "Monstrous elemental creations, evil horrors of the underworld, forms of the grotesque, insane, uncouth and fiendish aspect gathered around me and afflicted me with unimaginable repulsion."[4]

Then, suddenly, it was over. Brunton became aware of a new presence within the chamber—two tall figures wearing white robes and sandals, the regalia, Brunton decided, of an ancient Egyptian cult. One of these figures asked Brunton if he wished to continue on, even though he risked losing contact with the mortal world. When Brunton said yes, the speaker left, and the silent one told Brunton to stretch out on a stone.

Brunton fell into what he described as a total paralysis, and his soul separated from his physical being, entering, he was sure, into the realm beyond death. "I was but a phantom, a bodiless creature sojourning in space. I knew, at last, why those wise Egyptians of old had given, in their hieroglyphs, the pictured symbol of the bird to man's soul-form."[5] Brunton sensed he too had become a soul with the ability to exist apart from the body.

The old priest reinforced that notion. He spoke to Brunton, saying, "Thou hast learned the great lesson. *Man, whose soul was born out of the Undying, can never really die.* Set down this truth in words known to men."[6] He went on to tell Brunton of the lost records of an ancient civilization buried in the Great Pyramid, and explained that Atlantis sank because of the evil and spiritual blindness of its inhabitants. As if to prove his statement, the old priest conveyed Brunton out of the King's Chamber. "I knew perfectly well that I was inside or below the Pyramid, but I had never seen such a passage or chamber before. Evidently they [*sic*] were secret and had defied discovery until this day," Brunton wrote.[7]

The old priest reminded him that his journey led not only to a physical passage but also to a secret place within his own soul.

"The mystery of the Great Pyramid is the mystery of thine own self. The secret chambers and ancient records are all contained in thine own nature. The lesson of the Pyramid is that man must turn inward, must venture to the unknown centre of his being to find his soul, even as he must venture to the unknown depths of this fane to find its profoundest secret. Farewell!"[8]

Brunton awoke back in the King's Chamber, his soul returned to his body. He looked at his watch. Both hands rested on the 12; it was precisely midnight.

THE MUSICIAN
AND THE GEOMETRICIAN

In contemporary parlance, Paul Brunton experienced what we would call a vision quest—the spiritual pursuit that draws people to places like Sedona, Arizona, and Mount Shasta, California, to experience an internal awakening at a charged intersection of geography and psychology. There exist similar accounts. Taken together, I believe they indicate that there is something significant about the Great Pyramid: like other sacred sites in history— whether the imposing mounds contsructed by Native Americans, the megaliths produced by the early Celts, or the cathedrals that bridged the gap between the end of Rome and the dawn of European civilization—the pyramids pose an inexorable pull on the human psyche. The Great Pyramid is a sacred site.

Consider the experience of Drunvalo Melchizedek, a student of sacred geometry, who describes his encounter in the Great Pyramid in the second volume of his 2000 work *The Ancient Secret of the Flower of Life*. Melchizedek experienced his vision not alone in the King's Chamber like Napoleon and Brunton but with a group of colleagues in the Subterranean Chamber (which Melchizedek refers to as the "Well") and the Blind Passage off the Subterranean Chamber. When Melchizedek crawled into the Blind Passage, he became immediately aware of the mass of stone surrounding him and, with his flashlight turned off, of the absolute darkness enclosing him. Like Brunton, fear rose up, a loathing of poisonous snakes that could be working their cool, serpentine coils along that blacked-out passage. In conversation with Thoth and repeating the seven Atlantean words the ancient god had given him, Melchizedek realized that the passage was now filled with light. He could see the others who had come in with him, even though none of them had turned on their flashlights.

After an hour, the group had to leave. Back outside the pyramid, they began to talk. "We exchanged stories later, and it was clear that each person had a different experience—depending on what they needed, we assumed. My sister's story was extremely interesting to me. She talked about how she stood up in this little tunnel and was greeted by these very tall beings who took her into a special room for her initiation," Melchizedek wrote. "Life is more than we know."[9]

Another experience comes from the musician Paul Horn, a renowned jazz flautist who has played with everyone from Duke Ellington to Ravi Shankar. In the mid-1960s Horn embarked on a spiritual path that took him repeatedly to India. There he made a solo flute recording at night in the Taj Mahal and turned it into the hit album *Inside* (1968), which has since sold over 1 million copies and launched what is now known as New Age music.

The success of that album prompted Horn's music publisher to send him to Egypt to make a similar recording inside the Great Pyramid. One of the books Horn read before leaving was Brunton's *Search in Secret Egypt.* He also learned from an amateur Egyptologist that striking the coffer in the King's Chamber would give off an A note exactly two cycles lower than the standard western A.

Before playing and recording, Horn and his engineer performed a puja ceremony, a Hindu ritual for teaching meditation that is meant to eliminate the teacher's ego. He then meditated, and heard distant voices, " 'like angels softly chanting from far, far away.' "[10] Horn's engineer heard the same voices. Then, tapping the coffer, Horn heard that A note, exactly two cycles flat, and tuned his instrument to it. He wanted to be sure his music fit in.

Sitting on the floor in front of the coffer, with the stereo mike in the center of the room, I began playing alto flute. The echo sounded wonderful, lasting about eight seconds. I waited for the echo to decay, then played again. Groups of notes suspended in air and came back together as a chord. Sometimes certain notes stood out more than others, always changing. I listened and responded, as if I were playing with another musician.[11]

Horn felt he was playing in a way dictated by the place.

I gave myself up to the eons of vibrations and ghostly choirs present in the chamber, letting the music flow through me with a life of its own. . . . Many people have told me over the years that this pyramid music is especially meaningful to them. . . . Some people felt they experienced through the music the essence of the pyramids, without having been there. Others said the music brought back recollections of past Egyptian lives.[12]

THE SCIENCE OF THE VISION

At first glance, the experiences of Paul Brunton, Drunvalo Melchizedek, and Paul Horn have little in common. The one traveled out of his body into the zone of the undying. The next chatted with Thoth and saw darkness give way to spiritual light. The third played a jam session with ancient echoes. Yet, if you look a little deeper, something similar was happening in each case. All three had the experience of losing control and merging with what they perceived as the energy and atmosphere of the Great Pyramid. And each had a vision that made sense within the terms of his own background. Brunton's experience told him to turn inward, a path he was already following as a practitioner of Hindu meditation and yoga. Melchizedek had yet another conversation with his personal Egyptian god and went through a revelation of illumination. Horn discovered a music he didn't know he had, a music that told people what the Great Pyramid felt like and transferred that experience so powerfully that some of his listeners felt as if they had been there. The details of each vision differ; their impact and import for the people who experienced them do not.

Brunton, Melchizedek, and Horn represent three of many similar experiences related to the Great Pyramid that are found in the literature. Some of these are ostensibly factual, while others are speculative or couched in fiction—but each reiterates a core theme: the symbolic importance of the Great Pyramid. For example:

- In her popular 1960 novel *Initiation,* Elisabeth Haich has the figure of Ptahhotep* proclaim: "The pyramids will continue to stand for thousands of years, proclaiming to humanity the highest truths which have been built into them,"[13] and, according to Haich, it is through the study of the pyramids, among other means, that the individual can attain knowledge of the higher realms and humanity's place in the cosmos.

- In Roselis von Sass's 1999 novel *The Great Pyramid Reveals Its Secret,* the characters consider the Great Pyramid to be both a prophecy in stone, marking important events in the history of humanity along its passages (as many pryamidologists postulate), and a monument that encodes and preserves geographic, geodesic, and astronomical information.

- The ancient gods and goddesses instruct the initiate in the ways of the ancient mystery school associated with the Great Pyramid in *Initiation in the Great Pyramid,* a 1987 work by Earlyne Chaney, which, its author suggests, may either record her experiences in a previous life, may have been inspired by her master and instructor from the "Otherside of life," or may simply be a product of the author's imagination.

- Dorothy Eady (1904–1981), the English woman who came to be widely known as Omm Sety and believed that in a previous life she was a girl named Bentreshyt at the temple of Seti I in Abydos (c. 1300 B.C.), had many mystical and spiritual experiences and encounters around the Great Pyramid when she lived in Cairo,

---

*In ancient Egypt, Ptah was a god of craftspersons, as well as a creator god; Ptahhotep, or Ptah-hotep, was a name used in Old Kingdom times, and one historical Ptah-hotep was an inspector of the priests during the Fifth Dynasty, around the twenty-fourth century B.C., whose tomb is preserved at Saqqara (see West, 1985, p. 177).

including supposed meetings with ghosts and a spiritual entity that manifested itself as a blue light flame on the east face of the Great Pyramid, recounted by Jonathan Cott in the 1987 book *The Search for Omm Sety.*

However one may view these disparate writers and their work, whether with acceptance, interest, or skepticism, they each point to the same conclusion: the Great Pyramid has a profound and deep significance for humankind.

No doubt spiritual experiences like the ones Brunton, Melchizedek, Horn, and others describe spring at least in part from the dreaming portion of the mind. A dream, however, is not a hallucination. As we know from the pioneering work of Sigmund Freud and the even more significant studies of Carl Jung, dreaming represents the emergence of an aspect of the mind that knows, experiences, and feels in ways different from waking life. Dreaming is not so much unreal as a fresh take on reality.

Many ancient and earth-based cultures considered dreams and visions as one and the same, and treated them as messages from the gods and goddesses. In the Book of Genesis, for example, a dream warns Joseph in advance of seven years of abundant harvest followed by seven years of famine. In yet another dream, Jacob wrestles an angel and sees a ladder reaching up into heaven. In the Christian gospels, angels in dreams tell the magi to avoid returning to the murderous King Herod on their return trip from Bethlehem and order Joseph to flee with Mary and the infant Jesus to safety in Egypt. The *Iliad* and the *Odyssey* are filled with portentous dreams that have a way of predicting the future, often in strange symbolic ways. And Black Elk's visionary dream played a role in shaping the history of the Lakota before and after the battle of Little Big Horn.

Dreams, or visions, have something important to say. And the place where the dream or vision occurs can be a vital part of the substance of the dream or vision. Clearly, Brunton, Melchizedek, and Horn all felt that they were drawing on some energy or power inherent in the Great Pyramid. Although each had an experience that made sense in terms of the internal vocabulary he brought to the Great Pyramid, the experiences were specific to that structure. Elsewhere, they would have been different.

An interesting line of scientific research conducted in the School of Engineering/Applied Science at Princeton University provides a measure of how important place can be to experiences people describe as spiritual or religious. This research makes use of a device called a random event generator (REG). A REG uses a random physical process like radioactive decay to generate random numbers or random events. Developed for cryptography— where unwitting patterns can give away even a clever code—the REG has been adopted by the Princeton researchers as a way of measuring whether groups of people interacting in specific ways can shift a random series of numbers into a series with more pattern. The less random—or, conversely, the more patterned—the numbers, the stronger the energy created by the group consciousness (see further discussion in the appendices under "Selected Theories as to the Meaning and Purpose of the Great Pyramid: Site of Initiation and Sacred Mysteries").

The REG experimenters have made measurements in a wide variety of settings and gotten interesting results. Professional talks in academic or business settings typically exhibit little or no deviation from random. But the REG showed a significant deviation from random during certain religious rites and group rituals, and even during a worldwide meditation for peace in 1997. Roger Nelson, then of the Princeton Engineering Anomalies Research laboratories of Princeton University, traveled to Egypt in the 1990s with a portable REG—dubbed the FieldREG—and looked at the effects of focused group exercises in both various places in Egypt and at ancient sacred sites, such as the inner sanctums of Egyptian temples and the interior chambers of the pyramids. The data show that when the group engaged in communal spiritual activity, such as meditation or chanting in a mundane place like an airport or a sail repair shop, results deviated somewhat from random, but not enough to be statistically significant. In notable tourist sites that lack general religious meaning, as opposed to specific meaning for perhaps a certain pharaoh, such as Tutankhamen's treasure room or the tomb of Ramesses IV, chanting or meditation produced results that showed still less randomness, yet not enough to achieve statistic significance. That came only at sacred sites, such as the Great Pyramid, the temple of Hathor in Dendera, and the Great Sphinx. The sacred sites alone, without group activity, produced results in the same range as group activity in notable tourist sites. According to Nelson's studies, the most striking deviation from random came from group activity at sacred sites. It took both chanting or meditation, and the influence of the sacred site, to produce a significantly more patterned series of events from the FieldREG.

Of course, a single series of measurements is hardly definitive, and it would need to be replicated by other researchers in many other settings to be fully accepted as valid. Still, it is extremely interesting that the FieldREG results provide a measure for a type of religious experience in a sacred site that many people, including Napoleon, Brunton, Melchizedek, and Horn, have reported.

THE SHAPE OF THE SACRED

Widely considered the greatest scholar of comparative religion in the twentieth century, Mircea Eliade (1907–1986) spent his life probing the nature of the human impulse toward spirituality and religion. In his fascinating book *The Sacred and the Profane* (1937), Eliade details how a sacred space, like the Taj Mahal or the Great Pyramid, differs from a profane one, like the toolshed out back or your neighbor's garage. The profane space is built for some simple functional reason, like keeping hammers, saws, and automobiles out of the rain and snow. A sacred space may have practical uses, such as a burial ground or a communal gathering place, but what dictates its shape, form, and fundamental use is the intention to replicate the cosmos and thereby capture its sacredness.

A writer from a very different background than Eliade's, Manly P. Hall (1901–1990) made a similar point in his analysis of the Great Pyramid's internal passages. A Canadian who lived most of his life in Los Angeles, Hall began his career on Wall Street. There he witnessed something that changed his path: a man despondent over investment losses taking his own life. Realizing that everything was much less than it was cracked up to be, Hall entered upon a search for meaning. Largely self-taught, thanks to the bounty of the New York City Public Library and his ability to aquire then at affordable prices what are now rare and costly volumes, he wrote a book that is popularly known as *The Secret Teachings of All Ages* (first published

in 1928) to codify the results of his quest and pull together the most unusual aspects of myth, religion, and philosophy. In the course of covering
an extraordinary range of material, Hall looked at ancient Egypt and the
Great Pyramid. "Much of the information concerning the rituals of the
higher degrees of the Egyptian Mysteries has been gleaned from an examination of the chambers and passages in which the initiations were given,"
Hall wrote.[14]

Hall was making the same point as Eliade—and, even in their own cu-
rious ways, Charles Piazzi Smyth, Robert Menzies, Morton Edgar, and
David Davison. The key to understanding the purpose and meaning of the
Great Pyramid lies in understanding the sacred import of its shape.

Throughout this book we have encountered repeated evidence of the cosmic nature of the Great Pyramid and the Giza monuments—from the zo-
diacal star clock to the replication of Orion's Belt, from the perfect
northerly orientation to the Descending Passage's alignments with the celestial north pole. In addition, Stecchini's measurements show that the
Great Pyramid maps the Northern Hemisphere in exquisite geodesic detail. The ancient Egyptians went to a great deal of trouble to chart their
world, both heaven and earth, and create a cosmic sacred space in the Great
Pyramid.

Surely they carried that motivation over to the internal passages. This
wasn't a case of the builder changing his mind or losing courage at various
points in the process, as various Egyptologists have proposed. The internal
architecture of the Great Pyramid is no mistake; it is as much the product
of intention and plan as the external shape. The outside gives us the macro-
cosm; the inside, the microcosm. The one describes the universe; the other
the human soul.

Understanding the Great Pyramid in this way also answers a major
hanging question: Why of all the many pyramids that the ancient Egyptians built, does only the Great Pyramid contain such an intricate system of
passages and chambers? If the Great Pyramid, like all other pyramids,
served solely as a tomb to safeguard the body of the deceased pharaoh and
to conduct his soul into the afterlife, then every pyramid could be expected
to follow more or less the same design, both externally and internally. The
Great Pyramid's internal architecture is unique, however. Was Khufu so

special and distinct that his passage into the world beyond required special and distinct treatment? No; rather, something else was happening in the Great Pyramid. Once this structure was built and its purpose served, no similar structure was needed again. The Great Pyramid served a purpose apart from simply entombing a pharaoh. It was, in some manner, a temple, a sacred space in Eliade's terms, one that created an experience of ultimate, timeless reality.

In the late nineteenth century, W. Marsham Adams put out the idea that the Great Pyramid symbolized a body of rituals we know from the *Book of the Dead:*

> The intimate connection between the secret doctrine of Egypt's most venerated books, and the secret significance of her most venerable monument, seems impossible to separate, and each form illustrates and interpenetrates the other. As we peruse the dark utterances and recognize the mystic allusions of the Book, we seem to stand amid the profound darkness enwrapping the whole interior of the building. . . . [N]o sooner do we tread the chambers of the mysterious pyramid than the teaching of the Sacred Books seems lit up as with a tongue of flame.[15]

The eminent Egyptologist Gaston Maspero (1846–1916) agreed with Adams. "The Pyramids and the *Book of the Dead* reproduce the same original, the one in words, the other in stone," he wrote.[16]

Actually, there is no one *Book of the Dead.* The name is given to a group of New Kingdom mortuary spells written on sheets of papyrus covered with magical texts and elaborate illustrations called vignettes. There are approximately 200 spells in total, although no single surviving papyrus contains every one of them. Instead, various spells were chosen for a given individual, written and drawn on a papyrus, and buried with him or her. Wealthy people typically had highly customized collections, often with their own likeness included among the vignettes. People less well off could buy template papyri and write the names of the deceased in the blanks.

One of the best preserved versions of the *Book of the Dead* is the "Papyrus of Ani," which dates to 1240 B.C. and both shows and tells of the passage of the scribe Ani and his wife into and through the land of the dead.

Ultimately they come to the Hall of Ma'at, where their hearts are weighed against a feather and they are found worthy to enter the realm of the gods and become one with the stars. This is not an easy path, however. Ani must triumph in one ordeal after another, each requiring special knowledge and particular spells. By using the spells in the papyrus, Ani overcomes each obstacle and provides himself with food, drink, and everything else necessary to dwell in the land of eternity. By the end, he has gained such power and magic that he himself is a deity and can live among the gods.

While the "Papyrus of Ani" dates to the New Kingdom and is approximately 1,300 or 1,400 years younger than the Great Pyramid, it draws from a tradition that reaches well back into ancient Egypt. The *Book of the Dead* comes from the same original source as the so-called Coffin Texts of the Middle Kingdom and the Pyramid Texts of the Old Kingdom. Almost certainly, the tradition reaches back even farther, into the Predynastic Period in the fourth millennium B.C., to a time when most learning was oral and ritual texts were memorized rather than written down. We know this is true of the Greek epic poems, which existed in oral form for centuries before they were recorded, and of the *Epic of Gilgamesh*, which scholars suspect dates to least a millennium earlier than the oldest known written copy. There is no reason to suspect that the *Book of the Dead* is any different. Almost certainly these spells and the journey they describe are much older than their written versions.

The Egyptians had another name for the *Book of the Dead*—*prt m hrw*, which means "coming forth by day." The name refers to the freedom the dead enjoyed once they had passed through their various ordeals, mastered the knowledge they needed, and spoken the special spells. It could well be that the *Book of the Dead* isn't just about the dead, and that those who came forth by day could be numbered among the living as well as the deceased. Individuals who passed through a reenactment of the journey of the dead had a look into what happened on the other side of death. Seeing where they were headed, they possessed the freedom of knowing the way ahead. The living as well as the dead could come forth by day and enter the light of understanding. The *Book of the Dead* charted the path the individual soul could travel toward the freedom of knowing the true nature of both life and death.

Imagine arriving at the Giza Plateau as a pilgrim prepared to see a vision or to receive sacred wisdom rooted in the *Book of the Dead*. Imagine preparing with meditation and offerings, fasting and prayers over many days. Everywhere you turn, the cosmos is remade in stone and light. You make your way through the various stations and pyramids of the Giza Plateau, working through the labyrinthine passages and chambers with all their many orientations, angles, and dimensions, each with a unique meaning and significance. Imagine coming to the end of this long spiritual and metaphysical journey in the King's Chamber, where, like Ani in the Hall of Ma'at, your heart will be weighed against a feather. Prepared by meditation, fasting, physical exhaustion, and ritual days and nights filled with chanting, music, incense, and drumming, isolated from the rest of the world by those millions of tons of limestone and granite, you are left alone in the absolute darkness of the chamber with only the enigmatic granite coffer as company and no immediate way out. Imagine yourself there, immured within that mass of spiritually shaped rock, your defenses stripped and your fears dispelled. Know that the visions will come.

Twelve

A FRESH LOOK AT AN ANCIENT WONDER

THE BIGGEST, AND MOST COMMON, MISTAKE MADE IN attempting to unravel the mystery of the Great Pyramid is to assume that it is but one structure built at one time for one purpose. This error has been made again and again, from Smyth's biblical quest to conventional Egyptology's tomb-for-Khufu theory to Farrell's peculiar vision of a prehistoric death star. The reality is vastly more complex and, ultimately, much more interesting.

Not that our understanding is complete. There is much about the Great Pyramid we do not understand and may, in fact, never fully comprehend. Still, when I study the evidence at hand, a likely picture emerges, one that is very different from the standard explanation.

This picture begins with time. What we know as the Great Pyramid was built not all at once, in a single historical episode, but in stages across a long span of prehistory and history. What we see today isn't the product of one architectural genius or a single highly accomplished civilization but rather the end result of several rounds of construction, each successive phase elaborating on the ones before it. Indeed, the Egyptians rarely built something once and for all. The temples at Karnak and Luxor were rebuilt and refurbished repeatedly, and a dynastic pharaoh took it upon himself to recarve the head of the Great Sphinx and excavate its rump. In the case of the Great Pyramid, this process began well before the time of the Fourth Dynasty and Khufu.

I believe the evidence shows that the mound that underlies the Great Pyramid and was incorporated into it as part of the structure's foundation began serving as a sacred site no later than 5000 B.C. and possibly even as early as 7000 B.C. Use of the mound for ritual purposes, such as sacred astronomy, almost certainly dates to the time when the first structures were erected on the Giza Plateau—namely, the core body of the Great Sphinx and the Sphinx Temple. It is also likely that these same builders constructed the Valley Temple that lies to the south of the Sphinx Temple, the causeway leading to the Khafre Pyramid, a platform or base later incorporated into the Khafre Pyramid, and the core of what is now known as the Tomb of Queen Khentkawes (a queen of the late Fourth Dynasty whose tomb appears to have be an earlier structure that was refurbished and reused).

The next round of construction occurred in the middle of the fourth millennium B.C., in the Predynastic Period, centuries before Menes brought the Two Lands together. In this period, the Descending Passage was cut into the sacred mound following the angle of light falling from Alpha Draconis, which rested near the celestial North Pole at the time. These ancient builders of the second round also excavated the Subterranean Chamber at the end of the Descending Passage.

It is also possible, perhaps even likely, that these same builders laid the bottommost courses of the Great Pyramid. As the nineteenth-century British astronomer Richard Proctor demonstrated, the angles of the Descending and Ascending passages follow the same angle that would have been set by Alpha Draconis around 3500 B.C. Since neither passage rises above the level of the floor of the Queen's Chamber, it is possible that this lowest reach of the structure was built at about the same time that the Descending Passage was bored into the bedrock of the underlying mound. The resulting flat platform, with its nearly perfect orientation to the cardinal directions, would have made an excellent astronomical observatory, one that raised the ritual purpose of the site to a new level. Since the days before Nabta Playa and Giza's natural sacred mound, the people of ancient

Egypt had observed the skies and committed their observations to memory transmitted across generations. Now they had an even more sophisticated tool for carrying out this work.

Then, in the area of a millennium later, Old Kingdom Egyptians, quite possibly led by Khufu, built up from the base of the Great Pyramid. They added the Queen's Chamber and constructed the magnificent Grand Gallery to create an astonishingly elaborate astronomical observatory. The best evidence for this date comes from the star shafts emanating from the Queen's Chamber. As Robert Bauval has determined, the skies of the middle of the third millennium B.C. would have positioned Sirius—brightest star in the heavens and sacred to Isis—in line with the southern shaft, and four of the stars in the head or body of Ursa Minor (or Little Dipper) with the northern shaft.

The next round of construction finished the pyramid above the Grand Gallery. The King's Chamber, the Relieving Chambers, and the upper courses of stone were all added. Most probably this occurred during the Fourth Dynasty, perhaps later in the reign of Khufu, as is evidenced by the quarry marks in the Relieving Chambers and the alignments of the star shafts beginning in the King's Chamber.

At some point following this phase of building, the granite plugs were lowered into the base of the Grand Gallery, and access to the upper chambers was cut off. Why this was done is unclear. The standard explanation is that the barriers were meant to protect Khufu's mummy from grave robbers. I doubt this explanation, though, simply because there is little reason to believe that the Great Pyramid was intended primarily—or even secondarily—as a burial site. Some writers have suggested that the plugs made the upper reaches of the Great Pyramid a time capsule or repository of sacred information. That may be the case, although we currently have no way of knowing.

One other important event occurred at this time, too, I believe. The final outer casing of white Tura limestone was fitted to the Great Pyramid to give it an exterior polish that indicated the structure's completion.

Sometime later, perhaps in the Middle Kingdom, maybe in the New Kingdom, the Great Pyramid was reopened. The granite plugs remained in place—removing them was probably beyond the technology of the time—

but the Well provided a way to climb up from the Descending Passage into the Ascending, and from there into the Grand Gallery and King's Chamber. It may be that the Well was dug in the Old Kingdom period as an escape route for the workers who put the granite plugs in place and then was reopened later. Or it may be that the Well was excavated during the Middle or New Kingdom in order to enter the upper pyramid. We simply don't know which scenario holds true.

With access to the upper interior spaces of the Great Pyramid restored, the building could have been used as a site for ritual training and initiations. It may well have become what Saint Peter's is for Catholics, the Kaaba for Muslims, and Sedona for New Age seekers. During this period, from about 1500 to 500 B.C., the *Book of the Dead* was reworked again and again, in essence being retooled as a liturgy for use in the Great Pyramid— accordingly, as time passed, the book came to resemble more and more the interior of the Great Pyramid itself. Importantly, the final version of the *Book of the Dead* dates to the Twenty-sixth Dynasty, a time of economic prosperity that is also known as the Saite Period, for its devotion to Isis at the temple of Sais (recall Schiller's poem "The Veiled Image at Sais," discussed in chapter 11). At this time, too, the cult of Khufu again grew prominent. I doubt that this resurgence is a simple coincidence. Rather, the Great Pyramid figured importantly into the stages of Egyptian religious life.

Apparently, though, this period ended by the time Herodotus journeyed to Egypt, about a century in advance of Alexander the Great's army of Macedonian conquest. In the time between the Twenty-sixth Dynasty and Herodotus's arrival, the Persians conquered Egypt and turned it into a province of their empire. While folktales continued to pass on the surprisingly accurate scraps of the Great Pyramid's history that Herodotus recorded, his account provides no evidence that the Persian-ruled Egyptians of the time were still using the structure in the same ritual manner as their predecessors. The status of the Great Pyramid had shifted from ancient shrine to abandoned ruin in an occupied country.

And there it remained, through Macedonian, Roman, Christian, and Muslim invasion, until A.D. 820. In that year the ruler of Egypt, Abdullah al Mamun, organized a work party to tunnel into the Great Pyramid, promising the men a share of the treasure they were sure to discover inside.

Although the *Arabian Nights* ascribed magical qualities and heaps of gold to the Great Pyramid, al Mamun may have been more interested in the rumor that the ancient building included a secret room containing charts of the earth and sky. Al Mamun was a scholar and a sponsor of scholars, who paid 70 learned men to create an image of the earth and Islam's first astronomical chart. Whether al Mamun's motivation was for riches or intellect, his tunnel opened yet another stage in the Great Pyramid's history, the one that leads, through the medieval, Renaissance, and modern periods, to this very day.

When I step back from the Great Pyramid and put the stages and phases of its history into context, three key lessons appear to emerge.

- The first is the structure's remarkable antiquity. Ritual use of the oldest portion of the structure, the original natural mound rising up from the Giza Plateau, dates to at least 7000 to 5000 B.C., between 2,500 and 4,500 years before Khufu's workers levered the last facing stone into place. The origins of the Great Pyramid may be even older. Recall that astronomical alignments at Giza and Nabta Playa point as far back as circa 11,000 B.C. and 16,500 B.C., respectively. The Old Kingdom Egyptians didn't simply rise up full-blown from the desert as a mysteriously civilized people. Rather, they were the flower of a root that reached back 10 millennia or more into prehistory and that challenges our notions of civilization's beginnings.
- These people knew a great deal, which is the second lesson I draw from the Great Pyramid. By the time of Khufu, they had been watching and memorizing the skies for between eight and fourteen millennia. They understood the workings of the cosmos so well that they could align large structures with solstices, equinoxes, and the rising and setting points of stars and constellations. Using the north celestial pole as their reference, they oriented the Great Pyramid to the cardinal directions with an accuracy that makes modern-day civil engineers shake their

heads in wonder. They understood geometry so well that they could build pi and phi into the Great Pyramid. The size and shape of the earth were known to them, down to the size of a degree of latitude at the equator and the flattening of the planet at the poles. They knew so much that I wonder how much we have missed about their knowledge.

- The third lesson arises from the Great Pyramid's longevity and continuing mystery: throughout its long history, this structure has meant different things to different people. The ancient Egyptians, I am sure, were creating a scared space in Eliade's terms. The original mound, the first base, the astronomical observatory, and the finished pyramid itself all served to replicate the cosmos, to restate the mystery of existence within a universe we only dimly understand. Egyptians of the Middle Kingdom, New Kingdom, and Late Period Egyptians, who used the Great Pyramid for ritual and initiation, likewise understood its space as sacred. They created a somewhat different universe within it, one that existed less in a timeless, stony statement of knowledge than in the heart-opening power of ritual. In the Christian and Muslim eras, the Great Pyramid existed primarily as a reminder of the idolatry true religion sought to suppress. In our own time, the Great Pyramid has become a point of evidence in any number of arguments and theories—whether it is conventional Egyptology's unflattering view of the ancient Egyptians as talented but ignorant engineers, Sitchin's imaginations of extraterrestrial intervention, or Menzies's Bible-derived time line of salvation. Determined that the Great Pyramid must be what we are sure it is, we fail at the most challenging task of all: seeing the ancient Egyptians on their own terms.

René Schwaller de Lubicz attempted to do just that, and he becomes the figure who brings this book full circle. It was Schwaller de Lubicz's observation that only water could have caused the peculiar weathering pattern on the Great Sphinx of Giza that brought me to Egypt for the first time. The longer I study this place, the more I am convinced that Schwaller de

Lubicz offers an important insight into the ancient Egyptians. He understood something about the ancient Egyptians that deserves our attention.

His studies of the temple of Luxor made Schwaller well aware of the ancient Egyptians' intellectual sophistication. And he recognized that the new physics pioneered by Albert Einstein and Max Planck had overturned the clocklike mechanical universe of the nineteenth century. As Schwaller saw it, this new cosmology was leading us toward an understanding of the world more in line with the thinking of the ancients. The Egyptians, Schwaller believed, saw the world symbolically. They understood nature as an open book that revealed the metaphysical forces behind creation. This was a vision we need to regain, he believed.

But we cannot get there simply by using our heads. A consciousness based only on cognition—the data of scientific research, for example—divides the world into ever smaller pieces in its struggle to understand and control outer events. In its place, Schwaller argued for what he called functional consciousness: an awareness that comes from within, and one that, instead of dividing the world into pieces, seeks out the unity underlying its sometimes disparate appearance. For example, phi wasn't simply a handy mathematical constant to the ancient Egyptians. It was a key to reality's blueprint, a cosmic law that gave shape to the world and filled those who understood it with awe.

I feel that same awe whenever I lift my head from this writing to look again at the Great Pyramid. I feel awe that the ancients could build so remarkable a structure, that my own human ancestry includes not only a building of such beauty but also all the insights, observations, and spiritual experiences it has witnessed and incorporated. In a time of environmental degradation, extinction of species, terrorist warfare, and ethnic cleansing, we need to be reminded of both the magnificence of our heritage and our place in an interconnected universe. The Great Pyramid says all that, and more.

APPENDICES

by Robert M. Schoch

INTRODUCTION TO THE APPENDICES

The subject of the Great Pyramid is vast, and the volume of literature on the topic overwhelming. There exist more theories and minute details concerning the Great Pyramid than one could ever hope to cover in a single book. In the main text we have distilled what, in our opinion, are the most important elements and presented a unified narrative expressing one perspective on the Great Pyramid. The appendices provide significant details and relevant citations to support the main text, as well as noteworthy alternative hypotheses.

The appendix will allow this book to serve not only as a narrative about ways to interpret the Great Pyramid but also as a practical manual or reference to approach the study of this most magnificent and profound structure, a true wonder that has survived from ancient times.

A NOTE ON MEASUREMENT

In the literature on the Great Pyramid, four sets of linear units predominantly are used: (1) the standard metric system of millimeters, centimeters, and meters; (2) the British/American system of inches and feet; (3) "pyramid inches," "sacred cubits," and associated units; and (4) Egyptian cubits of various lengths. Direct measurements of the Great Pyramid have generally been taken either using the British/American inches and feet or the metric millimeter, centimeter, and meter. Pyramid inches, Egyptian cubits, and so forth have then been derived from the raw data. In the appendices I have reported raw data generally in terms of the units used by the original investigator, as this tends to be the most accurate way of presenting the data. To convert metric to British/American, and vice versa, the following equivalencies are useful (with some values rounded):

1 British/American inch = 25.4 millimeters = 2.54 centimeters = 0.0254 meters

1 foot = 12 inches = 304.8 millimeters = 30.48 centimeters = 0.3048 meters

1 cm = 0.3937007 inch = 0.0328083 foot

1 m = 100 centimeters = 1,000 millimeters = 39.370078 inches = 3.2808398 feet

The values for "Pyramid Inches," various cubits, and so forth vary from author to author and are discussed hereafter as appropriate.

In the Great Pyramid literature, angles are given in degrees (360° to a circle), but in some cases fractions of a degree are given decimally and in other cases using minutes (represented by ', where there are 60 minutes to 1 degree) and seconds (represented by ", where there are 60 seconds to 1 minute, and therefore 60 times 60, or 3600, seconds to 1 degree). As an example, 51° 53' 20" equals approximately 51.889°, but not exactly.

It is most accurate to report original data from sources using the units of the original source, and this procedure has generally been followed here.

EXTERNAL DIMENSIONS OF THE GREAT PYRAMID

Estimates of the basic dimensions of the Great Pyramid have varied considerably over the centuries (beginning in modern times with John Greaves; see Greaves, 1646, 1704, 1737), due in large part to the fact that the complete base of the pyramid was not exposed until the nineteenth and twentieth centuries. It is now generally assumed by many writers that, in terms of ancient units, the Great Pyramid was laid out to measure 440 cubits along each base (an assumption that may have originated with Petrie in the 1880s; see Petrie, 1883; Herz-Fischler, 2000, p. 193) and with a height of 280 cubits (an idea that apparently goes back to the work of Perring in the 1830s; see Herz-Fischler, 2000, p. 193).

The cubit, represented by a hieroglyphic picture of a forearm (transliterated as "mḥ," according to Herz-Fischler, 2000, p. 176), was a basic unit of length not only in ancient Egypt. The term *cubit* is derived from the Latin *cubitum* (elbow); an alternative or related term is *ell* (as in elbow, or the German *Ellbogen*). Cubit, ell, and related terms were used for various units of measure in many countries up through the nineteenth century (Herz-Fischler, 2000, p. 268). In ancient Egypt there were two basic cubits, the so-called royal cubit (generally the cubit, if not specified otherwise), which was divided into 7 palms (also known as hands; ancient Egyptian transliteration "šsp"), each palm consisting of 4 fingers (digits; ancient Egyptian transliteration "ḏbʿ"), and the short cubit, consisting of only 6 palms. The royal cubit was the cubit generally used in architecture and measuring land (Herz-Fischler, 2000, p. 176) and is the cubit referred to herein unless otherwise stated. Another related unit of measure was the remen (or upper arm), consisting of 5 palms (equals 20 fingers). (There was also a long unit of measure called the remen, equal to 50 cubits, and a measure of area known as a remen that was the surface area of a 50-by-100-cubit rectangle; see Herz-Fischler, 2000, p. 177.)

The length of a royal cubit, or simply a cubit, is variously given as about 523 to 526 millimeters (very nearly 524 mm, according to K. P. Johnson, 1998, 1999, and Flinders Petrie, cited in Stecchini, 1971, p. 315); "in the neighborhood of 52.3 cm" (according to Herz-Fischler, 2000, p. 12); 52.5 centimeters (according to Herz-Fischler, 2000, p. 176); 523.55 millimeters (according to Borchardt, as cited in Herz-Fischler, 2000, p. 192, n. 10). Petrie (1883, p. 181) says, "On the whole we may take 20.626 ± .01 [inches, or 523.748 mm] as the original value [of the cubit]." Kingsland (1932, p. 113) adopts "for the most part" 20.612 British inches [523.5448 mm] as the value of the "Egyptian cubit." Stecchini (1971, p. 320), however, based on studying the monuments and various ancient measuring rods, concludes that there were actually three values for the cubit (royal cubit) in use in ancient Egypt, measuring, respectively, 524.1483 millimeters, 525.0000 millimeters, and 526.3231 millimeters. According to Stecchini, the first value is the standard for the dimensions of the Great Pyramid, while the third value is the standard for the dimensions of the coffer in the Great Pyramid. The second value was the standard used for the dimensions of the Second (Khafre) Giza Pyramid (Stecchini, 1971, p. 320).

Using Stecchini's value of 524.1483 millimeters for the cubit, a 440-cubit base is equal to 230.625 meters, and a 280-cubit height is equal to 146.762 meters. Using Kingsland's value of 523.5448 millimeters for the cubit, a 440-cubit base is equal to 230.3597 meters, and a 280-cubit height is equal to 146.5925 meters.

The Cole Survey (1925) is the most recent and most definitive survey of the Great Pyramid. Based on this survey, the lengths of the four sides of the Great Pyramid, along with the corner-to-corner lengths, are as follows.

SIDE	LENGTH (METERS)
North	230.253 or 230.251 (There is a discrepancy in Cole's report as pointed out by Stecchini, 1971, p. 364; compare Cole, 1925, p. 6 to p. 8.)
South	230.454
East	230.391 (The value 230.381 was posted on the Internet [www.artifice-design.co.uk/kheraha/cole.html (accessed 30 June 2003)], but, comparing the posted version to an original copy of Cole, 230.391 is the correct value.)
West	230.357
N.E.–S.W.	325.699
N.W.–S.E.	325.868

The foregoing values are the actual lengths of the base sides, as measured by the Cole Survey, upon the socle (base or platform upon which the casing stones sit).

Pochan (1978, p. 10) cites the following values and attributions for the height of the platform at the top of the Great Pyramid above the base: 139.40 meters (Petrie), 139.117 meters (Jean Marie Joseph Coutelle, a member of Napoleon's expedition to Egypt; Tompkins, 1971, p. 44), and 138.30 meters (Edmé-François Jomard, another member of Napoleon's expedition; Tompkins, 1971, p. 44) and the length of a side of the platform as 11.7 meters (Petrie) or 9.96 meters (Coutelle) (note that all four sides are not necessarily the same length). As late as the early seventeenth century, the sides of the platform may have been only about 5 meters long (Pochan, 1978, p. 6), indicating that some of the top of the structure has been lost since then.

The Great Pyramid currently contains 203 courses of blocks. It is generally believed that it originally had 7 or 8 more courses, for a total of 210 or 211; presumably this is based on the concept that it came to a full point rather than ending in a platform. Some authors, such as Pochan (1978, p. 1) suggest that the pyramid originally was comprised of 210 courses, since 210 is a product of the first four prime numbers, namely 2 × 3 × 5 × 7. Today the Great Pyramid ends in a rough platform, approximately 25 to 30 feet on the side (Bonwick, 1877, p. 19), composed of limestone blocks (as used to build the rest if the pyramid's core), the tops of which are coarse and uneven. In 1874 the astronomers Sir David Gill and Professor Watson erected a steel mast on the top of the summit (DeSalvo, 2003, p. 10). Most researchers believe that the Great Pyramid came to a point at its summit and was capped with a pyramidion; some, however, disagree and contend: "It is certain that the Great Pyramid never ended in a point and was never capped with a pyramidion" (Pochan, 1978, p. 6; see also similar comments cited by Bonwick, 1877, p. 19). Pochan (1978, p. 245) cites Diodorus Siculus as saying that the Great Pyramid was intact in his day (first century B.C.) but ended in a platform 6 cubits (about 3 meters) long. The top platform of the Great Pyramid is today noticeably non-square (see aerial photo in DeSalvo, 2003, p. 10). It forms a distinct rectangle, and some researchers have suggested that perhaps it never held a pyramidion because a square-based pyramidion would not fit properly. Of course, it seems that a rectangular-based pyramidion could have been manufactured to specification so as to fit the platform.

The angle of inclination of the original sides, covered with their casing stones, of the Great Pyramid is a matter of uncertainty. Petrie (1885, p. 12) gives values that he measured on the few remaining in-place casing stones on the north face, as well as fragments found around the north face; he also gives one value for a casing stone on the south face. For the north face, Petrie's measurements range from 51° 44' 11" ± 23" (51.736° when converted to decimal form) to 51° 53' 20" ± 1' (51.889°), and for the south face he gives a value of 51° 57' 30" ± 20" (51.958°). As the north face mean, Petrie gives the value 51° 50' 40" ± 1' 5" (51.844°). Petrie (1885, p. 13) concludes: "On the whole, we probably cannot do better than take 51° 52' ± 02' [51.866°] as the nearest approximation to the mean angle of the Pyramid, allowing some weight to the South side." Assuming that the Great Pyramid originally came to a point at the top, Petrie (1885, p. 13) continues: "The mean base being 9068.8 ± .5 inches [230.3475 meters] this yields a height of 5776.0 ± 7.0 inches [146.7104 meters]."

Herz-Fischler (2000, p. 11) adopts the following values for his analyses and calculations: length of side: 230.4 meters; angle of inclination of the sides: 51.844°. From these, assuming that the pyramid came to a point, he calculates an original height of 146.6 meters. On the basis of these measurements, Herz-Fischler (2000, pp. 26–27) gives the following values for various relevant features of the Great Pyramid: the length of the diagonal line that connects two opposite corners of the base, 325.8 meters; the apothem, a line that connects the summit, vertex, or top point of the pyramid to a point at the base in the middle of one of the triangular faces, 186.5 meters; the arris, the line connecting the vertex or top of the pyramid to a corner, 219.2 meters; the angle of inclination of the arris relative to the level of the horizontal, 42.0°; the angle between an arris and a base line of the pyramid, 58.3°; the angle between adjacent faces, known as the dihedral angle, 112.4°; the area of each face, 21,481 square meters; the total surface area of the four faces plus the base, 139,008 square meters; and the volume of the Great Pyramid is 2,594,482 cubic meters. To this we can add that the area of the four sides, which would have originally been covered with the casing stones, is 85,924 square meters, and the area covered by the base of the Great Pyramid is 53,084 square meters.

THE CORNER SOCKETS OF THE GREAT PYRAMID

There are four corner sockets carved into the bedrock, one at each corner of the Great Pyramid (see Petrie, 1885; Cole, 1925; Davidson and Aldersmith, 1924; and especially Kingsland, 1932, pp. 15–19, where the sockets are photographically illustrated—they are currently not as easily defined in the bedrock as in Kingsland's time). At times, these sockets have been misinterpreted as defining the original four corners of the Great Pyramid, but this was not the case. The sockets are located at varying distances from both the true corners of the Great Pyramid and the edge of the base or platform underlying the casing stones of the Great Pyramid. Thus, the northern border of the northeast socket is about 85 centimeters north of the northeast corner of the Great Pyramid, whereas the northern border of the northwest socket is about 75 centimeters north of the northwest corner, according to the Cole Survey (1925). The depth of the sockets below the average level of the platform (base) of the Great Pyramid varies from 56.84 centimeters in the southwest socket to 104.69 centimeters in the southeast socket (Kingsland,

1932, p. 15). There is no certainty as to the purpose of the corner sockets, but one suggestion is that they were used to establish the original diagonals of the Great Pyramid (Kingsland, 1932, p. 16). Petrie (1885, plate 7) suggested that at the corners of the pyramid the corner casing stones did not sit on the platform or base as elsewhere but rather extended down to the bedrock and "locked" into the sockets, and the pavement here would then abut up against the sides of the corner casing stones. This is a hypothetical suggestion, however; other researchers have challenged it. Kingsland (1932, p. 18) writes: "If the angle [of the casing stone] were carried down right to the bottom of the Socket Hole it would not, even then— according to Sir Flinders Petrie's measurements—reach the outer edge of the Socket."

THE SOCLE, PLATFORM, OR BASE OF THE GREAT PYRAMID

The body of the Great Pyramid as measured above, at least as far as can be observed around the four sides as preserved today, sits on a platform (base or socle, referred to as a "pavement" in Cole, 1925) composed of fine white limestone similar or identical to that used in the casing stones. The distance from the bottom edge of the casing stones to the edge of the platform averages about 40 centimeters, but varies, "being 38 centimetres on the western side, 42 centimetres on the northern side, and 48 centimetres on the eastern side, at the places where it could be measured" (Cole, 1925, p. 1; see also Kingsland, 1932, p. 20). Not enough remained on the southern side to measure. Cole (1925, p. 5) reports that "the pavement is practically flat, but has a very slight slope of about 15 millimetres up from the N.W. corner to the S.E. corner." According to the calculations of Kingsland (1932, p. 19), the highest point of the platform is 2.15 centimeters above the lowest point, and this is over an area of 13 acres. The top surface of the platform (pavement) is about 60.4 meters above mean sea level, as measured at Alexandria (Cole, 1925).

The thickness of this platform is 55 centimeters or 21.6 inches, according to Fix (1978, p. 247) or 21½ inches, according to Kingsland (1932, p. 19). According to Pochan (1978, p. 12), the thickness of the platform (which Pochan refers to as the "socle") is "0.525 m. (exactly 1 cubit)." Generally, when people talk about the height of the Great Pyramid, they are referring to the height above the base, or platform; in some cases, however, the height of the platform may be included, and thus they are referring to the height of the Great Pyramid above the bedrock.

Herz-Fischler (2000), for instance, never takes the thickness of the platform into account in his various calculations and evaluations of theories related to the dimensions of the Great Pyramid.

THE EIGHT SIDES OF THE GREAT PYRAMID

The core masonry of the Great Pyramid is slightly indented, hollowed, or concave on each of the four major sides. This means that, in terms of the core masonry as exposed today, the Great Pyramid can be considered to actually have eight sides instead of four, in that each of the four major sides is divided in half. This hollowing or concavity is very subtle, however, and is rarely seen either in person or on photographs. If the conditions of light are just right, it can be seen quite dramatically, especially from the air, as is captured in an often-reproduced photograph first published by Groves and McCrindle (1926; for republications of the original, see for instance, Davidson, 1934; Haberman, 1935; Lepre, 1990; Pochan, 1978; Temple, 2000; Tompkins, 1971). It appears on all four faces. Petrie measured this hollowing during his survey of the Great Pyramid in 1880–1882 (originally published in Petrie, 1883, and quoted in Pochan, 1978, p. 114; see also Davidson and Aldersmith, 1924) and estimated that the hollowing consisted of a "concavity" or "indentation" in the amount of approximately 37 inches (0.94 meters) from a perfectly straight line along the base of the north side (Pochan, 1978, p. 114); Pochan (1978, p. 234) gives the value of 0.92 meters for the hollowing, meaning that the two planes of each "face" of the Great Pyramid meet at an angle of about 27' (about 0.45°) different from a perfectly flat plane. Petrie (1883) and (Kingsland, 1932, p. 26) believed that only the core of the pyramid had the hollowing effect, and the facing blocks were thicker in the middle of each of the four main sides and thinned toward the edges such that the final four faces of the pyramid were perfectly flat. Pochan (1978, pp. 132–133) and Davidson and Aldersmith (1924), in contrast, believe that the hollowing effect was present in the facing itself. This hollowing-in of the sides of the Great Pyramid alters the length of the perimeter of the structure, and the amount by which it is altered was referred to as the "displacement factor" by Davidson (Davidson and Aldersmith, 1924, n.d., p. 124; Kingsland, 1932, pp. 26, 57–58). Davidson utilized his so-called displacement factor in interpreting the Great Pyramid as encoding all sorts of scientific data, from the exact length of the year and the precessional cycle to the dimensions and shape of the earth's orbit (see Davidson and Aldersmith, n.d., pp. 124–137). For Davison, the displacement factor was also important in his prophetic interpretations of the Great Pyramid: "The Great Pyramid's Displacement Factor, 286, is the Key Number to the understanding of the Great Pyramid's Prophecy" (Davidson, [1931?], p. 1).

On the basis of an interpretation that the hollowing of the sides of the Great Pyramid was reflected in the final casing limestone, in September 1935 Pochan (see Pochan, 1978, pp. 230–233) introduced the concept that has seen become known as the "flash" phenomenon or effect. On the equinoctial day, at sunrise the sun's rays would be so aligned that they would illuminate the western side of the southern (or northern; it should work on both façades) façade of the Great Pyramid, while the eastern side would remain in shadow. This effect, Pochan believed, would be visible for four or five minutes in the morning, until the eastern side was also illuminated such that the entire façade would be in light. At sunset, the phenomenon would be reversed, the western side first going into shadow while the eastern remained illuminated for some minutes still as the sun continued to set. According to Pochan (1978, p. 232),

> this curious phenomenon is increasingly visible from March 21 to June 21, the summer solstice; at this date, when the sun is high on the horizon, it occurs at around 6:40 a.m. and 5:20 p.m. It occurs for the last time at the autumn equinox, at which date the phenomenon is seen only in the morning, at six o'clock, whereas at the spring equinox, it is seen only in the evening, at six o'clock.

Pochan (1978, p. 233) also suggests that "the singular phenomenon of the first 'flash' that I described might explain the comments made by Solinus, Ammianus Marcellinus, and Cassidorus to the effect that the pyramid *'absorbed'* its own shadow" (italics in the original). Instead of absorbed, we might say the Great Pyramid swallowed its own shadow.

BEDROCK CORE MOUND INTERNAL
TO THE GREAT PYRAMID

The area on which the Great Pyramid was built was not first leveled down to a flat bedrock foundation. Rather, a mound of rock, generally believed to be terraced to take the core blocks of the actual pyramid, was left in the middle. Various explanations for leaving this mound have been proposed. The most common, classical Egyptological, explanation is that it was simply a labor-saving means. Keeping a mound or core of bedrock in the center base of the pyramid meant that much less in the way of masonry that would have to be put into place.

Robert Bauval (personal conversation, May 2004), who is an engineer by training, disputes the notion that the Great Pyramid was built on and over the bedrock mound to save time and expense. He points out that from an engineering perspective, what is needed is a flat, level surface to enable the weight to be distributed evenly and to give clear lines of sight for surveying. Bauval speculates that the mound or knoll that lies under and within the pyramid's base was in very ancient (Predynastic) times considered a sacred site, and the Descending Shaft and Subterranean Chamber considerably predate the Great Pyramid superstructure. Bauval also believes the Old Kingdom Egyptians took an enormous risk of structural collapse building the Great Pyramid exactly where they did, so close to the edge of the plateau. He argues that they must have known it would have been much safer to move it 100 meters or so further away from the edge, so the fact that they built it where they did indicates they wanted it exactly there for some reason, and he thinks the reason is to cover and preserve and mark the sacred knoll or mound under and within, along with the much older subterranean chamber.

Davidson and Aldersmith (1924, n.d., p. 159) suggest that a terraced mound of bedrock was left internal to the Great Pyramid as a way of counteracting subsidence, the collapsing of caverns within the bedrock, tremors, and earthquakes.

THE CORE LAYERS OF STONE

In its current state, the Great Pyramid consists of 203 layers, or courses, of stone blocks. The thickness of the courses varies, but all of the blocks within a course are very closely of the same thickness. The base course is about 58 inches thick. From the base, the thickness of each course more or less decreases, until there is a sudden increase at the thirty-fifth course; the thirty-fourth course is 26.2 inches thick, and the thirty-fifth course is 49.8 inches thick (Kingsland, 1932, p. 25; see also table of course thicknesses in Davidson and Aldersmith, 1924, facing p. 120). Likewise, according to Kingsland (based on the work of Petrie; also see Davidson and Aldersmith, 1924, n.d.), there are marked increases at the 67th, 90th, 98th, 118th, and 144th courses; but the greatest increase is the one at the 35th course. Pochan (1978, p. 10) gives the average height of the courses as 0.685 meters (26.97 inches) and the average height of the top ten as 0.562 meters (22.1 inches).

Petrie (1885, p. 11) found that the mean azimuth of the core layers of the Great

Pyramid at its base is 5' 16" west of north, whereas the casing stones, according to Petrie's measurements are only 3' 43" west of north, suggesting that the final orientation of the Great Pyramid was adjusted very slightly when the casing stones were applied and cut to their final form.

THE NUMBER OF BLOCKS COMPOSING
THE GREAT PYRAMID

According to Pochan (1978, p. 1; see also Moyer, 2003), the Great Pyramid, composed predominantly of limestone but with some granite in the interior, has an estimated volume of 2.6 million cubic meters and a mass of 7 million metric tons. Typical estimates of the number of blocks composing the Great Pyramid are around 2.3 million (Petrie, 1885, p. 83 n., says there are 2.3 million blocks averaging 2.5 English tons each) to 2.5 million (DeSalvo, 2003, p. 2) or 2.6 million (Pochan, 1978, p. 10). However, according to DeSalvo (2003, p. 2), "recent quarry evidence indicates that there may only be about 750,000 blocks which weigh between ½ and 2 tons." Taseos (1990, p. 20) calculated that the Great Pyramid would be composed of 603,728 blocks if it were solid masonry, but subtracting his estimate of 13,016 blocks' worth of bedrock core in the center of the Great Pyramid, he concluded that the pyramid is composed of 590,712 blocks. Taseos, however, made very different assumptions about the sizes of the blocks relative to Petrie, for instance. On the other hand, using assumptions in the opposite direction, some researchers have estimated that there might be as many as 3.5 or 4 million blocks in the Great Pyramid (Moyer, 2003). In conversation with Zahi Hawass (Secretary General of the Supreme Council of Antiquities in Egypt and Director of the Giza Pyramids Excavation) on the Giza Plateau, December 5, 2003, he told me that a recent analysis estimated the number of blocks in the Great Pyramid to be 1.2 million.

Some authors have suggested that the Great Pyramid is not actually composed of blocks of stone per se but of blocks of concrete or a similar type of substance. Thus, back in 1877, James Bonwick (p. 9) wrote: "One reputed architect has informed the world that the whole was constructed of *pisé*. Water, by elaborate machinery, was led up to the required heights to mix with the sand, &c., to set in blocks of the needed size, and formed themselves tier by tier in the moulds." Originally writing in 1928, Manly P. Hall says: "The theory once advanced that both the

Pyramid and the Sphinx were built from artificial stones made on the spot has been abandoned" (Hall, 2003, p. 113). More recently, Joseph Davidovits (Davidovits and Morris, 1988) and Gadalla (2000) have promoted the idea that the Great Pyramid is composed of "synthetic stone" or "concrete." I have personally looked into to this issue firsthand, examining both the indisputably natural bedrock of the area and the stones of which the Great Pyramid is built, and I am convinced that the Great Pyramid is indeed composed of natural rock blocks that were quarried and set into place.

THE EXTERNAL CASING STONES

The interior or core of the Great Pyramid is composed of locally quarried limestone that varies in color and hardness, and in places contains abundant fossils of nummulites, reefal organisms, sea urchins, and other oceanic creatures, while the facing, or casing, was apparently composed of the finer and whiter Mokattam limestone (also known as Tura limestone; see Hawass, *Update to Petrie*, 1990, p. 105) quarried farther away on the other side of the Nile (Emery, 1960). Of the Mokattam limestone, Bonwick (1877, p. 16) writes: "The material came from the quarry of Mokattan [Mokattam, Mokhattam], beyond Cairo, and is commonly known as *swine-stone*, or *stink-stone*, from the odour proceeding from this marble [actually it is a limestone] when struck; but few fossils have been detected" (italics in the original). For a geological description of the Mokattam Formation and the layers above and below, see Said (1962, p. 136). Emery (1960) discusses the lithologies, weathering, and erosional features of the limestone rocks that compose the Great Pyramid. For a general modern description of the geology of the Giza Plateau, see Sampsell (2003, pp. 103–113). Granite used in the Great Pyramid and elsewhere on the Giza Plateau came from Aswan in southern (Upper) Egypt.

It is generally, if not universally, assumed that originally the Great Pyramid was completely covered with casing stones as finely worked, jointed, and polished as the few intact stones that were found at its base. Personally, I am not convinced that this is a valid assumption. It may well have been that the casing, while appearing finely worked from a distance, may not have been as carefully crafted high up on the completed pyramid where it could not be viewed close up. It has even been suggested that the majority of the Great Pyramid was never covered with any kind of actual casing, and smooth casing stones were placed just around the base to a certain (undetermined) height as a way of keeping people from attempting to climb the structure (see discussion in Bonwick, 1877, pp. 17–18).

Pochan (1978, pp. 219–223) contends that the casing stones of the Great Pyramid may originally (or at least at some point) have been painted red. He bases this contention primarily on chemical and spectrographic analyses of fragments of casing stone that apparently retained a reddish ochre-based paint on their external surfaces. I do not think it is inconceivable that at least some of the casing stones were painted at some point, perhaps even during a restoration of the Great Pyramid, but in my opinion Pochan has far from demonstrated that the pyramid was originally painted in its entirety. It should be noted, however, that Vyse (1840, 2:171; cited by Kingsland, 1935, p. 93), on the basis of some fragments of casing stone he found that appeared to be covered with red paint, also suggested that the Great Pyramid may have originally been painted red.

As to the incredible workmanship and tolerances exhibited by the casing stones, this is a matter that is taken on faith by many writers. Unfortunately, the few remaining casing stones *in situ* have suffered since the time they were uncovered in the 1830s by Howard Vyse's crew. Vyse commented on the magnificence of the finish of the casing stones, comparing it to modern (of course, early nineteenth-century) optical work (West, 1985, pp. 86–87).

It is worth quoting Petrie's (1883, p. 44) comments on the subject:

Several measures were taken of the thickness of the joints of the casing stones. The eastern joint of the northern casing stones is on the top .020, .002, .045 wide; and on the face .012, .022, .013, and .040 wide. The next joint is on the face .011 and .014 wide. Hence the mean thickness of the joints there is .020; and, therefore, the mean variation of the cutting of the stone from a straight line and from a true square, is but .01 on length of 75 inches up the face, an amount of accuracy equal to most modern opticians' straight-edges of such a length. These joints, with an area of some 35 square feet each, were not only worked as finely as this, but cemented throughout. Though the stones were brought as close as 1/500 inch, or, in fact, into contact, and the mean opening of the joint was but 1/50 inch, yet the builders managed to fill the joint with cement, despite the great area of it, and the weight of the stone to be moved—some 16 tons. To merely place such stones in exact contact at the sides would be careful work; but to do so with cement in the joint seems almost impossible.

EXTERNAL ORIENTATION AND LOCATION
OF THE GREAT PYRAMID

The Great Pyramid is located, along with two other major pyramids and another six smaller pyramids (three to the east of the Great Pyramid and three to the south of the Third, or Menkaure, Pyramid; these smaller pyramids are often referred to as Queen's Pyramids) on the Giza (Gizeh) Plateau on the west bank of the Nile outside of modern Cairo at the approximate apex of the Nile Delta. Also found on the Giza Plateau are the Great Sphinx, and a number of temples, tombs, boat pits, and other smaller structures.

Pochan (1978, p. 8) gives the geographic position of the Great Pyramid as:

Latitude 29°, 58', 51" North
Longitude 31°, 9' East

Pochan (1978, p. 8) says, without giving any references, that the previous determination was:

Latitude 29°, 59', 6" North
Longitude 31°, 7', 47" East

Smyth (1877, p. 70) gives the latitude of the Great Pyramid, according to his on-site measurements in 1865, as:

Latitude 29°, 58', 51" North

Gray (1953, pp. 114–115), basing his analysis on the work of Smyth, cites:

Latitude 29°, 58', 51" North
Longitude 31°, 9', 0" East

Schwaller de Lubicz (1961, p. 331) cites the astronomer Nouet as determining the Great Pyramid to be at:

Latitude 29°, 59', 48" North

The Cole Survey (1925) found the following orientations for the four sides and two diagonals of the Great Pyramid relative to true north (azimuths are read clockwise where true north is the 0° point).

SIDE	TRUE AZIMUTH		
North	89°	57'	32"
South	89°	58'	03"
East	359°	54'	30"
West	359°	57'	30"
N.E.–S.W.	44°	56'	45"
N.W.–S.E.	314°	57'	03"

Thus, we can see that the Great Pyramid overall is oriented very slightly west of the direction of true north (by the minuscule amount of about 3' 6" on average; see Pochan, 1978, p. 223). Petrie (1885, pp. 40–41) found this to be the case not only for the Great Pyramid and its passages but also for the Second Pyramid and its passages. To quote Petrie (1885, pp. 40–41) on this point:

The orientation of the Great Pyramid is about 4' West of North [Petrie's measurements differ slightly from the Cole Survey measurements, but the trend is the same]; a difference very perceptible [perceptible to Petrie at least; it is an incredibly small discrepancy for any building], and so much larger than the errors of setting out the form (which average 12"), that such a divergence might be wondered at. When, however, it is seen that the passage, which was probably set out by a different observation, nearly agrees in this divergence, it seems unlikely to be a mere mistake. And when, further, the Second Pyramid sides, and also its passages, all diverge similarly to the W. of North, the presumption of some change in the position of the North point itself, seems strongly indicated.

After discussing recorded changes in the precise position of the pole over the preceding century, Petrie speculates that such changes might be due to ocean currents, and finally concludes:

Thus the apparent change in the axis of rotation shown by the orientation of the Pyramids, is of the same order as a change actually observed. It is also far within the changes likely to be produced by known causes, and the uniform deviation is otherwise unaccountable in its origin. Hence it appears that it may legitimately be accepted as a determination of a factor which is of the highest interest, and which is most difficult to observe in any ordinary period. (Petrie, 1885, p. 42)

In an article published in *Science* in 1973, authored by G. S. Pawley of Edinburgh University, Scotland, and N. Abrahamsen of Aarhus University, Denmark (reprinted in Toth and Nielsen, 1985, pp. 59–63), it was tentatively suggested that at least part of the reason for the slight "misalignment" of the Great Pyramid from true north was not a builders' error, but might be due to continent drift (that is, plate tectonics).

BASALT PAVEMENT, TEMPLES, AND ENCLOSURE WALLS

On the east side of the Great Pyramid is found the remains of a basalt pavement, made from sawn and fitted basalt blocks that were laid upon a bed of limestone. According to Petrie (1885, p. 15), the north–south length of the basalt pavement is approximately 177 feet, and the east–west width was originally about 84 feet or more. This apparently formed the base or floor of the now destroyed Funerary Temple (also referred to as the Mortuary Temple) of King Khufu (see Hawass, *Update to Petrie*, 1990, p. 106).

Originally the complex of the Great Pyramid included the Funerary Temple on its east, which was connected by a causeway to the Valley Temple (Lower Temple) situated farther east, probably under what is now the modern village of Nazlet el-Samaan, which sits on the edge of the Giza Plateau (Hawass, *Update to Petrie*, 1990, p. 117). The Great Pyramid was surrounded on all four sides by two enclosure walls, referred to as *temenos* or *peribolus* walls (Hawass, 1990, p. 119). The inner wall was about 10.1 meters from the east, north, and south faces of the Great Pyramid, and about 10.5 meters from the west face; it was 3.25 to 3.6 meters thick (Hawass, 1990, p. 119). The outer wall, remains of which have been found on the north, south, and west sides of the Great Pyramid, was 7.6 to 8.75 meters thick, and was about 69.42 meters from the inner wall (Hawass, 1990, p. 119). Lehner (1997, pp. 108–109), in his text and reconstruction, mentions and illustrates only the inner enclosure wall.

BOAT PITS

Five boat pits have been found on the south and east sides and northeast corner of the Great Pyramid. The three on the east side were mapped by Lepsius in 1843 (Hawass, *Update to Petrie,* 1990, p. 111) and further studied by Petrie, who simply referred to them as trenches (Petrie, 1883, 1885). Two of these pits still contained funerary boats in modern times. In 1954 one of them was excavated, and the well-preserved remains of the cedar and acacia wood boat were rebuilt and housed in the Giza Boat Museum located alongside the Great Pyramid. This boat is 43.4 meters long by 5.9 meters wide in the beam (Hawass, 1990, p. 113). During excavation of this boat pit, cartouches of Djedefra, the son and immediate successor of Khufu, were found. The second pit, containing the apparently largely undisturbed remains of a boat, was inspected by video camera through a narrow drilled hole in 1987 but has not been excavated (Hawass, 1990, p. 112). These boats have been interpreted in different ways: as boats used during the pharaoh's lifetime for pilgrimages and various ceremonies; as boats to carry the deceased pharaoh to the cardinal points; or as boats that were used by the pharaoh and/or the god Ra to travel through the heavens, that is, so-called solar barques (Hawass, 1990, p. 115).

TRIAL PASSAGES NEAR THE GREAT PYRAMID

On the east side of the Great Pyramid, about 87.5 meters from the base (Hawass, *Update to Petrie,* 1990, p. 107), are a set of passages carved into the bedrock. These passages mimic in height, width, and orientation, but not in length, the Descending Passage, the Ascending Passage, the northern end of the Grand Gallery, and the beginning of the horizontal passage to the Queen's Chamber. There is also a vertical shaft that is basically the same size at the surface but does not extend to the same depth as the Well Shaft of the Great Pyramid. However, in contrast to the Great Pyramid, this vertical shaft extends down to the junction of the Descending and Ascending passages rather than extending down from the northern end of the Grand Gallery area (see Petrie, 1885, pl. 2).

Petrie (1883, 1885) considered these passages to be "trial passages" that acted as a model and practice for the construction of the actual passages of the Great Pyramid, an opinion that Hawass considers "most likely" (Hawass, 1990, p. 110). It has also been suggested that these passages may have been the substructure for a fourth Queen's Pyramid (in addition to the remains of the three so-called Queen's Pyramids still remaining east of the Great Pyramid), or it may have been a "satellite" or "ritual" pyramid for Khufu. Hawass (1990, p. 110) suggests that Khufu may not have even had a ritual pyramid, and he further points out that the function of so-called small ritual pyramids, when found with a larger pyramid, has been highly debated. Possible functions listed by Hawass (1990, p. 110) are: "symbolic burials of the king as ruler of Upper and Lower Egypt; tombs for the viscera; tombs for crowns; burials of placentas; burials for the king's ka; temporary storage of the body; solar symbols; and dummy tombs connected with the *Sed* festival" (italics in the original).

HEIGHTS OF THE SECOND AND THIRD PYRAMIDS ON THE GIZA PLATEAU

The second pyramid on the Giza Plateau, Khafre's (Khafra's or Chephren's) Pyramid, retains almost all of its apex and has a height of 471 feet (Lepre, 1990, p. 139; 472 feet ± 13 inches, according to Petrie, 1885, p. 32), a base length of 707 feet (Lepre, 1990, p. 139; mean of 706.24 feet, according to Petrie, 1885, p. 32), and a slope of 52° 20' (Lepre, 1990, p. 139) or a mean of 53° 10' ± 4' (Petrie, 1885, p. 32). The lowest course of casing stones, or possibly the two lowest, were of granite, while the remainder of the Second Pyramid was cased with Mokattam limestone (Petrie, 1885, p. 32). Given that the Great Pyramid lacks an apex, the Second Pyramid is currently taller than the Great Pyramid. Furthermore, the Second Pyramid's base is on higher ground than that of the Great Pyramid. Consequently, as seen today, the Second Pyramid is both taller than the Great Pyramid and reaches higher in the sky. When new, assuming that the Great Pyramid came to an apex, both the Great Pyramid and the Second Pyramid would have reached to approximately the same absolute altitude in the sky (see, for instance, measurements and diagrams in Vyse, 1840, 1842); or, in fact, the Second Pyramid may have been slightly higher. According to Vyse (and cited in Bonwick, 1877, p. 207), the base of the Second Pyramid is 33 feet and 2 inches above the base of the Great Pyramid. This means that, assuming the original height of the Great Pyramid was 481 feet, the Second Pyramid was about 10 feet shorter than the Great Pyramid, but since it was on an elevation of about 33 feet higher, it was actually about 23 feet higher than the Great Pyramid in absolute elevation.

The third pyramid on the Giza Plateau, Menkaure's (Menkara's, Mycerinus's) Pyramid, has a height of 218 feet (Lepre, 1990, p. 141; Petrie, 1885, p. 37, gives a height of 213.66 feet ± 15 inches), a base length of 356 feet (Lepre, 1990, p. 141; Petrie, 1885, p. 37, gives an average base length of 346.13 feet ± 3 inches), and a slope of 51° (Lepre, 1990, p. 141; Petrie, 1885, p. 37, gives 51° 0' ± 10'). The Third Pyramid was cased with granite on its lower parts (lower quarter? Petrie, 1885, p. 37, suggests that the granite casing only extended to the level of about 54 feet) and apparently with limestone above that, although it has also been suggested that it was originally to be cased entirely in granite (or possibly recased and restored in granite). The base of the Third Pyramid is set on even higher ground than that of the Second Pyramid (about 8 feet 5 inches higher; Bonwick, 1877, p. 207, citing Vyse), but it is much smaller overall.

PASSAGES AND CHAMBERS WITHIN
THE GREAT PYRAMID

In this section, some basic descriptions and comments on the various passages and chambers in the Great Pyramid are given. In the next section, basic measurements for these features are presented.

ENTRANCE

The Great Pyramid originally had a single entrance on the north, which occurs on the north face and slightly east of the middle of the pyramid (see hereafter for discussion of the eastern displacement of the passageways). Due to the loss of the external casing stones of the Great Pyramid, and probably the first few layers of the core stones in many areas, the floor of the remaining portion of the original entrance corresponds to the sixteenth layer of core masonry, but since the entrance passage is angled down toward the south, extending the passage up toward the north to find its original position would place the doorway as having come out at the nineteenth course (i.e., between the eighteenth and twentieth courses), according to Petrie (1885, pp. 16–17, pl. 7). Having established this position for the original entrance, Petrie calculated that the original entrance was approximately 668 inches above the pavement of the Great Pyramid, about 524 inches horizontally south of the north edge of the pyramid's casing, and its middle was 287 inches east of the center of the north face (Petrie, 1885, p. 17). As seen today with the outer casing stones removed, the original entrance has over it a huge gable made of massive limestone blocks.

Petrie (1885, pp. 72–73) argued that the Great Pyramid must originally have had a moveable stone flap door that pivoted out and up. He quotes Strabo as saying: "The Greater (Pyramid), a little way up one side, has a stone that may be taken out, which being raised up, there is a sloping passage to the foundations" (Petrie, 1885, p. 72). Petrie also points out that an Arab manuscript, written a couple of decades after Al Mamun (early ninth century A.D.) had forced his way into the Great Pyramid and thereby found the original entrance via entering the Descending Passage and working back to the original entrance, mentions a door.

From the original entrance one enters the Descending Passage.

DESCENDING PASSAGE

The Descending Passage extends for approximately 350 feet from the original entrance of the Great Pyramid to the Subterranean Chamber (the upper portion is through the masonry of the pyramid and the lower portion cut through the bedrock; Kingsland, 1932, p. 60, says that the bedrock is entered at a distance of approximately 1,350 inches, presumably measured from the position of the original entrance). This passage is remarkable in both its close orientation to true north and in its straightness and consistent angle of descent. Petrie (1885, p. 19) found that the mean axis of the entire length of the Descending Passage is west of true north by a mere 3' 44" ± 10", which is incredibly close to Petrie's (1885, p. 11) calculation of

The original entrance (top center) and the forced entrance made by Al Mamun (lower right) on the north face of the Great Pyramid. Photograph courtesy of Robert M. Schoch.

the average (mean) azimuth of the sides of the Great Pyramid at the base of the casing, namely 3' 43" ± 12". This is compatible with the concept that the Descending Passage was laid out first and then used to orient the entire Great Pyramid. Pochan (1978, p. 229) asserts that, "the Pyramid's entire interior layout was linked to the *impeccable* placement of the Descending Passage on a plane *strictly* parallel to the Pyramid's meridian plane" (italics in the original). Note that Petrie's azimuths for the overall orientation of the Great Pyramid differ slightly from those of the Cole Survey (1925). According to the Cole Survey, the Great Pyramid is oriented even closer to true north than Petrie's measurements indicate; the Cole Survey did not measure the azimuth of the Descending Passage, but on the basis of the consistency between the Petrie and Cole measurements, indications are that if the Cole Survey had dealt with the Descending Passage, it too would have found its azimuth to be approximately the same as the average azimuths for the sides of the Great Pyramid.

Petrie (1885, p. 19) found the angle of descent of the Descending Passage to be 26° 31' 23" ± 5"? (question mark in Petrie), and he noted: "The average error of straightness in the built part of the passage is only $\frac{1}{50}$ inch, an amazingly minute amount in a length of 150 feet. Including the whole passage the error is under $\frac{1}{4}$ inch in the sides, and $\frac{3}{10}$ on the roof, in the whole length of 350 feet, partly built, partly cut in the rock." Kingsland (1932, p. 52) calculated the mean angle for the Descending Passage as 26° 13' 37.4", trigonometrically based on his best estimates of the horizontal and sloping lengths of the Descending Passage, and the vertical distance between the entrance level and the level of the bottom of the passage. These measurements and calculations of the angle directly contradict Pochan (1978, p. 229) where he says: "constructing a slope gauge for digging the Descending Passage posed no problem (because its angle, 26° 34', corresponds to cotangent 2)." In fact, this is not the case; rather, the slope "is just slightly less than one in two" (Kingsland, 1932, p. 60) and not as simple to gauge as Pochan and some other researchers have suggested. This lends further credence to the idea that it was laid out astronomically by sighting on a star, as advocated by Proctor (1880, 1883). Note, too, that in order to measure the azimuths precisely, both Petrie and the Cole Survey made observations on the stars, in particular Polaris at elongation (the star closest to the north celestial pole in our own epoch).

The Descending Passage ends at a relatively short Horizontal Passage that leads to the Subterranean Chamber. About 20 feet from the point where the Descending Passage joins with the Horizontal Passage, a recess, or niche, opens on the western side for about 6 feet. Beyond the niche, it is about another 4 feet to the Subterranean Chamber.

About 25 feet from the end of the Descending Passage, on the western side, is a rough cavity that penetrates about 6 feet into the rock and then rises at a steep angle of about 63°; this is the bottom of the Well Shaft (Kingsland, 1932, p. 62). It should also be noted that the Descending Passage cuts through a couple of natural fissures or faults in the bedrock.

ASCENDING PASSAGE

The Ascending Passage commences from the Descending Passage at a distance of about 1,110 inches from the original entrance (Kingsland, 1932, p. 64). Petrie (1885, p. 22, apparently on the basis of Smyth's measurements; see Smyth, 1867) gives the angle of ascent of the Ascending Passage as 26° 2' 30", whereas Kingsland (1932, p. 49) calculated it trigonometrically as 26° 5' 0.2". These values are very close to the angle of the Descending Passage. Various authors, such as Edgar and Edgar (1910, 1923) and Davidson and Aldersmith (1924) have simply assumed that the Descending and Ascending passages have, or should have (that is, were designed to have), the same values, which Morton Edgar assumed was 26° 18' 9.7", and David Davidson assumed was 26° 18' 9.63" (see Kingsland, 1932, pp. 48–49).

Petrie attempted to determine the azimuth of the Ascending Passage but was frustrated that he could not measure it as accurately as he desired. Still, he concluded that the orientation of the Ascending Passages is very close to a true north–south line, just as are the sides of the Great Pyramid. In Petrie's own words (1885, p. 22):

> The determination of the azimuth has, unhappily, a large probable error, ±3' (owing to bad foundation for the theodolite in Mamun's Hole); and its direction –4' [that is, 4' west of true north], is so close to that of the Pyramid side, that it may be assumed parallel to that ±3'. This, on the passage length, = 1.2 inches for the probable error of the place of the upper end of the passage, in E. to W. direction in the Pyramid.

The cavity or tunnel of Al Mamun (discussed hereafter) opens to the base or north end of the Ascending Passage, and the way tourists and others currently enter the Great Pyramid today is through Al Mamun's tunnel to the general juncture where it meets the Ascending and Descending passages.

The workmanship exhibited in the Ascending Passage is of a very high quality, and not only is it composed of joined stones, as are all the other passages, but also it penetrates directly through three large stone blocks, which have come to be referred to as "Girdle Stones." In addition, along the walls of this passage are some stones that have been inset; it has been suggested that these inset stones are filling holes that were originally cut to hold beams or levers when the pyramid was actively used (see Kingsland, 1932, p. 70). The Ascending Passage ends at the lower (northern) end of the Grand Gallery.

GRANITE PLUGS IN THE ASCENDING PASSAGE

It has been suggested, and is still sometimes asserted, that all or the majority of passages in the Great Pyramid were plugged with stone blocks and possibly other materials after completion and interment of the body of the pharaoh (assuming the tomb theory). Concerning this theory, Petrie, who knew the Great Pyramid as well as almost anyone, having studied it carefully in the early 1880s prior to modern "cleaning and refurbishing," wrote:

> A theory which has obtained much belief, is that of the passages of each pyramid having been plugged up after the interment of the builder. But there is no evidence for this, and the passages of the pyramids show no trace of continuous plugging; nor indeed any plugging beyond the closing of the mouths of some passages, merely to prevent their being detected; on the contrary, there are incidental proofs, in the mortaring, etc., that no general plugging was ever introduced or extracted. (1885, p. 71)

Far from the Great Pyramid always being sealed up after the time of its presumed use for the burial of Khufu, Petrie even suggested that there may have always been a way, perhaps held as a secret by only a select few, for the ancient Egyptians to access the upper chambers, including the King's Chamber. When he studied the interior of the Great Pyramid in the early 1880s, Petrie (1883, p. 84) found that the coffer in the King's Chamber was tilted up at its southern end and resting on a "large pebble" of flint. On the basis of this observation, Petrie concluded:

> The flint pebble that had been put under the coffer is important. If any person wished at present to prop the coffer up, there are multitudes of stone chips in the Pyramid ready to hand. Therefore fetching a pebble from the outside seems to show that the coffer was first lifted at a time when no breakages had been made in the Pyramid, and there were no chips lying about. This suggests that there was some means of access to the upper chambers, which was always available by removing

loose blocks without any forcing. If the stones at the top of the shaft leading from the subterranean part to the gallery had been cemented in place, they must have been smashed to break through them, or if there were granite portcullises in the Antechamber, they must also have been destroyed; and it is not likely that any person would take the trouble to fetch a large flint pebble into the innermost part of the Pyramid, if there were stone chips lying in his path. (1883, p. 85; see also Petrie, 1885, p. 30)

As opposed to general wholesale plugging of the passages of the Great Pyramid, there were two places in particular where some plugging or barriers were used: the base (northern end) of the Ascending Passage was plugged with large granite blocks, and the entrance or Antechamber to the King's Chamber apparently contained a portcullis system of sealing the passage (discussed hereafter).

The northern portion, or lower end, of the Ascending Passage is blocked by three large granite "plugs" that together fill about 15½ feet of the passage. These granite plugs are very slightly wedge shaped, and the bottom of the Ascending Passage was formed the same way so that they would tightly fit but not slip any further. Today the end of the lowest granite plug can be seen in the roof of the Descending Passage, but originally a limestone block concealed it, so that when one passed down the Descending Passage one would never suspect the presence of the blocked Ascending Passage. According to tradition, this concealing limestone block was dislodged by the work of Al Mamun's men in the ninth century, they heard it fall, and then tunneled in the direction of the sound to ultimately discover the Descending and Ascending Passages. Some authors have suggested that more than three plug blocks originally blocked the Ascending Passage (see for instance Grinsell, 1947, p. 104 illus.), but others disagree (see Kingsland, 1932, p. 65).

GRAND GALLERY

The Grand Gallery continues upward at approximately the same angle as the Ascending Passage, but according to various measurements and calculations, the angle is very slightly greater than that of the Ascending Passage. Kingsland (1932, p. 49) quotes an angle of 26° 16' 40" from Petrie for the Grand Gallery (erratam sheet for Kingsland, 1932, p. 49, included in Kingsland, 1935), while Kingsland (1932, p. 49) calculates an angle of 26° 16' 43" for the Grand Gallery. According to Kingsland's calculations (1932, p. 49), the average value of the angle for the Ascending Passage and the Grand Gallery is 26° 11' 19.8", which is very close indeed to his calculated value of 26° 13' 37.4" for the Descending Passage.

The Grand Gallery is a magnificent hall, approximately 157 feet long and 28 feet high. At the base (northern end) is a horizontal passage leading to the Queen's Chamber, and at the top (southern end) is the so-called Giant Step, or Step, and then a horizontal passage leading to and through the Antechamber to the King's Chamber. Above the walls per se, making up the rest of the side walls and ceiling, are seven overlapping courses of stones that cause the Gallery to become narrower toward the ceiling. Just above the third overlap (about 5½ inches above the overlap) there is a groove about 6 inches wide and ¾ inch deep that runs the length of the Gallery. The uppermost course has ratchet teeth-like features that keep the slabs of stone that span the ceiling from sliding downhill. Kingsland (1932, p. 71) says there are 40 roofing stones in the Grand Gallery.

The actual floor of the Grand Gallery is as narrow as the roof, being about 41 inches wide, as there are two stone "ramps" or ledges on either side. The ramp or ledge on each side is about 20 or 21 inches wide, and they are about 23.5 inches high on average. Along each ramp is a series of 27 holes, or excavations (Kingsland, 1932, p. 72; Pochan, 1978, p. 30, gives the number as 28, and in fact it is difficult to determine, as some have possibly been obliterated, especially toward the lower, northern, end), occurring in pairs on either side, and alternating between longer ones of about 23.3 inches and shorter ones of about 20.5 inches. They are about 6¼ inches wide and cut to varying depths, usually 8 to 11 inches. In the walls above these holes are vertically arranged inset stones, each about 18 inches high and 13 inches wide, with a groove cut across each. The function of these ramps and slots or holes is enigmatic. Following Proctor (1883), if the Grand Gallery served as an astronomical observatory prior to being closed off, these slots might have been used to position benches and/or possibly a sort of viewing grid. Some Egyptologists have suggested that the slots were for the support of scaffolding and a platform that held plugging blocks up and back. Pochan (1978, p. 30) suggests that the Grand Gallery was a hall holding statues positioned at each slot, and specifically he thinks they were statues of Khufu's ancestors.

At the top (northern end) of the Grand Gallery is the Great or Giant Step, beyond which is the passage to the Antechamber, and then the King's Chamber.

ANTECHAMBER

From the step at the top (northern end) of the Grand Gallery there is a very short passage (a mere 52 inches) that leads to a small room known as the Antechamber.

The floor and ceiling of the Antechamber is composed of granite, as is the majority of the southern wall (a small portion at the top of this wall is composed of limestone), whereas the northern wall is solely of limestone. Thus the Antechamber marks the transition from the use of limestone for the Grand Gallery and majority of the pyramid to the use of granite for the King's Chamber.

The eastern and western sides of the Antechamber have a peculiar granite wainscoting that does not rise all the way to the ceiling. On each side this wainscoting has three vertical grooves (16¾ inches to 21½ inches wide and carved about 3¼ inches deep, while the vertical ridges, or pilasters, separating the grooves are about 5 inches wide; Kingsland, 1932, pp. 82–83), and north of these grooves is another set of similar grooves containing a "granite leaf" set in the grooves and suspended (this pair of grooves does not reach the floor) such that it does not reach the floor and can easily be passed under. The granite leaf is in two parts, a lower portion that contains a "boss" on its northern face and an upper portion that is broken at the top. The boss is a rough protrusion, rather semicircular in shape and about 5 inches long and wide, and raised from the surface of the granite about an inch. It is located approximately in the middle of the leaf horizontally, and about 5 inches above the lower edge of the leaf. In the nineteenth century, some pyramidists who accepted the concept of the "Pyramid Inch" believed this boss could be used as a standard of measure for the Pyramid Inch (see discussion in Kingsland, 1932, p. 82).

Returning to the wainscoting on either side of the Antechamber, it is not symmetrical. The eastern wall wainscoting is straight across the top, while the western wall wainscoting rises slightly higher than that of the eastern wall and contains semicircular cutouts, or hollows, above each of the three grooves beyond the first that holds the granite leaf. Above the wainscoting the side walls of the Antechamber recede, making the ceiling wider than the floor. The southern wall of the Antechamber has four vertical grooves, about 3.75 to 4.5 inches wide and 1.75 to 2.8 inches deep, carved into it (Kingsland, 1932, p. 82).

The function of these grooves in the Antechamber, and the purpose of the Antechamber itself, has been the subject of debate. The classical Egyptological view is that the grooves in the wainscoting held some sort of system of leaves (presumably of granite) that acted as a portcullis, in that they could be lowered or dropped once the mummy of the deceased pharaoh was safely placed in the coffer (sarcophagus) in the King's Chamber. Dunn (1998; see also Dunn, 2003, pp. 185–208) suggests that the eastern and western grooves in the Antechamber may have supported a system of cams and baffles that served as an adjustable acoustic filter for sound entering the King's Chamber (see hereafter for brief comments on Dunn's power plant theory of the Great Pyramid).

On the western wall of the Antechamber there is an excavation that was carried out by Caviglia in the early nineteenth century as he was searching for additional chambers in the Great Pyramid (Kingsland, 1932, p. 84).

KING'S CHAMBER

Leaving the Antechamber and passing through another narrow passage heading south, after traveling just 8½ feet, one enters the King's Chamber. One enters the King's Chamber from the northeast corner, and immediately sees that the long direction of the room stretches to the west. This room has become known as the King's Chamber simply because it has a flat ceiling. The custom among the Arabs was to bury men in tombs with flat ceilings and women in tombs with gabled ceilings (Tompkins, 1971, p. 11).

The King's Chamber is located at the fiftieth course of masonry, about 150 feet above the ground, and measures approximately 34 feet east to west and 17 feet north to south and is 19 feet high (Edgar and Edgar, 1923, p. 73). The floor, walls, and ceiling are completely lined with granite; the four walls are composed of 100 granite blocks in five courses, and the ceiling is composed of nine gigantic granite beams—the largest and heaviest known stone in the pyramid is one of them, measuring about 27 feet long by 5 feet by 7 feet, with an estimated weight of about 70 tons (Edgar and Edgar, 1923, p. 73).

The King's Chamber has been damaged. The floor has settled or inclined toward the southwest corner, and the granite ceiling beams are broken near the southern side, as are also various beams in the overlying Relieving Chambers (Edgar and Edgar, 1923, pp. 77–78; see hereafter for a description of these chambers). The base of the granite walls extends about 5 inches below the plane of the floor (see Smyth, 1877, p. 14). Explanations for this damage range from immediate settling during building that cracked the beams, settling of the structure over time, earthquake damage (for instance, a severe earthquake is reported as having occurred in 908 A.D.; some think it not only caused the damage to the King's Chamber and chambers above but also damaged the outer casing stones, making it easier for the medieval Arab Egyptians to strip them off and use them in building; Edgar and Edgar, 1923, p. 51), or an explosion in the King's Chamber during ancient times (Mehler, 2003, pp. 329–337).

The granite coffer, or sarcophagus, is currently located at the western end of the chamber, and its long axis is aligned approximately north–south. The coffer is lidless, but it was apparently designed to have a sliding lid that could be pinned in place; the remains of the lip for the lid and holes for the pins to be dropped into can still be observed. Dimensions of the granite coffer are given hereafter.

The north and south walls of the King's Chamber have shafts, or "airshafts" or "air channels" or "star shafts" (depending on one's interpretation), that lead to the exterior of the pyramid, at an upward angle. Unlike the shafts from the Queen's Chamber, there is no evidence that the interior ends of the shafts in the King's Chamber were ever blocked, and they also open to the exterior of the pyramid. The channels are 8 or 9 inches square. Petrie estimated the angle for the southern shaft at 44° 30′ 00″, whereas more modern measurements by Rudolf Gantenbrink place it at 45° 00′ 00″, and likewise Petrie estimated the angle of the northern shaft at 31° 00′ 00″, whereas Gantenbrink has placed it at 32° 28′ 00″. (Measurements reported in Bauval and Gilbert, 1994, p. 172; I believe these authors are being overly precise in their reporting of these angles. Petrie, 1885, p. 29, says: "The air channels leading from this chamber were measured on the outside of the Pyramid; the N. one varies from 30° 43′ to 32° 4′, in the outer 30 feet; and the S. one from 44° 26′ to 45° 30′, in the outer 70 feet.") These angles suggest to Robert Bauval that in the twenty-fifth century B.C., the southern shaft pointed to the star Al Nitak (Zeta Orionis) in the belt of the constellation of Orion, and the northern shaft pointed to Alpha Draconis (Thuban) in the constellation of Draco (Bauval and Gilbert, 1994, pp. 172–174). Note that the lower portion of the northern shaft has kinks in it at its base as it goes around the Grand Gallery (Bauval and Gilbert, 1994, p. 209, fig. 20).

RELIEVING CHAMBERS

Above the King's Chamber are five chambers or spaces that are often variously referred to as Relieving Chambers (after the idea that they serve the function of relieving the stress of the great weight over the King's Chamber) or Chambers of Construction. As far as can be determined, they were never meant to be entered once the Great Pyramid was completed, and indeed the top four were completely sealed up until they were opened by force in the early nineteenth century. Within these chambers are rough hieroglyphic inscriptions, including some cartouches, daubed on with a red paint (see the section entitled "Inscriptions on and within the Great Pyramid"), as well as various straight horizontal and vertical lines in red and black paint, apparently the remains of markings used by the quarrymen and builders in cutting, trimming, and arranging the blocks.

The floors of all of these chambers are composed of immense granite beams running north and south that form the smooth ceilings of the chambers below. The "floor" of each Relieving Chamber is rough and irregular, with some of the granite beams being considerably higher than the others. In the lower three chambers, the northern and southern side walls are also composed of granite, whereas they are limestone in the uppermost two chambers. The eastern and western ends are of limestone, and the gabled roof of the uppermost chamber is limestone.

The lowest of the Relieving Chambers was discovered and explored by Nathaniel Davison, British consul at Algiers, in 1765 (Kingsland, 1932, p. 97; DeSalvo, 2003, p. 42). Davison noticed a rectangular hole (about 28 inches wide by 32 inches high; dimensions from Kingsland, 1932) at the top of the southeastern corner of the Grand Gallery and arranged for a ladder to be erected so that he could climb up to it and explore. The hole (apparently formed by the removal of one entire stone in the Grand Gallery wall; Edgar and Edgar, 1923, p. 73) was the opening of a passage, much obstructed with dirt and bat dung, but Davison crawled into and along the passage for some 20 to 25 feet until he discovered the opening to the lowest Relieving Chamber, since then named Davison's Chamber in his honor. In the early nineteenth century, Caviglia is reported to have cleaned out Davison's Chamber and used it as a place to live while exploring the Great Pyramid. Today there is an inscription in Davison's Chamber that reads "1915 / 1st / AUSTRALIAN.-EXP. FORCE / CHAMBER."

In 1837 Howard Vyse made a complete examination of Davison's Chamber and, on the basis at least in part of the notion that there might be a concealed sepulchral chamber above (Kingsland, 1932, p. 97), excavated upward from the passage that Davison had found, through the masonry on the east side, and discovered the four remaining Relieving Chambers. On entering the highest chamber and observing the gabled ceiling of limestone rather than a flat ceiling of granite, presumably Vyse understood that this must be the last chamber. As Vyse discovered each chamber, they were named in honor of different people, and the names of the chambers were neatly painted in black letters inside each chamber. The chamber immediately above Davison's Chamber was thus christened Wellington's Chamber, followed by Nelson's Chamber, Lady Arbuthnot's Chamber, and finally Campbell's Chamber.

In their study of the Great Pyramid, the Edgar brothers (Edgar and Edgar,

1910) were initially unable to enter the Relieving Chambers. It was not until 1912 that Morton Edgar first visited their interiors, reporting that the distance from the floor of one chamber to the floor of the next above is on average 10 feet (Edgar and Edgar, 1923, p. 75 n.), and on the basis of Vyse, Morton Edgar says that the apex of the gabled roof of Campbell's Chamber is about 70 feet above the floor of the King's Chamber (Edgar and Edgar, 1923, p. 77).

QUEEN'S CHAMBER

Returning to the base (north end) of the Grand Gallery, one can follow a narrow passage for about 127 feet to the Queen's Chamber, located at the twenty-fifth course of masonry. The northern end of the Ascending Passage and the lower end (northern end) of the floor of the Grand Gallery are both cut down slightly, and there are holes in the side walls as one enters toward the horizontal passage to the Queen's Chamber. All of these features seem to indicate that originally there were cross-beams (composed of stone?) in the holes in the walls that supported stone slabs, which covered over and concealed the entrance to the horizontal passage to the Queen's Chamber. No remains of these slabs or cross-beams remain today. About 109 feet into the passage (heading south), there is a step down such that it is easier to stand. The passage leads into the northeast corner of the Queen's Chamber.

This room has become known as the Queen's Chamber simply because it has a gabled ceiling, and the custom among the Arabs was to bury men in tombs with flat ceilings and women in tombs with gabled ceilings (Tompkins, 1971, p. 11).

The Queen's Chamber is composed completely of limestone. The walls are relatively smooth and finished, but the floor is rather rough. The principle feature of this room is the niche or recess in the eastern wall. The center of the niche is about 25.19 inches south of the midline of the eastern wall (Kingsland, 1932, p. 77), and it is a little more than 15 feet high. The back of the niche shows evidence of excavation, presumably by hunters of more unknown chambers. The niche narrows toward the top with four overlaps before reaching its top, similar to the seven overlaps in the Grand Gallery. The floor of the Queen's Chamber is very rough, and there may have been a fine stone floor once in the chamber that has been removed, or perhaps was never put into place (see Petrie, 1883, p. 215).

Interesting features of the Queen's Chamber are the shafts, similar to the shafts of the King's Chamber, that occur on the north and south walls. These shafts

The east wall of the Queen's Chamber, showing the niche. Photograph courtesy of Robert M. Schoch.

were unknown until 1872, when Waynman Dixon was in the Queen's Chamber and noticed a crack in the south wall through which he could push a long piece of wire. Wondering what could be there, he had the stone broken away and discovered, concealed behind 5 inches of exterior stonework, a shaft measuring about 8 to 8.5 inches square, similar to that in the King's Chamber. Dixon next explored the north wall in the corresponding spot and discovered a similar northern shaft (Kingsland, 1932, p. 79; DeSalvo, 2003, p. 48). As far as is known, these shafts from the Queen's Chamber are not, unlike those of the King's Chamber, open to the exterior of the Great Pyramid. In fact, Gantenbrink found a "door" sealing the southern shaft (see hereafter). Petrie found the southern shaft of the Queen's Chamber to be at an angle of 38° 28' 00", whereas Gantenbrink found it to be 39° 30' 00" (values given in Bauval and Gilbert, 1994, p. 172; these authors may be overly precise in their reporting of these angles; Petrie, 1885, p. 24, gives a range of 38° 20' to 38° 35', with a mean of 38° 28'). Petrie (1885, p. 24) gives a mean value of 37° 28' (range of 37° 25' to 37° 33') for the northern shaft of the Queen's Chamber, whereas according to Bauval (Bauval and Gilbert, 1994, p. 173), Gantenbrink thought it might be closer to 39°. Bauval suggests that the southern shaft of the Queen's Chamber pointed to Sirius in the late twenty-fifth century B.C., whereas the northern shaft pointed to the center of the four stars forming the "head" in the constellation Ursa Minor at approximately the same epoch (Bauval and Gilbert, 1994, pp. 172–173). Note that the lower portion of the northern shaft has kinks in it at its base as it goes around the Grand Gallery (Bauval and Gilbert, 1994, p. 209, fig. 20).

Concerning the original use and contents of the so-called Queen's Chamber, Petrie (1883, pp. 216–217) writes:

It may be an open question whether the Queen's Chamber was not the sepulchre of Khnumu-Khufu, the co-regent of Khufu. Edrisi, in his accurate and observant account of the Pyramid (1236 A.D.), mentions an empty vessel in the Queen's Chamber; and that this was not a confused notion of the coffer now known, is proved by his saying that in the King's Chamber 'an empty vessel is seen here similar to the former.' Whether any fragments of a coffer remained there, among the great quantity of stone excavated from the floor and niche, it is almost hopeless to inquire, since that rubbish is now all shot away into various holes and spaces. Caviglia, however, did not find a coffer when clearing the chamber, but fragments might have been easily over-looked.

Pochan (1978) considers the Queen's Chamber to be the Great Pyramid's serdab, a secret room where the king's double was placed. This consisted of a statue (perhaps basalt or diorite) that was believed to be brought to life by the ritual of the opening of the mouth and eyes. K. P. Johnson (1998, 1999) believes that a pendulum "clock" was located in the niche of the Queen's Chamber and used in conjunction with astronomical observations of the skies.

SUBTERRANEAN CHAMBER

Following the Descending Passage below its junction with the Ascending Passage, we then come to the horizontal passage at the bottom. Passing through the horizontal passage past the recess (described earlier with the description of the Descending Passage), we enter the Subterranean Chamber from the northeast corner. Overall this is a large room, extending approximately 46 feet east–west and 27 feet north–south, very roughly hewn out of the bedrock limestone upon with the Great Pyramid sits. Across from the entrance to the Subterranean Chamber (sometimes known as the Pit), in the southeast corner, is a small passage (just over 2 feet high and 2 feet wide) that heads south for about 53½ feet and then just ends; accordingly, this is often referred to as the Blind Passage.

The Subterranean Chamber is about 100 feet below the level of the platform of the Great Pyramid, and approximately under the apex. The Subterranean Chamber is often referred to as "unfinished" or "partially excavated," and indeed it gives that appearance. Whereas the roof is relatively consistent (though very rough), the floor is incredibly inconsistent. At the western end, it is within 5½ feet of the roof, whereas on the eastern end, the floor is much lower, up to 16½ feet from the roof. In the approximate center of the eastern end of the Subterranean Chamber there is a vertical shaft in the floor. According to Kingsland (1932, pp. 63–64), the original depth of this shaft was about 5 feet, but Caviglia excavated in this area in 1817 to a depth of 10 feet, and then in the 1830s Vyse excavated down to a depth of 38 feet, searching for any unknown chambers, possibly the final resting site of Khufu on an island surrounded by water from the Nile as Herodotus described.

WELL SHAFT AND GROTTO

The so-called Well Shaft extends from the northwest corner (lower end) of the Grand Gallery nearly vertically down to the Grotto (an enlargement of the shaft or chamber at approximately the upper level of the bedrock under/within the Great Pyramid), and from the Grotto, the lower end of the Well Shaft extends down to and intersects with the western side of the Descending Passage toward the southern (lower) end of the Descending Passage.

The upper portion of the Well Shaft, as it originates at the base of the Grand Gallery, has been known at least since the ninth century A.D., when Al Mamun's men may have explored it. One Arab tradition (Kingsland, 1932, p. 73) is that a man fell down it and took three hours to reach the bottom! In the early nineteenth century, Caviglia attempted to explore the upper portion of the Shaft by clearing it of accumulated debris and descending down it using a rope, but he found the passage blocked by large stones. In 1817 Caviglia was working on clearing out the Descending Passage of debris and discovered the lower portion of the Well Shaft. He was then able to clear out the entire Well Shaft, starting from below, and make his way through it.

The Grotto may have been basically a natural feature, namely a fissure or cavity in the bedrock at or near the original surface of the plateau, and it was possibly packed with stones, sand, and gravel before building the Great Pyramid over it (see Kingsland, 1932, p. 74, and the photographs of the Grotto in Edgar and Edgar, 1910, 1923). The upper part of the Well Shaft, from the Grotto to the Grand Gallery, runs through the pyramid's masonry. The uppermost vertical 25 feet or so of the Well Shaft is sometimes reported to be very regular, leading some to believe that at least this portion was planned and built into the pyramid originally, whereas the lower portion down to the Grotto is more irregular and may have been cut through the masonry after it was in place (Kingsland, 1932, p. 74). Petrie believed that the Well Shaft was cut after the masonry through which it passes, writing:

> The shaft, or "well," leading from the N. end of the gallery down to the subter-
> ranean parts, was either not contemplated at first, or else was forgotten in the course

of building; the proof of this is that it has been cut through the masonry after the courses were completed. On examining the shaft, it is found to be irregularly tortuous through the masonry, and without any arrangement of the blocks to suit it; while in more than one place a corner of a block may be seen left in the irregular curved side of the shaft, all the rest of the block having disappeared in cutting the shaft. This is a conclusive point, since it would never have been so built at first. A similar feature is at the mouth of the passage, in the gallery. Here the sides of the mouth are very well cut, quite as good work as the dressing of the gallery walls; but on the S. side there is a vertical joint in the gallery side, only 5.3 inches from the mouth. Now, great care is always taken in the Pyramid to put large stones at a corner, and it is quite inconceivable that a Pyramid builder would put a mere slip 5.3 thick beside the opening to a passage. It evidently shows that the passage mouth was cut out after the building was finished in that part. It is clear, then, that the whole of this shaft is an additional feature to the first plan. (1883, pp. 214–215)

The portion of the Well Shaft from the Grotto to the Descending Passage is cut through the bedrock.

There is no universal consensus as to when the Well Shaft and Grotto were constructed, or what their purpose(s) were. One standard story, which was advocated by Smyth and Petrie, for instance (see also Hall, 2003, p. 112), is that the Well Shaft was a means for the workers to escape after they had blocked the Ascending Passage just below the lower end of the Grand Gallery with the granite plugs. Presumably they then retired down the Well Shaft, and the last person out dropped a block of limestone into place above his or her head to seal the upper entrance to the Well Shaft. The workers made their way down the Well Shaft to the Descending Passage, and came back up the Descending Passage and exited the pyramid through the entrance. Was the lower end of the Well Shaft also somehow blocked or sealed to prevent marauders from entering the Grand Gallery by the same means that the workers left, or was it thought that the steepness of the Well Shaft would preclude anyone from successfully making their way up it? It has been suggested that later pyramid robbers, to enter the upper chambers of the Great Pyramid, used this very "escape route." Alternatively, Hall (2003, p. 112) cites a Mr. Dupré who believed that the Well Shaft from the Descending Passage to the Grand Gallery was itself cut out by robbers (at an unknown date, but prior to Al Mamun's entry in the early ninth century A.D.), who first successfully entered the upper chambers when only the Descending Passage and Subterranean Chamber were known and open for entry; Hall (2003, p. 112) gives his opinion that "it is improbable that they [the robbers] used the descending passageway," although he does not explain how they would have entered the Subterranean Chamber otherwise (presumably through another, yet undiscovered, passageway?).

Davidson and Aldersmith (1924, and n.d., pp. 161–165) believe that the Well Shaft and Grotto were not original to the Great Pyramid but do date back to ancient times. According to these authors, the Great Pyramid suffered from subsidence and possible earthquake damage "not long after it was built, possibly within a few generations from the time of its construction, and certainly before precise details and measurements of its internal construction were lost or forgotten" (Davidson and Aldersmith, n.d., p. 161). In order to inspect the interior of the Great Pyramid to see what, if any, damage had occurred, according to Davidson and Aldersmith, the "keepers of the Pyramid" entered the original entrance, descended almost to the Subterranean Chamber, and then cut the Well Shaft from the bottom up to the lower end of the Grand Gallery in order to access the interior chambers. The reason they began so low in the Descending Passage was due to their desire to intersect and inspect two natural fissures in the rock before reaching the Grotto. Davidson and Aldersmith contend that the final stone to be removed in the Grand Gallery was forced up and out.

Pochan (1978, pp. 229–230) believes that the lower portion of the Well Shaft, up to the top of the bedrock, was excavated contemporaneously with the Descending Passage and the Subterranean Chamber. In his view, this portion of the Well Shaft was simply a means "to ensure that descending workers would not interfere with their fellow workers climbing back up the Descending Passage, bearing stone-cutting debris."

The top of the Well Shaft is currently (observation made in May 2004) covered with a cage and grate by the Egyptian authorities, who were hesitant to even allow me to photograph it from a distance. The site where the lower part of the Well Shaft intersects the descending passage, on the west side of the Descending Passage wall, is currently (observation made in May 2004) covered over by the Egyptian authorities, with plywood and other materials.

FORCED ENTRANCE AND PASSAGE

Today there are two entrances to the Great Pyramid: the original entrance just described and a forced entrance and tunnel that enters the pyramid on the north face at a level below and to the west of the original entrance. Most researchers ascribe this passage to Abdullah al Mamun (also known as simply Al Mamun, Al Mamoun, or Al Mamoon, entered the pyramid c. 810–830 A.D.); however, Pochan (1971; 1978, p. 4) contends that this is an old tunnel dating from the Seventh to Ninth Dynasty that was plugged up under Ramesses II and only reopened by Al Mamun's men in the early ninth century A.D. According to Pochan (1978, p. 130, footnote number 40), "'Al Mamun's' hole was not cleared until 1917. The members of the Commission d'Egypt Expedition [the French expedition under Napoleon, 1799–1801] were unaware of its existence."

Today there is a large gash on the southern side of the Great Pyramid where Howard Vyse in 1837 attempted to either force another entrance into the Great Pyramid or search for otherwise unknown chambers in the structure (DeSalvo, 2003, p. 88).

"Unknown" Chambers

Seiss (1877, pp. 10–11) postulated an undiscovered chamber in the center of the Great Pyramid (as viewed from the air) about halfway between the uppermost so-called Relieving Chamber (above the King's Chamber) and the apex of the pyramid. Holland (1885, p. 135) believed there is a currently unknown chamber above the Queen's Chamber and below the Antechamber of the King's Chamber. Hall (2003, p. 113) says: "Nearly all students of the subject believe that subterranean chambers exist beneath the Great Pyramid." Hall then quotes Ballard (1882) as saying:

> The priests of the Pyramids of Lake Moeris had their vast subterranean residences. It appears to me more than probable that those of Gizeh were similarly provided. And I may go further:—Out of these very caverns may have been excavated the limestone of which the Pyramids were built. . . . In the bowels of the limestone ridge on which the Pyramids are built will yet be found, I feel convinced, ample information as to their uses. A good diamond drill with two or three hundred fee of rods is what is wanted to test this, and the solidarity of the Pyramids at the same time.

H. S. Lewis (1936, 1939, 1945, 1994, pp. 126–127) suggests that there is an underground reception chamber and temple under and behind the Great Sphinx, and underground passages for this temple to each of the three major Giza pyramids.

Lewis obtained this information from "secret manuscripts possessed by archivists of the mystery schools of Egypt and the Orient" (Lewis, 1994, p. 181). D. H. Lewis (1980, p. 81) suggests there is a hidden entrance near the summit of the Great Pyramid that leads to a hidden staircase that runs down the center of the pyramid, past the King's and Queen's chambers, to a secret room below the Subterranean Chamber. The stairway continues even deeper into the bedrock, finally coming to another room that is connected to various tunnels and passages, including one that leads to the Great Sphinx (1980, p. 92).

In the context of hidden or formally unknown chambers, my colleague John Anthony West reports the following (2003, p. 232).

> A team of French engineers in the late 1980s found a mysterious cavity or void behind the masonry of the corridor leading to the Queen's Chamber. There was no entrance hidden or otherwise to this space, so that it was clear it was not intended to be used. A fiber-optic camera was inserted and showed the cavity empty of treasure but half full of sand, which upon testing proved to be radioactive! These finds were disclosed at an Egyptological meeting in Kansas, but thereafter, as far as I can determine, never published. All subsequent attempts to get more detailed information from the relevant authorities have been met with evasion and/or claims that I had been misinformed in the first place. Conspiracy theorists see a cover-up in progress. Certainly a cover-up is hardly out of the question, but for the moment it must remain just one of a number of possibilities. The cavity or void is acknowledged to exist but is considered a structural anomaly of no interest or importance.

Apparently referring to the same study, DeSalvo (2003, p. 58) reports that in 1986 two French architects, using "electronic detectors," found a 3-by-5-meter chamber under the passageway to the Queen's Chamber. They bored into this chamber and found it filled with 99 percent pure quartz sand that "may come from El Tur in southern Sinai" (DeSalvo, 2003, p. 58). According to DeSalvo (2003, pp. 58–59), in 1987 and 1988 Japanese researchers found similar cavities under or off the passageway to the Queen's Chamber, and they also detected a cavity or cavities behind the western end of the northern wall of the Queen's Chamber.

Melchizedek (2000, pp. 248–249) elaborates on these supposed rooms near and around the Queen's Chamber:

> they've [Melchizedek does not clarify who "they" refers to] found . . . more rooms in just the last several years (since 1994). Three more rooms off three walls of the

Queen's Chamber have been found. One room had nothing in it, another was filled from floor to ceiling with radioactive sand, and the third had nothing in it but a solid gold statue, which the Japanese allegedly removed. . . . This theft was followed by a silent alarm around the world. . . . There was a worldwide hunt for the gold statue, but they never found it, and as far as I know, they never found the people responsible. . . . The Japanese scientists were present when I was there in January 1990, and the statue was taken right after that.

DeSalvo (2003, p. 59) says:

In 1992, ground penetrating radar and microgravimetric measurements were made [he does not state who made them] in the Pit in the subterranean chamber and in the horizontal passage connecting the bottom of the descending passage with the subterranean chamber. A structure was detected under the floor of the horizontal passage. Another structure was detected on the western side of the passageway about 6 meters from the entrance to the subterranean chamber. Soundings studies seem to indicate it is a vertical shaft about 1.4 meters square and at 5 meters deep.

DeSalvo (2003, p. 179) also writes: "Recently remote sensing has detected an incredible large underground complex under the Giza Plateau with many tunnels and areas that we have no idea when and why they were constructed."

Yoshiki Su'e (1999), in postulating that the Great Pyramid is some sort of giant instrument for measuring vibrations and the rotation of the earth, suggests that there must be hidden control and measurement rooms in the structure. Just as I was putting the finishing touches on this manuscript, another report of suspected but unknown chambers came across the Internet. Two French amateur archaeologists, Gilles Dormion and Jean-Yves Verd'hurt, believe that there is a chamber under the Queen's Chamber that could be the true resting place of Khufu (Benoist, 2004).

Lepre (1990, p. 270) has suggested that there might be a possible western "entrance" or opening in the west wall of the King's Chamber of the Great Pyramid. Lepre (1990, p. 275) also postulates that there might be a second original entrance to the Great Pyramid, located on its north side, under the floorstones, where an offering shrine may have been located. In addition, Lepre (1990, pp. 275–278) has spotted what appears to his eye to be a 4-by-10-foot stone sunk into the foundation of the Great Pyramid on the northern side, 70 feet west of the pyramid's northeast corner. Originally this stone would have been covered by the external casing stones covering the pyramid, and thus would have been concealed. Lepre speculates that it conceals an entrance or cavity that may lead to the true burial chamber of Khufu under the Great Pyramid.

Alford (2003, 2004) believes that the intact tomb of Khufu is hidden in a network of caves beneath the Great Pyramid. Alford says (personal communication to Robert Schoch, November 26, 2004):

> In my view, the Subterranean Chamber played the role of a decoy burial chamber. Anyone entering the Pyramid and finding this room would have assumed that the king's body and burial treasure had already been discovered and stolen. The real tomb, in my opinion, lies in the Grotto or its vicinity. . . . The Grotto was originally accessed by the Well Shaft (the lower section), whose entrance in the Descending Passage took the form of a camouflaging plate of stone—in effect, a secret door. I hypothesize that the king's mummy (though not the coffin, as it would have been too big) was subjected to rituals in the Subterranean Chamber and then carried up the Well Shaft to be interred in the Grotto or its vicinity. Such a burial would have been ideal from a security point of view. . . . The purpose of the Grotto has always been something of a mystery. However, it strikes me that the position of this cave-like room—near the surface of the rocky outcrop of the Giza plateau—had pro-

The Grotto under the Great Pyramid, facing north, as seen in 1909. The stone-lined Well Shaft is on the right. (*From Edgar and Edgar, 1910, page 278.*)

found symbolic importance, representing the primeval mound of the Egyptian creation myth—a most auspicious place for the pharaoh to be buried."

GANTENBRINK'S EXPLORATIONS IN THE QUEEN'S CHAMBER

In 1993 Rudolf Gantenbrink used a small wheeled robot, that looked somewhat like a miniature military tank equipped with a video camera, to ascend the southern shaft originating in the Queen's Chamber (DeSalvo, 2003, p. 60). The shaft goes straight back from the wall for about 7 feet, then ascends. The robot, named Upuaut 2, traveled about 200 feet up the 9-inch-square shaft, where it encountered a stone "door" with two copper "handles" and could go no farther. In September 2002, another robot (not associated with Gantenbrink), designed by iRobot of Boston, ascended the shaft to the door, drilled through the approximately 3 inches of the door, and looked through with a camera. Behind the first stone door was a small, empty space, and then another stone door (DeSalvo, 2003, p. 62). The same robot was later sent up the northern shaft of the Queen's Chamber, where it encountered a stone door at 208 feet from the Queen's Chamber very similar to the stone doors found in the southern shaft (DeSalvo, 2003, p. 63).

DIMENSIONS OF THE INTERNAL PASSAGES, CHAMBERS, AND COFFER OF THE GREAT PYRAMID

Note: Unless otherwise stated, the following measurements (in British inches, as opposed to so-called pyramid inches), but not necessarily the descriptions, are from Kingsland's compilation (1932, pp. 113–117), with the exception of those for the Chambers of Construction, which are from Bonwick (1877, pp. 45–46), and the measurements of the coffer found in the King's Chamber, which are from Petrie (1885, p. 30).

All lengths of passages and chambers are floor lengths, unless otherwise stated. The value of the cubit used in the measurements that follow is the value adopted by Kingsland (1932), namely 20.612 British inches to a cubit. In some cases I believe that Kingsland's numbers are overly precise, but rather than round them I have reported them as he published them.

DESCENDING PASSAGE

Length of missing portion of entrance due to removal of the casing: 124.2 ± .3

Vertical height of original entrance above the platform of the Great Pyramid: 668.3

Length from original entrance to point of intersection with the Ascending Passage: 1110.64

Length from point of intersection to the bottom of the passage where it meets the short horizontal passage to the Subterranean Chamber: 3036.804

Total original length of the Descending Passage: 4147.444

Vertical depth of foot of Descending Passage below platform level: 1164.578

Average width of Descending Passage: 41.6

Average height taken perpendicular to floor and roof of the Descending Passage: 47.4

Average true vertical height of Descending Passage: 52.8

HORIZONTAL PASSAGE FROM THE BASE OF THE DESCENDING PASSAGE TO THE SUBTERRANEAN CHAMBER

Total length of this passage: 350.75

Average height of the passage: 34 (0.91 meters, according to Pochan, 1978, p. 13)

Average width of the passage: 34 (0.80 meters, according to Pochan, 1978, p. 13)

Distance of "recess" or "niche" from the southern end of the horizontal passage (Pochan, 1978, p. 13): 1.45 meters

Approximate length parallel to the passage of the "recess" or "niche" off of this passage (Pochan, 1978, p. 13): 1.85 meters

SUBTERRANEAN CHAMBER

Approximate east-to-west length: 553.07

Approximate north-to-south width: 325.904

Approximate height at the western end: 5.5 feet

Approximate height at the eastern end: 12–16.5 feet

Length of southern "Blind Passage": 53.5 feet

Average height of southern "Blind Passage": 28

Average width of southern "Blind Passage": 28

ASCENDING PASSAGE

Length from the intersection to the bottom of the Grand Gallery (75 cubits):
1,545.9

Horizontal length of Ascending Passage: 1,388.457

Vertical height of southern end of Ascending Passage above platform level:
850.396

Average width of Ascending Passage: 42.1

Average height of Ascending Passage perpendicular to floor and roof: 47.4

Average vertical height of Ascending Passage: 52.6

GRAND GALLERY

Length from north wall to south wall: 1,883.6

Horizontal length from north wall to south wall: 1,689.191

Length of the "Great Step" at the southern end: 61.32

Height of the "Great Step": 36.0

Height of the lower portion of the Grand Gallery above the platform level:
850.396

Height of the top of the "Great Step" above the platform level (82 cubits):
1,690.184

Width of the Grand Gallery over the side ramps (4 cubits): 82.448

Width between the side ramps (2 cubits): 41.224

Width of the Grand Gallery at the roof (2 cubits): 41.224

Width of each ramp (1 cubit): 20.612

Average height of ramps: 23.5

Average height of Grand Gallery: 28.5 feet

ANTECHAMBER

Length of passage from Grand Gallery to Antechamber: 52.02

Height of passage (2 cubits): 41.224

Width of passage (2 cubits): 41.224

Length of Antechamber: 116.08

Average width of Antechamber at floor level (2 cubits): 41.224

Average width of Antechamber at roof: 65.0

Average height of Antechamber: 149.35

Height of wainscoting on the east: 103.35

Height of wainscoting on the west: 112.1

KING'S CHAMBER

Length of passage from Antechamber to King's Chamber: 100.8

Average height of passage: 42.89

Average width of passage: 41.4

Length of King's Chamber (20 cubits): 412.24

Width of King's Chamber: (10 cubits): 206.12

Height of Granite walls in the King's Chamber: 235.2

Vertical height of floor above the platform level (82 cubits): 1,690.184

QUEEN'S CHAMBER PASSAGE

Total length of passage: 1,524.811

Length from north wall of the Grand Gallery to the step in the passage: 1,307.0

Length from the step to the Queen's Chamber: 217.811

Depth of the step (1 cubit): 20.612

Average width of the passage: 46.5

Average height of the passage at the northern end: 46.5

Average height of the passage at the southern end: 66.2

Vertical height of the northern portion of the passage above the platform level: 855.396

Vertical height of the southern portion above the platform level: 834.784

QUEEN'S CHAMBER

Length of the Queen's Chamber (11 cubits): 226.732

Width (10 cubits): 206.12

Average height of the north and south walls (9 cubits?): 184.47(?)

Average height to the ridge of the roof: 245.1(?)

Height of Niche: 183.9 (Kingsland, 1932, p. 117, lists 193.8, but this is an error; on p. 77 he cites it as 183.89 inches, and Petrie, 1885, p. 24, gives a value of 184 inches)

Width of Niche at the base (3 cubits?): 61.74(?)

Width of Niche at the top (1 cubit?): 20.3(?)

Average depth of the Niche (2 cubits?): 41.07(?)

Height of the floor of the Queen's Chamber above the platform level :834.784

COFFER IN THE KING'S CHAMBER

Outside length: 89.62

Outside width: 38.50

Outer height: 41.31

Inside length: 78.06

Inside width: 26.81

Inside depth: 34.42

Thickness at the northern end: 5.67

Thickness at the southern end: 5.89

Thickness of the eastern side: 5.87

Thickness of the western side: 5.82

Thickness of the bottom: 6.89

Volume of the inside: 72,030 cubic inches

Volume of the solid bulk of the granite: 70,500 cubic inches

Volume overall: 142,530 cubic inches

The volumes are calculated by Petrie (1885, p. 30), "omitting all notice of the attachments for the lid, employing the mean [average] planes."

CHAMBERS OF CONSTRUCTION

Length of passage from the entrance at the top of the Grand Gallery (southeast corner) to Davison's Chamber: 24.75 feet

Vertical height from the floor of the King's Chamber to the top of Campbell's Chamber: 69.25 feet

Length of Davison's Chamber: 38 feet 4 inches

Width of Davison's Chamber: 17 feet 1 inch

Height of Davison's Chamber: 2 feet 6 inches to 3 feet 6 inches

Length of Wellington's Chamber: 38 feet 6 inches

Width of Wellington's Chamber: 17 feet 2 inches

Height of Wellington's Chamber: 2 feet 2 inches to 3 feet 8 inches

Length of Nelson's Chamber: 38 feet 9 inches

Width of Nelson's Chamber: 16 feet 8 inches

Height of Nelson's Chamber: 2 feet 4 inches to 4 feet 10 inches

Length of Lady Arbuthnot's Chamber: 37 feet 4 inches

Width of Lady Arbuthnot's Chamber: 16 feet 4 inches

Height of Lady Arbuthnot's Chamber: 1 foot 4 inches to 4 feet 5 inches

Length of Campbell's Chamber: 37 feet 10 inches

Width of Campbell's Chamber: 20 feet 6 inches

Height of Campbell's Chamber: 5 feet 10 inches to 8 feet 7 inches

DISPLACEMENT OF THE PASSAGES TO THE EAST

All of the passages and chambers in the Great Pyramid occur in approximately a north–south oriented vertical plane that runs through the structure. This plane, however, is not aligned with the central axis of the Great Pyramid but rather is displaced slightly to the east. This displacement is cited as 7.29 meters by Pochan (1978, p. 12); on the basis of the data of Petrie (1883), Kingsland (1932, p. 57) gives it as about 100 inches (2.54 meters) for the center of the King's Chamber to about 287 inches (7.29 meters) for the center of the north entrance (original entrance). Davidson (see Davidson and Aldersmith, 1924) related his "displacement factor" to the displacement of the passages to the east of the central axis of the Great Pyramid, believing the two values to be numerically equal.

Pochan (1978, p. 12) explains the eastern displacement of the passage system as follows. "This displacement of the axis was necessary in order to avoid inundating the Subterranean Chamber, as each face's hollow constituted a vast gutter capable of draining more than 2,000 cubic meters of water during a rainstorm." I have never found this explanation tenable. Such storms were few and far between on the eastern edge of the Sahara; furthermore, the entrance to the Great Pyramid was apparently fitted with a tight stone door, so tight and inconspicuous that when knowledge of its exact location was lost, it could not easily be found again, resulting, for instance, in the forced passage of Al Mamoun (see hereafter). Such a tight-fitting door would hardly have let in enough water to inundate the Subterranean Chamber. Richard Proctor (1883) offers a better explanation for the eastern displacement of the passages, I believe. Proctor suggested that the partially completed Great Pyramid, built up to the level of the floor of the King's Chamber, served as a pretelescopic observatory. The Grand Gallery, open to the south, was the primary sighting tube for observations, but the flat, square, top of the partial pyramid, aligned to the cardinal points, would also have been used to make observations.

> An observer . . . should occupy the very centre of the square top of the, as yet, incomplete pyramid, so that the middle point of each side would mark a cardinal point, while the angles of the square would mark the mid-cardinal points. Also this central point ought not only to command direction-lines to the angles and bisections of the sides, but to be commanded, without obstruction, by direction-lines from these points. Thus the upper end of the Great Ascending Gallery [Grand Gallery] should not be exactly at the centre, but somewhat either to the west or to the east of the centre of the great square summit of the incomplete pyramid. (pp. 136–137)

INSCRIPTIONS ON AND WITHIN
THE GREAT PYRAMID

REPORTS OF EXTERNAL INSCRIPTIONS

According to some accounts, the original casing stones of the Great Pyramid were covered with hieroglyphic inscriptions. This may seem odd, given that no inscriptions (other than those in the relieving chambers) have been found inside the Great Pyramid. Indeed, it is not certain that there ever were any original inscriptions, as opposed to later graffiti, on the outside of the Great Pyramid.

On this point, Petrie (1883, pp. 217–219) elaborates:

> With regard to the many records of inscriptions on the outside of the Pyramid, a few words are necessary. From the time of Herodotus down to the 15th century, inscriptions are continually mentioned, and their great abundance is described with

astonishment by travellers. This has led to the supposition that the builders had left records inscribed on the outside, although not a letter is to be found on the inside. But against the possibility of this view, it must be remembered that no early inscriptions are found on the casing remaining at the Great Pyramid, nor on any of the innumerable fragments of those stones, nor on the remaining casing of the Second Pyramid, nor on that of the Third Pyramid, nor on the casing of the South Pyramid of Dahshur, nor on the casing of the Pyramid of Medum, nor on occasional blocks uncovered at the Sakkara Pyramids. In fact, not a single example of hieroglyphs has ever been seen on any casing, nor on any fragments of casing. The truth then about these numberless inscriptions appears to be that they were all travellers' graffiti. Strabo says that the characters were like old Greek, but were not readable; this points to Phoenician or Cypriote graffiti. The accounts of the inscriptions given by the Arabs also show that they were mere graffiti; Abu Masher Jafer (before 886 A.D.) mentions Mosannad (i.e., Himyaritic) letters; Ibn Khordadbeh (10th cent.) also mentions Musnad letters; Masudi (11th cent.) describes them as being in various different languages; Ibn Haukal (11th cent.) says they were in Greek. Abu Mothaffer (*alias* Sibt Al Jauzi, died 1250 A.D.) gives the fullest account, mentioning seven sorts of writing : (1) Greek, (2) Arabic, (3) Syriac, (4) Musnadic, (5) Himyaritic (or Hiritic or Hebrew in different MSS.), (6) Rumi, (7) Persian. William of Baldensel (1336 A.D.) mentions Latin; and Cyriacus (1440 A.D.) mentions Phoenician. Whether these travellers all understood exactly what they were talking about may be doubted; but at least none of them describe hieroglyphs, such as they must have been familiar with on all the tombs and other monuments; and they agree in the great diversity of the languages inscribed. The earlier travellers also do not describe such a great number of inscriptions as do the Arabic writers; suggesting that the greater part recorded in later times were due to Roman and Coptic graffiti.

Now among the hundreds of pieces of casing stones that I have looked over, very few traces of inscription were to be seen; this was, however, to be expected, considering that the pieces nearly all belonged to the upper casing stones, out of the reach of mere travellers. Three examples of single letters were found, two Greek and one unknown; and on the W. side, in one of the excavations, a piece was discovered bearing three graffiti, one large one attracting lesser scribblers, as in modern times. The earliest inscription was probably of Ptolemy X., showing portions of the letters Π T O .... C ω T .... ; the next was a Romano-Greek of a certain M A P K I O C K ...... ; and over that an Arab had roughly hammered in ..... maj ...... This is the only example of continuous inscriptions yet found, and it belonged to one of the lowest courses; it is now in the Bulak Museum. Thus, all the fragments and the descriptions point to the existence of a large body of graffiti, but do not give any evidence of original hieroglyphic inscriptions.

When one considers the large number of graffiti which are to be seen on every ancient building of importance, it seems almost impossible but that the Great Pyramid—one of the most renowned and visited of all—should not have been similarly covered with ancient scribbles, like the host of modern names which have been put upon it since the casing was removed. The statues of Ramessu II., at Abu Simbel, bear quantities of Greek graffiti, in fact, some of the earliest Greek inscriptions known, besides Phoenician and Roman; the top of the temple of Khonsu at Karnak is crowded with the outlines of visitors' feet, with their names and particulars appended, in hieroglyphic, demotic, and Greek; the inscriptions on the colossi of Amenhotep III. ("the Memnons") at Thebes, and on the Sphinx at Gizeh are well known; the long scribbles in demotic on the temple walls at Thebes have lately been examined; the corridors of Abydos bear early Greek graffiti; the passage of the S. Pyramid of Dahshur has two hieroglyphic graffiti, besides Greek; and there is scarcely any monument of importance in Egypt but what shows the scribbling propensities of mankind; be they Egyptians, Phoenicians, Greeks, Romans, or the worst sinners of modern times, Hellenes and Americans.

From about the ninth century A.D. on, the Great Pyramid (as well as the other pyramids and structures on the Giza Plateau) was used as a quarry, and much of the casing stone of the Great Pyramid is believed to have been removed to build the mosque of Sultan Hasan, around 1356 (see Petrie, 1885, p. 92). Since the stripping of the casing stones, the Great Pyramid has accumulated a prodigious amount of graffiti on the exposed core masonry. In the latter class, we may include the formal "hieroglyphic inscription" placed on the upper west side of the exposed "arch" over the original entrance by the German Egyptologist Karl Richard Lepsius in honor Kaiser Friedrich Wilhelm IV of Prussia (Smyth, 1877, p. 7 n.; Pochan, 1978, p. 4), apparently during his expedition of 1843–1844 (Verner, 2001, p. 191). As Pochan points out (1978, pp. 3–4), under the arch of the original entrance, inscribed in the space between the two "humps" of the "lintel," is a curious sequence of four "letters" (referred to as a tetragram by Pochan) that, to the best of my knowledge, have never been definitively deciphered. Being in an area that was originally covered with the casing stone, it is perhaps hard to conceive that they were inscribed earlier than medieval times, and in fact they may simply be modern (nineteenth or twentieth century) random graffiti. However, Kingsland (1932, p. 27) notes that approximately 25 feet of stone masonry has been removed from the area of the original entrance, and there may have been more blocks in front of the current surviving blocks that form a triangular arch over the entrance. If this was the case, there may have originally been a recess or chamber above the original entrance, and this four-letter inscription may have been carved in the southern end of the recess even before the casing was removed. Doreal (1938, 1992, p. 37) may be referring to this inscription when he writes:

> The entrance to the Great Pyramid is on the north side and consists of a square surmounted by a triangle. The square symbolizes the four-lettered word, Yod-He-Vau-He, the Tetragrammaton, the Lost Word through which the Divine Light created all things in the material plane. The triangle, a symbol of the immortality of the soul, rises to a point where it vanishes in Infinity.

Tastmona (1954, pp. 130–131) also refers to the Tetragrammaton, the Ineffable Name of God, the four consonants Y H V H, where the true vowels are unknown and therefore the pronunciation is unknown, the Shem Hammephorash. Tastmona (1954, p. 130) believes that Jehovah's identity is enciphered in the Giza pyramids, and it appears that, for Tastmona, Jehovah is a comet, or more specifically a triad

Four-letter inscription (tetragram) found over the original entrance of the Great Pyramid between the two "humps" of the carved stone under the gable. It is unclear when these four apparent letters, which have so far eluded interpretation, were placed there. They could be ancient, medieval, or modern. Photograph courtesy of Robert M. Schoch.

of comets. Tastmona also claimed to have discovered the correct pronunciation of the Tetragrammaton in the spring of 1933 (Tastmona, 1954, contents page, chap. 10 summary), although he did not publish this pronunciation. Whether or not the four letters under the lintel of the entrance to the Great Pyramid have anything to do with the Tetragrammaton is an open question, and not one explicitly addressed by Doreal or Tastmona.

Possibly the four "letters" of this tetragram on the Great Pyramid are related to the classical concepts of the four elements (earth, air, fire, and water) or properties (wet, dry, hot, and cold), or the Gnostic concept that nature, wisdom, and science rest on the four principles of Silence, Profundity, Intelligence, and Truth (Hall, 2003, p. 116, quoting Albert Pike).

HIEROGLYPHS CARVED INTO THE PYRAMID OR REPRESENTED BY PASSAGES
The ceiling of the Subterranean Chamber is not flat but has several similarly shaped irregularities in it that Pochan (1978, p. 14, and see his figure captions) in particular has interpreted as "mysterious letters" or "enigmatic marks carved in the rock." My sense is that these "mysterious letters" or "symbols" are simply the result of the techniques used to quarry out the ceiling area, the ceiling having never been smoothed and finished.

Marsham Adams (1933, p. 54 n.) suggested that the carved stone currently found immediately under the arch over the original entrance might represent the hieroglyph for the horizon ("Horizon of Heaven" in the words of Adams). Kingsland (1932, pp. 27–28) contends that, if anything, this stone resembles the hieroglyph for mountain, but ultimately Kingsland dismisses it as not an original form of the pyramid at all but simply the result of damage as explorers or vandals tried to hack into the pyramid. However, perhaps lending support to Adams's suggestion, Richard Wilkinson includes in his book *Symbol and Magic in Egyptian Art* (1999, pp. 166–167) a section entitled "Objects as Hieroglyphs and Hieroglyphs as Objects," in which he says (p. 167): "The importance of hieroglyphic forms as symbolic images in Egyptian culture cannot be overestimated, and the projection of such forms onto natural and constructed objects is extremely frequent." Wilkinson even discusses and illustrates the horizon hieroglyph specifically in this context, although not mentioning the form identified by Adams over the entrance of the Great Pyramid.

Adams also suggests that various passages and structures within the Great Pyramid form hieroglyphs, including a "sacred hieroglyphic symbol peculiar to

Thoth" (Adams, 1933, pp. 66–67) and hieroglyphs representing the Nile River, divinity, the territory of the holy dead, the ankh as a symbol of life, the scepter of Ptah as spirit of divine fire, the scepter of Anup, guide of the soul (Adams, 1933, pp. 90–91). For instance, consider the Well leading down to the Grotto,

> together with the line where the interior masonry is bounded by the natural rock through which entrance or initiation into the interior masonry is obtained from below—the entrance impassable by the postulant until the soul is restored to him. Then, if we indicate the image of the Well itself, shining in its own living but invisible waters, as seen by the soul from above, just as the Creator looks down on His own image in the universe, we obtain the symbol of the "Ankh," or mirror of Life. (Adams, 1933, p. 90)

INSCRIPTIONS IN THE RELIEVING CHAMBERS

I have entered the so-called Relieving Chambers twice, on the evening of November 24, 2003, and on the evening of May 20, 2004, to view the hieroglyphic inscriptions discovered by Howard Vyse and documented in his work *Operations Carried on at the Pyramids of Gizeh in 1837: With an Account of a Voyage into Upper Egypt, and an Appendix* (1840, 1:277–284). Most of the hieroglyphs occur in Lady Arbuthnot's Chamber and in Campbell's Chamber, and there are some prominent hieroglyphics (but no cartouches) on the western end of Nelson's Chamber. All of the hieroglyphs recorded by Vyse in the plates of his work appear to be present, although perhaps somewhat degraded and the worse for exposure since they were first uncovered in the 1830s. There is an incredible amount of nineteenth- and early twentieth-century graffiti defacing these chambers, indicative of the travails they have suffered at the hands of modern humans.

Having had a chance to see the chambers of construction and their inscriptions firsthand, I am convinced that (1) the inscriptions are genuinely ancient and contemporary with the construction of this part of the Great Pyramid, and (2) Howard Vyse and his associates did their best to accurately transcribe and record the inscriptions. Most of the inscriptions are upside down, and they were clearly done quickly and crudely, and before the limestone blocks were set in place (one can see that some of the inscriptions continue under other blocks that were set immediately on top of them or against them). Clearly these ancient inscriptions were never meant to be viewed in the future, and I agree with the assessment that they are "quarry marks." The ancient inscriptions have incrustations over them in places,

Inside Campbell's Chamber, the fifth and final Relieving Chamber above the King's Chamber. Photograph courtesy of Robert M. Schoch.

and are very different in appearance from the nineteenth- and twentieth-century inscriptions. I can imagine how difficult it must have been for Howard Vyse and his associates to even make out many of the inscriptions without modern electrical lighting techniques and given the filth when the chambers were first opened by blasting. Lepre (1990, p. 109) points out that it was in Campbell's Chamber in particular that numerous bats set up their nests in modern times. It would be understandable if the hieroglyphic inscriptions went unnoticed by Howard Vyse and his men initially when entering the chambers.

So to me the question is not whether or not the inscriptions are genuinely ancient—clearly, in my opinion, they are—but what do they tell us? I agree with the general assessment that they are workmen's marks, most likely painted on at the quarries (see Lepre, 1990, p. 108; S. Birch in Vyse, 1840, 1:279). Birch in particular suggested that these marks are found only on certain blocks transported from the Mokattam Quarries across the Nile, and are not found on blocks quarried locally on the Giza Plateau—this makes sense to me, and would explain why such quarry marks are not generally found throughout the Great Pyramid. Further, according to Birch, several of the marks found on the blocks are numbers indicating where the blocks were to be positioned. Some of the blocks have straight lines on them, oriented both horizontally and vertically, that were probably used in positioning the blocks correctly. According to Lepre (1990, p. 108), the hieroglyphics on some of the blocks can be interpreted as names of construction gangs or crews, and he cites as examples "The crew, the White Crown of Khnum-Khuf (Khufu) is powerful" and "The crew, Khufu excites love." Lepre (1990, p. 190) also says that one of the hieroglyphic lines refers to the seventeenth year of the reign of Khufu.

It seems that the inscriptions in the relieving chambers do support the attribution of at least this portion of the Great Pyramid to the Fourth Dynasty Pharaoh Khufu, or at least a "Khufu." I also have to question whether or not the lower portions of the Great Pyramid are actually contemporary with the Relieving Chambers and the upper portions of the pyramid. Could the base, and possibly up through the Grand Gallery, be earlier? This would be the case if Richard Proctor were correct in his assessment of the Great Pyramid as an observatory before it was "closed over."

Among the inscriptions in the Relieving Chambers are a number of cartouches, taking three different forms. There is one complete cartouche in Campbell's Chamber, and there are four relatively complete cartouches in Lady Arbuthnot's Chamber. There are also fragments of other cartouches, not complete enough to read alone but apparently partial versions of the complete cartouches found in the Relieving Chambers.

In the complete cartouche found in Campbell's Chamber, the name "Khufu" is easily read, on the basis of standard transliterations (see, for instance, Collier and Manley, 1998). Reading from bottom to top in the cartouche as it is found in the

Photograph of a hieroglyphic inscription that includes the cartouche of Khufu found in Campbell's Chamber. (*Photograph courtesy of Robert M. Schoch.*) Inset: Drawing of a hieroglyphic inscription that includes the cartouche of Khufu found in Campbell's Chamber. (*From Vyse, 1840, vol. 1, plate following p. 284; also reproduced in Kingsland, 1935, plate 2.*)

Photograph of a hieroglyphic inscription that includes the cartouche of Khnum-Khuf found in Lady Arbuthnot's Chamber. The inscription is shown upside down, the same way it appears in the chamber. Photograph courtesy of Robert M. Schoch. Inset: Drawing of a hieroglyphic inscription that includes the cartouche of Khnum-Khuf found in Lady Arbuthnot's Chamber. The inscription is shown upside down, the same way it appears in the chamber. (*From Vyse, 1840, vol. 1, plate following page 278; also reproduced in Kingsland, 1935, plate 3.*)

chamber, the round sieve symbol is transliterated as "kh" or a hard "ch," the bird is "w" or "u," the snake is "f," and the second bird is again "w" or "u."

In one of the complete cartouches from Lady Arbuthnot's Chamber we have, from left to right (viewing the cartouche as it is *in situ,* upside down), what have been interpreted as a jug and ram (Birch in Vyse, 1840, 1:281) followed by the sieve ("kh"), snake ("f"), and bird ("w" or "u"). The latter three make "Khfu" or "Khuf," which, given that the "w/u" was a weak sound and, according to Collier and Manley (1998, p. 127) "often not written," is basically the equivalent of "Khufu." The jug may be represented as issuing forth its contents as a libation (compare a similar hieroglyph in Collier and Manley, 1998, p. 140), and the jug and ram have been interpreted by Birch (in Vyse, 1840, 1:281) as the name of the god known variously as Chnoumis or Amoun-ra (or any of many other names). Amun (Amoun) is known from the Old Kingdom Pyramid Texts (Lurker, 1980, p. 25), and Amun could appear in the form of a ram and was worshiped under the name "Khnum" (Lurker, 1980, p. 99). Thus this cartouche can be read as "Khnum-Khuf," which is one of the names of the

Photograph of a hieroglyphic inscription that includes the cartouche of Khnum found in Lady Arbuthnot's Chamber. The inscription is shown upside down, the same way it appears in the chamber. Photograph courtesy of Robert M. Schoch. Inset: Drawing of a hieroglyphic inscription that includes the cartouche of Khnum found in Lady Arbuthnot's Chamber. The inscription is shown upside down, the same way it appears in the chamber. (*From Vyse, 1840, vol. 1, plate following page 278; also reproduced in Kingsland, 1935, plate 3.*)

pharaoh Khufu of the Fourth Dynasty (see Lepre, 1990, p. 61, where he spells it as "Khnum-Kheuf" and "Khnem-Kheuf," and p. 108, where he spells it "Khnum-Khuf"). Two of the other cartouches found in Lady Arbuthnot's Chamber also seem to read "Khnum-Khuf," although one is incomplete and the other seems to be either incomplete or a very crude version of this name.

A final complete cartouche found in Lady Arbuthnot's Chamber consists of a jug followed by an unclear form followed by a ram. This has been interpreted simply as the name "Khnum" ("Khnem," see Kingsland, 1935, p. 5).

IRON AND OTHER ANCIENT ARTIFACTS
FOUND IN THE GREAT PYRAMID

On May 20, 1837, Mr. J. R. Hill, working under Howard Vyse, found a flat piece of iron measuring approximately 12 by 4 inches by ⅛ inches in a joint in the masonry near the exterior mouth of the southern "air passage" originating in the King's Chamber. J. R. Hill wrote (quoted in DeSalvo, 2003, p. 64) that the iron plate "was taken out by me from an inner joint, after having removed by blasting the two outer tiers of the stones of the present surface of the Pyramid; and that no joint or opening of any sort was connected with the above-mentioned joint by which the iron could have been placed in it after the original building of the Pyramid" (italics in the original). The iron plate was sent to the British Museum. Petrie (1883, pp. 212–213) says:

> That sheet iron was employed we know, from the fragment found by Howard Vyse in the masonry of the south air channel; and though some doubt has been thrown on the piece, merely from its rarity, yet the vouchers for it are very precise; and it has a cast of a nummulite [a fossil organism of a type commonly found in the limestones of which the Great Pyramid is built] on the rust of it, proving it to have been buried for ages beside a block of nummulitic limestone, and therefore to be certainly ancient. No reasonable doubt can therefore exist about its being really a genuine piece used by the Pyramid masons; and probably such pieces were required to prevent crowbars biting into the stones, and to ease the action of the rollers.

In 1989 tests were conducted on this iron plate to determine if it was composed of meteoritic iron. The results were negative (although this may not prove definitively the origins of the iron), but traces of gold were found on its surface, suggestive of gold plating. If in fact this iron is from the middle third millennium B.C. and is nonmeteoritic in origin, it has the potential to change our views of how early and how extensively iron was smelted and utilized. Gold plating on this particular piece of iron, assuming it is genuinely ancient, could indicate that iron was a rare commodity and highly valued. Bonwick (1877, p. 46) suggested that this iron may have come "from the iron mines of the Wady Maghara, near Sinai," but he may have confused the copper and turquoise mines of this area of the Sinai with iron mines (no Old Kingdom iron mines are known from the Sinai).

In 1872 when Waynman Dixon discovered and opened the shafts in the Queen's Chamber, he found three objects in the northern shaft: (1) a granite ball weighing 1 pound and 3 ounces; (2) a piece of cedar about 12 centimeters long with notches cut into it that may have been some kind of measuring rod; and (3) a bronze instrument that had a double "hook" on the end (sort of like a snake's tongue) with a portion of a wooden handle still adhering to it (DeSalvo, 2003, p. 66; Bauval in DeSalvo, 2003, p. 218, with nineteenth-century illus.). Robert Bauval interprets the double hook object as a "Pesh-en-kef" instrument that was used in the ancient Egyptian "opening of the mouth" ceremony, and Bauval believes the same instrument, when used in conjunction with a plumb-bob, served as a sighting device for aligning a structure such as the Great Pyramid with the polar stars. These three items long remained with the Dixon family, until being donated to the British Museum in the 1970s, where they lay in obscurity until rediscovered in the 1990s, at which time the wooden artifact was missing (DeSalvo, 2003, p. 66).

In 1993, while exploring the northern shaft of the Queen's Chamber, Rudolf Gantenbrink discovered, via video from the robot, a metallic hook-like object and a long, thin piece of wood in the shaft beyond where W. Dixon had found the aforementioned three objects (DeSalvo, 2003, p. 67).

NOTES ON THE LAYOUT AND CONSTRUCTION
OF THE GREAT PYRAMID

A major point of contention is how the ancient Egyptians moved massive blocks of stone, whether it was for building pyramids and temples or raising obelisks. A novel approach has been suggested the amateur Egyptologist Maureen Clemmons: that the Egyptians may have harnessed wind power via kites and pulleys to raise large stones and set obelisks upright (Tindol, 2001; Wright, 2001). This controversial theory has received some support from experimental studies by researchers at California Institute of Technology demonstrating that using kites to raise large stones is possible. In several tests, for instance, they were able to lift a 3.4-ton obelisk off the ground in 25 seconds with a wind of only 15 miles per hour (Association for Research and Enlightenment, 2004). However, some Egyptologists have argued that there is no direct evidence for the use of either kites or pulleys in ancient Egypt. On the other hand, images of winged deities abound in Egypt, and it is certainly not inconceivable that the ancient Egyptians made and used kites.

Tastmona (1954) and Temple (2000; see also 2001) have both suggested that the ancients, and the ancient Egyptians in particular, had optical lenses that could be used not only for magnification of small, close objects but also to construct telescopes and what Temple refers to as "proto-theodolites" for precise surveying. Such ancient optical instruments could conceivably have been used to help accurately align various structures, including the Great Pyramid.

Concerning the orientation of the Great Pyramid, Proctor (1883, pp. 148, 149 n.) noted:

> We have seen that the Great Pyramid is so perfectly oriented as to show that astronomical observations of great accuracy were made by its architects. No astronomer can doubt this, for the simple reason that every astronomer knows the exceeding difficulty of the task which the architects solved so satisfactorily, and that nothing short of the most careful observations would have enabled the builders to secure anything like the accuracy which, as a matter of fact, they did secure. Many, not acquainted with the nature of the problem, imagine that all the builders had to do was to use some of those methods of taking shadows, as, for instance, at solar noon (which has to be first determined, be it noticed), or before and after noon, noting when shadows are equal (which is not an exact method, and requires considerable care even to give what it *can* give—imperfect orientation), and so forth. But to give the accuracy which the builders obtained, not only in the orientation, but in getting the pyramid very close to latitude 30° (which was evidently what they wanted), only very exact observations would serve.... In the first place, many seem quite unaware of the difficulty of orienting a building like the Great Pyramid with the degree of accuracy with which that building actually has been oriented. One gravely asks whether (as Narrien long since suggested) a plumb-line, so hung as to be brought into line with the pole-star, would not have served as well as the great descending passage. Observe how all the real difficulties of the problem are overlooked in this solution. We want to get a long line—a line at least 200 yards long—in a north and south position. We must fix its two ends; and as the pole-star is not available as a point along the line, we set our plumb-line at the northern end of the line, and our observing tube or hole, or whatever it may be (only it is not a telescope, for we are Egyptians of the time of Cheops, and have none), at the other. The pole-star being an altitude of 26½ degrees, the plumb-line should be nearly 100 yards long, to be seen (near the top), coincident with the pole-star, from a station 200 yards away..." Then its upper part (thus to be seen *without telescopic aid at night*) would be 260 yards away. The observer's eyesight would have to be tolerably keen. (italics in the original)

As already pointed out, Petrie (1883, 1885) and Cole (1925) sighted on the stars using modern instruments in order to determine true north and therefore determine the accuracy of the orientation of the Great Pyramid.

Hawass and other Egyptologists have suggested that the unusual layout of the chambers and passages in the Great Pyramid is simply the result of the ancient builders changing their minds a couple of times during construction. According to Hawass (*Update to Petrie*, 1990, p. 99):

> the first burial chamber of Khufu is located underneath the pyramid and was left unfinished. Next, the Overseer Of All The Works of Khufu moved the king's burial chamber up further within the pyramid to what is known as the queen's chamber. But for reasons I believe are connected to the cult change made by Khufu, the burial chamber, which contains the sarcophagus, was moved even higher up into the pyramid.

Hawass explains the cult change he refers to as follows.

> At all times, the kings was thought to be the reincarnation on earth of Horus, the Son of Ra. When the king died, he was believed to become Ra, the sun god and Osiris, king of the dead. I believe that Khufu changed this cult and became identified with Ra during his lifetime. Stadelmann suggested this idea because the name of Khufu's pyramid "Horizon of Khufu," as noted above, indicates that Khufu is placed with Ra, whose natural location is on the horizon. Furthermore, he notes that Djedefra and Khafra, the sons and immediate successors of Khufu, were the first kings to bear the title "Sons of Ra" suggesting that their father, Khufu, was Ra. (Hawass, 1990, p. 99)

PI AND THE EXTERNAL DIMENSIONS OF THE GREAT PYRAMID

Pi, π: Ratio of the circumference of a circle to its diameter, namely $C / d = \pi$ or $2\pi r = C$ (where r is the radius of the circle and thus $2r$ is the diameter); $3.14159 \ldots$ is the best six-digit approximation of π. Pi is an incommensurable number.

The pi theory of the Great Pyramid is that the shape of the pyramid was determined by setting the height of the pyramid equal to the radius of a hypothetical circle, and then making the perimeter of the base of the pyramid equal to the circumference of the same hypothetical circle; thus each of the sides of the pyramid (assuming all four sides are of equal length) will be one-quarter of the circumference of the circle defined by the height = radius of the pyramid; or let L be the length of one of these sides and let h be the height of the pyramid, then $2h\pi = 4L$, or $\pi = 2L / h$. Now let a be the distance from the middle of one side of the Great Pyramid along the horizontal to the point directly below the apex; then $2a = L$. Now substituting into the last equation, $\pi = 4a / h$. The tangent of the slope of the Great Pyramid, if built according to the pi theory, would be $h / a = 4 / \pi$ (by rearranging the last equation), so we can calculate the theoretical slope and compare it to the estimated "genuine" slope of the Great Pyramid. The theoretical pi-slope is 51.854° (Herz-Fischler, 2000, p. 67). Of course, this is based on a modern approximation of pi. If the ancient Egyptians applied the pi theory but used a different approximation of pi, such as $22 / 7 = 3.1428571$, then a different slope will ensue. Using $22 / 7$ as pi, the slope will be approximately 51.843°.

In the equation that summarizes the pi-theory for the Great Pyramid, $h / a = 4 / \pi$, this is basically the rise over the run. So if the rise is 4 for every run of π, the theory will be corroborated. Pi, however, is a pretty inconvenient number to cut or measure blocks to; it is much cleaner to have the rise and run in nice whole numbers for building purposes (and any units can be used, since in h / a units cancel out). If $22 / 7$ is used as an approximation for π, then $h / a = 4 / \pi = 4 / (22 / 7) = 28 / 22 = 14 / 11$, so use a rise of 14 for every horizontal run of 11, and one will be building a pi-theory pyramid. Petrie (1883, 1885) believed just this relationship holds in the Great Pyramid. $14 / 11 = 1.272727 \ldots$ which is the tangent of the angle 51.842767°, or approximately 51.843°, is remarkably close to the angle of $51.844 \pm .0180546°$ given by Petrie (see hereafter) for the north face mean of the Great Pyramid, or even his $51.866 \pm .0333°$ mean approximation.

The angle of inclination of the original sides, covered with their casing stones, of the Great Pyramid is a matter of uncertainty. Petrie (1885, p. 12) gives values that he measured on the few remaining in-place casing stones on the north face, as well as fragments found around the north face, and he gives one value for a casing stone on the south face. For the north face, Petrie's measurements range from 51° 44' 11" ± 23" (51.736° when converted to decimal form) to 51° 53' 20" ± 1' (51.889°), and for the south face he gives a value of 51° 57' 30" ± 20" (51.958°). As the north face mean, Petrie gives the value 51° 50' 40" ± 1' 5" (51.844°). Petrie (1885, p. 13) concludes: "On the whole, we probably cannot do better than take 51° 52' ± 02' [51.866°] as the nearest approximation to the mean angle of the Pyramid, allowing some weight to the South side." Assuming that the Great Pyramid originally came to a point at the top, Petrie (1885, p. 13) continues: "The mean base being 9068.8 ± .5 inches [230.3475 meters] this yields a height of 5776.0 ± 7.0 inches [146.7104 meters]."

Unfortunately, in a sense, the pi-theory is almost identical in practical terms to the so-called seked theory (Herz-Fischler, 2000, p. 30–45), and thus it is virtually impossible to distinguish which one is correct just on the basis of the data of the external dimensions of the Great Pyramid, and in fact it may not be that one is mutually exclusive of the other. The modern seked theory for the shape of the Great Pyramid is based on information and example problems in the Rhind Papyrus, an ancient Egyptian mathematical text. The actual manuscript probably dates from the Fifteenth Dynasty, a thousand or so years after the building of the Great Pyramid, but is apparently a copy of a Twelfth Dynasty text (which itself was still written about 700 years after the construction of the Great Pyramid). On the basis of the Rhind Papyrus, a seked can be considered the run relative to a rise of one cubit. A royal cubit, or simply a cubit, consisted of 7 palms (hands) consisting of 4 fingers (digits) each; thus a cubit was 28 fingers. According to the modern seked theory, the Great Pyramid was built with a seked of 5 palms and 2 fingers (equals 22 fingers), or, in modern terms, the rise was 1 cubit and the run was 5 palms and 2 fingers; this can be expressed as a rise of 28 fingers and a run of 22 fingers, which equals $28 / 22 = 14 / 11$, which is the same rise and run that would be used for the pi theory if the approximation of pi used is $22 / 7$.

One should note the comment of Herz-Fischler (2000, p. 34): "Despite having made an extensive search of the literature, I was unable to find unequivocal proof that the *seked* method was used [by the ancient Egyptians as an actual architectural and construction technique]." Still, "the assumption that the Egyptians used the *seked* method to determine the inclination of the faces of pyramids is widely accepted among Egyptologists" (Herz-Fischler, 2000, 43, italics in the original).

According to Herz-Fischler (2000, p. 70), the pi theory originated in 1838 with the publication by a certain H. Agnew of *Letter from Alexandria on the Evidence of the Practical Application of the Quadrature of the Circle in the Configuration of the Great Pyramids of Egypt.*

According to Herz-Fischler, Agnew applied the pi theory not to the Great Pyramid but to the Third (Menkaure) Pyramid, and it was later applied by Taylor (1859) to the Great Pyramid, although Taylor never acknowledged any debt to and never cited Agnew. Howard Vyse (1840) included a summary of Agnew's book. Herz-Fischler (2000, p. 72) says:

Taylor does not mention Agnew in his book, but we can be fairly certain that he was familiar with Agnew's work, because Taylor mentions Vyse's book several times and the latter has an explicit statement of Agnew's pi-theory. Another link to Agnew may have been provided by the mathematician De Morgan who had published a very short notice about Agnew's book and with whom Taylor was acquainted.

The pi theory was widely popularized by Smyth with the publication of *Our Inheritance in the Great Pyramid* (1864), which went through five editions (1864, 1874, 1877, 1880, 1890) and continues to be reprinted. Smyth was quite famous in his lifetime and immediately after his death for his Great Pyramid work and fantasies, and he is still well known today. There was even a fictionalized account of his life and work by Max Eyth, published in Germany: *Der Kampf um die Cheopspyramide* (The Struggle over the Pyramid of Cheops).

Mendelssohn (1974, p. 73) acknowledges the apparent pi relation found in the Great Pyramid but argues that it was an outgrowth of the practical way in which the Egyptians laid out the Great Pyramid, following an idea that was suggested to Mendelssohn "by an electronics engineer, T. E. Connolly" (Mendelssohn, 1974, p. 64). Mendelssohn says, relative to the theory he espouses:

> The explanation is based on the assumption that the ancient Egyptians had not yet formed the concept of isotropic three-dimensional space. In other words, whereas to us measures of height and vertical distance [apparently he meant "horizontal" rather than "vertical"] are the same thing, namely a length for which we use the same unit, this may not have been regarded as natural by the pyramid builders. (1974, p. 73)

He then suggests that the ancient Egyptians used cubits for height but what he calls a "rolled cubit" for horizontal distances, where a rolled cubit is one revolution on the ground of a drum that is 1 cubit in diameter. In terms of the Great Pyramid, if we apply Mendelssohn's hypothesis, we can suggest that it was designed to have a height of 280 cubits and a length on each side of 140 rolled cubits. The side length of 140 rolled cubits would be equal to $140 \times \pi = 439.8$ cubits. More important, using the foregoing terminology, $a = 70\pi$ cubits and $h = 280$ cubits, so $h / a = 280 / (70\pi) = 4 / \pi$, as is suggested by the pi theory. However, the downside of Mendelssohn's hypothesis is that there is no evidence "that the ancient Egyptians had not yet formed the concept of isotropic three-dimensional space" (I'm not sure how they would have achieved all of their amazing architectural and sculptural achievements if this were true), and it postulates a unit and way of measuring horizontal distances by the ancient Egyptians for which there is no independent evidence. As Herz-Fischler (2000, p. 226, n. 9) points out, it is not clear with Mendelssohn's theory how the ancient Egyptians either measured the vertical height up to 280 cubits so accurately, or rolled a drum so many times along the ground to measure the horizontal distance without any perceptible slippage. It is also not inconceivable that the ancient Egyptians used a variation on the scenario suggested by Mendelssohn for the very purpose of incorporating the pi relation into the Great Pyramid rather than the apparent pi relationship simply being an unexpected outcome of the way the Great Pyramid was laid out.

PHI AND THE EXTERNAL DIMENSIONS OF THE GREAT PYRAMID

Phi (or the Golden Number, Φ) is equal to (1 + square root of 5) / 2 = approximately 1.6180339 . . . (see West, 1979, pp. 74, 75).

Phi is obtained by dividing a line, AC, at a point B such that AC / AB = AB / BC. That is, the whole to the longer part is the same proportion as the longer part to the shorter part, both of which equal Φ. This is the Golden Section, or Primordial Scission (West, 1979, p. 74, discussing the work of Schwaller de Lubicz).

Take a square with a side of unit 1 and cut it in half from one side to the other to form two rectangles of 1 × ½. The diagonal of one of the rectangles plus ½ equals Φ. By the Pythagorean theorem, the length of the diagonal under consideration, call it W, bears the following relationship to the other two sides: $W^2 = 1^2 + (1 / 2)^2$. Or, $W^2 = 1.25$ and thus W = square root of 1.25, and Φ = square root of 1.25 + (1 / 2). However, the square root of 1.25 can be multiplied by 1 in the form of $\sqrt{4}$ /2 to arrive at $\sqrt{4 \times 1.25}$ / 2 = $\sqrt{5}$ / 2. Now substitute $\sqrt{5}$ / 2 for $\sqrt{1.25}$ in the equation $\Phi = \sqrt{1.25}$ + (1 / 2), and we arrive at $\Phi = (1 + \sqrt{5})/ 2$.

One of the important properties of Φ is that: $1 + \Phi = \Phi^2$

In the Fibonacci sequence—1, 1, 2, 3, 5, 8, 13, 21, 34, 55, 89, . . . —each number is the sum of the two preceding numbers. Ratios of successive terms give increasingly better approximations of phi (G, Golden number, Φ): for example, 55 / 34 = 1.61747, whereas phi is an irrational number 1.6180 . . . incapable of being expressed as a quotient of integers (see Herz-Fischler, 2000, p. 242; Tompkins, 1971, p. 192). It is through the Fibonacci series that phi is said to control many things in nature, such as growth curves of marine organisms (such as the outwardly spiraling shell of the Nautilus), seed whorls in composite flowers, or the structure of a spiral galaxy, and so on.

According to Schwaller de Lubicz (see Tompkins, 1971, p. 194), the ancient Egyptians had figured out that the relationship between π and Φ is $\pi = \Phi^2 \times 6 / 5$.

Take two approximations of Φ in the Fibonacci series in sequence and substitute them into this equation, and you can produce a good approximation of π (the π approximations get better as one goes further along in the Fibonacci series). As an example, an approximation of π apparently used in the Great Pyramid is:

$(34 / 21) \times (55 / 34) \times 6 / 5 = (55 / 21) \times (6 / 5) = (11 / 21) \times 6 = 66 / 21 = 22 / 7$

Stecchini, a modern researcher, has argued that the Great Pyramid was designed with phi in mind, at least in part. Let Y be the horizontal length from the middle of the northern side at the base to a point directly under the apex of the Great Pyramid; Y equals ½ of the standard base length of 439½ cubits (according to Stecchini; see hereafter) divided by 2 (230.363178 meters divided by 2 equals 115.181589 meters), according to Stecchini (1971, p. 368). To say that the northern face was designed with phi in mind means that Y divided by the square root of 1 over phi equals the height of the Great Pyramid, or 115.181589 meters $/ \sqrt{1 / 1.618}) = 146.512$ meters. This corresponds to what Herz-Fischler (2000, pp. 80–91) describes as the "Kepler Triangle Theory" of the shape of the Great Pyramid. If A is the apothem of a side of the Great Pyramid (the apothem is the length from the middle of the base of one side of the pyramid to the apex or summit of the pyramid; in the Great Pyramid the apothem would be approximately 186.5 meters if the summit came to a point; if the sides are not exactly the same, then each may have its own apothem value), then, according to the Kepler triangle theory, $A / Y = \Phi$.

The equivalence of these two approaches can be shown as follows.

$Y / \sqrt{1 / \Phi} = h$

By the Pythagorean theorem: $Y^2 + h^2 = A^2$. Substitute $Y / \sqrt{1 / \Phi}$ for h in the last equation, and one has

$Y^2 + \Phi Y^2 = A^2$ or $(1 + \Phi) Y^2 = A^2$

However, one of the properties of Φ is that $(1 + \Phi) = \Phi^2$ (Herz-Fischler, 2000, p. 83), so $\Phi^2 Y^2 = A^2$, or $\Phi Y = A$, and rearranging, $A / Y = \Phi$.

A Kepler triangle is a right triangle where the ratio of the hypotenuse to the larger side equals the ratio of the larger side to the smaller side; in a Kepler triangle, the hypotenuse divided by the smaller side equals Φ (Herz-Fischler, 2000, pp. 81–82). In the foregoing equation $A / Y = \Phi$, A is the hypotenuse, and Y is the smaller adjacent side. In the case of the Great Pyramid, if we use the following values for the apothem, height, and Y, respectively: 186.367 meters (apothem value calculated from the next two values using the Pythagorean theorem), 146.512 meters, 115.182 meters; then the ratio of the hypotenuse to the larger side is 1.270, and the ratio of the larger side to the smaller side is 1.272, which can be considered a fairly close match.

Related to the Kepler triangle theory, in that it gives ultimately the same result, namely that $A / Y = \Phi$, is the so-called equal area theory (Herz-Fischler, 2000, pp. 96–111). The core of the equal area theory is that the surface area of one face of the Great Pyramid is equal to the area of the square of the height. In terms of h, A, and Y used earlier, the equal area theory states that:

$$h^2 = (1 / 2)(2A)Y = AY$$

Using the Pythagorean theorem, we know that $h^2 + Y^2 = A^2$.

Rearranging, $h^2 = A^2 - Y^2$, and substituting into the equation $h^2 = AY$, we have:

$$A^2 - Y^2 = AY$$

Divide both sides by Y^2, and we have $(A / Y)^2 - 1 = A / Y$, then add 1 to each side, and we have $1 + A / Y = (A / Y)^2$, remembering that $1 + \Phi = \Phi^2$.

This means that $A / Y = \Phi$, which is the same ultimate result as the Kepler triangle theory.

If $A / Y = \Phi$, then $1 / \Phi = Y / A$, and by trigonometry, the theoretical slope of a side of the Great Pyramid is equal to the inverse cosine of $1 / \Phi = 1 / 1.6180 = 0.6180$, which is approximately 51.827°.

Note that in terms of the slope angle each predicts, the pi theory can be considered closer to the actual observations of the slope of the Great Pyramid than the Kepler triangle theory or equal area theory. All three, however, really give remarkably close results to the actual observations (which observations may include some degree of inaccuracy from the slopes and angles possibly intended by the original architects).

The equal area theory was also espoused by Taylor (1859), and was at least partially suggested, but not developed, by Agnew (1838, as quoted by Herz-Fischler, 2000, p. 98). Herz-Fischler thinks it is "not unlikely" (p. 99) that Taylor was inspired by Agnew's comments. If anyone deserves credit for fully developing the equal area theory, I think it is Taylor.

Agnew and Taylor both based their concepts (or, in Agnew's case, protoconcept) of the equal area theory on a reinterpretation of Herodotus. Herz-Fischler (2000, p. 98) quotes a translation of the relevant passage from Herodotus's *Histories*, book 2, chapter 124, as follows: "The pyramid itself was twenty years in the making. Its base is square, each side is eight plethra long and its height is the same; the whole is of stone polished and most exactly fitted; there is no block of less than thirty feet in length."

Taken literally in terms of linear dimensions, Herodotus's statement cannot be correct. The length of the sides of the Great Pyramid are not equal to its height, and the lengths of the sides are not even equal to their apothems or the arris of the Great Pyramid (the arris is the length of the edge between two sides, from the corner of the pyramid to the vertex, about 219 meters in the Great Pyramid). Taylor suggested that the term *plethron* (plural *plethra*) was being used here by Herodotus as a measure of surface area, not as a linear measure, and indeed it could be used in either sense in antiquity (as *plethra* was used elsewhere by Herodotus as a measure of surface area). It is relatively easy to see how the surface area of each side can be measured in terms of surface area, but what does it mean to measure the height in terms of surface area? Taylor suggested that what Herodotus means is that the square of the height (a surface area that is $h \times h$) must be equal to the surface area of one side.

In terms of this interpretation, it is unclear to me exactly what a plethron was in terms of modern units. Herz-Fischler (2000, p. 100) equates 8 plethra with 7,589 square meters, but I am not convinced this is correct. What is important for the equal area theory, however, is the closeness of the fit of the area of a side to h^2. If we use a value of 146.6 meters for h, then $h^2 = 21,492$ square meters. Using 230.4 meters for the length of one side, and 186.5 meters for the length of an apothem, the surface area of a side is 21,485 square meters. (The values used here for height, side length, and apothem are those used by Herz-Fischler in his book.) This is a discrepancy of only 7 square meters, so the theory and the calculations are very close.

Stecchini (1971, pp. 370–372) traces other ancient accounts of the dimensions of the Great Pyramid back to Agatharchides of Cnidus, of the late second century B.C., who served under the Ptolemaic kings of Egypt. According to Stecchini's interpretation of these writings, the "surface area interpretation" of Herodotus is correct.

Smyth, in the first edition *Our Inheritance in the Great Pyramid* (1864) never mentioned the equal area theory, despite being the foremost champion of Taylor's

work on the Great Pyramid. Smyth only mentions the equal area theory in footnotes in later editions. Instead, Smyth promoted and supported the pi theory.
Robert Ballard (1882) concluded that Y / A (apothem to half the length of a side)
is 34 / 21, which is a close approximation to Φ, and he used this to support a version
of the equal area theory. Martin Gardner (1957, p. 178), the well-known debunker,
apparently accepted the equal area theory for the Great Pyramid, saying:

> The only Pyramid "truth" which cannot be explained easily in terms of such jug-
> gling is the value *pi*. The Egyptians may have purposefully made use of this ratio,
> but it seems more likely that it was a by-product of another construction. Herodotus
> states that the Pyramid was built so the area of each face would equal the area of a
> square whose side is equal to the Pyramid's height. If such a construction is made,
> it fits the Pyramid perfectly, and the ratio of height to twice the base will automat-
> ically be a surprisingly accurate value for *pi*. (italics in the original)

Most Great Pyramid researchers assume that initially the structure was at least
intended to have a perfectly square base and sides that rose to the apex at equal angles. Stecchini (1971), on the basis of his analysis, questions these fundamental assumptions. Stecchini (1971, p. 368) believes that a starting point for the design of
the Great Pyramid may have been a base length of 440 cubits and a height of 280
cubits, but that this was then modified in the final plan and construction. According to Stecchini (1971, p. 364), the basic length of each side was modified to 439.5
cubits (230.363 meters, using Stecchini's value of 524.1483 millimeters for the cubit used in the Great Pyramid). The perimeter of the Great Pyramid was therefore
meant to be 1,758 cubits (921.453 meters), which, according to Stecchini (1971,
p. 365) is half the value of a minute of latitude at the equator, as calculated by the
ancient Egyptians as 3,516 cubits (1,842.905 meters; Stecchini, 1971, p. 365, cites
1,842.925 as a modern calculation of the same entity).

Stecchini (1971, p. 364) interprets data from the Cole Survey (1925) to indicate
that the sides of the Great Pyramid were not off from a perfect square due to acci-
dents or inaccuracies in the layout but that the base was purposefully designed to
be slightly different from a perfect square. Stecchini believes the western side was
laid out (the line for its alignment drawn) first, and the northern side was made to
be as perfectly perpendicular to it as possible. The eastern side, however, was intended to be an angle of 3' greater than perpendicular to the northern side (i.e., the
northeast corner was meant to be 90° 03' 00"), and the southern side was intended
to be ½' greater than perpendicular (i.e., the southwest corner was meant to be 90°

00' 30"; see Stecchini, 1971, pp. 364–365). Furthermore, using the data from the Cole Survey on a small line found on the pavement at the base of the Great Pyramid near the middle on the north side, which some have assumed to be the original axis of the Great Pyramid, Stecchini (1971, pp. 366–367) concludes that the north–south axis of the pyramid was off center, and accordingly the apex was off center, by about 35.5 millimeters to the west (the line in question is located 115.090 meters from the northwest corner and 115.161 meters from the northeast corner). The foregoing information would indicate that the four faces of the Great Pyramid have slightly different slopes from each other, as was suspected but not actively pursued by Petrie (1883, 1885).

On the basis of his novel assumptions and analysis, Stecchini (1971, p. 367) concludes that the western face of the Great Pyramid was designed using the factor pi (π, approximately 3.14) while the northern face was designed using the factor phi (Φ, or the irrational Golden Number, approximately 1.618; see earlier). Furthermore, Stecchini (1971, p. 367) "concluded that the height of the [Great] Pyramid was either 279.53 cubits = 146,515.174 millimeters or a figure very close to 279.53 cubits."

Let Z be the horizontal length from the middle of the western side at the base to a point directly under the apex of the Great Pyramid, which equals 115.090 meters, according to the Cole Survey (1925), as interpreted by Stecchini. To say that the western face was designed with pi in mind means that 2 times value Z times 4 divided by 2 times pi equals the height of the Great Pyramid, or (2×115.090 meters $\times$ 4) / (2×3.14) = 146.6 meters. If a more accurate value of pi is used in this equation, such as 3.14159, then the calculated height is 146.537 meters. Using the approximation of 3.1420 for pi, the calculated height is 146.518 meters.

Note that these concepts of the Kepler triangle theory and the equal area theory discussed earlier, the former of which Stecchini uses to relate the length of the northern face to the height using phi, are very different from the "side : height = Golden Number" concept discussed by Herz-Fischler (2000, pp. 92–95). According to the Cole Survey (1925), the northern side has a length of 230.251 meters, and 230.251 meters divided by a height of 146.515 meters, as used by Stecchini, equals 1.5715182, a far cry from the value of phi. The side : height = phi theory yields a theoretical slope of 51.027° for the sides of the Great Pyramid. Let s be the length of a side. To calculate the theoretical angle for this relationship, we can use the tangent of the height over one-half the side length: $\Phi = s / h$, so $h = s / \Phi$, $s = h\Phi$, and $s / 2 = h\Phi / 2$, so $h / (s / 2) = h / (h\Phi / 2) = 2 / \Phi$; $2 / \Phi = 1.2360679$, and the cotangent of 1.2360679 is 51.02655°, a value that is not particularly close to the actual value calculated for the Great Pyramid.

LATITUDE AND POLAR FLATTENING EXPRESSED
IN THE SHAPE OF THE GREAT PYRAMID

After much astute analysis, Stecchini (1971, p. 378) summarizes his conclusions as follows:

> The basic idea of the Great Pyramid was that it should be a representation of the northern hemisphere, a hemisphere projected on flat surfaces, as is done in mapmaking. . . . The Great Pyramid was a projection on four triangular surfaces. The apex represented the pole and the perimeter represented the equator. [Actually, even according to Stecchini's writings elsewhere, in the appendix to Tompkins, this is not really correct. Metaphorically the perimeter may represent the equator, but in actual point of fact it represents a great circle through the poles perpendicular to the equator.] This is the reason why the perimeter is in relation to 2π with the height. The Great Pyramid represents the northern hemisphere in a scale of 1:43,200; this scale was chosen because there are 86,400 seconds in 24 hours. But then the builders became concerned with the problem of indicating the ratio of polar flattening of the earth and the length of the degrees of latitude which depends on the ratio of this flattening. Next, they incorporated into the Pyramid the factor Φ as the key to the structure of the cosmos.

According to Stecchini's (1971, p. 365, 373) interpretations of ancient Egyptian geodesy, his analysis of the Great Pyramid directly, and his research on ancient authors, drawing from the comments of Agatharchides on the Great Pyramid, the perimeter of the base of the Great Pyramid was specifically designed to be one-half minute of latitude at the equator, which the Egyptians calculated as 3,516 cubits. Thus the perimeter of the Great Pyramid is 1,758 cubits (average of 439.5 cubits per side times four sides). The ancient Egyptians were interested in latitude, not longitude, in this case because they were concerned with the length and shape of the north–south meridian, from the equator to the North Pole, or more generally the nature of a great circle through the poles that describes the shape of Earth and also determines the polar diameter of Earth. If the perimeter of the Great Pyramid describes, or contains a unit of measure of, a great circle through the poles of Earth, and the pi relationship holds for the Great Pyramid, then the height of the Great Pyramid is indeed a measure of the polar radius, and therefore also the diameter (2 times radius = diameter), of Earth. The Egyptian value of 3,516 cubits = 1,842.905 meters for a minute of degree of latitude at the equator is incredibly close to the modern 1,842.925 meters cited by Stecchini (1971, p. 365).

A great circle through the poles is not a perfect circle, however. There is a minor flattening at the poles. According to Stecchini's analysis of the Great Pyramid, which he calculates rose to a final height at the apex of 279.53 cubits or thereabouts (Stecchini, 1971, p. 367), the ancient Egyptians were not only aware of the polar flattening and its magnitude to a very fine degree but they incorporated this information into the design of the Great Pyramid. He believes that the original design for the Great Pyramid called for a height of 280 cubits to the apex, but this was reduced to about 279.5 cubits as an indication of the polar flattening and its order of magnitude (which is very slight and was not demonstrated in modern times until the eighteenth century, although Newton had predicted the polar flattening in the late seventeenth century).

ANCIENT NAMES FOR THE GREAT PYRAMID

Hawass (*Update to Petrie*, 1990, p. 98) says that the original name for the Great Pyramid was "Horizon of Khufu," and this may indicate, according to Hawass (1990, p. 99), that Khufu was associated with Ra, the sun god, who of course rose from and set into the horizon. According to Pochan (1978, p. xiii), the name of the Great Pyramid was "Akhet Khufu" (Khufu's Luminous Horizon). Pochan (1978, p. xiii) argues that "the Great Pyramid was both the tomb of Cheops and the temple of the sun god Khnum." Adams (1895, p. vii; 1933, p. 23) says that the Great Pyramid was "called by the Egyptians of old" "Khut" (Lights). D. H. Lewis (1980, p. 9) says that the ancient Egyptian name for the Great Pyramid was "Khuti," meaning "the Lights." Adams (1895, 1898, 1933; see also Hall, 1945, 2003, p. 117) also refers to the Great Pyramid as "the House of the Hidden Places." Baines and Málek (1980, p. 140) give the ancient name of the Great Pyramid as "The Pyramid which is the Place of Sunrise and Sunset" (this corresponds to the same hieroglyphic inscription that Pochan translated as "luminous horizon"). According to Baines and Málek (1980, p. 140), the second (Khephren or Khafre) pyramid of Giza was known as the "Great Pyramid" by the ancient Egyptians, and the third (Menkaure) pyramid was known as the "Divine Pyramid." According to Pochan (1978, p. xv) the second and third pyramids were known as "Khefra the Great" and "Menkaura the Divine," respectively. Wake (1882, p. 38) says: "From the inscriptions, it would seem to have been called 'the Great Temple of Shofo [Khufu or Cheops],' and within its precinct to have been dedicated at one time to the worship of that king."

THE ATTRIBUTION OF
THE GREAT PYRAMID TO KHUFU

The ancient writers Herodotus (fifth century B.C.) and Diodorus (first century B.C.) both clearly attribute the Great Pyramid to the pharaoh now commonly known as Khufu. Sandys (1621, p. 129) accepted the attribution to Khufu (Cheops). Greaves (1704, p. 704) assigned the Great Pyramid to "Cheops or Chemmis," the second Giza pyramid to "Cephren or Chabryis," and the third to "Mycerinus." Greaves thought that these three kings should be assigned to the Twentieth Dynasty, and he calculated that the beginning of the reign of Cheops could be dated to 1,266 years "before the beginning of the Years of our Lord" [i.e., 1266 B.C.]. Since the time of Greaves, the vast majority of Egyptologists have attributed the Great Pyramid to Khufu.

IMAGES OF KHUFU

It is often said (for instance, by DeSalvo, 2003, p. 3; also Fix, 1978, p. 82) that the only known representation of Khufu is a small (approximately 3 inches tall, according to Lepre, 1990, p. 61, but "barely two inches tall," according to El Mahdy, 2003, p. 82; I have seen it behind glass, and my guess would be about 2½ inches) ivory seated figure found by Petrie in a temple at Abydos in 1909 (Lepre, 1990, p. 62; see Petrie, 1923, *Arts*, p. 134, fig. 123; Petrie, 1923, *History*, p. 57), and now housed in the Egyptian Museum in Cairo. However, this is not precisely true, as a stylized image of Khufu was found carved into a rock cliff face in Wady Maghara [Maghâreh], in the Sinai (Lepre, 1990, p. 61; see also Petrie, 1906, p. 46, where he says that not long before he studied the area the "Khufu sculptures were smashed up" by recent miners, and p. 259, where Petrie notes: "we secured a piece [among the fragments of stone collected in the wake of the modern mining] that showed the face of the king [Khufu]"). It has also been suggested that the face of the Great Sphinx represents Khufu (see, for instance, Stadelmann, 2000), in part on the basis of the reputed similiarity between the Great Sphinx's face

Ivory statuette portrait of Khufu. (*From Petrie,*
1923, Arts and Crafts of Ancient Egypt, *facing*
page 136.)

and the ivory statuette. Returning to the ivory statuette from Abydos, El Mahdy (2003, p. 82) writes: "As for Cheops [Khufu] himself, only one image of him survives as King. This tiny ivory figurine . . . bears his name, although recently even this has been questioned." She includes a photograph of the figurine, and her caption reads: "This tiny ivory figurine is the only surviving image of Cheops, although some authorities are now questioning its authenticity." So what did Khufu look like? We really don't know precisely. El Mahdy (2003, p. 31) says: "In images of Snofru and his son, Cheops, their faces are African." The same appears to apply to known images of other relatives of Khufu, such as his brother Rahotep.

THE NAMES OF KHUFU

Lepre (1990, p. 61) lists the following as names of the pharaoh commonly known as Cheops or Khufu: Metheru ("The Energetic"—so called "Hawk name" and "Vulture-and-Cobra name"), Khufu ("He Protects"—so called "Set or Hawk-of-Nubi name" and "Reed-and-Hornet name"), Chembres, Chemististes, Chemmis, Cheop, Cheops, Comastes, Khembes, Khemmes, Kheop, Kheops, Kheuf, Khnem-Kheuf, Khnum-Kheuf, Khnum-Khuf, Khuf, Khufu, Khufui, Khufwey, Kouf, Koufou, Nem-Shufu, Noh-Suphis, Saoph, Saophis, Sen-Suphis, Shofo, Shufu, Shure, Soris, Suph, Suphis, Surid, Xufu. Pochan adds Saurid and Khoufou to this list (1978, p. xiv and title page, respectively). Bonwick (1877, pp. 75–76) adds Xeopos, Khoofoo, Soyoof, Souphis, and Shoopho. D. H. Lewis (1980, p. 14) lists the names Khupfu and Saophia. Other variants on the foregoing forms are found in the literature. Bonwick (1877, p. 76, italics in the original) says: "Eratoshtenes speaks of King Saophis, the many-haired; and, in Coptic, *shoo* is *many,* and *pho* is *hair.* Bonwick (1877, p. 75, quoting Mr. Gliddon) also cites the tomb of a certain "Eimei, chief priest of the habitations of King Shoopho" as having been discovered near the Great Pyramid, and suggests that this Eimei may have been the architect of the Great Pyramid.

According to Herodotus and Diodorus Siculus, Khufu reigned for 50 years; however, Mantheo wrote that "Suphis reigned 68 years. He built the largest Pyramid. He was also called Peroptes" (Kingsland, 1935, p. 2).

According to Pochan (1978, p. xiii), the full name of Khufu, with the title "Hrw" before it, based on inscriptions in the so-called Relieving Chambers and also an inscription found at Wadi Magharah on the Sinai (illustrated by a drawing in Fix, 1978, p. 86) is "Hrw-Khnum-Khufu" ("the most high"—"Khnum protects me"). The simplified cartouche by which he is more commonly known reads, according to Pochan (1978, p. xii), simply "Khufui" ("He protects me"). Pochan (1978, pp. xiii–xiv) contends that the Fourth Dynasty originated in Upper Egypt and was associated with the ram-headed sun god of Elephantine known as Khnum (and associated with Ra and Amon in New Kingdom times). Further north in Egypt, around the Memphis and Heliopolis area (in the region of the Giza Plateau), the god Khnum was considered an intruder relative to the native gods, so the pharaoh's name was often shortened to be less offensive, reading simply "He protects me," and the "He" could be considered to refer to any of the gods. Pochan (1978, p. xiv) further suggests that the names Saurid, Surid, and Soris, sometimes applied to Khufu, derived from the Egyptian "Sri" ("ram"), as Khnum was a ram-headed god.

During the nineteenth and early twentieth centuries, many Egyptologists suggested that the names "Khufu" and "Khnum-Khufu" might refer to two different persons, especially since they occur together in the same inscription on the Sinai (see discussion and quotations from Petrie and Gaston Maspero in Fix, 1978, pp. 85–87; see Petrie, 1923, *History,* p. 62), and it was only in the later twentieth century that opinion solidified around the notion that both refer to the same man, the pharaoh Khufu of the Fourth Dynasty. Fix (1978, p. 89) suggests that these are not even the names of a person or persons but rather either two different names for a single god or the names for two different gods. He further hypothesizes (p. 89) that "if there ever was a King Khufu he lived long after the Pyramid was built and *was named after the Pyramid*" (italics in the original). Fix (1978, p. 93) further suggests, based both on the attributes of various gods, their symbolism, and etymological similarities, that "Khnum, Khnoum, Khufu, Souphis, Khnoubis, Chnouphis, Tehuti, Thoth, Mercury, Enoch, Hermes, and possibly 'Christos' are simply different representations of the same figure and power that finds remarkably similar expression in cosmologies extending over many thousands of years."

WHERE WAS KHUFU ACTUALLY BURIED?

The standard Egyptological view is that the Great Pyramid was built as the tomb of the pharaoh Khufu. Even if this was indeed the case, if being the intended tomb of Khufu does not exclude the possibility that it was used for other purposes as well, such as an astronomical observatory, before being completed (Proctor, 1883), or as a site of initiatory rites (Adams, 1895, 1898), it is not necessarily true that Khufu was actually buried in the Great Pyramid upon his death. Indeed, the classical writer Diodorus said that the Great and Second Pyramids were designed as tombs for the pharaohs Chemmis (Khufu) and Cephren (Khafre), but that neither one was actually buried there (Greaves, 1646; Kingsland, 1935, p. 32),

> for the people being exasperated against them by reason of the toilsomeness of their works, and for their cruelty and oppression, threatened to tear in pieces their dead bodies, and with ignominy to throw them out of their sepulchres. Wherefore both of them dying, commanded their friends privately to bury them in an obscure place. (Diodorus as quoted by Kingsland, 1935, p. 34)

Although generally dismissed by western Egyptologists and historians, there exists a medieval Arab tradition of a body having been found in the Great Pyramid, as explained by Wake:

> As to the Great Pyramid, if we are to believe those [Arab] writers, an embalmed human body was actually discovered in the so-called King's Chamber when it was

opened by the Caliph Mamoon. This is said to have taken place in the year 820 A.D., and Arab historian, Abd-el-Hôkm, relates that "a statue resembling a man was found in the sarcophagus, and in the statue (mummy case) was a body with a breast-plate of gold and jewels, bearing characters written with a pen which no one understood." Alkaisi gives much the same story, and he adds that the case stood at the door of the king's palace at Cairo in the year 511—that is, 1133 A.D. It may be doubted, however, whether this had anything to do with the Great Pyramid. Dr. Ebers mentions that in the middle of the 15th century, "an Emir caused the destruction of the much admired 'green shrine,' which was formed out of a single block of a stone as hard as iron, and ornamented with figures and inscriptions. It was smashed to pieces." He adds, "the golden statue, with eyes of precious stones, which had once been enshrined in this marvel of art—dedicated probably to the Moon-god Chonsu—had long before disappeared." In this shrine and statue we have no doubt the case and body mentioned by Abd-el-Hôkm, as Alkaisi when referring to these speaks of an image of a man in green-stone, containing a body in golden armour with a large ruby overhead. It must be admitted, therefore, that there is no reliable evidence of any human body having been found in the Great Pyramid. Nevertheless this is not any proof that the building was *not* used as a tomb. The Arab writer Abd Allatif refers to an early statement that when the Persians conquered Egypt they took away great riches from the Pyramids, which were the sepulchres of the kings, and, therefore, no doubt the receptacle of their treasures. Moreover, according to Sir Gardner Wilkinson, the Egyptians themselves had in many instances plundered the tombs of Thebes and he seems to think that the Great Pyramid met with the same fate at their hands. (1882, pp. 49–50)

According to Herodotus, Khufu was buried in an underground chamber that included a canal flowing in from the Nile such that his tomb sat on an island surrounded by water (Wake, 1882, p. 40). There is a tomb located south and slightly east of the Great Pyramid and west and slightly north of the Great Sphinx that was called Campbell's Tomb (named by Vyse for Colonel Campbell), which Smyth (see Smyth, 1877; Tastmona, 1954, pp. 30–31) considered to be Khufu's actual tomb, "fulfilling the description of Herodotus, as to the place where King Cheops was buried; viz. 'not in Gr[eat] Pyramid at all, but in a subterranean Island, surrounded by the waters of the 'Nile,' which filter through the intervening rock up to their level in the River at the time" (Smyth, 1877, part of caption on p. 15).

Concerning this tomb, Petrie (1883, pp. 138–139) says:

The very remarkable tomb known as Campbell's tomb, requires some notice here, as it has been associated with the name of Khufu by some writers. . . . We may state the general form of it as a large square pit in the rock, 26 by 30 feet, and 53 feet deep; outside this there is a trench, running all round it at 9 to 22 feet distant; this is 5 feet wide and 73 feet deep. Bars of rock are left at intervals across this trench. Altogether about 10,000 tons of limestone have been excavated here.

The gold ring found here, bearing the cartouche of Khufu, only belonged to a priest of that king in late times, and the king's name on it is only introduced incidentally in the inscription, which does not profess to be of early period. But there is, nevertheless, ground for believing this excavation to be the remains of a tomb of the Pyramid period.

When this pit was cleared out by Vyse, he found a tomb built in the bottom of it; but this cannot have been the original interment, for the following reasons. On the sides of the pit may be seen the characteristic marks where the backs of lining blocks have been fitted into the rock . . . and on the surface round the pit and the trench are numerous traces of the fitting of stones, and of plastering, and even some remaining stones let into the rock. Hence this pit has been lined with fine stone, and a pavement or a building has existed above it at the ground level. This lining would so far reduce the size of the pit, from 315 width to probably about 206 inches, that it could be roofed either with beams or with sloping blocks. But the object of such a deep pit seems strange, as it would form a chamber 50 feet high. Perhaps the great rock-pit of the Pyramid at Abu Roash explains this; as Vyse says that in his day, there were signs that it had been filled up with successive spaced roofs, like those over the King's Chamber.

The remaining indications then show that this pit is merely the rough shell of a fine-stone chamber, probably roofed with successive ceilings for its greater security, and having some pavement, or probably a great mastaba chapel, on the surface above it. The access to it was perhaps down the square shaft in the rock, which still remains. It is certain, then, that the tomb of the twenty-sixth dynasty, built of small stones in the bottom of the great pit, after all the lining had been removed, and when it was again a mere shell, cannot have been the original interment. And from the character of the design, and its execution, there can be but little hesitation in referring the original work to the fourth dynasty. Though it may not have been the tomb of Khufu himself, as some have suggested, yet the trench around it may at high Nile have readily held water, insulating the central pit; and it may thus be the origin of the description of Khufu's tomb, given by Herodotus.

Following the account of Herodotus, Pochan (1978, p. 287) believes that the body of Khufu (Cheops) was laid in a crypt, where it presumably rests to this day, located 58 meters beneath the Great Pyramid's base and 27 meters below the Subterranean Chamber. Pochan (1978, p. 287) passionately writes:

> To me, this is more than a mere hypothesis, for while crawling along the blind passage, surrounded by bats, I have repeatedly had the strange impression that by striking the floor with a simple key, I made the entire Pyramid tremble! This extraordinary resonance was probably the reason why Howard-Vyse [many authors, including Pochan, hyphenate this name] had the primitively squared lustral well deepened by 9 meters. But the depth reached was clearly not sufficient to lead to the vault of the royal hypogeum.

For additional suggestions as to the location of Khufu's burial chamber, see the earlier section on "Unknown" Chambers in "Passages and Chambers within the Great Pyramid."

WAS KHUFU GOOD OR BAD?

According to Herodotus (fifth century B.C.), Khufu was a tyrannical and criminal king whose memory instilled hate long after his death. He was said to have closed all of the temples and outlawed sacrifices, and furthermore made the populace work for him building the Great Pyramid (Wake, 1882, p. 39). Supposedly, according to Herodotus, when Khufu's funds ran out, he put his own daughter to work as a prostitute: she took on lovers, each of whom was required to donate a stone block toward the construction of the Great Pyramid (Bonwick, 1877, p. 75). Khufu, according to Herodotus, reigned for 50 years and was then succeeded by his brother Khafre (Khafra or Chephren), who reigned another 56 years and continued the evil ways of his brother (Wake, 1882, p. 40). (In the probable Twelfth Dynasty Westcar Papyrus, however, Khafre is referred to as a son of Khufu; see Petrie, 1999, p. 5.) Supposedly, the memory of these monarchs was so odious that the Egyptian priests of Herodotus's time did not want to even speak their names, "and for this reason they call the Pyramids after the shepherd Philitis [also referred to as Philition; see Kingsland, 1935, p. 3], who at the time of their erection used to feed his flocks near this spot" (Herodotus as quoted by Wake, 1882, p. 40). According to Herodotus, Khafre was followed by Mycerinus, a son of Khufu, who built the third (and much smaller) Giza pyramid and also ordered the temples opened, ended the cruelties of his father and uncle, and was viewed by the Egyptians as a fair and just king. As a side note, some authors such as Smyth have equated Philitis with Melchizedek, King of Salem and a priest of God (see Kingsland, 1935, p. 4; Genesis 14:18; Salem is sometimes equated with Jerusalem, Viening, 1969, p. 660), and in turn some have suggested that it was Melchizedek (Melchisedek) who built the Great Pyramid. It has also been suggested that Melchizedek was actually Jesus Christ (Bonwick, 1877, p. 80, quoting, but not advocating, the opinion of a writer named Captain Tracey).

In contradiction to the account of Herodotus that Khufu "plunged into every kind of wickedness," Mantheo says that he "was translated to the Gods, and wrote the sacred book" (both quotations from Kingsland, 1935, p. 1). Kingsland (1935) suggests that Mantheo, being an Egyptian, is a better authority here than Herodotus. Furthermore, both the Great Pyramid and Second Pyramid have temples associated with them, which is contrary to Herodotus's assertion that Khufu and Khafre closed all of the temples. It is also possible that the statements of both Herodotus and Mantheo are to some extent true, depending on one's perspective. That is, Khufu may have introduced a new religion or supreme god, and in that sense was considered "wicked" by the standards of the old religion, while revered by the adherents of the new religion (compare the suggestion made along the same lines by Pochan, 1978, p. xiii). Fix (1978, p. 89) says that cartouches of Khufu are found on many tombs and monuments, some dating to the last centuries before the Christian era. "Egyptologists explain that Khufu's name had become 'a powerful charm,' and was put on monuments as a sign of sanctity and protection. In other words, it was used in later times as the sign of the cross has been used in Christian countries for nearly two thousand years" (Fix, 1978, p. 89). The cult of Khufu may have lapsed during the Middle and New Kingdoms, but it was revived during the Twenty-sixth Dynasty, also known as the Saite Period (Hawass, *Update to Petrie*, 1990, p. 98).

The Westcar Papyrus (named after the former owner, Henry Westcar, and purchased by the Berlin Museum), a probable Twelfth Dynasty document but containing possibly older tales, contains a story known as "Tales of the Magicians," in which the sons of Khufu relate stories to their father (Petrie, 1895, 1999, p. 21). The royal son Hordedef also brings the living magician Dedi to Khufu. Khufu asks Dedi, "And is it true what is said, that thou knowest the number of the designs of the dwelling of Tahuti?" and Dedi responds that he knows where they are (Petrie, 1999, p. 15). According to Petrie (1999, p. 25), "the translation of 'the designs of the dwelling of Tahuti' is not certain; but the passage seems to refer to some architectural plan which was desired for the [Great] pyramid."

THE RELATIONSHIPS OF THE PHARAOHS
OF THE FOURTH DYNASTY

According to Baines and Málek (1980, p. 36) the pharaohs composing the Fourth Dynasty and the dates of their approximates reigns (all B.C.) were as follows (note that spellings vary from author to author).

Snofru: 2575–2551

Khufu (Cheops): 2551–2528

Ra'djedef: 2528–2520

Khephren (Ra'kha'ef): 2540–2494

Menkaure' (Mycerinus): 2490–2472

Shepseskaf: 2472–2467

The gap in this list between Khafre (Khephren) and Menkaure was filled by the short reign of the pharaoh Shero, or Sheiru, a son or Khafre, according to Lepre (1990, pp. 139–140), or by the short reign of a pharaoh named Nebka (Nabka) or Bikka (possibly the Bicheris of Mantheo; see Edwards, 1985, p. 144), who was responsible for the so-called Unfinished Pyramid at Zawiyet el-Aryan. Bikka may have been a son of Ra'djedef (Djedefre; Edwards, 1985, p. 144).

Sneferu (Snofru) married Hetepheres, the daughter of Huni (El Mahdy, 2003, p. 77), the briefly reigning last pharaoh of the Third Dynasty, and so became the founder of the Fourth Dynasty. Possibly Sneferu and Hetepheres were brother and sister, or half-brother and half-sister (El Mahdy, 2003, p. 77). According to El Mahdy (2003, see diagram of reconstructed lineage, p. 9), Khufu (Cheops) was the son of Sneferu and Hetepheres. Khufu himself married at least two of his sisters, Meritetes and Henutsen, and had many children by them, including his intended heir, the crown prince Kawab, who died before the end of Khufu's twenty-three-year reign (El Mahdy, 2003, p. 78). Another son of Khufu, Redjedef (Ra'djedef, Rededef, Djedefra, Djedefre: see Lepre, 1990, p. 132), became his direct successor as pharaoh, and upon Redjedef's death, Redjedef's half-brother Khafre (Chephren) took the throne (El Mahdy, 2003, diagram p. 9). Menkaure was apparently of a later generation, with Khafre being possibly the uncle of Menkaure and Khufu being Menkaure's grandfather (see El Mahdy, 2003, diagram p. 9).

Lepre (1990, p. 61), who considers Sneferu to be the last pharaoh of the Third

Dynasty and begins the Fourth Dynasty with Khufu, believed that both Khufu and Khafre were sons of Sneferu, and that Redjedef was a son of Khufu, as was Menkaure (Mycerinus), who inherited the throne after the death of his uncle, Khafre (see Lepre, 1990, p. 139, who says he is following ancient hieroglyphic texts in this respect). Shepseskaf, according to Lepre (1990, p. 61), was a son of Menkaure, and Imhotep (not the Imhotep of the Third Dynasty) and Queen Khentkawes, the two of whom ruled for about two years after Shepseskaf, were a son and a daughter of Menkaure (Lepre, 1990, p. 150). The Tomb of Khentkawes is one of the structures found on the Giza Plateau, and it is very likely that her tomb actually consists of an older (Predynastic or very early Dynastic) structure that was refurbished and reused.

DATING THE GREAT PYRAMID

If the Great Pyramid can be attributed to the reign of the pharaoh Khufu, then the dating of the Great Pyramid is essentially synonymous with the dating of Khufu's reign. Baines and Málek (1980) give the reign of Khufu as 2551–2528 B.C. Other researchers have given the reign of Khufu as "about 4748–4685 B.C." (Petrie, 1923, *History*) or, on the extreme young side, as the tenth century B.C. (Wathen, 1843, p. 64). Lepre (1990, p. 61) gives Khufu's reign as 2789–2767 B.C. Pochan (1978, p. xi), according to his "reestablished" Egyptian chronology, dates the Great Pyramid to 4800 B.C. and gives the reign of Khufu (referred to as "Suphis I" in his table, p. 263) as 4829–4766 B.C. Taseos (1990), basically adopting the nineteenth-century dating scheme of Lepsius for the various dynasties, estimates the date for the Great Pyramid as 3104 B.C. El Mahdy (2003, p. 26) suggests that the Fourth Dynasty may have begun about 2450 B.C. and that Khufu's father and predecessor ruled for 24 years (p. 51); thus the Great Pyramid would date to circa 2425 B.C. While not giving me actual dates, in a conversation with Zahi Hawass on the Giza Plateau, December 5, 2003, he told me that recent evidence suggest that Khufu reigned for 32 or 33 years.

Smyth (1877) dates the Great Pyramid to 2170 B.C. on the basis of his calculation that Alpha Draconis would shine down the Descending Passage when it crossed the meridian below the north celestial pole in that year. Proctor (1883) suggests a date of around 3440 to 3350 B.C. for the base or lower portion of the Great Pyramid, based on a similar analysis (see hereafter). Macnaughton (1932) accepts the theory of Proctor (1883) that the Great Pyramid was built in two stages: the lower portion, which served as an astronomical observatory, and the upper portion, which closed it over. On the basis of astronomical evidence and his interpretations of such, Macnaughton (1932, p. 98) dates the base of the Great Pyramid, up through the Grand Gallery, to about 5600–5100 B.C.

Radiocarbon dating of organic materials in the mortar of the Great Pyramid has tended to give dates one to a few centuries earlier than the now standard date of circa, 2551–2528 B.C. (Baines and Málek, 1980; see discussion in Schoch with McNally, 2003, pp. 14–16). Farrell (2003, p. 52) dismisses even the theoretical use of carbon dating, "since radiation occurring within the structure at any time would massively distort any obtained results," and Farrell believes that the Great Pyramid was the target of a nuclear war, among other things (see further discussion hereafter).

Many "unorthodox" or "revisionist" analyses of the Great Pyramid place it in remotest antiquity (e.g., Farrell, 2001, 2003; DeSalvo, 2003). According to the Edgar Cayce readings, the Great Pyramid was built in 10,490 B.C. (Lehner, 1974, p. 131; see Robinson, 1958, p. 32, who says that the Great Pyramid was begun in 10,490 B.C. and completed in 10,390 B.C.). Ralph Ellis (cited in Brennan, 2001, p. 39), on the basis of supposed erosion rates and temporal scaling of the paving stones around the Great Pyramid and other structures, dates the Giza complex to 38,000 B.C. I disagree with these results; I don't believe Ellis has taken human-induced damage and other factors adequately into account. On the basis of her research, as yet unpublished, the Argentinian math teacher and astronomer Carmen Cusó has speculated that the Great Pyramid (or a core structure later incorporated into the Great Pyramid) was built in two stages, separated by one precessional cycle of 25,920 years (personal e-mail correspondence from Carmen Cusó to Robert Schoch, November 26, 2004, and December 10, 2004). Thus the she dates the earliest portions of the Great Pyramid to some 30,000 years ago or more.

In my assessment, no single date can be assigned to the Great Pyramid as a whole, since I believe it was built in stages: (1) first the Descending Passage and Subterranean Chamber were built into a preexisting natural "sacred mound" that now underlies and is within the Great Pyramid's superstructure; (2) the base of the Great Pyramid, up through the Grand Gallery, was built and used for some period of time as an ancient astronomical observatory; (3) the King's Chamber, Relieving Chambers, and superstructure above the Grand Gallery were built, and the interior of the Great Pyramid, other than the Descending Passage and Subterranean Chamber, was sealed up; (4) the Well and access to the upper chambers of Great Pyramid were opened or reopened; (5) Al Mamoun's tunnel was cut into the Great Pyramid.

I tentatively suggest the following as possible dates for these various stages.

1a. The preexisting mound held a special, sacred position back in the midst of

Predynastic times, at least circa 5000 B.C. or earlier, contemporaneous with the earliest stage of the Great Sphinx (see Schoch with McNally, 2003).

1b. The Descending Passage and Subterranean Chamber were carved in Predynastic times, perhaps in the mid–fourth millennium B.C. (Proctor, 1883, p. 59, suggests that Alpha Draconis would have shined down the Descending Passage in 3440 B.C., although on p. 100 he gives the date as around 3350 B.C.)

1c. The core of the lower portion of the base, up through the level of the floor of the Queen's Chamber, may have been built at around the same time as the Descending Passage and Subterranean Chambers were carved out. The final, finished casing stones on the base and the rest of the pyramid may not have been put in place until later, during the final completion of the Great Pyramid during the Fourth Dynasty.

2. The upper portion of the base of the Great Pyramid, up through the level of the floor of the King's Chamber, was built in Old Kingdom, Fourth Dynasty times, quite possibly under Khufu. The orientations of the shafts originating from the Queen's Chamber would support this contention.

3. Construction of the King's Chamber, Relieving Chambers, and superstructure, along with the sealing of the Great Pyramid above the Descending Passage and Subterranean Chamber, took place later in Khufu's reign, and was perhaps even completed after he was deceased.

4. The Well and access to the upper chambers was opened or reopened in ancient times, perhaps during the Middle Kingdom, or possibly not until the New Kingdom, or even the Late Period. At any rate, once access to the upper chambers was regained in ancient times, the interior of the Great Pyramid was quite possibly used for ritualistic and initiatory purposes, and the final Saite Recension (c. 600 B.C.) of the *Book of the Dead* (see the following section) may have been based in part on the use of the Great Pyramid, such that the *Book of the Dead* was reworked to conform to the interior of the Great Pyramid. It was during the time of the Twenty-sixth Dynasty (or Saite Period) that the cult of Khufu was revived (Hawass, *Update to Petrie*, 1990, p. 98).

5. In the ninth century A.D., Al Mamun's tunnel was cut into the Great Pyramid.

THE PYRAMID TEXTS, COFFIN TEXTS, AND THE *BOOK OF THE DEAD*

The Pyramid Texts are hieroglyphic inscriptions found on the walls of the sarcophagus chamber, and also usually on the walls of the antechamber and horizontal passage, and occasionally in the accompanying vestibule, in pyramids of the Fifth and Sixth dynasties (late Old Kingdom), such as those of Unas (also known as Wenis, Fifth Dynasty) and Teti, Pepy I, Mernere, and Pepy II (Sixth Dynasty). Such texts have also been found in the pyramids of queens and in private tombs. So-called Pyramid Texts have been found dating to the Middle Kingdom, and also as late as the Late Period (Saitic Period; see Grinsell, 1947, p. 84). Most of the Pyramid Texts consist of "utterances," which were spells believed to have been spoken by the priests during the mortuary rituals. Maspero discovered the first Pyramid Texts in the pyramid of Pepy I in 1880; Breasted (1912) discusses the Pyramid Texts, and a recent compilation and translation is provided by Faulkner (1969).

During the Middle Kingdom, the Pyramid Texts were supplemented by more texts and spells, written using either hieroglyphics or the "cursive" hieratic script within the coffins of officials and commoners (as opposed to the Pyramid Texts that had at first been restricted to the tombs of royalty). These texts are, accordingly, commonly called the Coffin Texts. One of the larger compositions within the general category of the Coffin Texts is referred to as "the Book of the Two Ways." It was the Coffin Texts that were the direct predecessors of the various texts written on papyri and buried with the deceased, beginning in New Kingdom times (the earliest such papyri date to the mid–fifteenth century B.C.) and collectively referred to as the *Book of the Dead* (Carol Andrews, introduction to Faulkner, 1990; see Budge, 1967 [1895] for an earlier translation of the *Book of the Dead*). Early versions of the *Book of the Dead*, with little regularity in the order and number of chapters in any particular copy, are often referred to as the "Theban Recension," whereas the *Book of the Dead* papyri of the Twenty-sixth Dynasty and later are characterized by a regular order and number of the chapters and are commonly known as the Saite Recension (Andrews, introduction to Faulkner, 1990).

Although the earliest known recorded Pyramid Texts date to the late Fifth Dynasty (c. 24th century B.C.), they include some material that originated hundreds, perhaps thousands, of years earlier. For instance, there are allusions and references to burial practices dating back to Predynastic times, before circa 3100 B.C., and also to earliest Dynastic times. The Pyramid Texts consist of hymns and supplications to the gods, magical recitations, material referring to the "Opening of the Mouth" ceremony performed on the mummy or certain tomb statues, and various other rituals carried out on behalf of, and for the benefit of, the deceased. Andrews (introduction to Faulkner 1990, p. 11) says: "The *Pyramid Texts* also reflect a belief in an astral afterlife among the circumpolar stars which predates the ideas of the pyramid-builders who believed in a solar afterlife spent in the company of the sun-god" (italics in the original). In effect, Andrews is arguing that the Pyramid Texts contained beliefs older than and different from those actually held by the pharaohs who occurred earlier, in the Fourth Dynasty for instance, or even by those in whose pyramids they are found, a theory held by many Egyptologists but not universally accepted. Another interpretation is that the pyramid builders of the Fourth Dynasty placed more emphasis on the stars than has generally been accepted. The possible use of the Great Pyramid as an astronomical observatory before "completion," as suggested by Proctor (1883), supports the latter view.

Following an emphasis on the stars, reflected in the Pyramid Texts, and then the apparent ascension of the supremacy of the sun god, with whom the deceased might travel through the sky and the underworld, by the Middle Kingdom Coffin Texts, the god Osiris had taken a prominent role as the ruler of the underworld, judge of the deceased, and the entity with whom the dead were to be joined or assimilated. It should be noted, however, that Osiris is often mentioned even in the Pyramid Texts, as is the sun god (see Faulkner, 1969). By the Middle Kingdom, it was generally believed that the deceased would have to carry out various daily and agricultural tasks, and the shabti, or ushabti, figurines were buried with the deceased to carry out manual labor in the "Field of Reeds." In the *Book of the Dead* found in New Kingdom and later times, the three differing traditions of (1) an astral afterlife, (2) the supremacy of the sun god, and (3) the prominence of Osiris as ruler of the dead are found (Andrews, introduction to Faulkner, 1990, p. 12). The title "Book of the Dead" is a modern conception; the ancient Egyptians referred to the texts as the "Book of Coming Forth by Day," in reference to the idea of the spirits of the deceased being granted the freedom to continue to live and "come and go as they pleased in the afterlife" (Andrews, introduction to Faulkner, 1990, p. 12).

ETYMOLOGY OF THE WORD "PYRAMID"

Different etymologies have been proposed for the word "pyramid," as summarized by Pochan (1978, p. xiv). According to some, it is derived from the Greek root *pyr* (fire), as a pyramid resembles the shape of a flame (Sandys, 1621, p. 127). It has been proposed that the word derives from the Hebrew *bur a-mit* (the vault of the dead, or the tomb; Pochan, 1978, p. xiv). Or *pyramid* may be derived from the Greek version of the Egyptian *peri m uisi* (or *per-em-us,* see Herz-Fischler, 2000, p. 38), a mathematical phrase found in the Rhind Papyrus, possibly referring to the ridge of the pyramid where two sides meet. Ebers ([1879–1888?], 1:117 n.) says: "The hieroglyphic word 'per-am-us' (edge of the Pryamid) is the supposed origin of the word to which many fanciful derivations have been given. The solid content was called 'abumir,' the word 'peramus' meaning the four lines of the angles of the face or edge." Pochan (1978, p. xv) says that the ancient hieroglyphic word for pyramid was *mr* (stairway), but he does not think this is the derivation of our word *pyramid.* Rather, Pochan believes it may derive from the Egyptian *pr m it* (abode of laments, or house of the dead), or possibly *pr m mwt* (abode of the sarcophagus). Petrie (1911, p. 683, n.1) says: "The vertical height [of an ancient Egyptian pyramid] was named by the Egyptians *pir-em-us* . . . hence the Greek form *pyramis,* pl. *pyramides* (Herod[otus].), used unaltered in the English of Sandys (1615 [see Sandys, 1621, pp. 127–129]), from which the singular *pyramid* was formed" (italics in the original).

D. H. Lewis (1980, p. 9) says "the Greek word 'pyramidos' . . . is derived from a composite of Phygian and Phoenician form of 'Purimmiddah' of the Chaldeau . . . [these ellipses in the original] a Hebrew word for 'Urimmiddin.' . . . The word 'Urim' means 'Lights' or a revelation; and 'middin' carries the meaning of measures; thus denoting a revelation in measures."

Hall (1945, 2003, p. 118) notes that a popular derivation of the word *pyramid* is from the Greek "fire," as noted earlier, "signifying that it is the symbolic representation of the One Divine Flame, the life of every creature" (see also Hall, 1922). Hall (1945, 2003) further notes that John Taylor (1859) believed the word *pyramid* to mean "a measure of wheat" (from the Greek *puros,* wheat, and *metron,* measure; Bonwick, 1877, p. 22), and C. Piazzi Smyth (1864) thought it might derive from the Coptic for "a division of ten" (*pi-re-mit;* Bonwick, 1877, p. 22). H. S. Lewis (1936, 1939, 1945, 1994, p. 95) writes:

we must remember that the very name Pyramid as given to these great structures in Egypt was symbolic, because the word is really Greek and not Egyptian. In the Greek language the *pyra* means fire, or light, or illumination that reveals something or makes things visible in darkness as well as giving heat. The word *midos* means measures. The Greeks had derived these words from the Phoenician word *purimmiddoh,* which means "light-measures." Even in the Hebrew language there was a word very similar, which meant measures that revealed something, or revelation measures. Therefore, the Pyramid itself meant something that constituted measured revelations or revelations through measurements. (italics in the original)

Bonwick (1877, pp. 20–22) cites other possible etymologies for *pyramid*. The pyramids were sometimes referred to in Arabic as Haram or Alehram, signifying old age or an old structure. Other variations of this were El-Haram and Pi-Haram. It was also suggested that Haram could mean a holy place. The Coptic phrases *pirá-mona* and *pi-re-mi* are said to both mean "splendor of the sun." Some authors also suggested that pyramid may be derived from the Coptic *ramas* (rich), *pouro* (king), and or *mici* (birth). *Piromes* was also said to refer to statues of kings and priests. Another derivation suggests that it was originally *pooramis*, where *pour,* or *bour,* is prison or sepulcher, and *amit* means "of the dead," thus prison, cave, or sepulcher of the dead.

In certain numerological interpretations, 7 is the unity of spirit and matter, represented respectively by 3 (the trinity, which far predates Christianity) and 4 (the four elements of earth, air, fire, and water; the four principles or characteristics of cold, dry, hot, wet). The pyramid represents 7, with a square base (4) and triangular sides (3); that is, a pyramid represents matter giving rise to spirit.

Alan Alford, author of *Pyramid of Secrets* (2003), has suggested (private e-mail from Alford to Schoch, January 9, 2004) that

> the generic name for the true pyramid "mr" meant "place of ascension" not just in the sense of the king ascending to the sky but also in the sense of the king re-enacting the rising of the creator-god (personification of the cosmos evolving from the proto-earth and primeval waters) into the sky. You have to appreciate, of course, that Egyptian cosmogony and cosmology were geocentric, not heliocentric.

ARAB TRADITIONS CONCERNING THE GREAT PYRAMID

A number of Arab stories or traditions concerning the Great Pyramid existed during medieval times, covering a period of about a thousand years, most of which were variations on the same basic themes (see Greaves, 1646, 1704, 1737; Kingsland, 1935; Vyse, 1840, vol. 2). In outline, many of the Arab traditions attributed the Great Pyramid or the Giza Pyramids more generally to the king of Egypt Saurid (or Saurid Ibn Salhouk, or Surid, or a variation on this theme), said to have lived 300 years before the Flood (i.e., the Noachian flood or its equivalent). Saurid had a prophetic dream in which he saw the stars wandering from their courses and falling from the sky (comets and cometary action?) and the earth in upheaval, after which Saurid assembled his priests (the high priest is sometimes referred to as Philimon or Iklimon), the deluge was foretold, and Saurid had the pyramids built as vaults to preserve treasures; writings, artifacts, symbols, talismans preserving knowledge and wisdom; and the bodies of ancestors and deceased priests. Statues or idols that had magical powers guarded each of the pyramids; furthermore, the pyramids were said to be haunted by living spirits who would keep out all intruders other than those worthy of admission (apparently these spirits included, according to some legends cited by Tompkins, 1971, p. 21, "a naked woman with large teeth," who, after seducing trespassers, drove them insane).

These Arab traditions are often simply dismissed outright, as for instance by Greaves (1646; quoted in Kingsland, 1935, p. 101): "Thus far the *Arabians*, which traditions of theirs are little better than a Romance, and therefore leaving these, I shall give a more true and particular description out of mine own experience and observation" (italics in the original). Kingsland (1935, pp. 103–104), however, suggests that the Arab traditions do have meaning, but they are not referring to the Giza Pyramids literally, or to a true historical tradition in terms of a king named Surid or Saurid, and so on. Rather, the Arab tales refer in veiled terms to occult knowledge and the ancient mysteries and initiatory rites of the Egyptians.

> It is quite evident that we cannot accept this description [of the Arab traditions] of all the wonderful things which the Pyramids were said to contain as actually applying to the Gizeh structures; and what I suggest here is simply this: that in these narratives the word *Pyramid* is a symbol for the mighty structure of occult knowledge which has been built by the Adepts and Initiates from the very commencement of Man's evolution on this Globe; and that the reputed connection of it with the actual structures at Gizeh is simply a "*blind,*" giving in an apparent and historical basis. (Kingsland, 1935, p. 104; italics in the original)

THE ISRAELITES AND THE GREAT PYRAMID

There is sometimes a popular conception that the Israelites, or proto-Israelites, as slaves of the Egyptians, built the Great Pyramid. In fact, there is no good evidence to support this contention, and the time of Moses and the Exodus was over a millennium after the erection of the Great Pyramid. In the first century A.D., the Jewish historian Josephus promulgated this Israelite–pyramid connection by writing:

"The Egyptians inhumanly treated the Israelites, and wore them down in various labours, for they ordered them to divert the course of the river (Nile) into many ditches, and to build walls, and raise mounds, by which to confine the inundations of the river; and, moreover, vexed our nation in constructing foolish pyramids" (quoted in Bonwick, 1877, p. 72).

THE GREAT PYRAMID AND MASONRY (FREEMASONRY)

Various authors have traced Freemasonry back to the ancient Egyptians, and to the Great Pyramid in particular in some cases (see for instance Churchward, 1898; Cornish, 1986, 1990; Fellows, 1877; Hall, 1937; Higgins, 1923; Holland, 1885; Rowbottom, 1880). One concept, in simplified form, is that Masonry/Freemasonry actually originated with the very masons and stonecutters who worked on the Great Pyramid and, in the course of building the structure, could not help but learn the secrets and were thus themselves compelled to protect the sacred knowledge.

Palmer (1994, p. 138) says that the Great Pyramid was built as a "Freemasonic or Rosicrucian temple" and in it was celebrated the "Rite of the Little Dead." In this rite the initiate was said to spend three days in the "Pit" (Subterranean Chamber) in the total darkness without food or water, and a limited supply of air, during which time he or she would experience altered states of consciousness (compare discussions in Horgan, 2003), and ultimately the ego would die. After three days, the initiate would be reborn and taken to the King's Chamber for an initiation ceremony.

PYRAMID INCHES, PRIMITIVE INCHES, SACRED CUBITS, AND PYRAMID CUBITS

The concepts of "Pyramid Inches," "Primitive Inches," "Sacred Cubits," and "Pyramid Cubits" are due to nineteenth and twentieth-century "Biblical Pyramidists" (Kingsland, 1932, p. 38; other authors have referred to them less sympathetically as "pyramidiots"—see, for instance, Cottrell, 1963, p. 183) such as C. Piazzi Smyth, Morton Edgar, and D. Davidson. Considering the Great Pyramid to be a building that was directly inspired by God, Smyth reasoned that the "profane cubit" of the ancient Egyptians was either not used in the Great Pyramid or was supplemented by a different "Sacred Cubit." Smyth apparently derived this idea of a Sacred versus Profane Cubit from the work of Isaac Newton (see Newton in Greaves, 1737), who had sought to identify the cubit used by the ancient Israelites.

According to Smyth (1864, 1867, 1874, 1877, 1880, 1890), the Sacred Cubit essentially equivalent to the Pyramid Cubit, as it was termed by some authors, for instance Davidson, in Davidson and Aldersmith, 1924, was 25.025 British inches (or simply inches), and the Sacred Cubit was divided into 25 Pyramid Inches (essentially equivalent to the Primitive Inches of Davidson, for instance); thus a Pyramid Inch was equal to 1.001 British inches. What was the basis of the Pyramid Inch and Sacred Cubit? It was divinely inspired, based on the polar diameter of Earth (from the North Pole to the South Pole). The contention was that the polar diameter of Earth equals exactly 500 million (500,000,000) Pyramid Inches, or 20,000,000 Sacred Cubits. Part of the allure of the so-called Pyramid Inch and the Sacred Cubit is that they would be truly Earth-commensurable units of measurement rather than simply arbitrary lengths. Who should know the true dimensions of Earth better than God?

Depending on the value of the polar diameter of Earth used, and various assumptions made, the value of the Pyramid Inch or Primitive Inch and Sacred Cubit or Pyramid Cubit varies from author to author (see summary in Kingsland, 1932, pp. 40–42). Compared to the values of Smyth, Morton Edgar (see Edgar, 1924; Edgar and Edgar, 1910, 1923) used a value of 1.001001 British inches for the Pyramid Inch (accordingly, his Sacred Cubit equals 25.025025 British inches). Davidson (see Davidson and Aldersmith, n.d., p. 92; 1924) uses a Primitive Inch equal to 1.0011 British inches (and thus a Sacred Cubit or Pyramid Cubit of 25.0275 British inches).

SELECTED THEORIES AS TO THE MEANING AND PURPOSE OF THE GREAT PYRAMID

Tomb Theory

The most common theory as to the purpose of the pyramids, including the Great Pyramid, is that they were first and foremost tombs for the deceased. Even following this standard Egyptological dogma, to see them as primarily tombs may be an oversimplification. Kemp (in Trigger, Kemp, O'Connor, and Lloyd, 1983, p. 85) says:

Whilst it is common to emphasize the mortuary character of pyramids and to see them primarily as tombs with temples ancillary to them, the way in which they were in fact organized and referred to suggests that the emphasis should be reversed, and they be regarded first and foremost as temples for the royal statue with a royal tomb attached to each, which, acting as a huge reliquary, gave enormous authority to what was, in essence, an ancestor cult and an important factor in the stability of government."

PUBLIC WORKS PROJECT

It has been argued that in some ways the building of the pyramids in ancient Egypt was essentially a public works project that employed and channeled labor and resources that had the effect of increasing the overall prosperity of Egypt. Building a pyramid reinforced the authority of the pharaoh and the ruling power structure, as well as developing and solidifying administrative hierarchies and bureaucratic apparatuses that could be put to use for other purposes, be it collecting taxes, asserting control over the provinces, settling land disputes, waging war, or any of many other functions of government. Pyramid building was an industry that "provided jobs," as it were; created demand for consumable goods, whether goods to be buried with the deceased or goods to supply the laborers on the project; required the training of craftsmen, who could then apply their skills to other purposes; and led to improvements in technology as ways had to be developed to efficiently quarry stone, carve it, transport it, and erect it into gigantic structures. In addition, the building and decoration of associated temples and so forth would inspire technological and artistic innovations.

The relative size (volume) of pyramids during the Old Kingdom Fourth Dynasty has sometimes been suggested as a crude measure of economic activity. As compiled by Kemp (in Trigger et al., 1983, p. 88), the pyramid with the largest volume is the Great Pyramid, followed by the North Pyramid (Red Pyramid) of Sneferu at Dahshur, the Second or Khafre Pyramid of Giza, and the South Pyramid (or Bent Pyramid) of Sneferu at Dashur. Note that while the Great Pyramid may be the largest single pyramid of those listed, the combined volume of the pyramids at Dahshur is considerably greater than that of the Great Pyramid. This might suggest an even greater amount of economic activity under Sneferu (assuming that both Dahshur pyramids are correctly attributed to Sneferu) than his successor Khufu.

ASTRONOMICAL OBSERVATORY

The suggestion that the Great Pyramid might have served to make astronomical observations is a very old idea. The biblical Tower of Babel was in ancient times believed to have been used to observe the heavens (Bonwick, 1877, p. 144), and Arab legends viewed the Great Pyramid as an observatory (West, 1985, p. 91). Bonwick (1877, p. 145) quotes Edmé-François Jomard (one of the *savants* with Napoleon; see Tompkins, 1971, p. 44) as remarking that "it is very remarkable that the openings of pyramids are all to the north"; thus the "true tube" of a passage could be used for observing the stars, and "one could at the lower point see the circumpolar stars pass the meridian, and observe exactly the instant of that passage." Most writers, however, dismissed the idea of the Great Pyramid as an observatory, since its smooth sides could not be easily ascended (thinking in terms of the pyramid supplying a raised platform from which to make observations) and its passages and entrance were blocked off once it was completed. But what if the Great Pyramid served as an astronomical observatory before it took the shape we see today? The Neoplatonic philosopher Proclus, of the fourth century A.D., mentioned in passing that the Great Pyramid had functioned as an astronomical observatory before it was completed (see Proctor, 1883, p. 177). Arab legends associated the Great Pyramid with astronomy and astronomical knowledge (see for instance Davidson and Aldersmith, 1924, n.d., p. 90). The British astronomer Richard A. Proctor (1880, 1883) argued cogently that a partially completed Great Pyramid, where the southern end of the Grand Gallery was exposed to the night sky, would make an excellent pretelescopic astronomical observatory. K. P. Johnson (1998, 1999) has more recently shown how certain of the shafts from the King's and Queen's Chambers could also have been used for astronomical observations.

SURVEYING POINT

Ballard (1882; see also Tompkins, 1971, pp. 117–120) suggested that the Giza pyramids could serve as a point of reference, or essentially a huge theodolite in reverse (theodolites are instruments used by surveyors for measuring angles), for a land surveyor along the Nile within view of the Great Pyramid. According to Ballard, the changing relative positions of the three pyramids, as viewed from different areas around the Giza Plateau, could be used to determine angles and therefore allow triangulation and establishment of land boundaries and parcels. This would be especially important in ancient Egypt, as the annual inundation of the Nile along its river plain would destroy marked land boundaries that would have to be restored.

CALENDAR AND ALMANAC

Cotsworth (1905) was convinced that the Great Pyramid (as well as other pyramids, pyramid-like structures, obelisks, and various stone erections around the world) served as a giant "sun dial" or "almanac," the changing shadow cast throughout the year being used not only to tell daily time but also to determine the seasons, the times of the equinoxes and solstices, and the exact length of the year. Cotsworth says

> these sharp pointed stones were purposefully selected to cast an easily-marked pointed shadow which would indicate the hour of the day, etc. Further, the stones were required in solid blocks to ensure stability, and cast the longest possible shadows from a fixed vertical height to trace the progress of the Seasons by the differentiation of their shadows, which vary so slightly and gradually that they could not be traced and studied with the requisite accuracy from smaller erections. . . . the real object of the Pyramids was to determine that most vital factor of human knowledge—the length of the Year and the Seasons, so essential to the welfare of Nations growing in population, and thus forced to develop a higher civilization with assured regularly increasing crops to meet the growing needs of its people. (1905, pp. 3–4 of the section "The Pyramids of Egypt, Mexico, Etc.: Their Solution— Showing why they were built")

Pochan (1978, p. 287) summarized his ideas about the calendar function of the Great Pyramid as follows.

> The Great Pyramid, unlike the other pyramids, was not topped by a black basalt pyramidion, but ended in a platform, in the center of which was a raised gnomen (spherical, I believe), whose shadow, cast on the pavement of the northern esplanade, marked true solar noon on the various days of the year. The maximal and minimal elongations of this shadow distinguished, respectively, the winter and summer solstices. Moreover—and this is an important detail that has eluded the Egyptoplogists who have dealt with the Great Pyramid—the faces are not at all flat, but are hollowed in such a way that for half a minute, at sunrise and sunset during the two equinoxes, only half of the north and south faces are illuminated.

STANDARD OF MEASURES

Going back to at least the seventeenth century, with the work of Greaves and Newton (see Greaves, 1646, 1704, 1737), the Great Pyramid has been regarded as either a standard of measures (including linear measure, volume, weight, and in some cases even temperature) or at least a record of the measures used by the ancient Egyptians (see Bonwick, 1877, for a review). One of the driving beliefs behind this type of research during the seventeenth through nineteenth centuries among certain researchers was that the standards of measure used by the ancients were more accurate and meaningful—in the sense of, for instance, being Earth commensurate, based on natural entities like the "fixed" diameter of the planet—than the diverse modern measures then in common usage. There was also a strong amount of both nationalism and religiosity involved in such researches (see for instance, Day, 1868, 1972 [reprint of an 1870 work]; Gray, 1953; Seiss, 1877; Smyth, 1864, 1867; Taylor, 1859). Taylor (1859) was heavily concerned with the issue of British measures, and the first edition of *Our Inheritance in the Great Pyramid* (Smyth, 1864) is heavily focused on deriving Earth-commensurate, divinely inspired weights and measures in the Great Pyramid that just so happen to be almost identical with certain traditional British measures. Indeed, Smyth (1864, p. ix) said that the *Our* of his title was "being used in a national [i.e., British] sense," and he goes on to say:

> that particular *inheritance* of our nation did not come to pass by accident or chance—but was, on the contrary, the result of settled intention and high purpose, arranged from the beginning of the world! In partial demonstration whereof it may be mentioned, that the remarkable length alluded to, of *twenty-five* such unit inches [so-called Pyramid Inches or Primitive Inches; see earlier] (increased by 1/1000th on the present Parliamentary inch), formed in early ages *the sacred cubit of the Jews*; and was specially maintained by them for important purposes, in antagonism to the measures of profane nations, during all the period of Divine Inspiration to the chosen of their race. (p. x, italics in the original)

Commenting on the concept of the reputed standards found in the Great Pyramid being the result of divine inspiration, as asserted by Smyth, Bonwick (1877, p.127) commented:

> But that which has intensified the interest in the excitation of the marvelous in man by the announcement that this said standard was an ordinance from heaven— *a gift from God.* By bringing the religious faculty into the arena of discussion, a vast increase of force has been acquired. Argue as philosophers will upon materialism, they are confronted with the practical reply, from all the ages, of the *intuitive* in humanity. There is a something at the back of all that cannot be accounted for by the

rude logic of facts. There is in man a perception, however obscure and ill-defined, of spiritual existence, that sometimes comes with such power as to sweep away all dykes of reason and philosophy, and stir to the very depths the hearts of nations as of individuals. The mass are, and perhaps ever will be, governed more or less by a feeling of the supernatural. The alliance, therefore, of religion with the pyramid idea of measurement at once lifted the theory from the field of abstract, scientific enquiry into the domain of sympathetic belief. (italics in the original)

SOLAR TEMPLE

Pochan (1978, p. 286) contends that, among other functions, the Great Pyramid "was also a solar temple dedicated to the ram-headed god Khnum, for whom were reserved two of the four solar barques discovered at its base. The Pyramid—as well as the head of Sphinx, (Harmachis, the watchful guardian of the rising sun)—was painted red, the color of the sun as it sets in the crimson west."

PYRAMIDOLOGY AND THE GREAT PYRAMID AS PROOF OF GOD

In our day of modern research it has been discovered that the Great Pyramid of Giza in Egypt is something more than just a great tomb of a pharaoh. This colossal monument of antiquity has been found to portray the Christian religion upon a scientific basis in a manner most appropriate to our present scientific age. Pyramidology is the science that deals with the Great Pyramid's scientific demonstration of Biblical truth, true Christianity and the Divine plan respecting humanity on this planet. (Rutherford, 1970–1986, 1:[first published in 1957]11)

Pyramidology is the science which co-ordinates, combines and unifies science and religion, and is thus the meeting place of the two. When the Great Pyramid is properly understood and universally studied, false religions and erroneous scientific studies will alike vanish, and true religion and true science will be demonstrated to be harmonious. (Rutherford, 1970–1986, 1:13)

"In that day shall there be an altar to the Lord in the midst of the land of Egypt, and a pillar at the border thereof to the Lord." Isaiah 19:19 (quoted from the cover of Ferris, 1939). Some have interpreted the Great Pyramid as the altar and pillar referred to in this biblical passage (for instance, Capt, 1986, p. 9).

Many writers have considered the Great Pyramid to be divinely inspired and thus proof of God, and most commonly the Judeo-Christian God specifically, as indicated in the foregoing quotations. Riffert (1952, originally published 1932) titled his book *Great Pyramid Proof of God,* and more recently Zajac (1989) has made the same argument. This concept of the Great Pyramid as proof of God is closely related to the concept of the Great Pyramid's structure being prophetic if interpreted correctly (see the later section, "Prophecies").

ENCODING OF MATHEMATICAL, ASTRONOMICAL, AND GEODESIC DATA

Using a variety of different measurements and units (various forms of inches, cubits, and so forth), subject to a wide range of mathematical manipulation, different authors have claimed to find many pieces of information encoded in the Great Pyramid, such as pi, phi, and other mathematical relationships; the radius, circumference, and polar flattening of the earth; the distance to the sun, moon, and even planets; the density of the earth; the processional cycle; the length of the year; the shape of the earth's orbit; the law of gravity; the speed of light and other physical constants; and so forth (see, for instance, various discussions in Adams, 1933; Bonwick, 1877, who summarizes much of this thinking up to his time; Davidson and Aldersmith, 1924; Day, 1868, 1972; Edgar and Edgar, 1988 [originally published 1923–1924]; Gill, 1984, 1997; Gray, 1953; Smyth, 1864, 1867, vol. 3; Stecchini, 1971; Taylor, 1859; Tompkins, 1971; review of certain theories along these lines in Kingsland, 1932, pp. 99–112).

In relation to the concept of ecoding geographic knowledge, Smyth (1877, 1880, 1890) and many subsequent authors have contended that the Great Pyramid sits in the middle of the landmass of the entire Earth ("Geographic Centre of the Land Surface of the Whole World," to quote from Smyth, 1877, pl. 20) and it also sits at the exact apex of the Nile Delta. Indeed, I have long hypothesized that the Giza Plateau, with the proto-Sphinx (the Predynastic portions of the Great Sphinx) and other Predynastic structures and sites, such as the mound underlying the Great Pyramid, may have been both a very sacred site and also a politically important site marking the apex of the Nile Delta and the an early boundary between Upper (to the north) and Lower (to the south) Egypt.

THE GREAT PYRAMID AS TIME CAPSULE AND SYMBOL OF CREATION

Alford (2003, 2004; see also Alford, 2000; DeSalvo, 2003, p. 107) has suggested that the Great Pyramid was a symbol and memorial to the creation of the universe.

It served as tomb in its subterranean parts, but the upper sealed portions were a sort of a museum, repository, or time capsule. The coffer in the King's Chamber, in Alford's view, contained meteoritic iron representing the seed of the creator god. From the King's Chamber, low-frequency sound may have been broadcast to the Giza Plateau, via the so-called airshafts. Alford has suggested in his 2004 book *The Midnight Sun* that the Great Pyramid was part of an ancient "cult of creation," the primary aim of which was a celebration and reenactment of the myth of the creation of the cosmos. In Alford's view, the Great Pyramid was a simulacrum of the cosmos in its intial stages of coming-into-being, whereas various Egyptain temples symbolized later or final stages of coming-into-being (Alford's term). Alford suggests that restorative rituals were carried out at both pyramids and temples that helped ensure the continuity and ultimate immortality of the world. In this conception, the Great Pyramid in particular was infinitely important to the cosmos.

Doreal (1938) and Edgar Cayce (see Lehner, 1974; Robinson, 1958; Cayce, 2004) are among the spiritual leaders who viewed the Great Pyramid as having a connection with the lost continent of Atlantis and a possible Hall of Records for the Atlantean civilization. Doreal (1938/1992, pp. 2–3) explicitly says that the Great Pyramid, besides being "used as a temple of initiation by the priests of Thoth, in fact, is still used as such. . . . It was also used as a storehouse for the records brought from Atlantis when the Atlantean Islands sank beneath the waves, which had happened some 12,000 years before the building of the Great Pyramid."

PYRAMID PHYSICS

As best summarized by DeSalvo (2003), following in the footsteps of Antoine Bovis, who in the 1930s believed there was evidence that the Great Pyramid helped to preserve organic remains, such as dead animals, and Karl Drbal, who in the 1940s developed a method that he believed could preserve and even sharpen razor blades utilizing a pyramid shape, research on "pyramid power" and "pyramid physics" continues to this day. A leader in this field since the 1970s is Patrick Flanagan (1975; DeSalvo, 2003, p. 251), who has done numerous experiments with "pyramid energy" ("biocosmic energy"; see also DeSalvo, 2003, p. 168), such as the effects on food, razor blades (claiming to have duplicated successfully Drbal's experiments along these lines), growing plants, and so forth.

The Ukraine physicist Dr. Volodymyr Krasnoholovets has also been working with pyramid shapes and their properties, and has reputedly found that the pyramid shape, when the orientation is correct, can affect the fine structure of metals, including the result that razors are sharpened (see discussion in DeSalvo, 2003, pp. 143–152). According to DeSalvo (2003, p. 147), Krasnoholovets believes

> the Great Pyramid was build to intentionally amplify basic energy fields of the Earth on a subatomic, quantum level. He calls these fields inerton fields or waves and has measured them in model pyramids. He proposes that the Great Pyramid is a resonator of these fields produced by the earth. It would be a new physical field like the electromagnetic or gravitational field. This field is what affects the materials placed in the pyramids and caused the sharpening of the razor blades.

In Russia, a series of large fiberglass pyramids, up to 144 feet tall, has been erected, and experiments involving nonorganic and organic materials, as well as living organisms, are being carried out in them (DeSalvo, 2003, pp. 117–141). Pyramids are also being used in Canada, India, and elsewhere for meditation and health purposes (DeSalvo, 2003, pp. 169–173).

Another prominent researcher in the field of "pyramid physics" is Joe Parr, a man who has twice spent a night on top of the Great Pyramid taking electrical, magnetic, and radioactive measurements in 1977 and 1987 (DeSalvo, 2003, p. 153). It has been noticed since at least the nineteenth century by some people that anomalously large electrical charges may build up on the summit of the Great Pyramid. DeSalvo (2003, p. 12; see also Tompkins, 1971, pp. 278–279) relates the account of the nineteenth-century British inventor Sir William Siemens, who, at the top of the pyramid, felt a prickling sensation and received an electrical shock. Reputedly on the spot, Siemens made a Leyden jar (which will store static electricity) out of a wine bottle and newspaper. He was able to charge the Leyden jar by holding it up over his head, and it started to emit sparks. It then discharged toward one of the Arab guides, giving him a shock that knocked him to the ground.

From both studying the Great Pyramid and from working with small pyramids and pyramid-shaped materials in his lab, Parr has suggested that "mass particles" (which have inertia but are not subject to normal quantum laws: see DeSalvo, 2003, p. 155) can potentially be trapped by pyramid shapes. As these mass particles are trapped, Parr believes an energy field bubble forms around the pyramid that shields the pyramid and mass particles inside of it. Parr experimentally induces this phenomenon by rotating small pyramids through an alternating magnetic field in the laboratory. As the energy field bubble builds up around the pyramid, according to Parr (see DeSalvo, 2003, pp. 153–165), objects inside the pyramid are shielded from external fields, including the gravitational field, and therefore become weightless. Furthermore, Parr believes that as the bubble around the pyramid closes completely, the pyramid (and any contents) leave the normal space-time continuum of three dimensions plus time that we are used to in everyday life, and the pyramid enters what he terms hyperspace. Speculatively, once the pyramid is in hyperspace, it may be able to travel through ordinary matter and through time, as we know it, perhaps allowing so-called time travel backward and forward.

Parr suggests that the field bubbles around pyramids are sensitive to external astronomical events, such as the sun's 11-year sunspot cycle and when the earth, the sun, and the constellation of Orion are lined up. He believes that at such times of sun-earth-Orion alignment, there is a conduit of neutrinos moving from the sun past and through the earth, and into space in the direction of Orion. These moving neutrino particles seem to cause small spinning pyramids to break away from the rotating arm they are attached to and presumably fly toward the direction of Orion. All of this type of research is of course extremely controversial and calls out for independent verification by other researchers. Another physicist, Dan Davidson, has repeated many of Parr's experiments and says that he has gotten similar results (see DeSalvo, 2003, pp. 161, 289–304).

POWER PLANT THEORIES

Miller, Sloan, and Wilson (2001, p. 35) suggest that the Great Pyramid was a plutonium mill. In their words:

> We propose here that the Great Pyramid was a nuclear fission production mill, and that it was a technical and financial success. It did not create energy but packaged energy within artificially created isotopes of plutonium. . . . The approach is to drop preconceptions about religion and culture, and look upon the Great Pyramid as a business investment.

In other words, they impose a certain twenty-first-century business/capitalistic mentality and set of assumptions on this ancient structure. Furthermore, since there was no known need for plutonium on Earth in ancient times, Miller, Sloan, and Wilson (2001, p. 41) suggest that the most likely destination for the plutonium was Mars.

Christopher Dunn (1998) has developed an elaborate hypothesis that the Great Pyramid was a power plant that generated electricity through an elaborate system of resonators ultimately tuned to the frequency of Earth, electrons moving from one level to another within the hydrogen atom, and so forth. Even more speculatively, Dunn suggests that the ancient Egyptians had power tools that they used for machining stone and other materials.

Farrell (2001, 2003, and see discussion hereafter) also believes that the Great Pyramid was used as a means to generate enormous amounts of power. However, as he points out (2003, pp. 52–53), "the Great Pyramid would, on the basis of an analysis in terms of standard contemporary physics, and barring unknown fields and forces, be capable of only a few milliamps of power output, hardly enough to light a small light bulb." Clearly, the implication is that if the Great Pyramid was a generator of power, it did not use simply physics, fields, and forces as we know them today.

WEAPON OF MASS DESTRUCTION

Farrell (2001, 2003), following up on the work of Dunn (1998) and others asserting that the Great Pyramid was a source of power, believes that this power was not used for good but for evil (my terms). Farrell considers the Great Pyramid to be part of a very ancient gigantic military weapon system that was actually used. To do justice to his theory, it is best to quote Farrell (2003, p. 51) directly:

> I have posited a scenario in which, its many difficulties notwithstanding, there was a paleoancient Very High Civilization possessed of a highly unified physics, a corresponding "unified technology," and a capability for mass destruction greatly exceeding our own. In this scenario, the Great Pyramid was a weapon of mass destruction, and the focal point of a war fought with nuclear weapons, a war fought at least in part either to destroy it or render it permanently non-operational. . . . It is *possible* that this scenario may have been even more gruesome, that the Very High Civilization may have been interplanetary in nature, and that "the Great Weapon" may have been used to create system-wide planetary destruction on Mars and the Moon, and perhaps elsewhere. (italics in the original)

Discussing Farrell's hypothesis, DeSalvo (2003, p. 106) says that the ancients apparently had knowledge of "zero point energy" (see McTaggart, 2002) and learned to put it to practical and destructive use.

THE GREAT PYRAMID AS A WATER PUMP

That the Great Pyramid may have something to do with water moving through its passages and chambers dates back to at least the nineteenth century, when it was suggested that it might have severed as a "Filtering Reservoir." "A Swedish philosopher gave it as his opinion that pyramids were simply contrivances for purifying the water of the muddy Nile, which would pass through their passages" (Bonwick, 1877, p. 111). More recently, several authors and researchers have championed the theory that the Great Pyramid was a huge water pump used to move Nile water from lower elevations to higher elevations, both as a means of construction (blocks of stone could be moved on barges or by means of attached floats through locks, brought to the worksite, and put into place) and for the distribution of water for agricultural and related purposes. Edward J. Kunkel conducted research along these lines from the middle 1930s through the late 1970s, and his research is currently being championed by Steven Myers and the Pharaoh's Pump Foundation (Kunkel, n.d; see discussions of Kunkel's work in Valentine, 1975 [who misspells his name "Kunkle"], and Noone, 1997; see DeSalvo, 2003, pp. 367–368, for information on Steven Myers and Pharaoh's Pump Foundation). Recently, John Cadman has continued the research of Kunkel regarding the possibility that the Great Pyramid served as a giant water pump (see Cadman, 2003, pp. 339–350).

Somewhat related to water pump theories is the hypothesis of Yoshiki Su'e (1999) that the passages and certain chambers of the Great Pyramid were partially filled with water to form some kind of huge instrument that acted somewhat like a giant pendulum and could measure the rotational speed and various vibrations of the Earth.

EVIDENCE OF EXTRATERRESTRIAL VISITATION OF EARTH

Benavides (1974, p. 157) says boldly: "The Great Pyramid is a good example if evidence is needed to support the theory of extraterrestrial visitors in the past." Similar sentiments, or discussions of extraterrestrials and ancient Egypt, can be found in Brennan (2001), Bramley (1993), von Däniken (1969, 1996), Farrell (2001, 2003), Hoagland (2001), Herschel (2003), and Temple (1998). Zecharia Sitchin (cited and discussed in Farrell, 2003, p. 281; see Sitchin, 1985) has viewed the Great Pyramid as a "beacon" for interplanetary travelers. Miller, Sloan, and Wilson (2001) suggest that plutonium packaged at the Great Pyramid was transported off the planet, most likely to Mars. Mehler (2001; see also DeSalvo, 2003, pp. 181, 235, 329) has suggested that the ancient dynastic Egyptians were preceded by a

"Khemetian" or "Khemitian" civilization that had connections with both Atlantis and "star people." Herschel (2003) suggests that pyramids around the world, including the Great Pyramid, represent stars. The pyramids' arrangements on Earth are star maps of the heavens, possibly pointing toward the extraterrestrial origin of the "gods" of ancient religions. Furthermore, according to Herschel (2003), humankind's ancestors may have originated from the colonization of our planet by extraterrestrial beings.

PROPHECIES

There is one general school of "pyramidologists" who view the passages and chambers within the Great Pyramid as a chronological representation of both the past and a prophecy of the future. This school of thought originated when the Scottish ship-builder Robert Menzies wrote to C. Piazzi Smyth in 1865 (as he was on site at the Great Pyramid, studying it firsthand; see Seiss, undated, 14th edition, p. 129; Smyth, 1880, p. 461; Tompkins, 1971, p. 93; interestingly, Smyth did not mention or adopt Menzies's theories in his 1867 *Life and Work at the Great Pyramid*, although beginning with the 1874 edition of *Our Inheritance in the Great Pyramid* he did) and was adopted and expanded upon by Smyth and others (for example, Capt, [1971], 1986; Casey, 1883; Davidson, 1925, 1934; Davidson and Aldersmith, 1924 and n.d.; Edgar, 1924; Edgar and Edgar, 1910, 1923, 1988; Ferris, 1939; Fish, 1880, first and second editions; Ford, 1882; Foster, 1979/1988; Gardener, 1944, 1948; Garnier, 1905; Gray, 1953; Haberman, 1935; Knight, 1933; Landone, 1940; Lemesurier, 1977, 1999; D. H. Lewis, 1980; H. S. Lewis, 1936; Marks, [1879?]; McCarty, 1907; Nicklin, 1961; Riffert, 1952; Russell, 1915; Rutherford, 1970–1986; Seiss, 1877; Smith, 1934; Smyth, 1874, 1877, 1880, 1890; Stewart, 1935; Toth, 1988; Webber and Hutchings, 1985; Zajac, 1989; Roselis von Sass used this concept in part in her novel *The Great Pyramid Reveals Its Secret*).

Here it is appropriate to quote Smyth (1880, pp. 461–462) concerning Menzies's original suggestion, which set the stage for all subsequent studies along these lines.

From the north beginning of the Grand Gallery floor, said Robert Menzies (who was called to his rest in the end of 1877), there, in southward procession [traveling up the Grand Gallery], begin the years of the Saviour's [i.e., the Christian Jesus] earthly life, expressed at the rate of a Pyramid inch to a year. Three and thirty inch-years, therefore, or thereabout, bring us right over against the mouth of the well, the type of His death, and His glorious resurrection too; while the long, lofty Grand Gallery shows the dominating rule in the world of the blessed religion which He established thereby; over-spanned above by the 36 stones of His months of ministry on earth, and defined by the floor-length in inches, as to its exact period to be. The Bible fully studied, shows that He intended that first Dispensation to last only for a time; a time, too, which may terminate very much sooner than most men expect, and shown by the southern wall *impending*. (italics in the original)

Smyth (1880, pp. 462–465) further says:

The first ascending passage, moreover, he [Robert Menzies] explained, as representing the Mosaic Dispensation. I measured it, and found it to be, from the north beginning of the Grand Gallery, the assumed natal year of Christ, to its junction with the roof of the entrance-passage northward and below, or to some period in the life of Moses, 1,483 Pyramid inches: and when produced across that passage, so as to touch its floor, 1,542 inches.

But the chief line of human history with Robert Menzies was the floor of the entrance-passage. Beginning at its upper and northern end, it starts at the rate of a Pyramid inch to a year, from the Dispersion of mankind, or from the period when men declined any longer to live the patriarchal life of Divine instruction, and insisted on going off upon their own inventions . . . until it ends, at a distance from the top of the passage equal probably to 4,404 Pyramid inches, in the symbol of the bottomless pit; a chamber deep in the rock, well finished as to its ceiling and the top of its walls, but without any attempt at a floor.

One escape, indeed, there was in that long and mournful history of human decline; but for the chosen few only, when the Exodus took place in the first ascending passage, which leads on into the Grand Gallery: showing Hebraism ending in it original prophetic destination—Christianity. . . .

But it was not Hebrews alone, descended from those under Moses, who were to be saved by Christ; for besides the special Hebrew passage,—another, though far less conspicuous mode of escape from the descent into the bottomless subterranean pit, was also eventually provided, to prevent *any* immortal soul being necessarily lost. For, before reaching the dismal abyss, there is a possible entrance, though it may be by a strait and narrow way, to the one and only gate of salvation through the death of Christ—viz. the peculiar, deep but dry, well representing His descent into Hades.

This Hades locality is not the bottomless pit of idolaters and the wicked, lying at the lowest point to which the entrance-passage subterraneously descends, but a natural grotto, rather than artificial chamber, in the course of the well's further progress to the other place. It is in fact the Paradise of the dead, which is stated to be within the earth; and where they wait in unconscious condition, either the rapturous awakening to meet their Lord in the air, before His visible return to all men as Millennial King; or, the final trump of the day of Judgment and the great white throne.

Meanwhile here at the Pyramid, the stone which once covered that well's upper mouth is blown outwards into the Grand Gallery with excessive force (and was once so thrown out, and is now annihilated), carrying part of the wall with it, and indicating how totally unable was the grave to hold Him beyond the appointed time.

Thus we see how Menzies, Smyth, and their followers have interpreted the passages of the Great Pyramid in terms of their understanding of Judeo-Christian prophetic history and furthermore have used the continuations of the passages and chambers to prophesy the future history of humankind. For instance, Lemesurier (1977, pp. 135, 137) gives the following reading based on the Subterranean Chamber:

in around 2004, "the bottom will fall out of the world." Both world-civilisation and its technologies will quickly collapse to rock-bottom by 2010, and will remain at that level for at least fifteen years. . . . By around the year A.D. 2025, world-civilisation will be reestablished, and by 2055, with material conditions at last rapidly improving, human technology will revive to at least its former level. Then, in around 2075, there will be a sudden explosion of progress on all fronts, and a new civilization of extraordinary vigour will arise whose physical aspects will last until the year A.D. 2100, and whose spiritual achievements—which may be of unprecedented magnitude—may even endure until the very end of the era predicted. This is dated at A.D. 2132–3, just prior to the second Messianic visitation.

Based on the Great Pyramid, D. H. Lewis (1980, p. 33) predicted that Armageddon would occur in the year 2000, and our current civilization would end approximately three-quarters into the year 2001 (on September 17, 2001, exactly; D. H. Lewis, 1980, p. 34).

Kingsland (1935) includes a chapter on the "Biblical Theory" of the Great Pyramid and its attendant prophecies, pointing out the numerous times that members of this school have failed in their predictions of future events. Many members of the school of biblical prophecy from the Great Pyramid have interpreted the events presumably recorded in the chronologies of the passages of the Great Pyramid not just in terms of world events but more specifically in terms of events in Great Britain and America (giving rise to what is sometimes known as the British Israelite movement or Anglo-American Israelite moment, or by similar terms). Why? As Kingsland (1935, pp. 58–59) says: "The reason that is given to-day by the modern Biblical theorists for selecting events connected with Great Britain—even to the significance of our unemployment figures!—is, that we are the 'lost tribes of Israel.'" As an example of just this school of thought, we may cite Ferris (1939, p. 12) who says: "The purpose of the following pages is to demonstrate the manner in which the Pyramid is such a '*sign and witness*,' i.e., HOW ITS MESSAGE IDEN-TIFIES THE ANGLO-SAXON RACE AS ISRAEL" (italics and capitalization in the original). Another example of such thinking is Foster (1979/1988), who also confirms that Britain and America are part of Israel, having descended from the lost tribes.

SITE OF INITIATION AND SACRED MYSTERIES

Egyptian initiatory rites and secret mysteries are discussed and hypothetically re-constructed by such authors as Anonymous (1785), Brunton (1936), Hall (1922, 1937, 1945), Kingsland (1935), Pochan (1978), and Spence (1915, [1933]). In their best developed, or most popular, form (especially during the late period and Greco-Roman times), the Egyptian Mysteries consisted of two phases: the Lesser Mysteries (associated with the cult of Isis) and the Greater Mysteries (associated with the cult of Osiris). The mystic drama enacted the life and death of Osiris and the his-tory of Isis, in some ways equivalent to the mystery plays of Christian medieval times; it was not simply theatre or drama. The Osirian Cycle can be viewed as the Passion Play of ancient Egypt. Variations and portions were performed for the public; other portions were performed solely for neophytes, postulants, and initi-ates; and the true Egyptian Mysteries, restricted to elite priests and spectators, were performed in isolated buildings, secret chambers, and crypts away from the public view. The Mysteries used not only words but gestures, symbolic acts, symbols, and allegorical representations to convey the divine (Spence, [1933]). The *CRATA REPOA, or Initiations to the Ancient Mysteries of the Priests of Egypt* (*CRATA REPOA. Oder Einweihungen in der alten geheimen Gesellschaft der Egyptischen Priester* [Anonymous, 1785; see Hall, 1937]) was composed and compiled from fragments of ancient authors, attempting to restore the ancient initiatory rites used for the Egyptian Mysteries. "No one is so strong on the mysteries of antiquity as a German," commented Gerard de Nerval (in *The Women of Cairo: Scenes of Life in the Orient* (2 vols. [London: Routledge, 1929]); de Nerval describes a Prussian officer's description of how he imagined ancient initiation rites taking place in the Great Pyramid (quoted by Pochan, 1978, p. 104). According to the *CRATA REPOA*, the initiate could pass through up to seven grades or levels (not all persons could achieve the highest grades). At each grade, the initiate would both receive instruction and undergo physical and mental/spiritual tests. The fundamental idea underlying initiatory rites was a new birth or re-birth into a higher phase of life. To regain knowledge of our own spiritual nature and powers, the resurrection from the spiritually dead condition of the common or ordinary person, this was (and is) the objective of genuine initiation, be it in the Egyptian Mysteries or any of various other mysteries (Kingsland, 1935, p. 118).

Adams (1895, 1898, 1933) is probably the author who has most explicitly depicted the Great Pyramid as a place in which initiatory rites were actively carried out, according to formulas recorded in the so-called *Book of the Dead*. Other authors have adopted Marsham Adams's ideas more or less wholesale (for instance, Capt, 1986, pp. 239–245; Churchward, 1898; DeSalvo, 2003, chap. 8; Holbrook, n.d.; Purucker, 2003; Van Auken, 1999, chap. 6; see also Doreal, 1938, although I am not certain that Doreal's ideas along these lines came from Marsham Adams's work directly; and Chaney, 1987, who, in what I consider to be a fictional piece, was clearly influenced, either directly or indirectly, by Marsham Adams's work) and in some cases elaborated upon his work (for instance, Davidson and Aldersmith, 1924; Palmer, 1924; Stewart, 1929). Kingsland (1935), while open and favorable to the idea that the Great Pyramid may have played a role, albeit this is not known for certain, in the enactment and propagation of the Egyptian mysteries, he is not convinced by the arguments of Marsham Adams making a direct connection between the Great Pyramid and the *Book of the Dead*. Kingsland wrote (1935, p. 131): "It is highly probable . . . that we must look to these ancient *Mysteries* for the key to the *symbolism* of the [Great] Pyramid in its various structural features, if not to its actual use for initiation ceremonies" (italics in the original).

Building on the work of Marsham Adams, Davidson and Aldersmith (1924, n.d., p. 88–90) have the following to say:

> every possible attempt was made by the compilers of the various chapters of the
> *Book of the Dead* to refer back the origin of the ritual and symbolism to the Pyra-

mid Kings of Memphis—the builders of the Pyramids of Gizeh. . . . Now it was during the XXVIth (Saïte) Dynasty that the order of chapters of the *Book of the Dead* was drawn up, and when, as Breasted [in *A History of Egypt*, 1919] states, "the worship of the (Pyramid) kings, who ruled at Memphis in these remote days, was revived. . . . Their Pyramids were extensively restored and repaired. The archaic titles . . . in the government of the Pyramid builders again brought into requisition, and in the externals of government everything possible was done to clothe it with the appearance of remote antiquity." . . . Essentially geometrical in form, the Pyramids, by influencing the expression of theological conceptions, supplied religious allegory with an unfailing source of geometrical symbolism. It is this allegory of which a corrupt survival exists in the Egyptian *Book of the Dead.* It is from the *Book of the Dead* that the Coptic descendants of the ancient Egyptians derived the mystical and allegorical element which was introduced into early Christian gnosticism. The literature of early Christian gnosticism abounds in mystical pyramid figures and associated astronomical conceptions and constellations. . . . It is . . . such texts as the *Book of the Dead* which picture the passages and chambers of the Standard Pyramid of the Dynastological Lists, or Secret House of the *Book of the Dead* as lined with instructions and formulae, and with mythical figures and stars. It is to these that the traditions refer, and from such texts as these that the traditions obtained authority for identifying the Standard Pyramid of the Dynastological Texts with the Great Pyramid of Gizeh. The fact therefore remains that Coptic tradition associates the Great Pyramid with the symbolizing of astronomical and geometrical figures, just as the Egyptian Ancestors of the Copts associated the Great Pyramid with their ideal secret houses in the *Book of the Dead,* and with their geometrical Dynastology, cosmical year circle, and Sothic cycle mythology. (italics in the original)

Supporting the contention that the ways and structures of the Old Kingdom were revered and revived during the Late Period (including the Twenty-sixth Dynasty) is the evidence of the Third (Menkaure) Pyramid on the Giza Plateau. Close to the entrance on the north face is a hieroglyphic inscription carved in the granite that dates from the Late Period (Verner, 2001, p. 243). In the upper antechamber of the Menkaure Pyramid, Howard Vyse found a wooden coffin, bearing Menkaure's name and containing human bones (separate from the basalt sarcophagus he found in the room considered the main burial chamber, that sarcophagus having been lost at sea in 1838 when the ship carrying it back to England sank between Malta and Spain), that some have seen as a substitute or reconstruction from the Saite period (Twenty-sixth Dynasty) or later. According to radiocarbon dating, the bone fragments may be less than 2,000 years old (Verner, 2001, p. 245).

Manly Palmer Hall (2003, originally published in 1928) is very clear in his belief that the Great Pyramid was used for, among other things, ritual initiations and includes a chapter in his book titled "The Initiation of the Pyramid." Hall (2003, p. 162) quotes a manuscript by Thomas Taylor that says Plato was initiated into the "Greater Mysteries" at the age of 49 in the "subterranean halls" of the Great Pyramid. Hall (2003, p. 108; see also Kingsland, 1935, p. 2) suggests that Herodotus "was an initiate of the Sacred Schools and consequently obligated to preserve inviolate the secrets of the ancient order" and therefore "concocted a fraudulent story to conceal the true origin and purpose of the Great Pyramid."

Lehner (1974) encapsulated the views developed in the Edgar Cayce readings relative to the Great Pyramid: "Hermes, a cryptic figure in the [Edgar Cayce] readings, became the construction architect of the Great Pyramid. . . . The Pyramid was to be a monumental repository of knowledge and prophecy, and also serve as the Temple of Initiation for the White Brotherhood" (Lehner, 1974, p. 86). Also following the Cayce readings, Robinson (1958, p. 32) says: "The Great Pyramid was built as a hall of initiation, the 'House Initiate' for those dedicating themselves to special services in the secrets of the mystery religion of Egypt. Here the masters performed their vows, consecrating themselves to holy service. Its purpose, therefore, was far greater than that of a burial place." Lewis (1936, 1939, 1945, 1994 ed., p. 181) speaks of "secret manuscripts possessed by archivists of the mystery schools of Egypt and the Orient . . . telling of the ancient forms of initiations held in the Sphinx [presumably under the Sphinx, where Lewis believes there is a chamber] and the Great Pyramid." Melchizedek (2000, p. 250) and Doreal (1938/1992, pp. 2–3) also view the Great Pyramid as a place of initiation.

Summarizing his views of the religious and initiatory importance of the Great Pyramid, Pochan (1978, p. 287) wrote:

the minor isiac initiatory trials and rites took place in the chaotic Subterranean Chamber, with its uterine passage and lustral well, while the Pyramid's central chamber with its granite sarcophagus, was used as the setting for the supreme initiation (reserved exclusively for the king, under the first six dynasties), during the transferal of the divine *ka* from the body of the deceased pharaoh into that of his successor. (italics in the original)

Farrell (2001, p. 16), quotes Hancock (1995, pp. 142–143) to the effect that the "opening of the mouth ceremony" performed on the deceased pharaoh in ancient times, and thought to be necessary to ensure resurrection in the heavens, may have been carried out in "one of the chambers" of the Great Pyramid.

At the Princeton Engineering Anomalies Research (PEAR) laboratories, electronic random event generators (REGs) were developed with the explicit purpose of identifying and detecting genuine pyschokinesis (also known as PK, telekinesis, or psychoenergetics; the influence of consciousness on physical and biological systems: see Jahn, 1982; Jahn and Dunne, 1987). Nelson (July 1997) took a portable FieldREG to a number of sacred sites in Egypt and obtained very interesting results. For instance, in the Holy of Holies (the inner sanctums) of most ancient temples he would detect major anomalous effects. It seemed that some kind of residual consciousness, an empirical measure of sacredness, could be detected in the temples. Nelson found one exception: the Holy of Holies in the Temple of Isis at Philae showed no anomalous results. However, the Temple of Isis at Philae is no longer in its original position. When the British built the first Aswan Dam at the turn of the nineteenth–twentieth century (see Ward, 1900, for photographs and a description of the building of the first Aswan Dam), the temple was partially flooded, and with the building of the Aswan High Dam in the 1960s, the temple was slated to be entirely covered by the waters of Lake Nasser. An international consortium raised the money to move the temple to the higher island of Algikia, orienting it exactly and even carving the island to look like the original home for the temple (West, 1985, p. 426). Still, on the basis of Nelson's REG study, it seems the "sacredness" of the temple was lost in the move.

Nelson (February 1997; McTaggart, 2002, p. 207) also visited the Great Pyramid with his REG machine. Conventional wisdom would suggest that he should have picked up the strongest deviation, the most powerful anomaly, in the King's Chamber, famous for its powerful effect on the famous (remember Napoleon) and anonymous alike. Science does not always give the expected result, however. Dr. Nelson found little, if any, REG activity in the King's or Queen's Chambers; but in the Subterranean Chamber the machine became very "excited." The REG machine showed a strong anomalous deviation that Nelson interpreted as a strong objective indication that the Subterranean Chamber was an extraordinary site. The Subterranean Chamber also personally moved Nelson, and there he had a personal insight. Perhaps, he suggests (Nelson, February 1997), the strange architecture found in the Subterranean Chamber is actually a ritualistic map of the land of

Egypt. A path down the middle of the room represents the Nile River, with the land and mountains to each side. In the area of Memphis on the "map" is a throne where the pharaoh might take his seat. And the lower part of the room, where the "Nile" empties, represents the delta and the Mediterranean Sea. A high priest, Dr. Nelson suggests, might enter the Subterranean Chamber in humility through the low passage entranceway on hands and knees, seeking help from the gods.

In a conversation with Graham Walker (a British police officer with a passion for Egyptology) on the evening of November 29, 2003 (in Elena Konstantinou's room in the Sheraton Sharm Hotel, Al Pasha Coast, Sharm El Sheikh, Egypt), he said he viewed the Great Pyramid as the "House of Osiris," which was used for initiatory rites (see Adams, 1895, 1898, 1933; Holbrook, n.d.; Purucker, 2003). Walker also believes that both the Great Pyramid and the *Book of the Dead,* when properly interpreted and decoded, point to a cavern ("Hall of Records"?) in the Sinai (see Walker, 2003). We drove out to Walker's "cavern" (or more specifically, what he believes is a mound over the entrance to the cavern) on November 30, 2003. Once off the road, it is a distance of about 35 kilometers (according to Walker) up the wadi through sand and rocks, with four-wheel drive necessary at times. The cavern mound is essentially, as far as I could tell, a heavily weathered, probably pre-Cambrian, granite mound, with other debris (all the rocks are igneous and metamorphic in this area, except for later Tertiary/Holocene sediments). I was not

View of the Subterranean Chamber, facing toward the southwest corner. In the ceiling can be seen a couple of examples of what some writers have interpreted as carved symbols in the rock. Photograph courtesy of Robert M. Schoch.

convinced that it is artificial, to Walker's disappointment. Still, I cannot completely dismiss Walker's analysis. He may be onto something—perhaps there is a cave or underground chamber or simply a sacred site near the area/site he has located, or perhaps he is correct in his interpretation that the Great Pyramid and sacred writings of the ancient Egyptians points to a location but has misinterpreted the clues and come up with the wrong location.

In a conversation in Al Mamun's forced passage on November 24, 2003, Emil Shaker (who has studied Egyptology and works for Mohamed Nazmy of Quest Travel, Giza, Egypt—Mohamed made the arrangements for us to enter the Great Pyramid and was there with us) expressed his opinion that, looking at a map of Egypt, the outlines of the country can be compared to a man (specifically Osiris) with raised and outstretched arms. The head of Osiris is the Great Pyramid, the body and legs are the Nile stretching to the south, the delta is the up-stretched arms that touch the Mediterranean Sea, representing the sky.

RITUAL SEND-OFF OF THE PHARAOH TO THE STARS

The Orion Theory of Robert Bauval (see Bauval, 2000; Bauval and Gilbert, 1994; Hancock and Bauval, 1996; see also DeSalvo, 2003, pp.105–106) suggests that the three major pyramids of the Giza Plateau and the Nile River form a map on the ground of the three stars in Orion's belt plus the Milky Way in the sky. Orion represented Osiris for ancient Egyptians, and in the King's Chamber, the southern so-called airshaft pointed to Orion (Osiris); the southern shaft of the Queen's Chamber pointed toward the star Sirius, associated by the ancient Egyptians with Isis (the sister and wife of Osiris). The Great Pyramid is thus seen as a way for the deceased pharaoh to be ritually sent to the constellation of Orion and be transformed into Osiris.

THE TAROT AND THE GREAT PYRAMID

Although many believe that the Tarot dates back to no earlier than late medieval times, there is a tradition in some circles that the Tarot has its origins and predecessors in ancient Egypt and the wisdom of Thoth/Hermes:

> Papus, in his *The Tarot of the Bohemians*, a classical book about the mystery of the Major and Minor Arcana [the two sets of cards composing the Tarot deck], tells us in legend, that the whole initiatory wisdom of Ancient Egypt was recorded in the

symbols of the Tarot cards as a last attempt to preserve this wisdom for future generations, and was made just before Egypt was invaded and destroyed by the advancing hordes of the Persian king. (Sadhu, 1962, pp. 11–12, italics in the original)

(See also Benavides, 1974; Mebes, n.d.; Ouspensky, 1928, 1976 [originally published in 1913]; Uxkull, 1922).

Cornish (1986, 1990) explicitly ties together the Tarot, initiatory rites of the ancient Egyptians, the Great Pyramid, and Christianity. Quotations from this author explain how.

The Book of Thoth is the Tarot and Tarot murals are the very substance of the Mysteries of the Great Pyramid. . . . Originally the Greater Arcana portion [of the Tarot deck] assumed the form of 22 murals or panels which could be raised or lowered as the candidate made his ascent or descent in the Pyramid's Hall of Illumination [Grand Gallery]. It is this enormous (150 ft long), narrow but high-ceilinged passageway which connects the Hierophant's (also known as the Queen's) chamber with the King's chamber. These murals represent the gist of essence of the 22 initiations which constitute the timeless Mysteries. (Cornish, 1990, p. 13)

"Let it be said at the outset that The Gospel According to St. Matthew is based and structured directly upon the mystery initiations of the Great Pyramid" (Cornish, 1986, p. 13), and Jesus the Christ himself passed through the Isiac-Osirian mysteries, as revealed in the Great Pyramid and Tarot. "The mysteries are in two parts, the Isiac and the Osirian, dealing with man's outer and inner consciousness, respectively" (Cornish, 1986, p. 13). In other terms, one can refer to these as matter-consciousness and spirit-consciousness.

THE KABBALA AND THE GREAT PYRAMID

Some authors have attempted to link the Jewish mystical writings and secret teachings of the Kabbala (Kabala, Caballa, Cabala, Quabalah, Quabala, Quabbala, Quabbalah), and the Kabbalistic interpretation of the Hebrew scriptures, with the Great Pyramid (see, for instance, Doreal, 1938; see Hall, 2003, for a discussion of the Kabbala more generally). A key method of kabbalism is to use gematria, "the art of discovering the secret sense of a (Hebrew) word by means of the numerical equivalents of each letter, each letter in Hebrew being also a number" (Kingsland, 1935, p. 86). Given the emphasis that researchers from Greaves (1646) to Smyth

(1867) to Petrie (1883) to Cole (1925) to Stecchini (1971) have placed on the exact measurements of almost every aspect of the Great Pyramid, this is a subject that would inevitably cry out for Kabbalistic interpretation. J. Ralston Skinner supplied this in the nineteenth century (Skinner, n.d., but originally published in 1875 according to Kingsland, 1932, p. vii). Skinner developed an elaborate correlation between numbers of Kabbalistic significance and various measurements of the Great Pyramid. Kingsland (1935, pp. 85–92) reviewed Skinner's work along these lines, concluding that the basic measurements he used for the Great Pyramid were incorrect, and therefore any correspondences Skinner seems to have found between numerical values of Hebrew words and scriptural passages and measurements of the Great Pyramid do not, at least in their specifics, hold up well to scrutiny. However, Kingsland (1935, p. 92) did say that personally he was "inclined to believe that there should be a connection on the basis of both the Kabala and the Pyramid containing to a certain extent a numerical and geometrical symbolism as Key to the Cosmic Principles taught in the Ancient Mysteries."

THE GREAT PYRAMID AS A RESONANCE MACHINE OR
A GIANT MUSICAL INSTRUMENT

On the evening of November 24, 2003, Elena Konstantinou, Leila Makeeva, John Anthony West, I and my students (Logan Kaye Danielle Yonavjak [Logan] and Jessica Brady Hahn [Brady]), the documentary film crew working for Elena and Leila, and various other persons that joined the group had the opportunity to spend over four hours in the Great Pyramid, leaving shortly after midnight. We had a chance to go through almost all of the passages and chambers of the Great Pyramid; unfortunately, we could not view/enter the Well Shaft, the Grotto, or the passage from the Grotto to the lower portion of the Descending Passage (these have been rather permanently blocked off and are not currently accessible—I have never been in them).

West propounded his version of the theory that one of the major reasons the Great Pyramid's interior was built the way it was is for resonance purposes—to carry or transmit sound throughout; essentially it can be viewed as a giant musical instrument (my analogy). The chambers above the King's Chamber would be for resonance purposes, and he suggested that the oddly cut pit or Subterranean Chamber at the bottom of the descending passage may have been a way to "tune" the pyramid; bits of rock would be carved out here and there to tune it precisely, thus giving rise to the odd, higgledy-piggledy floor of the pit. We tested the resonance theory after a fashion, by having West go to the King's Chamber and chant an "Om" while I stood in the pit; even with my poor hearing (I suffer a hearing loss from when I had the mumps as a child), I could hear West chanting. (Logan Yonavjak has independently suggested to me that perhaps priests may have stood in each of the chambers simultaneously to meditate and hum, setting up mutual resonance of sounds throughout the pyramid.)

Later that evening, standing in Al Mamun's forced passage, Elena astutely suggested that if the Great Pyramid has, or had, resonance properties, if it acted as a musical instrument, then it has been damaged by the forced passage and also by the forced entry into the Relieving Chambers, such that it can no longer function properly. She suggested that in order to test the resonance theory, these later forced passages should be filled in or at least stuffed and blocked off acoustically. At that point we were all assuming that the Well Shaft and Grotto, with the passage from the Grotto down to the Descending Passage, were part of the original construction of the Great Pyramid.

On November 27, 2003, John Anthony West and I were talking in the Temple of Osiris (Seti I, Nineteenth Dynasty) in Abydos and looking at the reliefs on the walls of the temple that apparently, methodically and systematically, had certain portions chiseled out and defaced, while other portions have been left untouched suggesting that this is not late vandalism or Christian defacing but specific or ritualistic defacing that was done purposefully by the ancients to "kill" the temple or neutralize its magic when the end of the life of the temple, or when the cycle of the temple, came to a close. Quick inspection on my part suggested that the same chisel was used with fair accuracy to take out only certain portions of the reliefs, such as the faces, hands, or feet of particular deities and figures, across a wall, not just random smashing with hammers or mallets. It then occurred to me that perhaps the Well Shaft and Grotto complex of the Great Pyramid served a similar function. If the Great Pyramid served resonance functions, if it is was essentially a huge "musical instrument," then it may have been decommissioned purposefully in ancient times at the end of its life cycle by the opening up, carving out, and/or unsealing (was it partially already dug/carved out previously?) of the Well Shaft and Grotto complex; this would have the effect of disrupting the resonance and harmonic properties, and so on, of the Great Pyramid and making it relatively "useless" for such purposes. J. A. West immediately took to this suggestion and thought it fit in well with the "resonance" theory of the Great Pyramid.

All of the foregoing is, I believe, compatible with an initiatory function for the Great Pyramid. Although they did not study the Great Pyramid, Jahn, Devereux, and Ibison (1995) report on acoustical resonance behaviors that they found in various ancient structures.

Miscellaneous Theories

Besides the suggestions summarized heretofore relating to the purpose of the Great Pyramid, a number of other suggestions have been offered (many of which are succinctly summarized in Bonwick, 1877). A few of these include:

1. The pyramids in general served as barriers against the desert sands.
2. The Great Pyramid is a copy of, or possibly the same base dimensions as, the Tower of Babel.
3. The Great Pyramid has the same base dimensions as Noah's Ark.
4. The Great Pyramid was built to preserve knowledge in the wake of the Deluge. This is perhaps not unrelated to the concept that the Great Pyramid was built by Atlanteans to preserve something of their knowledge and heritage for posterity (with perhaps a Hall of Records under or near the Great Pyramid), as it was clear that their civilization would be destroyed.
5. The Great Pyramid was constructed after the Deluge as a memorial to the incident.
6. The Great Pyramid was the abode of Satan.
7. The Great Pyramid served as Joseph's granary, a notion that can be traced back to medieval times.
8. The Great Pyramid specifically, and various pyramids and Egyptian monuments in general, served as a way to monitor the levels of the Nile, Mediterranean, and Red Sea relative to the land.
9. The Great Pyramid has been considered a phallic symbol, a symbol for the Sun or the Sacred Fire, or as a place (a human-made mountain) atop which an alter was set for sacrifices.

A NOTE ABOUT CAVIGLIA

Giovanni Battista Caviglia (1770–1845) was arguably one of the most colorful explorers of the Great Pyramid in modern times, and possibly the person who had in some respects the best intuitive feel and understanding for this structure in modernity. A Genoese mariner and owner of a vessel based on Malta, Caviglia took an interest in Egypt in the early nineteenth century and explored the Great Pyramid and Sphinx, undertaking excavations; it was he who cleared out the complete passage from the Well to the Descending Passage near the Subterranean Chamber. He also worked with and for Howard Vyse (Vyse, 1840), in charge of several hundred excavators (see Tompkins, 1971, p. 386). For a time Caviglia even lived in Davison's Chamber, just above the King's Chamber in the Great Pyramid.

Bonwick (1877, pp. 223–224) relates the following comments about Caviglia.

Lord Lindsay met him at Gizeh, admired and honoured him. He was, as he himself expressed it, *"tout à fait pyramidale."* His lordship wrote, "We are told that in Ceylon there are insects that take the shape and colour of the branch or leaf they feed upon; Caviglia seems to partake of their nature, he is really assimilating to a pyramid." This was not said in ridicule. He described him as "happy with his pyramid, his mysticism, and his Bible." Even then, at sixty-six years of age, he had, we are told, "reared a pyramid of the most extraordinary mysticism—astrology, magnetism, magic (his favorite studies), its corner-stones; while on each face of the airy vision he sees inscribed, in letters of light, invisible to all but himself, elucidatory texts of Scripture."

Mr. Ramsay has this account:—"He has strange, unearthly ideas, which seem to open up to you, as he says them, whole vistas of unheard-of ground, which close up again as suddenly, so that one can hardly know what his theories are. He says, it would be highly dangerous to communicate them, and looks mystical."

One who knew something about *Lost Secrets* wrote thus of him:—"By studying the remains of Pagan antiquity in the only way they can be profitably studied, namely, through the medium of the occult sciences, Caviglia had discovered the long-lost secret of the pyramids. And with the discovery of the central mystery of Egyptian paganism the great central truth of Christianity, historically considered, had revealed itself to him."

One who studied such questions for half a century, and who lately left this Babel of ours for the "dimly-shadowed shore," told the writer [i.e., Bonwick] that there were untold secrets of value in the Great Pyramid, and that the pyramid builders possessed the secret of all philosophical mysticism on the basis of astronomical fact.

There is something in the pyramid; and men who see what others cannot, would not, see, if derided for their second sight, may yet be proved to have a vision true and clear. (italics in the original)

SEEKING WISDOM ON THE GIZA PLATEAU

Note: This is a speculative piece that I wrote in 2003. I include it here for its possible heuristic value.

Might we find ancient wisdom encoded or enshrined in the Great Sphinx? This is a question I have often asked myself while studying the great monument. Standing between the paws of the Sphinx, sometimes I cannot help but have the sense that there is something important and profound to be learned from her (unlike many people, I consider the Sphinx to be female—indeed, a female of African or Nubian ethnicity—despite the false beard, surely a later addition, that was once attached to her chin). The seismic analysis Dr. Thomas Dobecki and I performed around the Sphinx in 1991 revealed what might be a chamber or room carved into the limestone under the left paw of the Sphinx, hailed by some as the "Hall of Records" of the lost continent of Atlantis. To the best of my knowledge, this cavity has never been probed or explored, so we don't know what it might contain, if anything. But my sense of importance and profundity is not linked to finding some secret store of knowledge, stash of treasure, or ancient technological marvel. To simply be in the presence of the Great Sphinx, or even to ponder the statue and all its possible implications from afar, can be a moving experience.

I first came face to face with the Great Sphinx at 8:30 a.m. local time on June 17, 1990 (I know people who believe there is astrological significance to this time and date, but it has never been explained to me). Many more trips would follow over the years. I am a geologist, and I had come to look at the Sphinx specifically with a geologist's eye. The question posed to me by my colleague and friend, the heretical independent Egyptologist John Anthony West (author of the classic work on R. A. Schwaller de Lubicz and the Symbolist interpretation of ancient Egypt *Serpent in the Sky: The High Wisdom of Ancient Egypt*), was: What is the age of the Great Sphinx? Is the attribution of the Great Sphinx to the time of the pharaoh Khafre (a.k.a. Chephren), circa 2500 B.C., reasonable, on the basis of the geology and geomorphology of the Giza Plateau, where the Great Pyramid (attributed to Khufu, a.k.a. Cheops, circa 2540 B.C.), Second Pyramid (attributed to Khafre), the comparatively small Third Pyramid (attributed to Menkaure, a.k.a. Mycerinus, circa 2480 B.C.), and Sphinx stand?

Studying the weathering and erosion of the limestone that makes up the body of the Sphinx, analyzing subsurface weathering patterns that we documented seismically, and comparing the ancient climatic history of the Giza Plateau with the features of the rocks led me to one conclusion: the origins of the Great Sphinx are not only antecedent to the time of Khafre but appear to go well back into Predynastic times, circa 5000 B.C. or earlier. What is more, the so-called Sphinx Temple, sitting directly in front of the Great Sphinx, also dates back to this earlier time. There is a connection between the Sphinx and her temple and the pharaohs Khufu and Khafre of the Fourth Dynasty (Old Kingdom Egypt), but it is one of appropriation and adoption by these pharaohs of much older, indeed what they may have thought of as ancient (and no doubt sacred), structures. The Fourth Dynasty Egyptians repaired and refurbished the Sphinx and associated buildings, and at some point during early dynastic times the head of the Sphinx appears to have been recarved (the head of the Great Sphinx is actually out of proportion to the body; it is too small, as would be expected if an earlier and badly weathered head was recarved; there is no way now to determine what the original head of the Great Sphinx looked like).

To suggest that the origins of the Sphinx go back to Predynastic times, before the modern Sahara Desert even existed (the Sphinx and associated pyramids today sit on the eastern edge of the Sahara Desert across the Nile from modern Cairo) was heresy of the first order. I was told by mainstream academic Egyptologists that no people were sufficiently civilized and sophisticated to carve the Sphinx, or even a proto-Sphinx, at such an early date. My redating of the Sphinx, if true, would necessitate a rethinking of the origin of civilization. Obviously, my critics argued, despite my geological evidence, my conclusions must be flawed. I diligently wrote articles on the subject and presented talks at geological and Egyptological conferences, and despite the animosity toward the implications of my analysis, the analysis itself stood up to scrutiny. Indeed, independent geological studies of the Sphinx have now vindicated my analysis.

As a result of my work on the Great Sphinx, I've taken my share of both abuse and praise. Is the Sphinx trying to teach me a lesson? If so, it is a lesson for all of us. Initially I was a lonely voice, a persona non grata at Egyptological meetings for suggesting the impossible, but gradually I noticed that my work and ideas began to slowly take hold, even among those most antagonistic. The battle is not yet won, but more and more ground is being taken every day. Is the lesson persistence? Is it an example of the usefulness of trials and tribulations in fortifying the spirit? Is the Sphinx representative of the duality of mind, spirit, rationality, higher consciousness, and the divine versus matter, animal life, and beastly urges (sometimes thought of as the Leo-Aquarian opposition), both of which are manifested in humans to various degrees and are typically expressed in conflict, be it intellectual sniping or armed war between nations?

Not only does the geological evidence support my analysis and redating of the Great Sphinx, but also so does the astronomical work of my colleagues Robert Bauval and Thomas Brophy. Robert Bauval has suggested that the three major pyramids of the Giza Plateau correlate with the stars in Orion's belt and commemorate an epoch of circa 10,500 B.C. (see Bauval and Gilbert, 1994). Thomas Brophy has found significant correlations between the Giza monuments and celestial phenomena dating to the twelfth through tenth millennia B.C. (Brophy, 2002, finds alignments at 11,772 B.C. and 9420 B.C., for instance). Furthermore, Brophy suggests that the Giza monuments form a grand zodiac clock tied to precessional cycles.

To put it in crude modern terms, Earth wobbles as it spins on its axis, and thus the sky changes over the centuries and millennia. At present, on the vernal equinox (spring equinox in the northern hemisphere, when the sun crosses the celestial equator from south to north, around March 20–21) the sun rises against the constellation of Pisces, as it has done for about 2000 years. We live in the astrological Age of Pisces. In the not-too-distant future (within the next couple of centuries, depending on where one draws the boundary between Pisces and Aquarius) the sun will rise against Aquarius on the vernal equinox, and it will be the Age of Aquarius. Three thousand years ago, the sun rose against Aries on the vernal equinox, thus the world was in the Age of Aries. In his book, Brophy marshals evidence to support his hypothesis that the Giza monuments served, among other functions, as a testimony to and marker of the end of the Age of Virgo and the beginning of the Age of Leo, circa 10,909 B.C. The motif of the Great Sphinx can be interpreted in this light: the human head represents Virgo, the lion's body represents Leo, and the Sphinx faces due east to watch the rising sun on the vernal equinox. Certainly, Brophy's analysis is compatible with the gist of my redating of the Great Sphinx.

Through the ages, the Great Sphinx has been both feared and revered. When fully exposed (the Sphinx, if left to the elements, is quickly covered with desert sands up to her neck), the Sphinx stands some 66 feet high and 240 feet long from the tips of her outstretched paws to her rump. One Arab tradition refers to the Sphinx as *Abou el Hôl,* or the *Father of Terrors,* and it is reported that in about 1379 A.D. a fanatical sheik damaged the nose of this heathen idol in his zeal to proclaim Allah the one true god (see Bonwick, 1877). The Sphinx was also reported to give responses at sunrise to questions placed before it, perhaps not literally speaking but conveying information in subtle and mysterious ways. In New Kingdom Egypt, as well as during Greco-Roman times, the Great Sphinx was often revered as a beneficent deity. Her face was painted red, an altar was positioned between her paws, offerings were made to her, and votive tablets were left to her.

Why was the Great Sphinx carved in the location where she sits? Often the Sphinx is seen as the sentinel or guardian of the pyramids, but in fact I believe the Great Sphinx (or proto-Sphinx) predates the present Giza pyramids. The Giza Plateau essentially marks the apex of the Nile delta and the very ancient division between Upper and Lower Egypt, a delineation that goes back into the far mists of Predynastic times.

One cannot fully fathom the meaning of the Great Sphinx without considering the adjacent pyramids. Were these monstrous structures merely tombs for maniacal pharaohs, or do they have another story to tell? Even if they served as the final resting places for dead men (and women), and this is far from proven, do the pyramids represent something more? Might the nineteenth-century royal astronomer of Scotland, C. Piazzi Smyth, and his colleagues have been on the right track when they suggested that the Great Pyramid in particular encodes and acts as a repository for sophisticated metrological, mathematical, geometric, geographical, and astronomical data? (I take exception to many of the strong Christian fundamentalist aspects of certain forms of "pyramidology," but that doesn't mean we should throw the entire baby out with the bathwater.) Elsewhere, I have suggested that the Great Sphinx and pyramids record, and were raised in response to, periodic encounters of Earth with comets and space debris, which at times wreaked havoc on the surface of our planet (see Schoch with McNally, 1999, 2003).

The strange and bizarrely designed but consummately built interior passageways and chambers of the Great Pyramid, and the connection between the pyramids and the Great Sphinx, have so far eluded any simple explanation. A theory that I believe has merit combines the astronomical and astrological significance of the orientations of the Sphinx, pyramids, and their internal passageways, with a hypothesis of initiation rites (including the passing-on of sacred and profane knowledge that may be encoded in the structures) that culminated in an ultimate mystical experience for those fortunate enough to achieve such a status.

The celestial alignments of the Giza structures have been empirically demonstrated. The vast literature on the sophisticated knowledge of the ancients cannot be ignored (see, for instance, Stecchini, 1971). To this day, many people who visit the Giza Plateau can innately "feel" the mystery of the setting, and to enter the Sphinx Temple or Great Pyramid even without preparation can be a very moving experience. It is well known that Napoleon experienced something very strange and inexplicable when he was alone in the King's Chamber on August 12, 1799; to his dying day, he refused to relate the experience.

Imagine traveling to the Giza Plateau prepared for a potential mystical vision or to receive sacred wisdom. In ancient times, adepts may have come from all parts of the globe to learn wisdom at the feet of the Sphinx. Imagine preparing with meditation and offerings, fasting and prayers over many days, in the Sphinx Temple. You face the enigmatic representation of the divine manifested in the mundane. You make your way up to and through the various stations and pyramids of the Giza Plateau, working thorough multifarious and labyrinthine passageways and chambers of diverse orientations, angles, and dimensions, each with their unique meaning and significance. The culmination of a long spiritual and metaphysical journey, for those with the stamina and fortitude to complete it, may have been experienced in the so-called King's Chamber of the Great Pyramid. Prepared by meditation and fasting, physical exhaustion and mental endeavor, aided by the acoustical, tactile, and olfactory properties of the granite insulation lining the chamber deep in the heart of the pyramid (drumming, chanting, music, and incense may have been used as part of the ritual), and perhaps followed by induced sensory deprivation, as one was left locked alone in the absolute darkness of the chamber with only the enigmatic granite coffer as company and no way to exit (dependent totally on one's colleagues to ultimately be retrieved), mystical experiences occurred.

Using sophisticated but now poorly understood means, the Sphinx and pyramids may have allowed adepts to accomplish what others have tried to achieve through ingesting mescaline (the active ingredient of peyote) and other drugs, kundalini yoga, study of the Kabbala, Transcendental Meditation, or any of numerous other presumed roads to enlightenment (see Horgan, 2003). The Sphinx and pyramids served as a vehicle, a means, to experience true mystical states, a way to gain that insight that cannot be described (sometimes referred to as the "oneness" or "void"), a method to glimpse ultimate reality.

What is the ancient wisdom that the Sphinx and pyramids have to impart? Perhaps it eludes all words, all language, and can only be attained by traveling the path to its ultimate consummation.

THE SEVEN WONDERS OF THE ANCIENT WORLD

In Greco-Roman times the concept of seven awe-inspiring works of art and architecture commonly known as the Seven Wonders, had wide currency. Lists of the Seven Wonders in some cases differed from one writer to another, but the seven most generally agreed upon were as follows (see Anonymous, 1965; Horowitz, 2004).

1. THE COLOSSUS OF RHODES
This gigantic brass statue, dedicated to the sun god, stood some 109 feet in height and was completed around 282 B.C. It overlooked the harbor of Rhodes until it was thrown down by an earthquake around 226 B.C.

2. THE SHRINE TO DIANA
The Temple of Artemis (Diana) was built in the city of Ephesus in the sixth century B.C. The main structure was constructed of marble, with a roof supported by 127 columns, each 60 feet high and weighing over 150 tons. About 356 B.C. the temple was damaged or destroyed by fire, but then rebuilt. It was finally destroyed by the Goths, as they sacked the city, in about A.D. 262.

3. STATUE OF ZEUS
Dating to the fifth century B.C., this statue was an estimated 40 feet or more high and stood in the temple dedicated to Zeus in Olympia. In late Roman times, it was apparently moved to Constantinople, where it was destroyed by a fire in the late fifth century A.D.

4. THE LIGHTHOUSE AT ALEXANDRIA
Constructed in the early third century B.C., the lighthouse off the harbor of the Egyptian city of Alexandra was reputedly constructed of white marble and stood 400 or more feet high. It lasted into medieval times; it was destroyed by an earthquake in the thirteenth century.

5. THE MAUSOLEUM AT HALICARNASSUS

This magnificent structure was erected about 350 B.C. by Queen Artemisia in memory of her dead husband King Mausolus, the late king of Caria, in Asia Minor. According to some descriptions, the building was 114 feet long and 92 feet wide and was divided into five major sections and surmounted by a pyramid. It was damaged by an earthquake in the fifteenth century and then disassembled.

6. THE HANGING GARDENS OF BABYLON

These may date to around 600 B.C. and are often attributed to Nebuchadnezzar II, although there is disagreement among the ancient sources. They have sometimes been described as a series of planted terraces, connected by marble stairways, rising along the banks of the Euphrates River.

7. THE GREAT PYRAMID

This is the only one of the Seven Wonders that has survived to modern times, located on the Giza Plateau in Egypt.

ACKNOWLEDGMENTS

First and foremost, I wish to acknowledge the generosity and support that I have received from my two dear friends and colleagues, Elena Konstantinou and Leila Makeeva. Without them, I don't know that I could have written this book. Elena, Leila, and I made two amazing trips together to visit the Great Pyramid. Together we explored the interior at length, including the so-called Relieving Chambers above the King's Chamber. I have been to Egypt many times over the years, and I can honestly say that my best and most productive trips have been with Elena and Leila. Thank you.

Joining Elena, Leila, and myself on one or both of the trips to Egypt were Shareen der Parthogh, Yervant der Parthogh, Andreas Wallach, Valeria Sanina, Ze'ev Gilad, Vitaly Lenskiy, David Wilkie, Andrew Martin, Chance Gardner, my old friend John Anthony West, David Hands, Leigh Cunningham, Graham Walker, Nicholas Hadjipavlou, and my Boston University students Jessica Brady Hahn and Logan Kaye Danielle Yonavjak (Logan has since moved on to the University of North Carolina at Chapel Hill). Although college freshpersons at the time, Brady and Logan both played significant roles in our November–December 2003 trip to Cairo, Upper Egypt, and the Egyptian Sinai. They were often mistaken for upper-level college or graduate students. Logan has since worked with me continuously on Egypt-related material and other projects and is always willing to help me when I need her assistance. Logan brought to my attention the Thoreau quotation used in the epigraph to this book (the Sandys quotation is from Sandys, 1621, p. 127). Through Logan, I have gotten to know her mother, Liane Salgado, who has also helped me with my research in many ways and provided constructive criticism of many of my ideas. In Egypt, my good friend Mohamed Nazmy provided logistical and moral support; Emil Shaker helped me in numerous ways; and

I also had the opportunity to meet with Dr. Zahi Hawass, whose kind permission allowed us access to the Great Pyramid and other sites.

My webmaster, Steve LeMaster (the website address is currently www.robertschoch.net, however, this is subject to change; it can be found by searching "Robert Schoch" on any good search engine), has provided me with unfailing support and helped me to collect information. It was an absolute pleasure meeting Michael McCleery in Cairo during November 2003, and I thank him for his assistance inside the Great Pyramid and for his generosity in sharing his photographs with me. Robert Bauval, who has always been a source of great help and encouragement, chatted with me about the Great Pyramid when we had the good fortune to meet in Cairo in May 2004, as did Steven Myers on the same trip. I have had many discussions with Richard Noone over the phone, and he has been an inspiration to me over the years.

During Boston University's spring recess in March 2004, my fine friend and "brother," Stratton Horres, and I were coleaders of a group trip to Egypt. Furthermore, he and I played the roles of Osiris and Set, respectively, in a modern rendition of the sacred story of Osiris, Isis, Set, and Horus. Participants in the March 2004 trip were Stratton's wife, Deborah J. Horres; Stratton's children Rachel L. Horres, Caroline M. Horres, and Stratton Jamison Horres; and Boston University students Aaron Manders, Jeffrey A. Gilfillan (Anubis in our rendition), Amanda J. Scobie (who took the role of Nephthys), Blanca D. (Daisy) Romero, Megan E. Hodes (who was Isis in the play), Danae Maragouthakis, Lori Danielle LaCroix, Molly F. Beitchman, Mallory E. Glenn, Natalie Grigorian, and Natasha Chander. Also participating in this trip were Betsyanne Tippette, Martha W. Potter, Patricia G. Arredondo, Bradley J. Trapnell (Horus in the play), Patricia M. Harris, Mary F. Driver, Kathleen P. Carmer, Maria L. Carmer, Michelle Escuriex, and John P. Cole. I especially thank Natalie Grigorian, Aaron Manders, and Jeffrey A. Gilfillan for their assistance during this trip. In Egypt Soha Mohmoud and Ashraf William joined us. I want to thank all of them for making the trip an outstanding success.

Of course, there are many people who have helped me or provided support other than those with whom I have traveled to, or worked in, Egypt. In this category are various friends, acquaintances, and family members, including, Alan Alford (author of *The Midnight Sun: The Death and Rebirth of God in Ancient Egypt*); Cheryl Baxa (always supportive of my endeavors, she helped me locate books in the early stages of my research); Noah Chatham; Laura Cortner; Carmen Cusó (a math teacher and astronomer in Argentina with whom I have exchanged ideas about the Great Pyramid); Brenda J. Dunne; Robert and Zoh Hierondimus; James Arthur Jancik; Helen Landis; Tom Manney (a pseudonym for someone who prefers to be anonymous); Roger D. Nelson; Liliane Roth (my friend in France who translated *Voyages of the Pyramid Builders* into French); Ashley Shelby; Don Yonavjak; my parents, Milton and Alicia Schoch; my parents-in-law Robert and Anne Pettit; my sister Rita Schoch; my constituents and fellow elected officials in the city of Attleboro, Massachusetts, where I am currently a city councilor; my colleagues and students at the College of General Studies of Boston University (in particular, Dean Linda Wells has always been very supportive of my research endeavors), where I have taught full-time since 1984; and of course my wife, Cynthia Pettit Schoch, and my two sons, Nicholas and Edward Schoch.

I must also express a debt of gratitude to all the Great Pyramid researchers of the past and present, many of whom are mentioned in this book or their works are cited in the bibliography. The field is so vast that no single volume can give every aspect of the Great Pyramid equal justice, so I have had to pick and choose from the available material. I apologize to those researchers whose work I lacked room to cover in this book.

This book would not be possible without the warm enthusiasm, encouragement, and fine editorial input that our editor at Tarcher, Mitch Horowitz, has always provided. I also extend personal thanks to my coauthor, Robert Aquinas McNally. This is our third book together, and it is always a pleasure to work with him. Our fine literary agents, Sarah Jane Freymann and Judith Riven, nurtured and believed in *Pyramid Quest*. Finally, I must thank readers like you for making it possible for this book to exist. Without readers, there is perhaps no point in writing.

Robert M. Schoch
Attleboro, Massachusetts
January 2005

NOTES

CHAPTER 1. A DISTANT MIRROR

1. The original reads: *"ce Sphinx dont tout le corps léonin, à l'exception de la tête, montre une indiscutable érosion aquatique"* (Schwaller de Lubicz, 1961, p. 119); translated by Robert Aquinas McNally.

CHAPTER 2. THE STANDARD STORY

1. Verner, 2001, p. 189.
2. Quoted in Kingsland, 1932, p. 6.

CHAPTER 3. THINKING OUTSIDE THE SARCOPHAGUS

1. Drbal, 1985, p. 121.
2. Drbal, 1985, p. 116.
3. Drbal, 1985, p. 119.
4. Quoted in Valentine, 1975, p. 164.
5. See Petrie, 1883, 1885.
6. Farrell, 2001, p. 2.

CHAPTER 4. A CERTAIN AGE

1. Tompkins, 1971, p. 61.
2. Translation as given by Hassan, 1949, pp. 222–223.
3. See Nakhla et. al, 1999.
4. Lehner, 1991, p. 33.
5. Coxill, 1998, p. 16.

CHAPTER 5. NAMING THE BUILDER

1. Valentine, 1975, p. 7.
2. Quoted in Tompkins, 1971, p. 72; italics Taylor's.
3. Quoted in Tompkins, 1971, p. 76.

4. Quoted in Tompkins, 1971, p. 76.

5. Smyth, 1880/1978, p. xii; italics in the original.

6. Smyth, 1880/1978, p. xi.

7. Quoted in Kingsland, 1932, pp. 6–7.

8. See El Mahdy, 2003, pp. 113–115.

9. El Mahdy, 2003, p. 131.

10. See for instance, Emery,1960; Said, 1962; Sampsell, 2003.

11. Petrie, 1883, 1885.

CHAPTER 6. TRACKING THE HEAVENS

1. Isler, 2001, p. 173.

2. Proctor, 1880, pp. 62–63.

3. See Petrie, 1883, 1885, and Kingsland, 1932.

4. Quoted in Tompkins, 1971, p. 165.

5. Bauval and Gilbert, 1994, p. 192.

6. Bauval and Gilbert, 1994, pp. 192–193.

7. Hertaus, 2004.

8. Edge, 1995, 1998.

CHAPTER 7. BOUNDARIES OF SEASONS AND THE EARTH

1. Quoted in Calter, 1998/2004.

2. Stecchini, 1971, p. 289.

3. According to Herz-Fischler, 2000, p. 176.

CHAPTER 8. GOD'S NUMBERS

1. Quoted in Shalev, 2002, p. 569.

2. Quoted in Shalev, 2002, p. 570.

3. Quoted in Kingsland, 1932, p. 2.

4. Smyth, 1880/1978, p. xx, capitals in original.

5. Quoted in Tompkins, 1971, p. 92.

6. Quoted in Tompkins, 1971, p. 93.

7. Smyth, 1880/1978, p. 621.

8. Smyth, 1880/1978, p. xi.

9. Smyth, 1880/1978, p. xi.

10. Smyth, 1880/1978, p. xii; italics in original.

11. Smyth, 1880/1978, p. xii.

12. Smyth, 1880/1978, p. 623.

13. Quoted in Tompkins, 1971, p. 108.

14. Davidson and Aldersmith, n.d., p. 383.

15. Russell, 1915, p. 315; italics in original.

16. Russell, 1915, pp. 315–316.

17. Russell, 1915, p. 326.
18. Russell, 1915, p. 342.
19. Lewis, 1994, p. 97.
20. Lewis, 1994, pp. 176–177.
21. Lemesurier, 1977, p. 295.
22. Lemesurier, 1977, p. 242.

CHAPTER 9. PI AND THE GOLDEN SECTION

1. Quoted in Herz-Fischler, 2000, p. 144.
2. See Schwaller de Lubicz, 1985, pp. 104–105.

CHAPTER 10. SECRET KNOWLEDGE

1. Said, 1979, p. 70.
2. Quoted in West, 1985, p. xi.
3. Lucius Apuleius, 1951, pp. 264–265.
4. See Hornung, 2001.
5. Hornung, 2001, p. 117.
6. See Hornung, 2001, pp. 119–120.
7. Anonymous, 1785; Hall, 1937.
8. Quoted in Hornung, 2001, p. 147.
9. Quoted in Hornung, 2001, p. 148.

CHAPTER 11. AN ENTRY INTO THE MYSTERIES

1. Tompkins, 1971, p. 50; Cott, 1987, p. 50.
2. Brunton, 1936, 1969, p. 65.
3. Brunton, 1936, 1969, p. 65.
4. Brunton, 1936, 1969, p. 69.
5. Brunton, 1936, 1969, p. 73.
6. Brunton, 1936, 1969, p. 74; italics in the original.
7. Brunton, 1936, 1969, p. 76.
8. Brunton, 1936, 1969, p. 77.
9. Melchizedek, 2000, p. 277.
10. Horn, 2003, p. 283.
11. Horn, 2003, p. 284.
12. Horn, 2003, p. 286.
13. Haich, 1974, p. 233.
14. Hall, 1928/1945; 2003, p. 62.
15. Quoted in DeSalvo, 2003, pp. 109–110.
16. Maspero quoted in Adams, 1933, p. 12.

BIBLIOGRAPHY

These references include works cited in both the text and appendices and materials that I consulted during my studies and that I recommend as further reading and reference for any Great Pyramid devotee. Sources are divided into two categories. Some sources from the Internet/World Wide Web are listed at the end of the bibliography. Since on-line sources can change quickly, I have kept these to a minimum. Interested readers should use any of the many on-line search engines to find useful and relevant Great Pyramid materials. Biblical quotations in the text are taken from *The Jerusalem Bible*, Reader's Edition (Jones, 1968).

This bibliography makes no claims to completeness, but it is relatively comprehensive. Some of the works cited are relatively rare, but with diligence the majority can be found either for sale or in libraries, and many of the more critical works have been reprinted. I include relevant bibliographic details under some entries in order to clarify certain confusing issues regarding various editions of important works. Even though I do not agree with their analyses and conclusions, *Great Pyramid Passages*, vol. 1, by John and Morton Edgar (1910, 1923, and various reprints of the 1923 edition; personally I prefer the 1910 edition) is an invaluable source of photographs taken in and around the Great Pyramid at the beginning of the twentieth century before many modern restorations had been made and conveniences (such as railings for tourists) had been installed. Likewise, the multivolume set *Pyramidology* by Adam Rutherford is worth perusing for the photographs alone.

BOOKS AND OTHER PAPER SOURCES

Adams, W. Marsham. *The Book of the Master of the Hidden Places: The True Symbolism of the Great Pyramid Revealed by the Book of the Dead.* Edited by E. J. Langford Garstin. London: Search, 1933.

Adams, W. Marsham. *The Book of the Master, Or the Egyptian Doctrine of the Light Born of the Virgin Mother.* London: John Murray, 1898.

Adams, W. Marsham. *The House of the Hidden Places: A Clue To The Creed of Early Egypt from Egyptian Sources.* London: John Murray, 1895.

Agnew, H. *Letter from Alexandria on the Evidence of the Practical Application of the Quadrature of the Circle in the Configuration of the Great Pyramids of Egypt.* London: Longman, Orne, Brown, Green, and Longman's, 1838. Citation from Herz-Fischler (2000).

Aldred, Cyril. *The Egyptians*. Rev. and enl. ed. London: Thames and Hudson, 1984.

Alford, Alan F. *The Midnight Sun: The Death and Rebirth of God in Ancient Egypt*. Walsall, England: Eridu Books, 2004.

Alford, Alan F. *Pyramid of Secrets: The Architecture of the Great Pyramid Reconsidered in the Light of Creational Mythology*. Walsall, England: Eridu Books, 2003.

Alford, Alan F. *When the Gods Came Down: The Catastrophic Roots of Religion Revealed*. London: Hodder and Stoughton, 2000.

Angell, Christopher. "Inside the Pyramids of the Pharaohs." In *The World's Last Mysteries*. Pleasantville, N.Y.: Reader's Digest Association, 1978, pp. 188–201.

Anonymous. *28. The Sphinx, Pyramid and Kneeling Camel, Cairo, Egypt*. Stereograph view card. N.p., n.d. [1900?].

Anonymous [attributed to Carl Friedrich Koeppen, or Köppen, ed., sometimes with Johann Wilhelm Bernhard von Hymmen; see Hornung, 2001, p. 120.]. *CRATA REPOA. Oder Einweihungen in der alten geheimen Gesellschaft der Egyptischen Priester*. [Berlin]: n.p., 1785.

Anonymous [sometimes attributed to Iamblichus]. *Egyptian Mysteries: An Account of an Initiation*. York Beach, Maine: Samuel Weiser 1988.

Anonymous. "Seven Wonders of the World." In *Encyclopedia Americana*, international ed., 24:610a–610b, 611. New York: Americana, 1965.

Anonymous. *The Theosophical Movement, 1875–1925: A History and A Survey*. New York: Dutton, 1925.

Association for Research and Enlightenment (A.R.E.). *A.R.E.'s Annual Mysteries Conference 2004, Mu, Atlantis, and Egypt: Pole Star Aligns and Soul Groups Return. October 7–10, 2004*. Announcement brochure. Virginia Beach, Va.: Association for Research and Enlightenment, 2004.

Aziz, Philippe. *The Mysteries of the Great Pyramid*. Translated by John Derek Megginson. Geneva: Editions Ferni, 1977.

Badawy, Alexander. *A History of Egyptian Architecture*. Vol. 1. *From the Earliest Times to the End of the Old Kingdom*. London: Histories and Mysteries of Man, 1990. Originally published 1954.

Baines, John, and Jaromír Málek. *Atlas of Ancient Egypt*. New York: Facts on File, 1980.

Ballard, Robert. *The Solution of the Pyramid Problem or, Pyramid Discoveries. With a New Theory as to Their Ancient Use*. New York: Wiley, 1882.

Barber, F. M. *The Mechanical Triumphs of the Ancient Egyptians*. London: Kegan Paul, Trench, Trübner, 1900.

Bauval, Robert. *Secret Chamber: The Quest for the Hall of Records*. London: Arrow Books, 2000.

Bauval, Robert, and Adrian Gilbert. *The Orion Mystery: Unlocking the Secrets of the Pyramids*. New York: Crown Trade Paperbacks, 1994.

Bedford, Francis. See Smyth, 1864.

Benavides, Rodolfo. *The Prophetic Tarot and the Great Pyramid*. Mexico City, Mexico: Editores Mexicanos Unidos, 1974.

Bernard, Jean-Louis. *Aux Origines de L'Égypte*. Paris: Éditions Robert Laffont, 1976.

Besant, Annie. *The Ancient Wisdom: An Outline of Theosophical Teachings*. New York: Theosophical Publishing, 1897.

Birch, S. *Ancient History from the Monuments. Egypt from the Earliest Times to B.C. 300.* London: Society for Promoting Christian Knowledge, 1890.

Blackden, M. W., translator and editor. *Ritual of the Mystery of the Judgment of the Soul.* London: For the Societas Rosicruciana in Anglia by Bernard Quaritch, [1914].

Blavatsky, H. P. *Isis Unveiled: A Master-Key to the Mysteries of Ancient and Modern Science and Theology.* 2 vols bound as one. New York: J. W. Bouton, 1877. Reprint, Los Angeles: Theosophy, 1931.

Blavatsky, H. P. *The Secret Doctrine: The Synthesis of Science, Religion, and Philosophy.* 2 vols bound as one. London: Theosophical Publishing, 1888. Reprint, 1925.

Bonwick, James. *Egyptian Belief and Modern Thought.* London: C. Kegan Paul, 1878.

Bonwick, James. *Pyramid Facts and Fancies.* London: C. Kegan Paul, 1877. Reprint, as *The Great Pyramid of Giza: History and Speculation,* Mineola, N.Y.: Dover, 2002.

Borchardt, Ludwig, and Herbert Ricke. *Egypt: Architecture, Landscape, Life of the People.* N.p., n.d. [1929?], [date of the introduction and latest date of some of the photographs in the book]. Marked "Orbis Terrarum" and "Printed in Germany." Herz-Fischler, 2000, p. 277, gives the city and publisher as "New York: Westermann" but may be referring to a different edition of this book.

Bowles, J. *The Gods, Gemini, and the Great Pyramid.* Grass Lake, Mich.: Gemini Books, 1998.

Bramley, William. *The Gods of Eden.* New York: Avon Books, 1993.

Breasted, James Henry. *Development of Religion and Thought in Ancient Egypt.* London: Hodder and Stoughton, 1912. Reprint, New York: Harper, 1959.

Brennan, Herbie. *Martian Genesis: The Extraterrestrial Origins of the Human Race.* New York: Dell, 2000.

Brennan, Herbie. *The Secret History of Ancient Egypt: Electricity, Sonics, and the Disappearance of an Advanced Civilization.* New York: Berkley Books, 2001.

Brophy, Thomas G. *The Origin Map: Discovery of a Prehistoric, Megalithic, Astrophysical Map and Sculpture of the Universe.* With foreword by Robert M. Schoch and afterword by John Anthony West. New York: Writers Club Press, 2002.

Brunton, Paul [pen name of Raphael Hurst; see Feuerstein, 2003]. *A Search in Secret Egypt.* New York: Dutton, 1936. Reprint, New York: Weiser, 1969. Page citations are to the Weiser reprint.

Budge, E. A. Wallis. *The Egyptian Book of the Dead (The Papyrus of Ani).* London: Trustees of the British Museum, 1895. Reprint, New York: Dover, 1967.

Budge, E. A. Wallis. *The Mummy.* New York: Causeway Books, 1974. Originally published 1894.

Bunsen, Christian C. J. *Egypt's Place in Universal History: An Historical Investigation in Five Books.* 5 bks. bound in 4 vols. Translated from the German by Charles H. Cottrell. London: Longman, Brown, Green, and Longmans, 1848, 1854, 1859, 1860.

Busch, Moritz (translated by W. C. Wrankmore). *Hand-book for Travellers in Egypt and Adjacent Countries Subject to the Pascha.* Trieste: Austrian Lloyd, 1864.

Cadman, John. "The Subterranean Chamber Hydraulic Pulse Generator and Water Pump." In *The Complete Pyramid Sourcebook,* edited by John DeSalvo. Bloomington, Ind.: 1stBooks, 2003, pp. 339–350.

Capt, E. Raymond. *The Great Pyramid Decoded.* Thousand Oaks, Calif.: Artisan Sales, [1971].

Capt, E. Raymond. *Study in Pyramidology.* 1986. Reprint, Muskogee, Ok.: Artisan, 2002.

Casey, Charles. *Philitis: Being a Condensed Account of the Recently Discovered Solution of the Use and Meaning of the Great Pyramid.* 5th ed. Dublin: Carson Brothers, 1883. Reprint, photocopy, n.p.: Kessinger, [2004?].

Cavalli, Thom F. *Alchemical Psychology: Old Recipes for Living in a New World.* New York: Jeremy P. Tarcher/Putnam, 2002.

Cayce, Edgar. *The Essential Edgar Cayce.* Edited and with an introduction by Mark Thurston. New York: Penguin, 2004.

Ceram, C. W. [pen name of Kurt W. Marek]. *Gods, Graves, and Scholars: The Story of Archaeology.* New York: Knopf, 1952.

Chaney, Earlyne C. *Initiation in the Great Pyramid Book.* Upland, Calif.: Astara's Library of Mystical Classics, 1987.

Chase, J. Munsell. *The Riddle of the Sphinx: A Key to the Mysteries and a Synthesis of Philosophy.* San Francisco: J. Munsell Chase, 1915.

Churchward, Albert. *Origin and Antiquity of Freemasonry and its Analogy to the Eschatology of the Ancient Egyptians, as Witnessed by the "Book of the Dead," and the Great Pyramid of Ghizeh, the First Masonic Temple in the World.* London: Sir Joseph Causton and Sons, 1898.

Churchward, Albert. *The Origin and Evolution of Primitive Man—Lecture Given at the Royal Societies Club, St. James's Street, February 1912.* London: George Allen, 1912.

Clancy, Flora Simmons. *Pyramids.* Montreal: St. Remy Press, 1994.

Clymer, R. Swinburne. *The Mysteries of Osiris or Ancient Egyptian Initiation.* Quakertown, Penn.: Philosophical Publishing, 1951.

Cohane, John Philip. *The Key.* New York: Crown, 1969.

Cole, J. H. *Determination of the Exact Size and Orientation of the Great Pyramid of Giza.* Survey of Egypt paper no. 39. Cairo: Government Press, 1925. See also on-line at: www.artifice-design.co.uk/kheraha/cole.html (June 30, 2003), for an incomplete and inexact copy.

Collier, Mark, and Bill Manley. *How to Read Egyptian Hieroglyphs.* London: British Museum Press, 1998.

Collins, Andrew. *Gateway to Atlantis: The Search for the Source of a Lost Civilization.* New York: Caroll and Graf, 2000.

Collins, Andrew. *Gods of Eden: Egypt's Lost Legacy and the Genesis of Civilization.* Rochester, Vt.: Bear, 2002.

Coppens, Philip. *The Canopus Revelation: Stargate of the Gods and the Ark of Osiris.* Enkhuizen, Netherlands: Frontier, 2004.

Cornish, Norman Charles. *The Great Pyramid.* Vol. 1. *The Ancient Mysteries.* Vancouver: Thomas Chatterton Press, 1990.

Cornish, Norman Charles. *The Matthew Connection: Pyramid and Cross.* Vancouver: Thomas Chatterton, 1986.

Coryn, Sidney G. P. *The Faith of Ancient Egypt.* New York: Theosophical, 1913.

Cossette, Thomas L. *The Way of Melchizedek.* N.p.: Xulon Press, 2003.

Cotsworth, Moses B. *The Rational Almanac. Tracing the Evolution of Modern Almanacs from Ancient Ideas of Time and Suggesting Improvements.* York, England: privately printed, 1905.

Cott, Jonathan, with Hanny El Zeini. *The Search for Omm Sety: A Story of Eternal Love.* Garden City, N.Y.: Doubleday, 1987.

Cottrell, Leonard. *The Mountains of Pharaoh: Two Thousand Years of Pyramid Exploration.* London: Pan Books, 1963.

Coxill, David. "The Riddle of the Sphinx." *InScription: Journal of Ancient Egypt.* (spring 1998), pp. 13–19. Coxill's name is misspelled "Coxhill" in the byline.

Darwin, Charles. *On the Origin of Species by Means of Natural Selection, or the Preservation of Favored Races in the Struggle for Life.* 5th ed., with additions and corrections. New York: D. Appleton, 1871. First ed. published November 24, 1859; see p. 16 of 1871 ed. for citation.

David, A. Rosalie. *The Pyramid Builders of Ancient Egypt: A Modern Investigation of Pharaoh's Workforce.* London: Routledge, 1996.

Davidovits, Joseph, and Margie Morris. *The Pyramids: An Enigma Solved.* New York: Hippocrene Books, 1988.

Davidson, Dan. "Experimental Research on Shape Power Energies." In *The Complete Pyramid Sourcebook,* edited by John DeSalvo, Bloomington, Ind.: 1stBooks, 2003, pp. 289–304.

Davidson, David. *The Current Crisis in the Great Pyramid's Prophecy.* Flyer. N.p. [1931?].

Davidson, D. *The Great Pyramid's Prophecy on the Current Economic Oppression.* Leeds: privately published, 1931.

Davidson, David. *The Hidden Truth in Myth and Ritual.* London: Covenant, 1934.

Davidson, D. *Talks on the Great Pyramid. No. 3, Pyramid Prophecy and Current Events.* 2nd rev. ed. London: Williams and Norgate, 1925.

Davidson, D., and H. Aldersmith. *The Great Pyramid, Its Divine Message: An Original Coordination of Historical Documents and Archaeological Evidences. Vol. I.—Pyramid Records.* 1st ed. London: Williams and Norgate, 1924. [This is the first edition of this often-reprinted work; Vol. 1 is complete unto itself.]

Davidson, D., and H. Aldersmith. *The Great Pyramid, Its Divine Message.* London: Williams and Norgate, 1925. Reprint, n.p.: Kessinger, n.d. [2003?].

Day, St. John Vincent. *On Some Points in Certain Theories Concerning the Purpose and Primal Condition of the Great Pyramid of Jeezeh: Being a Paper Read to the Philosophical Society of Glasgow, February, 1868, and in Chief Part a Reply to a Lecture Delivered to the Royal Society of Edinburgh, January 20, 1868, by Sir J. Y. Simpson, Bart., M.D.* Glasgow: Bell and Bain, 1868.

Day, St. John Vincent. *Papers on the Great Pyramid.* Edmonston and Douglas, Edinburgh: 1870. Reprint, Mokelumne Hill, Calif.: Health Research, 1972.

DeRosa, Neil. *Apocryphal Science: Creative Genius and Modern Heresies.* Dallas: Hamilton Books/University Press of America, 2004. [Includes a chapter on Robert Schoch's research in Egypt.]

DeSalvo, John, ed. *The Complete Pyramid Sourcebook.* Bloomington, Ind.: 1stBooks, 2003.

D'Hooghe, Alain, and Marie-Cecile Bruwier. *The Great Pyramids of Giza.* Paris: Vilo, 2000.

Doreal, [M.] *The Emerald Tablets of Thoth the Atlantean.* Sedalia, Colo.: Brotherhood of the White Temple, 1939.

Doreal, [M.] [Tibetan initiation name of Claude Maurice Dodgin]. *An Interpretation of the Emerald Tablets Together with the Two Extra Tablets.* Sedalia, Colo.: Brotherhood of the White Temple, 1948.

Doreal, M. *Kabbalistic Alchemical and Occult Symbolism of the Great Pyramid.* Sedalia, Colo.: Brotherhood of the White Temple, 1938. Reprint, Castle Rock, Colo.: Brotherhood of the White Temple, 1992.

Drbal, Karl. "The Struggle for the Pyramid Patent." In *Pyramid Power: The Secret Energy of the Ancients Revealed,* by Max Toth and Greg Nielsen. Rochester, Vt.: Destiny Books, 1985, pp. 114–123.

Dunn, Christopher. "The Mighty Crystal." In *The Complete Pyramid Sourcebook,* edited by John DeSalvo, Bloomington, Ind.: 1stBooks, 2003, pp. 185–208.

Dunn, Christopher. *The Giza Power Plant: Technologies of Ancient Egypt.* Rochester, Vt.: Bear, 1998.

Ebers, Georg. *Egypt: Descriptive, Historical, and Picturesque.* 2 vols. Translated by Clara Bell. Introduction and notes by S. Birch. London: Cassell, [1879 to 1888?].

Edgar, John, and Morton Edgar. *The Great Pyramid Passages and Chambers.* Vol. 1. Glasgow: Bone and Hulley, 1910.

Edgar, John, and Morton Edgar. *The Great Pyramid Passages and Chambers.* Vol. 1. Glasgow: Bone and Hulley, 1923. The two editions of this book vary substantially, and each includes materials not found in the other.

Edgar, John, and Morton Edgar. *Great Pyramid Passages.* 3 vols. bound as one. Chester Springs, Pa.: Laymen's Home Missionary Movement, 1988. Reprint of John and Morton Edgar, *The Great Pyramid Passages and Chambers,* vol. 1 (Glasgow: Bone and Hulley, 1923); John and Morton Edgar, *The Great Pyramid Passages and Chambers,* vol. 2 (London: Marshall Press, 1924); Morton Edgar, *The Great Pyramid and Its Scientific Features,* (Glasgow: Maclure MacDonald, 1924); and Morton Edgar, "Pyramid Discourse— 1929."

Edgar, Morton. *The Great Pyramid: Its Spiritual Symbolism.* Glasgow: Bone and Hulley, 1924.

Edge, Frank. "Aurochs in the Sky: Dancing with the Summer Moon. A Celestial Interpretation of the Hall of Bulls from the Cave of Lascaux." Unpublished manuscript. December 1995.

Edge, Frank. "Les Aurochs de Lascaux Dansant avec la Lune d'Été." *Kadath: Chroniques des Civilisations Disparues,* no. 90 (spring–summer 1998), pp. 20–34.

Edwardes, Michael. *The Dark Side of History: Magic in the Making of Man.* New York: Stein and Day, 1977.

Edwards, I.E.S. *From the Pyramids to Tutankhamun: Memoirs of an Egyptologist.* Oxford: Oxbow Books, 2000.

Edwards, I.E.S. *The Pyramids of Egypt.* New York: Viking Press, 1972. Reprint, Middlesex, England: Penguin Books, 1985.

El Mahdy, Christine. *The Pyramid Builder: Cheops, The Man behind the Great Pyramid.* London: Headline Book, 2003.

Eliade, Mircea. *The Sacred and the Profane: The Nature of Religion.* Translated from the French by Willard R. Trask. New York: Harcourt, Brace and Jovanovich, 1959.

Emery, K. O. "Weathering of the Great Pyramid." *Journal of Sedimentary Petrology* 30, 1 (1960), pp. 140–143.

Emery, Walter B. *Archaic Egypt.* Middlesex, England: Penguin Books, 1961.

Evans, Humphrey. *The Mystery of the Pyramids.* New York: Crowell, 1979.

Eyth, M. *Der Kampf um die Cheopspyramide.* Heidelberg: Carl Winter, n.d. A 1902 edition of this book published by Carl Winter is cited by Herz-Fischler (2000, p. 280); Herz-Fischler indicates that he did not actually consult this work.

Fagan, Brian M. *Quest for the Past: Great Discoveries in Archaeology.* Reading, Mass.: Addison-Wesley, 1978.

Fagan, Brian M. *The Rape of the Nile: Tomb Robbers, Tourists, and Archaeologists in Egypt.* New York: Scribner's, 1975.

Fakhry, Ahmed. *The Pyramids.* Chicago: University of Chicago Press, 1969.

Farrell, Joseph P. *The Giza Death Star Deployed.* Kempton, Ill.: Adventures Unlimited Press, 2003.

Farrell, Joseph P. *The Giza Death Star: The Paleophysics of the Great Pyramid and the Military Complex at Giza.* Kempton, Ill.: Adventures Unlimited Press, 2001.

Faulkner, R. O. *The Ancient Egyptian Book of the Dead.* Edited and with an introduction by Carol Andrews. Austin: University of Texas Press, 1990.

Faulkner, R. O. *The Ancient Egyptian Pyramid Texts.* Oxford: Oxford University Press, 1969. Reprint, Wiltshire, England: Aris and Phillips, n.d.

Fellows, John. *Mysteries of Freemasonry; Or, an Exposition of the Religious Dogmas and Customs of the Ancient Egyptians; Showing from the Origin, Nature, and Object of the Rites and Ceremonies of Remote Antiquity, Their Identity with the Order of Modern Masonry, with Some Remarks on the Metamorphosis of Apuleius, with Numerous Illustrative Woodcuts.* London: Reeves and Turner, 1877.

Ferris, A. J. *The Great Pyramid: A Simple Explanation of the Divine Message of the Great Pyramid to the Anglo-Saxon Race.* 6th ed. London: Clarendon, 1939. Originally published 1934.

Fish, Everett W. *Egyptian Pyramids: An Analysis of a Great Mystery.* Chicago: C. H. Jones, 1880.

Fish, Everett W. *Egyptian Pyramids: An Analysis of a Great Mystery.* 2nd ed. Chicago: Everett W. Fish, 1880. Reprint, Mokelumne Hill, Calif.: Health Research, 1972.

Fix, William R. *Pyramid Odyssey. Dramatic New Evidence—Decoded for the First Time—of an Ancient Civilization as Advanced as our Own.* New York: Mayflower Books, 1978.

Flanagan, G. Pat. *Pyramid Power.* Glendale, Calif.: Pyramid, 1975.

Ford, S. H. *The Great Pyramid of Egypt: The Historic, Geographic, Scientific, Prophetic, and Eschatologic Disclosures of the Oldest and Most Gigantic of All the Works of Man.* St. Louis, Mo.: Office of Ford's Christian Repository, 1882.

Foster, Thomas. *Great Pyramid Power: The World's Wonder Building Explained.* Burwood, Victoria, Australia: Crusade Centre, 1979/1988.

Gadalla, Moustafa. *Pyramid Handbook.* 2nd rev. ed. Greensboro, N.C.: Tehuti Research Foundation, 2000.

Gardener, Harry J. *1948 What's Next*. Los Angeles: Harry J. Gardener, 1948. (Includes "Mystical Construction of the Great Pyramid" B. H. Reddy, pp. 8–12.)

Gardener, Harry J. *Re-Creation*. Monograph no. 27. Los Angeles: Harry J. Gardener, 1944.

Gardner, Martin. *Fads and Fallacies in the Name of Science*. New York: Dover, 1957.

Garnier, Colonel J. *The Great Pyramid: Its Builder and Its Prophecy. With a Review of the Corresponding Prophecies of Scripture Relating to Coming Events and the Approaching End of the Age*. London: Robert Banks, 1905.

Gaunt, Bonnie. *The Magnificent Numbers of the Great Pyramid and Stonehenge*. Jackson, Mich.: Bonnie Gaunt, 1985 (second printing, 1988).

Gibbon, Edward. *The Decline and Fall of the Roman Empire*. London: Dent, 1910. New York: Dutton, 1910.

Gilbert, Adrian. *Magi: Uncovering the Secret Society That Read the Birth of Jesus in the Stars*. Montpelier, Vt.: Invisible Cities Press, 2002.

Gilbert, Adrian. *Signs in the Sky: The Astrological and Archaeological Evidence for the Birth of a New Age*. New York: Three Rivers Press, 2000.

Gill, Joseph B. *The Great Pyramid Speaks to You*. New York: Philosophical Library, 1984.

Gill, Joseph B. *The Great Pyramid Speaks: An Adventure in Mathematical Archaeology*. New York: Barnes and Noble Books, 1997.

Gillispie, Charles Coulston, and Michel Dewachter. *Monuments of Egypt: The Napoléonic Edition*. Princeton, N.J.: Princeton Architectural Press, 1987.

Ginenthal, Charles. *Pillars of the Past: History, Science, Technology as These Relate to Chronology*. Forest Hills, N.Y.: Velikovskian, 2003.

Good, Frank M. *No. 98. EGYPT.—The Great Pyramid and Excavated Temple*. Stereograph view card. London: Frank M. Good, [1880?].

Gordon, John. *Egypt Child of Atlantis: A Radical Interpretation of the Origins of Civilization*. Rochester, Vt.: Bear, 2004.

Gray, Julian T. *The Authorship and Message of the Great Pyramid*. Cincinnati: Steinmann, 1953.

Greaves, John. *Miscellaneous Works of Mr. John Greaves, Professor of Astronomy in the University of Oxford: Many of which are now first Published. I. PYRAMIDOGRAPHIA; or a Description of the Pyramids in Egypt. With a Great Many Additions and Alterations, from a Copy corrected by the Author. II. A Discourse of the Roman Foot, and Denarius; [etc.]. III. Tracts upon various Subjects, [etc.]. IV. A Description of the Grand Seignor's Seraglio. To which are added, I. Reflections on the Pyramidographia, written by an anonymous Author, soon after the Publication of the Book. II. A Dissertation upon the Sacred Cubit of the Jews, and the Cubits of the several Nations, [etc.]. Translated from the Latin of Sir ISAAC NEWTON, Not yet published. Adorn'd with SCULPTURES. To which is prefix'd, An Historical and Critical Account of the Life and Writings of the Author*. 2 vols. Edited by Thomas Birch. London: printed by J. Hughes, published by Thomas Birch, 1737. Vol. 1 contains "Pyramidographia: or, a Description of the Pyramids in Aegypt," with a separate title page reading, "London: J. Brindley, 1736."

Greaves, John. *Pyramidographia: Or a Description of the Pyramids in Ægypt*. London: George Badger, 1646. Herz-Fischler (2000, p. 281), notes that according to the *National Union Catalog (Pre-1956)* [London: Mansell, 1968–1981] of the Library of Congress, there was a 1641 edition of this book but other sources do not cite such an edition; Herz-Fischler himself apparently never saw a copy, although he cites "Greaves (1641)," p. 48. This mistaken citation may be based on Greaves (1704), which is a separately bound reprint; a copy of this 1704 reprint deaccessioned from the College of Librarianship Library, Wales, and currently in the possession of R. M. Schoch, has an old (nineteenth or twentieth century) label on the spine that reads "PYRAMIDS—1641"; in addition, the 1704 *Pyramidographia* contains a printed version of a letter by Greaves dated 1641.

Greaves, John. *Pyramidographia: Or a Description of the Pyramids in Ægypt.* In *A Collection of Voyages and Travels,* compiled by Awnsham Churchill. London: A. and J. Churchill, 1704, pp. 688–736, bound separately.

Greenlees, Duncan. *The Gospel of Hermes.* India: Theosophical Publishing, 1949. [Copy not seen; citation taken from an Internet database.]

Greer, John Michael. *Inside a Magical Lodge: Group Ritual in the Western Tradition.* St. Paul, Minn.: Llewellyn, 1998.

Grinsell, Leslie V. *Egyptian Pyramids.* Gloucester, England: John Bellows, 1947.

Groves. P.R.C., and J. R. McCrindle. "Flying over Egypt, Sinai, and Palestine." *National Geographic* 50, no. 3 (September 1926), pp. 312–355.

Haag, Michael von. *Guide to Egypt.* London: Travelaid, 1981.

Haberman, Frederick. *The Great Pyramids Message to America.* 3rd ed. St. Petersburg, Fla.: Kingdom Press, 1935.

Haich, Elisabeth. *Initiation.* Palo Alto, Calif.: Seed Center, 1974.

Hall, Manly Palmer. *An Encyclopedic Outline of Masonic, Hermetic, Qabbalistic and Rosicrucian Symbolical Philosophy: Being an Interpretation of the Secret Teachings concealed within the Rituals, Allegories and Mysteries of all Ages.* 8th ed. Los Angeles: Philosophical Research Society Press, 1945. Reprint, as *The Secret Teachings of All Ages: Reader's Edition,* New York: Penguin, 2003. Commonly referred to by the title *The Secret Teachings of All Ages.* Originally published 1928.

Hall, Manly Palmer. *Freemasonry of the Ancient Egyptians, to Which Is Added an Interpretation of the Crata Repoa Initiation Rite.* Los Angeles: Philosophical Research Society, 1937.

Hall, Manly Palmer. *Freemasonry of the Ancient Egyptians, to Which Is Added an Interpretation of the Crata Repoa Initiation Rite and the Initiation of Plato.* 2nd ed. Los Angeles: Philosophical Research Society, 1952. Includes "The Initiation of Plato."

Hall, Manly Palmer. *The Initiates of the Flame.* Los Angeles: Premier, 1922.

Hancock, Graham. *Fingerprints of the Gods.* New York: Crown, 1995.

Hancock, Graham, and Robert Bauval. *The Message of the Sphinx: A Quest for the Hidden Legacy of Mankind.* New York: Crown, 1996.

Hardy, Dean, Mary Hardy, Marjorie Killick, and Kenneth Killick. *Pyramid Energy: The Philosophy of God, the Science of Man.* Allegan, Mich.: Delta-K Products, 1987.

Hart, George. *Pharaohs and Pyramids: A Guide through Old Kingdom Egypt.* London: Guild, 1991.

Hassan, Selim. *The Sphinx: Its History in the Light of Recent Excavations.* Cairo: [Egyptian] Government Press, 1949.

Hawass, Zahi. Foreword to Horres and Perreault (2001).

Hawass, Zahi. *The Pyramids of Ancient Egypt.* Pittsburgh: Carnegie Museum of Natural History, 1990.

Hawass, Zahi. Update to Petrie (1990), pp. 97–136. Unless otherwise stated, this is the "Hawass, 1990" reference cited in the text and appendices.

Heath, Richard. *The Matrix of Creation: Technology of the Gods.* St. Dogmaels, Pembrokeshire, Wales: Bluestone Press, 2002.

Herschel, Wayne, with Birgitt Lederer. *The Hidden Records.* N.p., Printability (www.thehiddenrecords.com), 2003.

Herz-Fischler, Roger. *The Shape of the Great Pyramid.* Waterloo, Ontario, Canada: Wilfrid Lauer University Press, 2000.

Hieronimus, Robert. *America's Secret Destiny: Spiritual Vision and the Founding of a Nation.* Rochester, Vt.: Destiny Books, 1989.

Higgins, Frank C. *Ancient Freemasonry: An Introduction to the Study of Masonic Archaeology.* New York: Pyramid, 1923.

Hoagland, Richard C. *The Monuments of Mars: A City on the Edge of Forever.* 5th ed. Berkeley, Calif.: North Atlantic Books, 2001.

Hodges, Henry. *Technology in the Ancient World.* New York: Knopf, 1970. Reprint, New York: Barnes and Noble Books, 1992.

Hodges, Peter. *How the Pyramids Were Built.* Longmead, England: Element Books, 1989.

Hoffman, Michael A. *Egypt before the Pharaohs.* New York: Knopf, 1979.

Holbrook, Isabel B. *Egyptian Studies: The Path of Light in the House of the Hidden Places.* N.p., n.d. [circa 1930s?].

Holland, Thomas. *Freemasonry from the Great Pyramid of Ancient Times.* London: Thos. Holland, 1885.

Horgan, John. *Rational Mysticism: Dispatches from the Border between Science and Spirituality.* Boston: Houghton Mifflin, 2003.

Horn, Paul. "Inside the Great Pyramid." In *The Complete Pyramid Sourcebook,* edited by John DeSalvo. Bloomington, Ind.: 1stBooks, 2003, pp. 277–287.

Hornung, Erik. *The Secret Lore of Egypt: Its Impact on the West.* Translated from the German by David Lorton. Ithaca, N.Y.: Cornell University Press, 2001.

Horres, E. Stratton, Jr. *I Am You Are Me.* With a foreword by Robert M. Schoch. Dallas: Turtle Creek Press, 2003.

Horres, Stratton, and Michala Perreault. *Showing Up! An Action Plan for Personal Growth and Following Your Bliss.* With a foreword by Zahi Hawass. Dallas: Brown Books, 2001.

Ihek, Fernand. *"La Pyramide de Chéops a-t-elle Livré son Secret?"* Paris: C.E.L.F., 1951.

Isler, Martin. *Sticks, Stones, and Shadows: Building the Egyptian Pyramids.* Norman: University of Oklahoma Press, 2001.

Ivimy, John. *The Sphinx and the Megaliths.* New York: Harper and Row, 1975.

Jackson, Kevin, and Jonathan Stamp. *Building the Great Pyramid.* Toronto: Firefly Books, 2003.

Jahn, Robert G. "The Persistent Paradox of Psychic Phenomena: An Engineering Perspective." *Proceedings* Institute of Electrical and Electronics Engineers (IEEE) 70, no.2, (1982), pp. 136–170.

Jahn, Robert G., Paul Devereux, and Michael Ibison. *Acoustical Resonances of Assorted Ancient Structures.* Technical report 95002. Princeton, N.J.: Princeton Engineering Anomalies Research, March 1995.

Jahn, Robert G., and Brenda J. Dunne. *Margins of Reality: The Role of Consciousness in the Physical World.* San Diego: Harcourt Brace Jovanovich, 1987.

Jones, Alexander, gen. ed. *The Jerusalem Bible.* Reader's Edition. Garden City, N.Y.: Doubleday, 1968.

Keller, G. *De Wonderen der Wereld: Kunstwerken der Natuur en der Menschheid. Afleveringen 11, 12, 13, 14* [sections on Egypt with many photographs]. Leiden: A. W. Sijthoff [1911–1912?].

Kemp, Barry J. *Ancient Egypt: Anatomy of a Civilization.* London: Routledge, 1989.

Keystone View Company. *Climbing the Great Pyramid of Khufu, Egypt.* Stereograph view card no. 9758. Meadville, Pa.: Keystone View Company, 1899.

Keystone View Company. *The Great Sphinx of Gizeh, the Largest Royal Portrait Ever Hewn—Egypt.* Stereograph view card no. 2544. Meadville, Pa.: Keystone View Company, n.d. Card produced c. 1900s or 1910s[?]; the same photographic image appears on an Underwood and Underwood stereograph view card dated 1896—see D'Hooghe and Bruwier (2000), p. 69.

Keystone View Company. *Looking up an Angle of the Great Pyramid, Showing the Difficulties of its Ascent, Egypt.* Stereograph view card no. 9869T. Meadville, Pa.: Keystone View Company, n.d.

Kilburn, B. W. *Pyramid of Khephren, original polished top, Cairo, Egypt.* Stereograph view card no. 12510. New York and Littleton, N.H.: James M. Davis / B. W. Kilburn, 1898.

Kingsland, William. *The Great Pyramid in Fact and in Theory. Part 1. Descriptive.* London: Rider, 1932.

Kingsland, William. *The Great Pyramid in Fact and in Theory: Part 2. Theory.* London: Rider, 1935. Includes errata sheet for Kingsland (1932).

Kingsland, William. *The Great Pyramid in Fact and [in] Theory. Part 1.* Kila, Mont.: Kessinger, [2003?]. Originally published 1932.

Kirchenhoffer, H. *The Book of Fate, Formerly in the Possession of Napoleon, Late Emperor of France; And Now First Rendered into English, from a German Translation, of an Ancient Egyptian Manuscript, Found in the Year 1801, by M. Sonnini, in One of the Royal Tombs, near Mount Libycus, in Upper Egypt.* 6th ed. London: C. S. Arnold, 1824.

Knight, Charles S. *The Mystery and Prophecy of the Great Pyramid.* 2nd ed. San Jose, Calif.: Rosicrucian Press, 1933.

Knight, Christopher, and Robert Lomas. *Uriel's Machine: Uncovering the Secrets of Stonehenge, Noah's Flood, and the Dawn of Civilization.* Gloucester, Mass.: Fair Winds Press, 1999.

Krupp, E. C., ed. *In Search of Ancient Astronomies.* Garden City, N.Y.: Doubleday, 1977.

Kunkel, Edward J. *Pharaoh's Pump.* 1978. Coquille, Ore.: Pharaoh's Pump Foundation, n.d. According to Noone (1997, p. 386), this book was first self-published by Kunkel in 1962.

Lamy, Lucie. *Egyptian Mysteries: New Light on Ancient Spiritual Knowledge.* New York: Crossroad, 1981.

Landone, Brown. *Prophecies of Melchi-Zedek in the Great Pyramid and the Seven Temples.* New York: Book of Gold, 1940.

Landsburg, Alan, and Sally Landsburg. *In Search of Ancient Mysteries.* New York: Bantam Books, 1974.

LaViolette, Paul A. *Earth under Fire: Humanity's Survival of the Apocalypse.* Fresno, Calif.: Starlane, 1997.

Lawton, Ian, and Chris Ogilvie-Herald. *Giza: The Truth: The People, Politics, and History behind the World's Most Famous Archaeological Site.* Montpelier, Vt.: Invisible Cites Press, 2001.

Layard, Austen Henry. *Nineveh and Babylon: A Narrative of a Second Expedition to Assyria during the Years 1849, 1850, and 1851.* London: John Murray, 1867.

Lehner, Mark. *The Complete Pyramids: Solving the Ancient Mysteries.* London: Thames and Hudson, 1997.

Lehner, Mark. "Computer Rebuilds the Ancient Sphinx." *National Geographic* 179, no. 4 (April 1991), pp. 32–39.

Lehner, Mark. *The Egyptian Heritage: Based on the Edgar Cayce Readings.* Virginia Beach, Virginia: A.R.E. Press, 1974.

Lemesurier, Peter. *Decoding the Great Pyramid.* Shaftsbury, Dorset, England: Element Books, 1999.

Lemesurier, Peter. *The Great Pyramid Decoded.* Longmead, England: Element Books, 1977.

Le Plongeon, Augustus. *Queen Móo and the Egyptian Sphinx.* London: Kegan Paul, Trench, Trübner, 1896.

Lepre, J. P. *The Egyptian Pyramids: A Comprehensive, Illustrated Reference.* Jefferson, N.C.: McFarland, 1990.

Lewis, David H. *Mysteries of the Pyramid.* St. Petersburg, Fla.: 6th ed. Science Research, 1980. Originally published 1978.

Lewis, H. Spencer. *The Symbolic Prophecy of the Great Pyramid.* San Jose, Calif.: Supreme Grand Lodge of the Ancient and Mystical Order Rosae Crucis, 1936. Second ed. 1939; 3rd ed. 1945. Also published by the Grand Lodge of the English Language Jurisdiction, AMORC, San Jose, Calif., 1994.

Little, Lora H., Gregory L. Little, and John Van Auken. *Secrets of the Ancient World: Exploring the Insights of America's Most Well-Documented Psychic, Edgar Cayce.* Virginia Beach, Va.: A.R.E. Press, 2003.

Lockyer, J. Norman. *The Dawn of Astronomy: A Study of the Temple Worship and Mythology of the Ancient Egyptians.* New York: Macmillan, 1894. Reprint, with a preface by Giorgio de Santillana, Cambridge, Mass.: MIT Press, 1964.

[Long, George]. *The British Museum Egyptian Antiquities.* Vol. 1. London: M. A. Nattali, 1849.

Lucius Apuleius. *The Golden Ass.* Translated by Robert Graves. New York: Farrar, Straus and Giroux, 1951. (Paperback edition, eleventh printing, 1975.)

Lurker, Manfred. *The Gods and Symbols of Ancient Egypt: An Illustrated Dictionary.* London: Thames and Hudson, 1980.

Lynch, Jeremiah. *Egyptian Sketches.* New York: Scribner and Welford, 1890.

Lythgoe, Albert M., and Caroline L. Ransom. *The Tomb of Perneb.* New York: Metropolitan Museum of Art, 1921. Originally published 1916.

Macnaughton, Duncan. *A Scheme of Egyptian Chronology.* London: Luzac, 1932.

Malkowski, Edward F. *Sons of God, Daughters of Men: Genesis: A Clash of Cultures.* Champaign, Ill.: Bits of Sunshine, 2004.

Manning, Samuel. *Egypt Illustrated with Pen and Pencil.* New York: Hurst, 1891.

Marks, T. Septimus. *The Great Pyramid: Its History and Teachings. With a Diagram. 2nd ed.* London: S. W. Partridge, [1879?].

Mariette-Bey, Auguste. *The Monuments of Upper Egypt.* Translated by Alphonse Mariette. Boston: J. H. Manfield and J. W. Dearborn, 1890.

McCarty, Louis P. *The Great Pyramid of Jeezeh.* San Francisco: McCarty, 1907.

McTaggart. Lynne, *The Field: The Quest for the Secret Force of the Universe.* New York: Quill, 2002.

Mebes, G. O. *Os Arcanos Maiores do Taro: Curso de Enciclopedia do Ocultismo.* Sao Paulo, Brazil: Pensamento, n.d.

Mehler, Stephen S. *The Land of Osiris.* Kempton, Ill.: Adventures Unlimited Press, 2001.

Mehler, Stephen. "Was There an Explosion in the Great Pyramid in Antiquity?" In *The Complete Pyramid Sourcebook,* edited by John DeSalvo. Bloomington, Ind.: 1stBooks, 2003, pp. 329–337.

Melchizedek, Drunvalo. *The Ancient Secret of the Flower of Life.* Vol. 2. Flagstaff, Ariz.: Light Technology, 2000.

Mencken, August. *Designing and Building the Great Pyramid.* Baltimore; privately printed, 1963.

Mendelssohn, Kurt. *The Riddle of the Pyramids.* New York: Praeger, 1974.

Mertz, Barbara. *Temples, Tombs, and Hieroglyphs: The Story of Egyptology.* New York: Coward-McCann, 1964.

Michell, John. *The New View over Atlantis.* London: Thames and Hudson, 1983.

Miller, Erica, Sean Sloan, and Gregg Wilson. "Great Pyramid at Giza." *Meta Research Bulletin* 10, no. 3, September 15, 2001, pp. 35–45.

Miller, Reg T. *Pyramid Truth Gateway Universe: The Purpose, Intent, and Overview of Extraterrestrial Visitations.* Blue Hill, Me.: Medicine Bear, 1998.

Mills, Thomas O. *The Truth.*: N.p., 1998.

Morley, Jacqueline, Mark Bergen, and John James. *An Egyptian Pyramid.* New York: Peter Bedrick Books, 1991.

Murray, Margaret A. *The Splendor That Was Egypt.* New York: Philosophical Library, 1949.

Nakhla, Shawki, Zahi Hawass, Georges Bonani, Willy Wölfli, Herbert Haas, Mark Lehner, Robert Wenke, and Wilma Wetterstrom. "Dating the Pyramids." *Archaeology* 52, no. 5 (September–October 1999), pp. 26–33. Available on-line at: www.he.net/~archaeol/9909/abstracts/pyramids.html (November 25, 2004).

Nelson, Kit, and associates. *Holocene Settlement of the Egyptian Sahara.* Vol. 2. *The Pottery of Nabta Playa.* New York: Kluwer, 2002.

Nelson, Roger D. FieldREG Measurements in Egypt: Resonant Consciousness at Sacred

Sites. Technical note 97002. Princeton, N.J.: Princeton Engineering Anomalies Research, July 1997.

Nelson, Roger D. The Subterranean Chamber of the Pyramid of Khufu: A Ritual Map of Ancient Egypt? Technical note 98001. Princeton, N.J.: Princeton Engineering Anomalies Research, February 1997.

Nelson, R. D., G. J. Bradish, Y. H. Dobyns, B. J. Dunne, and R. G. Jahn. "FieldREG Anomalies in Group Situations." *Journal of Scientific Exploration* 10, no. 1 (1996), pp. 111–141.

Nelson, R. D., R. G. Jahn, B. J. Dunne, Y. H. Dobyns, and G. J. Bradish. "FieldREG II: Consciousness Field Effects: Replications and Explorations." *Journal of Scientific Exploration* 12, no. 3 (1998), pp. 425–454.

Newton, Isaac. See Greaves, 1737.

Nicklin, J. Bernard. *Testimony in Stone.* Merrimac, Mass.: Destiny, 1961.

Noone, Richard W. *5/5/2000, Ice: The Ultimate Disaster.* Rev. ed. New York: Three Rivers Press, 1997. Originally published 1982.

Novak, Peter. *The Lost Secret of Death: Our Divided Souls and the Afterlife.* Charlottesville, Va.: Hampton Roads, 2003.

Nunn, John F. *Ancient Egyptian Medicine.* Norman: University of Oklahoma Press, 1996.

Oakes, Lorna, and Lucia Gahlin. *Ancient Egypt: An Illustrated Reference to the Myths, Religions, Pyramids and Temples of the Land of the Pharaohs.* London: Hermes House, 2003.

Oliver, George. *The History of Initiation.* London: Richard Spencer, 1841.

Ostrander, Sheila, and Lynn Schroeder. *Psychic Discoveries behind the Iron Curtain.* Englewood Cliffs, N.J.: Prentice-Hall, 1970.

Ouspensky, P. D. *The Symbolism of the Tarot.* New York: Dover, 1976. Originally published 1913.

Ouspensky, P. D. *Tertium Organum: The Third Canon of Thought; A Key to the Enigmas of the World.* London: Kegan Paul, Trench Trubner, 1928.

Palmer, Ernest C. *The Secret of Ancient Egypt.* London: William Rider, 1924.

Palmer, M. Dale. *True Esoteric Traditions.* Plainfield, Ind.: Noetics Institute, 1994.

Perring, [J. S.] *Perring's Manuscript Communications on the Measurements of the Pyramids.* In *Egypt's Place in Universal History: An Historical Investigation in Five Books* by Christian C. J. Bunsen. Translated from the German, by Charles H. Cottrell. London: Longman, Brown, Green, and Longmans, vol. 2, 1854, pp. 633–645.

Petrie, W. M. Flinders. *The Arts and Crafts of Ancient Egypt.* Edinburgh: T. N. Foulis, 1923.

Petrie, W. M. Flinders. *A History of Egypt. Vol. 1. From the Earliest Kings to the Sixteenth Dynasty. 10th ed. rev.* London: Methuen, 1923.

Petrie, W. M. Flinders. *The Pyramids and Temples of Gizeh.* London: Field and Tuer, 1883.

Petrie, W. M. Flinders. *The Pyramids and Temples of Gizeh.* 2nd ed. London: Field and Tuer, 1885. Reprint, with an update by Zahi Hawass, London: Histories and Mysteries of Man, 1990. The two editions of this book vary substantially, and each includes materials not found in the other.

Petrie, W. M. Flinders. "Pyramid." In *Encyclopaedia Britannica,* 11th ed. (New York: Encyclopaedia Britannica Company, 1911), 22: 683–685.

Petrie, William Matthew Flinders. *Researches in Sinai.* With chapters by C. T. Currelly. New York: Dutton, 1906.

Petrie, W. M. Flinders, ed. *Egyptian Tales: Translated from the Papyri.* Illustrated by Tristram Ellis. Series 1 and 2. 2 vols. London: Methuen, 1895. Reprint, Mineola, N.Y.: Dover, 1999.

Picknett, Lynn, and Clive Prince. *The Stargate Conspiracy: The Truth about Extraterrestrial Life and the Mysteries of Ancient Egypt.* New York: Berkley Books, 1999.

Pochan, André. *L'énigme de la Grande Pyramide.* Paris: Robert Laffont, 1971.

Pochan, A. *The Mysteries of the Great Pyramids.* New York: Avon Books, 1978.

Proctor, Richard A. *The Great Pyramid: Observatory, Tomb, and Temple.* London: Chatto and Windus, 1883. London: Longmanns, Green, and Co., 1888. London: Longmanns, Green, and Co., 1898.

Proctor, Richard A. *Myths and Marvels of Astronomy.* London: Chatto and Windus, 1880. Chapters 2 and 3 reprinted in Richard A. Proctor, *The Mystery and Religion of the Great Pyramid.* East Sussex, England: Andrew, n.d.

Putnam, James. *Egyptology: An Introduction to the History, Culture and Art of Ancient Egypt.* New York: Crescent Books, 1990.

Randall, D. A. *The Handwriting of God in Egypt, Sinai, and the Holy Land: The Records of a Journey from the Great Valley of the West to the Sacred Places of the East.* Philadelphia: Potter, 1862.

Rawlinson, George. *History of Egypt.* Vol. 1. New York: Lovell, Coryell, n.d. Preface dated December 31, 1880.

Reader, C. D. "A Geomorphological Study of the Giza Necropolis, with Implications for the Development of the Site." *Archaeometry* 43, no. 1 (2001), pp. 149–159.

Reddy, B. H. "Mystical Construction of the Great Pyramid." In Gardener (1948).

Redford, Donald B. *Egypt, Canaan, and Israel in Ancient Times.* Princeton, N.J.: Princeton University Press, 1992.

Riffert, George R. *Great Pyramid Proof of God.* Haverhill, Mass.: Destiny, 1952. Originally published 1932.

Roberts and Fellows. *Photographing the Pyramids—Egypt.* Stereograph view card no. 111. Philadelphia: Roberts and Fellows, [1880–1900?]. Shows third pyramid, Sphinx, and part of second pyramid.

Robinson, Lytle W. *The Great Pyramid and Its Builders: A Study of the Edgar Cayce Readings Regarding Early Egyptian History and the Great Pyramid.* Virginia Beach:,Va.: Edgar Cayce Publishing, 1958.

Rothenberg, Beno. *God's Wilderness: Discoveries in Sinai.* London: Thames and Hudson, 1961.

Rowbottom, W. *The Origin of Masonic Ritual and Tradition As Manifested by the Geometrical Design and Symbolism of the Great Pyramid, the Everlasting Pillar, or Temple, of Witness to the Most High: A Lecture.* Alfreton, England: published by the author, 1880.

Russell, Charles T. *Studies in the Scriptures. Series 3. Thy Kingdom Come.* Brooklyn: International Bible Students Association, 1915. Originally written in 1891; copyrighted 1891 by the Watch Tower Bible and Tract Society.

Russell, Michael. *View of Ancient and Modern Egypt; With an Outline of Its Natural History.* New York: J. and J. Harper, 1831.

Rutherford, A. *The Great Pyramid; Its Christian Message to All Nations; Its Divine Call to the British Empire and U.S.A. (with Iceland)*. London: privately published, n.d. Introduction is dated December 1942.

Rutherford, Adam. *The Great Pyramid: A Scientific Revelation*. London: published by the author, 1939.

Rutherford, Adam. *Pyramidology*. 4 vols. Hertfordshire, England: Institute of Pyramidology, 1970–1986. First printings of the four volumes/books listed in book 1 are as follows: bk. 1, 1957; bk. 2, 1962; bk. 3, 1966; bk. 4, 1972.

Sadhu, Mouni. *The Tarot: A Contemporary Course of the Quintessence of Hermetic Occultism*. London: Allen and Unwin, 1962.

Said, Edward W. *Orientalism*. New York: Vintage Books, 1979.

Said, Rushdi. *The Geology of Egypt*. Amsterdam: Elsevier, 1962.

Sampsell, Bonnie M. *A Traveler's Guide to the Geology of Egypt*. Cairo: American University Press in Cairo, 2003.

Sandys, George. *A Relation of a Journey Begun An: Dom: 1610. Foure Bookes. Containing a Description of the Turkish Empire, of Ægypt, of the Holy Land, of the Remote Parts of Italy, and Ilands Adjoyning*. 2nd ed. London: Barrett, 1621. First edition, 1615.

Santillana, Giorgio, de. Preface to Lockyer (1964).

Santillana, Giorgio de, and Hertha von Dechend. *Hamlet's Mill: An Essay on Myth and the Frame of Time*. Boston: Gambit, 1969.

Sarolides, G. Photographs "No. 109. Route des Pyramides," and "No. 117. Le Sphinx armachis." N.p., [1870s–1880s?]

Sass, Roselis von. *The Great Pyramid Reveals Its Secret*. Embu, Brazil: Ordem Do Graal Na Terra, 1999.

Schoch, Robert M. Forward to Brophy (2002).

Schoch, Robert M. Forward to Horres (2003).

Schoch, Robert M. "Redating the Great Sphinx of Giza." *KMT: A Modern Journal of Ancient Egypt*, vol. 3, no. 2 (summer 1992), pp. 52–59, 66–70.

Schoch, Robert M., with Robert Aquinas McNally. *Voices of the Rocks: A Scientist Looks at Catastrophes and Ancient Civilizations*. New York: Harmony Books, 1999.

Schoch, Robert M., with Robert Aquinas McNally. *Voyages of the Pyramid Builders: The True Origins of the Pyramids from Lost Egypt to Ancient America*. New York: Tarcher/Putnam, 2003.

Schwaller de Lubicz, R. A. *The Egyptian Miracle: An Introduction to the Wisdom of the Temple*. Translated by André and Goldian VandenBroeck. Illustrated by Lucie Lamy. Rochester, Vt.: Inner Traditions International, 1985.

Schwaller de Lubicz, R. A. *Esoterism and Symbol*. Translated by André and Goldian VandenBroeck. New York: Inner Traditions International, 1985.

Schwaller de Lubicz, R. A. *Le Roi de la Theocratie Pharaonique*. Paris: Flammarion, 1961.

Schwaller de Lubicz, R. A. *Propos sur ésotérisme et symbole*. Paris: La Colombe, 1960.

Schwaller de Lubicz, R. A. *Sacred Science: The King of Pharaonic Theocracy*. Translated by André and Goldian VandenBroeck. New York: Inner Traditions International, 1982.

Schwaller de Lubicz, R. A. *Le Temple dans L'Homme*. Cairo: Schindler, 1949.

Schwaller de Lubicz, R. A. *The Temple in Man: Sacred Architecture and the Perfect Man.* Translated by Robert and Deborah Lawlor. Illustrated by Lucie Lamy. Rochester, Vt.: Inner Traditions International, 1981.

Schwaller de Lubicz, R. A. *The Temple of Man: Apet of the South at Luxor.* Translated by Deborah Lawlor and Robert Lawlor. Illustrations by Lucie Lamy. 2 vols. Rochester, Vt.: Inner Traditions International, 1998.

Scranton, Laird. *Hidden Meanings: A Study of the Founding Symbols of Civilization.* N.p. [Xlibris], 2002.

Seiss, Joseph A. *A Miracle in Stone: or The Great Pyramid of Egypt.* Philadelphia: Porter and Coates, 1877. ("Sixth edition enlarged," Philadelphia: Porter and Coates, no date other than "1877" referring to the first edition [circa 1880(?); the ninth edition of this book is cited in Wake, 1882.] "Fourteenth edition enlarged" (very close to, or identical with, the sixth edition), New York: Charles C. Cook, no date other than "1877" referring to the first edition.)

Sellers, Jane B. *The Death of Gods in Ancient Egypt: A Study of the Threshold of Myth and the Frame of Time.* Rev. ed. N.p.: Lulu, 2003. Revised edition of a book first published by Penguin Books, London, 1992.

Shalev, Zur. "Measurer of All Things: John Greaves (1602–1652), the Great Pyramid, and Early Modern Metrology." *Journal of the History of Ideas* 63, no. 4 (2002), pp. 555–575.

Siliotti, Alberto. *The Pyramids: Egypt Pocket Guide.* Cairo: American University in Cairo Press, 2002.

Siliotti, Alberto, and Zahi Hawass. *The Illustrated Guide to the Pyramids.* Cairo: American University in Cairo Press, 2003.

Silverberg, Robert, ed. *Great Adventures in Archaeology.* New York: Dial Press, 1964.

Simpson, J. Y. *Archaeology: Its Past and Its Future Work. Being the Annual Address to the Society of Antiquaries of Scotland, Given January 28, 1861.* Edinburgh: Edmonston and Douglas, 1861.

Sitchin, Zecharia. *The Wars of Gods and Men. (Book III of the Earth Chronicles).* New York: Avon Books, 1985.

Skinner, J. Ralston. *Key to the Hebrew-Egyptian Mystery in the Source of Measures Originating the British Inch and the Ancient Cubit By Which Was Built the Great Pyramid of Egypt and the Temple of Solomon; And through the Possession Use of Which, Man, Assuming to Realize the Creative Law of the Deity, Set It Forth in a Mystery, among the Hebrews Called Kabbala,* and *Supplement to Source of Measures* (bound together). Philadelphia: David McKay, n.d. This may be the 1931 reprint listed by Kingsland (1932, p. 120); table of contents dated 1875, chart to supplement dated 1876. This book was first published in America in 1875, according to Kingsland (1932, p. vii).

Smith, Worth. *Miracle of the Ages: The Great Pyramid of Gizeh.* Holyoke, Mass.: Elizabeth Town, 1934; New York: Wm. H. Wise and Company, 1937.

Smyth, C. Piazzi. *Life and Work at the Great Pyramid during the Months of January, February, March, and April, A.D. 1865; With a Discussion of the Facts Ascertained.* 3 vols. Edinburgh: Edmonston and Douglas, 1867.

Smyth, Charles Piazzi. *Our Inheritance in the Great Pyramid.* London: Alexander Strahan, 1864. Includes mounted photograph of the Great Pyramid taken by Francis Bedford on March 5, 1862.

Smyth, Charles Piazzi. *Our Inheritance in the Great Pyramid.* 2nd ed. London: W. Isbister, 1874.

Smyth, Charles Piazzi. *Our Inheritance in the Great Pyramid.* 3rd ed. London: Daldy, Isbister, 1877. Reprint, Bauvelt, N.Y.: Rudolf Steiner, 1977.

Smyth, Charles Piazzi. *Our Inheritance in the Great Pyramid.* 4th ed. London: Daldy, Isbister, 1880. Reprint, as *The Great Pyramid: Its Secrets and Mysteries Revealed,* New York: Gramercy Books, 1978. This reprint includes a new foreword by Fatma Turrkan [spelling on title page] or Fatma Turkkan [spelling at end of foreword] and various photographs not found in the original edition.

Smyth, Charles Piazzi. *Our Inheritance in the Great Pyramid.* 5th ed. New York: Anson D. N. Randolph, [1890–1891?]. London: Charles Burnet, 1890.

Spence, Lewis. *The Mysteries of Egypt or the Secret Rites and Traditions of the Nile.* London: Rider, [1933].

Spence, Lewis. *Myths and Legends of Ancient Egypt.* London: George G. Harrap, 1915.

Spivey, Thomas Sawyer. *Lavius Egyptus. Or the Unveiling of the Pythagorian Senate.* Cincinnati: Thomas Sawyer Spivey, 1903.

Stadelmann, Rainer. "The Great Sphinx of Giza—A Creation of Khufu/Cheops." *Minerva* 42 (July–August 2000), p. 43.

Stecchini, Livio Catullo. "Notes on the Relation of Ancient Measures to the Great Pyramid." Appendix to Tompkins (1971), pp. 287–382.

Steiner, Rudolph. *Fruits of Anthroposophy: An Introduction to the Work of Dr. Rudolph Steiner.* Compiled and edited by George Kauffman. Highland, N.Y.: AnthropoSophic Press, 1922.

Steiner, Rudolf. *Fruits of Anthroposophy.* London: Rudolf Steiner Press, 1986.

Steiner, Rudolf. *Knowledge of the Higher Worlds and Its Attainment.* 2nd ed. New York: Anthroposophic Press, 1961. Originally published 1947.

Steiner, Rudolf. *Man's Being, His Destiny and World Evolution.* 2nd ed. New York: Anthroposophic Press, 1966. Originally published 1952.

Stewart, Basil. *History and Significance of the Great Pyramid and the Theories and Traditions Held about It from the Earliest Days down to the Present.* London: John Bale, 1935.

Stewart, Basil. *The Mystery of the Great Pyramid: Traditions concerning It and Its Connection with the Egyptian Book of the Dead.* London: Routledge, 1929.

Stewart, Desmond. *The Pyramids and Sphinx.* New York: Newsweek, 1971.

Story, Ronald. *The Space-Gods Revealed.* With a foreword by Carl Sagan. New York: Harper and Row, 1976.

Sullivan, William. *The Secret of the Incas: Myth, Astronomy, and the War against Time.* New York: Crown, 1996.

Tarrell, J. "The Great Pyramid Courses." *Ancient Egypt.* British School of Archaeology in Egypt. Macmillan and Co., London and New York. Egyptian Research Account, Chicago, June 1925, pt. 2, pp. 36–39.

Taseos, Socrates G. *Back in Time 3104 B.C. to the Great Pyramid.* Charlotte, N.C.: SOC Publishers, 1990.

Tastmona, Thothnu [pseudonym of Paul T. Platt (see Tompkins, 1971, p. 400)]. *SECRET: The Gizeh Pyramids.* 2nd ed. New York: Comet Press, 1954.

Tastmona, Thothnu [pseudonym of Paul T. Platt]. *The Secrets of SECRET: Being the Gist of the Conclusions Deriving from the Discoveries in SECRET: The Gizeh Pyramids.* New York: Tothmona, 1955.

Taylor, John. *The Great Pyramid. Why Was It Built? & Who Built It?* London: Longman, Green, Longman, and Roberts, 1859. The date of this work is usually given as 1859, and that is indeed the date on the title page. However, this book actually consists of two parts: "Why Was It Built?" and "Who Built It?" The 4-page preface to the second part, between pp. 198 and 199, is dated March 12, 1860. A copy in the University of Chicago Library has an inscription in Taylor's hand dated "May 1860"; a copy in the possession of R. M. Schoch has an inscription in Taylor's hand dated "Oct. 1860."

Temple, Robert. *The Crystal Sun: Rediscovering a Lost Technology of the Ancient World.* London: Century, 2000.

Temple, Robert. *The Sirius Mystery: New Scientific Evidence of Alien Contact 5,000 Years Ago.* Rochester, Vt.: Destiny Books, 1998.

Thompson, Joseph P. *Photographic Views of Egypt, Past and Present.* Boston: John P. Jewett, 1854.

Thoreau, Henry David. *Walden* (originally published in 1854; reprinted in *Walden and Other Writings by Henry David Thoreau*, edited and with an Introduction by Joseph Wood Krutch. New York: Bantam Books, 1981).

Time-Life Books, editors of. *Mystic Places.* Alexandria, Va.: Time-Life Books, 1987.

Tompkins, Peter. *Mysteries of the Mexican Pyramids.* New York: Harper and Row, 1976.

Tompkins, Peter. *Secrets of the Great Pyramid.* With an appendix by Livio Catullo Stecchini. New York: Harper and Row, 1971.

Toth, Max. *Pyramid Prophecies.* Rochester, Vt.: Destiny Books, 1988.

Toth, Max, and Greg Nielsen. *Pyramid Power: The Secret Energy of the Ancients Revealed.* Rochester, Vt.: Destiny Books, 1985.

Trigger, B. G., B. J. Kemp, D. O'Connor, and A. B. Lloyd. *Ancient Egypt: A Social History.* Cambridge: Cambridge University Press, 1983.

Underwood and Underwood. *Climbing Cheops, the Greatest of the Pyramids, Egypt.* Stereograph view card. New York: Underwood and Underwood / Strohmeyer and Wyman, Publishers, 1896.

Underwood and Underwood. *From the summit of the Great Pyramid E. over the Valley of the Nile, Egypt.* Stereograph view card. New York: Underwood and Underwood, 1904.

Underwood and Underwood. *Looking up the N.E. Corner of the Great Pyramid Where Tourists Ascend, Egypt.* Stereograph view card. New York: Underwood and Underwood, 1904.

United States, Continental Currency of September 26, 1778. Fifty-dollar bill. Printed by Hall and Sellers, [Philadelphia], 1778. A step-pyramid is shown on the obverse face of this bill.

Uxkull, Woldemar v. *Eine Einweihung im alten Ägypten. Nach dem Buch Thoth geschildert.* Munich: Roland-Verlag Dr. Albert Mundt, 1922.

Valentine, Tom. *The Great Pyramid: Man's Monument to Man*. New York: Pinnacle Books, 1975.

Van Auken, John. *Ancient Egyptian Mysticism and Its Relevance Today*. Virginia Beach, Va.: A.R.E. Press, 1999.

Van Sertima, Ivan, ed. *Egypt Revisited*. New Brunswick, N.J.: Transaction, 1989.

Verner, Miroslav. *The Pyramids: The Mystery, Culture, and Science of Egypt's Great Monuments*. New York: Grove Press, 2001.

Viening, Edward, ed. *The Zondervan Topical Bible*. Grand Rapids, Mich.: Zondervan, 1969.

von Däniken, Erich. *Chariots of the Gods? Unsolved Mysteries of the Past*. London: Souvenir Press, 1969.

von Däniken, Erich. *The Eyes of the Sphinx: The Newest Evidence of Extraterrestrial Contact in Ancient Egypt*. New York: Berkley Books, 1996.

Vyse, Colonel Howard. *Appendix to Operations Carried on at the Pyramids of Gizeh in 1837. Containing a Survey by J. S. Perring, Esq. Civil Engineer, of the Pyramids at Abou Roash, and to the Southward, Including Those in the Faiyoum*. London: John Weale and G. W. Nickisson, 1842. On page xi of this volume Vyse refers to Vyse (1840) as having been published in 1841, although it bears the date 1840 on its title page.

Vyse, Colonel Howard. *Operations Carried on at the Pyramids of Gizeh in 1837: With an Account of a Voyage into Upper Egypt, and an Appendix*. 2 vols. London: James Fraser, 1840. Vyse (1842) is essentially the third volume of this work. Richard William Howard Vyse (1784–1853) is often cited in the literature as "Howard-Vyse," "Howard Vyse," or "Vyse"; in this 1840 work he lists himself on the title page as "Colonel Howard Vyse" without a hyphen, so "Vyse" is used herein.

Wake, C. Staniland. *The Origin and Significance of the Great Pyramid*. London: Reeves and Turner, 1882. Reprint, San Diego: Wizards Bookshelf, 1987.

Ward, John. *Pyramids and Progress: Sketches from Egypt*. With an introduction by Prof. Sayce. London: Eyre and Spottiswoode, 1900.

Wathen, George H. *Arts, Antiquities and Chronology of Ancient Egypt: From Observations in 1839*. London: Longman, Brown, Green and Longmans, 1843.

Watson, Philip J. *Egyptian Pyramids and Mastaba Tombs of the Old and Middle Kingdoms*. Aylesbury, England: Shire Egyptology, 1987.

Webber, David, and N. W. Hutchings. *New Light on the Great Pyramid*. Oklahoma City: Southwest Radio Church, 1985.

Wendorf, Fred, Romuald Schild, and associates. *Holocene Settlement of the Egyptian Sahara. Vol. 1. The Archaeology of Nabta Playa*. New York: Kluwer, 2001.

West, John Anthony. Afterword to Brophy (2002).

West, John Anthony. *Serpent in the Sky: The High Wisdom of Ancient Egypt*. New York: Harper and Row, 1979.

West, John Anthony. "Sphinx and Pyramid Update." In *The Complete Pyramid Sourcebook*, edited by John DeSalvo. Bloomington, Ind.: 1stBooks, 2003, pp. 219–234.

West, John Anthony. *The Traveler's Key to Ancient Egypt: A Guide to the Sacred Places of Ancient Egypt*. New York: Knopf, 1985.

Westcott, W. Wynn, ed. *Egyptian Magic. Vol. 3 of Collectanea Hermetica.* London: Theosophical Publishing Society, 1896.

Wilkinson, J. Gardner. *Popular Account of the Ancient Egyptians.* Vols. 1 and 2. New York: Harper, 1854.

Wilkinson, Richard H. *Symbol and Magic in Egyptian Art.* London: Thames and Hudson, 1994.

Wilson, Colin. *From Atlantis to the Sphinx: Recovering the Lost Wisdom of the Ancient World.* New York: Fromm International, 1999.

Wilson, Colin, and Rand Flem-Ath. *The Atlantis Blueprint: Unlocking the Ancient Mysteries of a Long-Lost Civilization.* New York: Delta Trade Paperbacks, 2000.

Witherby, H. Forbes. *Light from the Land of the Sphinx.* London: Elliot Stock, 1896.

Wirth, Diane E. *Parallels: Mesoamerican and Ancient Middle Eastern Traditions.* St. George, Utah: Stonecliff, 2003.

Zajac, John. *The Delicate Balance: Coming Catastrophic Changes on Planet Earth.* Lafayette, La.: Prescott Press, 1989.

ON-LINE SOURCES

The dates given after the Internet/World Wide Web addresses (URLs; uniform resource locators) are the dates when I accessed these websites and web pages using the given URLs. Some of these sites and pages may no longer be active, and URLs may have changed. In such cases, it may be possible for the interested reader to find the applicable or comparable material through a search engine.

Anonymous. "Ancient Egyptian Texts." www.crystalinks.com/egyptexts.html. August 22, 2004. Ellie Crystal's Metaphysical and Science website.

Anonymous. "Pyramidology." www.greatdreams.com/pyramid.htm. June 14, 2003. Dreams of the Great Earth Changes Website, Dee Finney and Joe Mason.

Astronomical Society of Edinburgh. "A Guide to Edinburgh's Popular Observatory." www.astronomyedinburgh.org/publications/booklet/. July 4, 2003. Astronomical Society of Edinburgh website.

Benoist, Annick. "Uncovering the secrects of the Great Pyramid." www.iol.co.za/index. php?set_id=1&click_id=588&art_id=qw1093769284459B216. August 29, 2004.

Calter, Paul. "The Golden Ratio and Squaring the Circle in the Great Pyramid." www. dartmouth.edu/~matc/math5.geometry/unit2/unit2.html. August 25, 2004. (Article bears a 1998 copyright.)

Dudley, Underwood. Review of *The Shape of the Great Pyramid* by Roger Herz-Fischler. www.maa.org/reviews/pyramid.html. June 30, 2003. Mathematical Association of America website.

Feuerstein, Georg. "Paul Brunton: From Journalist to Gentle Sage." www.yrec.org/brunton. html. September 29, 2003. Article bears a 1997 copyright. Yoga Research and Education Center website.

Fournier, Jim. "Critical Notes on Stecchini and Tompkins." www.geoman.com/jim/critical. html. December 22, 2003. James L. Fournier's website.

Fournier, Jim. "Precession and the Pyramid: Astronomical Knowledge in Ancient Egypt." www.geoman.com/jim/pyramid.html. December 22, 2003. Article dated May 5, 1996. James L. Fournier's website.

Great Pyramid of Giza Research Association. "The Relationship between the Great Pyramid of Giza and the Book of the Dead." www.gizapyramid.com/book.htm. July 25, 2004.

Hawass, Zahi. "The Three Secret Doors and the Magician Djedi." www.guardians.net/ hawass/articles/three_secret_doors_and_the_magician_djedi.htm. January 1, 2004. Guardian's Egypt website.

Hertaus, Jeff. "Nabta Playa." www.mnsu.edu/emuseum/archaeology/sites/africa/nabtaplaya. html. June 6, 2004. Minnesota State University, Mankato, website.

Herz-Fischler, Roger. "The Shape of the Great Pyramid. Additional Drawings and Photographs." www.wlu.ca/~wwwpress/. October 4, 2003. Search under "Herz-Fischler" and *The Shape of the Great Pyramid* at the Wilfrid Laurier University Press website.

Horowitz, Mitch. "Can You Name the Seven Wonders of the World?" www.mitchhorowitz. com/seven-wonders.html November 24, 2004. Mitch Horowitz's website.

Johnson, Charles William. "The Great Pyramid." www.earthmatrix.com/serie77/pyramid. htm. July 4, 2003. Earthmatrix, Science in Ancient Artwork website.

Johnson, Charles William. "The Great Pyramid: Measurements." www.earthmatrix.com/ great/pyramid.htm. July 4, 2003. Earthmatrix, Science in Ancient Artwork website.

Johnson, Keith P. "The Key to the Great Pyramid." http://home.globalcrossing.net/ ~kjohnson/index.html. May 26, 2004. Documents dated 1998 and 1999.

Lachman, Gary. "René Schwaller de Lubicz and the Intelligence of the Heart." www. theosophical.org/theosophy/questmagazine/januaryfebruary2000/lubicz/. September 22, 2003. Originally published in *Quest Magazine,* January–February 2000. Theosophical Society in America website.

Moyer, Ernest. "Calculation of the Number of Stones in the Great Pyramid." www. world-destiny.com/numberofstones.htm. June 30, 2003. Ernest Moyer's website.

Oderberg, I. M. "Gateway to the 'Horizon of Heaven.'" www.theosophy-nw.org/theosnw/ world/med/my-imo6.htm. October 25, 2003. Originally published in *Sunrise,* June/July 1973. Northwest Branch of the Theosophical Society website.

Parsons, Marie. "Khufu." www.touregypt.net/featurestories/khufu.htm. January 1, 2004. Tour Egypt website.

Plato. "Timaeus and Critias (English translations by Benjamin Jowett)." www.activemind. com/Mysterious/Topics/Atlantis/timaeus_and_critias.html. September 9, 2004. The Active Mind website.

Pratt, David. "The Great Pyramid." http://ourworld.compuserve.com/homepages/dp5/ pyramid.htm. October 9, 2003.

Purucker, G. de. "The Pyramid Initiation." http://ourworld.compuserve.com/homepages/ dp5/pyrinit.htm. October 9, 2003. Originally published in *Theosophical Forum,* January 1948, pp. 20–22.

Rappenglueck, Michael. See Whitehouse, David.

Reynolds, Mark. "A Comparative Geometric Analysis of the Heights and Bases of the Great Pyramid of Khufu and the Pyramid of the Sun at Teotihuacan." www.nexusjournal.com/Reynolds.html. June 5, 2003. Nexus Network Journal website.

Schoch, Robert M. "Ancient Wisdom and the Great Sphinx of Giza." www.robertschoch.net/articles/Ancient_Wisdom_and_the_Great_Sphinx.html. January 9, 2005. Also published, in slightly modified form, in *Psychic Reader* 28, no. 10 [October 2003], pp. 10–11. Robert Schoch's website.

Seawright, Caroline. "Tales of Magic in Ancient Egypt." www.touregypt.net/featurestories/magic.htm. January 1, 2004. Tour Egypt website.

Su'e, Yoshiki. "Hypothesis [concerning the Great Pyramid]." www22.ocn.ne.jp/~p-inpaku/pyramid/sub80.htm. August 25, 2004. Document dated 1999.

Temple, Robert. "Lost Teachings of the Ancients: The Crystal Sun." www.newdawnmagazine.com/Articles/Crystal_Sun.html. October 9, 2003. Originally published in *New Dawn* 65 (March–April 2001). New Dawn Magazine website.

Tindol, Robert. "Researchers Lift Obelisk with Kite to Test Theory on Ancient Pyramids." (Story dated July 6, 2001.) http://news.nationalgeographic.com/news/2001/06/0628_caltechobelisk.html. November 15, 2003. National Geographic News website.

Walker, Graham. "Cavern In the Sinai: A Solution to Giza." www.robertbauval.com/articles/cis1.html. September 10, 2003. Robert Bauval's website.

Whitehouse, David. "'Oldest star chart' found." http://news.bbc.co.uk/1/hi/sci/tech/2679675.stm. January 29, 2003. BBC News website.

Wright, David. "Unlocking the Mystery: Scientists Try to Figure Out How Pyramids Were Built." Story dated June 24, 2001. http://abcnews.go.com/sections/wnt/DailyNews/wnt_pyramid010624.html. November 15, 2003. ABC News website.

INDEX

ABOUT THE AUTHORS

ROBERT M. SCHOCH, a full-time faculty member at the College of General Studies at Boston University since 1984, earned his Ph.D. in geology and geophysics at Yale University. Dr. Schoch is known internationally for his work in Egypt; he has been quoted extensively in the media with reference to the Great Sphinx and ancient civilizations; and he has been featured in a number of documentaries, including the Emmy Award–winning *The Mystery of the Sphinx*. Dr. Schoch's website is located at www.robertschoch.net.

ROBERT AQUINAS MCNALLY is a writer and poet whose early education in classical Latin blossomed into a lifelong fascination with ancient civilization and mythology. Schoch and McNally have previously collaborated on the books *Voices of the Rocks: A Scientist Looks at Catastrophes and Ancient Civilizations* (1999) and *Voyages of the Pyramid Builders: The True Origins of the Pyramids from Lost Egypt to Ancient America* (2003).